...- for

Love, Hickory

Enjoy Mother's (~~second~~) first 50 years,

Tommy

Thomas J. Pérez

01 - 26 - 2016

Love, Hickory

A Southern Lady Prevails at 99

Part One: The First Fifty Years

Thomas Joseph Perez

Outskirts Press, Inc.
Denver, Colorado

Love, Hickory
A Southern Lady Prevails at 99
Part One: The First Fifty Years

Outskirts Press, Inc.
http://www.outskirtspress.com

ISBN: 978-1-4327-7161-4

Outskirts Press and the "OP" logo are trademarks belonging to Outskirts Press, Inc.

PRINTED IN THE UNITED STATES OF AMERICA

Fawn River
South Mobile County, Alabama
January 21, 2012

I CAN'T BE certain, of course, but I'm betting my daughter will see her 100th birthday next year.

Like a lot of folks her age, her short-term memory is failing a bit and she gets confused about which day her sister-in-law picks her up to play bridge—it's every Thursday—yet she still can bid and make a grand slam if dealt a decent hand.

Her blood pressure is normal and her heart is fine. She has no sign of diabetes or cancer. Other than her fragile knees which require a walker, she's in pretty good shape—as long as she holds on to that three-wheel walker.

At nine this morning I stood over her recliner as she dozed in her nightgown and robe, waiting for my grand-daughter to come downstairs and escort her mother to the breakfast table upstairs. The journey from bed to recliner across the four-room spacious apartment had tired her out. But no matter how quickly she fades, it's apparent that—despite declaring once a week "I'm ready to leave"—my daughter has no intention of going anywhere.

When I appeared from the deck outside the apartment, I gave the sliding glass door a noisy push to awaken her in the chair. As she stirred, I positioned myself at the front window in my black gabardine trousers— the seat shiny from wear—hoping she would recognize me from the photograph on her bedroom wall. I was wearing a wrinkled white broad- cloth shirt topped with a detachable collar which should have given me away. But if she didn't recognize the Edwardian collar, all she had to do was glance at my feet to notice the high-top, black calfskin shoes—laced to my ankle, then buttoned up the rest of the way.

"Were you out on the end of the wharf?" finally she opened her eyes a little bit.

"I stopped by to see where you've been living since you left Spring View Retirement Center."

"Who let you in? . . . Mickey? . . . Pal?"

"I let myself in."

"Did you close that door tight? . . . It's cold in here!"

"You're always cold—even in the summer."

"I've been cold all my life! . . . But only my family knows that about me."

"I know everything about you."

"You're gonna freeze to death in that flimsy shirt."

"It's all I've got," I pointed at the collar to see if she noticed.

"When I was a child, all the men wore collars like that. Where'd you get it?"

"I've had it a while. . . . Time for you to get dressed for your birth- day party. You turn ninety-nine today, don't you?"

"Yes," she laughed and closed her eyes. "I never thought I'd live this long. I've outlived all that insurance money Rappy left me. . . . All that bank stock! . . . And I'm tired, just tired."

"Nobody ever died from being tired," I hoped not to aggravate her by sounding too philosophical.

"Maybe I'll be the first," she chuckled, her eyes remaining closed. "I'm ready to leave."

"You're too curious to leave yet. *Nosy,* some would say. Besides, they're already planning your 100th birthday party."

"I've gotta get through this one first."

"Which means you've gotta get out of that chair! Is your daughter coming downstairs to help you dress?"

"I guess so. . . . I hate that I've become such a *burden*!"

"If we live to be ninety-nine, we're gonna be dependent."

"That's why I prayed for the Lord to take me before this happened! I'd planned to die in my own apartment back at that retirement residence, where they call it *independent* living!"

"But you were alone most of the time, weren't you?"

"I *liked* living alone! After raising eleven children, I was *ready* for some peace and quiet," she opened her eyes slowly and glared at me.

"Your family was afraid you'd fall again. You would've ended up totally dependent, probably in a nursing home!"

"Step away from that window! I can't see the river."

"You enjoy it here on the water, don't you?"

"We don't have a wide view of the bay like we did from Uncle Joe Midgette's wharf, but I like looking at the river marsh. If you get out of my line of view, I'll be able to tell you if that blue heron's made it back."

"Why do you like to look out over the water?"

"*Horizons*. . . . I like to view the horizon, don't you?"

"Indeed, I do."

"You resemble one of my sons, Tommy, but he's way past sixty. You're too young to be Tommy. How old are you, anyway?"

"Twenty-six. . . . My name's Tommy also."

"When Tommy was in his twenties, he looked just like my father in that wedding photo with Mama—the one in my bedroom hanging on the wall next to the vanity."

"*I'm* the young man in that photo."

"*You?*" her eyes blinked several times as she tried to focus on my face.

"I'm your father."

"No, you're not. . . . Besides, I never had a father."

"Look at my face closely," I nervously jingled the six silver dimes in my trousers pocket.

"I don't believe in ghosts!"

"Do you believe in spirits? Your own spirit?"

"I don't know exactly what the Church calls a spirit, but they say I have a *soul*."

"I understand the Catholics don't use the word 'ghost' anymore. You say 'spirit'."

"You mean, like 'Holy Ghost'?" she furrowed her brow.

"Yes, . . . and of the Son, and of the Holy *Spirit* . . . "

"You're right—they don't say 'Holy Ghost' anymore."

"So, could I be a spirit?" I asked tentatively.

"If this is a dream, I'm gonna have to ask you to leave!"

"Did you really say 'I'm gonna have to *ask* you to leave'? . . . You don't have to act the Southern Lady, you know? If it's a dream, you can *make* me leave."

"All right, then! Get outta here!"

"You've been searching for me all your life."

"No, I haven't," she closed her eyes.

"And, now I'm here."

The Southwest Corner of
Bayou and Savannah

TWO DAYS AFTER the stock market crashed in 1929, as Alyce Hicks prepared for Confession in her school chapel, she received her first hint that the event was catastrophic. But at the time she had no inkling how the crash—and its aftermath—would affect her own life.

"Three more people jumped out of the Merchants National Bank!" Modeste Friedhoff couldn't stop giggling in spite of the dreadful news. She made a sloppy Sign of the Cross while genuflecting next to the front pew of Convent of Mercy day-school's chapel, sprang from her knees, and sidled in next to Alyce.

"They just dedicated that building two weeks ago! . . . Did you say *three* people?" Alyce whispered. She squirmed on the hard wooden kneeler as she waited to enter the Confessional next to the statue of the Blessed Virgin Mary. She welcomed Modeste interrupting the five steps for her weekly Confession: 'First, you must *Examine Your Conscience* to recall your sins.'

"And two the night before! Alyce, why are all these bankers jumping out the window?" Modeste fingered the crystal beads on her rosary as if she were praying.

"My brother says the stock market crashed."

"I have no idea what a stock market is," Modeste giggled, "and I don't care!"

"Something to do with high finance in New York, and Bubber

says a 'crash' is when they lose all their money cuz everybody sells at once, but I don't understand a word of it!"

"Me neither! . . . But at least Mobile's finally got a building tall enough for folks to jump *out* of. They finished that bank building just in time for the stock market crash," Modeste guffawed at her own cynicism.

"Modeste Friedhoff!" Alyce admonished. "We can't laugh at this! We're high school seniors! Bubber says the whole economy's just gonna collapse! This is something *serious*, isn't it?"

"Don't you read the newspaper, Alyce? People are jumping off buildings all over the damn country!"

"You just cussed in front of the Blessed Sacrament right up there on this altar! You're gonna have to confess that!"

"Sure, Alyce! And you make sure you confess 'entertaining impure thoughts' about Clark Gable and Romeo Novarro."

"*Ramon* Novarro . . . not Romeo! Monica and I are going to see him this Saturday in "Devil May Care"—it's his first talking movie! And if you go with us, you'll have to confess 'entertaining impure thoughts' too! . . . I *guarantee* it!"

"Ramon Novarro is a *Mexican*! . . . Ugh! . . . I mean, hell, Alyce! If you're gonna 'entertain impure thoughts' about a foreign picture star, then choose Charles Boyer—he's French!"

♪♪♪

When the stock market crashed in October of 1929, Alyce Hicks had just started her final year of high school in Mobile, Alabama. Few of her classmates at the Convent of Mercy day-school had any inkling that businessmen were jumping from buildings all over the country. Not only were most of the Catholic teenagers at the all-girls school oblivious to the oncoming financial crisis, but most folks in Alabama's only port city on the Gulf were equally unaffected by the stock market crash. For a while, that is.

Mobile was not a financial center, nor did it boast any manufacturing prowess. The port city ambled along as usual for a year or so. It wasn't until late 1930 that unemployment figures crept up and tonnage at the port began to decrease. It was then that the unemployed were seen bounding off freight cars after riding the Gulf Mobile & Ohio railroad to the Gulf Coast to escape from sleeping outside in the northern winters.

For four years the country's economy struggled under President Hoover. Then, in 1933 Franklin Roosevelt was inaugurated as the new president. On March 5—the day after being sworn into office—President Roosevelt declared a 'bank holiday', which forced the closure of the nation's banks for four days and halted all financial transactions. The 'holiday' stopped the frantic run on banks and gave the president time to push the Emergency Banking Act through Congress. But that didn't occur until three and one-half years after the Crash of '29.

By the time Roosevelt took over the presidency with his New Deal, Alyce Hicks had graduated from high school and was working as a secretary for the Mobile Chemical Company making $6 a week, half of which she gave to her mother to help with household expenses in the south part of town where Alyce lived with her mother, brother, and invalid grandmother.

At the Merchants National Bank around the corner from Mobile Chemical, Rappy Perez—at age twenty-four and the starting short-stop on the bank's baseball team—had just begun his third year with the official title of 'bank clerk'. He courted Alyce Hicks, a lively and petite brunette, with the help of the bank's office-boy who delivered documents among the several downtown banks. In exchange for the privilege of serving as bat-boy at all home games, the office-boy made a detour to Mobile Chemical each afternoon to exchange love-letters between Rappy and Alyce.

Dear Hickory   *Monday, 8:45 a.m.*

> *Forgive me for getting tight at that party Saturday night. I think Goober slipped something into that moonshine. When they repeal Prohibition, we can buy Canadian Club like my daddy taught me to drink and then I'll be able to behave myself. You know I'd never hurt you. Promise!*

It all started off with an innocent smacker—I didn't mean for it to go any further than that. You know I'd never take advantage of you. I love and respect you so much.

I'm looking forward to the dance Friday night. I've already got the OK from Julius to use his car so I'll pick you up at 7:30 sharp. I'll be on time. Promise!

All my love,
Rappy

Dear Sweet,   *Monday, 10:45 a.m.*

Gosh, Sweet, I'm so sleepy I can hardly keep my eyes open. I've been posting and I went to sleep about five times. My head just fell down on the ledger so I decided that if I got up and wrote to you, I might wake up. But it's going to be short 'cause I've got lots of work to do.

Honey, I'm sorry about last night. I hope we will be good after this. We will try real hard anyway, won't we? Dear, I know that you hate all that foolishness just as much as I do, and I know that you can't help it either. We just love each other too much, I guess. Sweet, I do love you so much—it even hurts. We'll be happy some day 'cause Our Lord made us for each other, didn't He?

I won't see you till tomorrow night. Such a long time, no? Try not to worry about last night.

All my love,
Hickory

As their romance bloomed, the financial crisis around the country deepened. The entire world entered into a profound economic de-

6

pression. Originally Alyce and Rappy had planned to marry in June of 1933, but they were forced to postpone the wedding for a full year until the following June.

♪♪♪

Alyce leaned back in the porch swing on the verandah of her family's 1880's cottage at the southwest corner of Bayou and Savannah streets in a working-class neighborhood of downtown Mobile. She let herself relax after a boring day at work filing delinquent accounts as Rappy stood behind her in the dark and pushed the swing. It was a rare moment for her—allowing herself to be indulged. Usually she was the one waiting hand-and-foot on Bubber, her only brother, so he wouldn't be disturbed from his homework at Spring Hill College. Or, unless she had a date with Rappy for the picture-show at the Saenger, she spent the evenings helping her mother sew tiny satin-covered buttons down the back of eight bridesmaids' dresses that were behind schedule for a society wedding next month.

"And don't worry about spilling another glass of iced-tea!" Rappy whispered into her ear as he leaned forward and gave the swing a firm push.

"Well, don't sit me in the middle of the table! Then I won't have to pass the serving dishes back and forth to all your brothers!" she tossed her head to force her short dark bob to bounce as the swing lunged forward.

"Now, Hickory, don't get so excited—it's just Sunday dinner."

"And don't call me 'Hickory' in front of your family—especially your daddy!"

"But you *know* how hard-headed you are!" he raised an eyebrow hoping for a friendly fight. "And the hardest wood *does* come from the hickory tree!"

"Well," she pretended to pout, "you can call me 'Hickory' but only in front of our friends, and *never* in front of your family—especially your daddy!"

"Aw, Papa's not so bad," Rappy slid into the swing and put his arm around her shoulder.

"I just can't get close to your daddy."

"*Nobody's* close to him—he's Spanish."

"Spanish!? . . . But he's not dark like Ramon Novarro."

"My daddy's family came from the Canary Islands where a lot of folks are blonder."

"Ah, so that's why you're not dark and handsome like Ramon Novarro?" she teased while she played with the lace at her wrist.

"And my mother's family came from Ireland," he massaged her shoulder.

"Didn't everybody's? . . . I'm Irish on both sides!" she glanced through the window into the living room to make sure her grand-mother was concentrating on her crochet and not spying on her. If Rappy was ready to kiss her, she didn't want her grandmother to catch them. She had just turned twenty and Rappy was twenty-four, both old enough to sit on the verandah without a chaperone glaring out the window—but both came from Irish Catholic families where nice people didn't show affection outside the bedroom.

By 1933 the courting rules for the younger generation had changed dramatically. During the Roaring Twenties Alyce's crowd grew up at the Saenger Theater watching picture-shows of flappers dancing the racy Charleston on nightclub tabletops while swigging bootleg whisky. And now that the country was in the middle of a Great Depression, there were more important things to worry about than sweethearts stealing kisses on the front porch.

♪♪♪♪

Three years earlier Alyce Hicks graduated from Convent of Mercy high school as part of the Class of '30. She wasn't at the top of the class, nor was she at the bottom. Following the advice of her older brother, 'the Brain in the Family', she took the Classical Course which consisted of four years of Latin, two years of Spanish, and several Mathematics cours-es including Algebra. She'd rather had completed the General Course, consisting of Typing, Shorthand, Home Economics, and Sewing, but Bubber insisted the Classical Course would 'prepare her for life.'

Not one girl in the graduating class mentioned the possibility of going to college. If a classmate had even considered college sometime during her senior year, she certainly dropped the idea upon June graduation. Seven months after that disastrous stock market crash, bad times were now felt in the port city. In downtown Mobile no middle-class Catholic family—much less the working-class—could afford to send a son to local Spring Hill College, much less send a daughter to Dominican or Ursuline in New Orleans.

One of Alyce's classmates, Mary Margaret O'Hara, announced that she was entering a convent to become a Sister of Charity, but the other twenty-four assumed they would fulfill the destiny of any Good Catholic Girl—get married and have children. But if she considered herself 'modern', a Good Catholic Girl didn't have to get married right away upon graduation. If she didn't have a serious beau, she could play the field. She could get a job, if she could find one during the Great Depression, to earn enough money to buy a couple of pretty frocks and a pair of nice high-heels and date a lot of different young men until she fell in love. She hoped her heartthrob would be suitable for marriage. If nothing else, he would need to have a job.

Alyce was in no hurry to marry. In high school she never went on a real date—not one where the boy picked her up at the front door and brought her home after the dance. Yet she attended many dances with her brother, Tommy, whom she called 'Bubber'. He was a bit bookish and shy. Only two years younger than he, Alyce adored him. Being the only two children in a house with their mother and maternal grandmother, the two Hicks children felt no need for sibling rivalry. They were loved and cared for. With no father in the house, Bubber was the male who earned Alyce's love and respect because he always looked out for her. So, at the beginning of her junior year when Bubber offered to escort her to a Knights of Columbus dance, Alyce jumped at the opportunity.

As valedictorian of his high school class at McGill Institute, Tommy Hicks had won a full scholarship to Spring Hill College, the local liberal arts college founded in 1830 and operated by the Jesuits ever since. At

Saturday night dances sponsored by the Knights of Columbus and local Catholic churches, Tommy's college friends didn't give Alyce a chance to sit down between dance-numbers. She was whirled around the floor by college boys who made sure that Tommy's little sister didn't become a wallflower. And when one college boy was dancing with her, a second stood by waiting to cut-in half way through the dance-number by tapping her partner on his shoulder.

"Look at that Alyce Hicks!" Monica Bridges pouted as she leaned against the wall sipping a Coca-Cola out of a waxed cup. "She's the most popular girl in our class!"

"Because she never sits out a dance?" Modeste Friedhoff asked. "Hell, there're two boys here for every girl. It's easy to be popular!"

"But she gets *cut-in* during every dance number!" Monica sulked.

"*That's* because her brother brings half of Spring Hill College with him, silly!"

"My mother says that if at least one boy doesn't cut in during each dance-number, then you're just not *popular*!"

"Damn, I'm glad she's not *my* mother!"

"I guess I need an older brother with lots of friends."

"You need to be 5'2", like Alyce, with a pretty face and a real cute figure!"

"She had those bosoms in the 8th grade! . . . And look at my chest! It's just not fair!"

"Being flat-chested, Monica, was fashionable in the Twenties, but nobody binds her chest with wide cotton bandages anymore! Boys like *bosoms*!"

"Mama says I should lift encyclopedias," Monica stared wistfully across the dance-floor.

"*Encyclopedias*?"

"One in each hand . . . like this!" she demonstrated as if she were lifting a dumbbell in each hand, alternately, over her head.

"That might help! But you've got to develop some *personality*!"

"There's nothing wrong with my personality!" Monica snapped.

10

"Boys like personality, Monica . . . and Alyce has a personality that just won't quit!"

）ﾉﾉﾉ､

Immediately after high school graduation in June of 1930, Alyce discovered dating with a vengeance. When word got around that her mother no longer insisted on Bubber escorting Alyce to dances, the boys descended upon the Hicks home. On the corner of Bayou and Savannah, it appeared to be raining boys.

By the middle of the summer Alyce stopped to catch her breath and take stock of how dramatically her life had changed—and how the stock market crash only nine months earlier had transformed life in her working-class community in downtown Mobile.

Men were losing jobs all over Alyce's neighborhood. Miss Alice's income as a professional dressmaker had fallen appreciably. Weddings and Mardi Gras ball gowns—plus Catholic school uniforms—were the bread-and-butter for Miss Alice's dress-making business. Everybody, even rich girls in the fashionable Spring Hill neighborhoods, were postponing their weddings because their merchant fathers couldn't afford a big church wedding with eight bridesmaids. As the summer of 1930 progressed into July, Alyce noticed that there were fewer and fewer bridesmaids' dresses hanging from the tall French doors in the spacious dining room.

As tough times got worse at the Hicks household on the corner of Bayou and Savannah, Alyce learned quickly what 'living on credit' meant. Although she was contributing half of her $6/week paycheck from her secretarial job to her mother each week, they still didn't have enough money to pay the grocery bill—even with Tommy working two summer jobs between semesters at Spring Hill College. Luckily, the Toenes Grocery across the street empathized with the whole neighborhood struggling to make ends meet. It helped that the Toenes family lived next door to their grocery store and were part of the community.

Every afternoon Alyce returned home from her job at Mobile Chemical Company and picked up the grocery list her mother had

11

left on the kitchen table. On the list were only items necessary to prepare two meals for the day. Breakfast was hot tea with buttered toast, and lunch was a sandwich or hot soup. Alyce crossed the street and handed the list to Mercedes Toenes who filled Alyce's wicker basket with the ordered items.

"You wanna put this on credit, Alyce?" Mercedes avoided eye contact as she deftly arranged the canned goods in the basket.

"If it's all right!" Alyce tried to hide her embarrassment with a cheery smile. "Mama's expecting a big wedding order next week—some society girl whose Daddy works for Waterman Steamship is marrying a rich boy from New Orleans. She's gonna have six bridesmaids so Mama hopes to pay off this whole bill next month, maybe even sooner if—"

"Alyce," Mercedes gently rested her hand on Alyce's fist clutching the basket's handle, "there's no reason to be embarrassed about these hard times, honey! Everybody's hurting these days. If we didn't have this grocery store, I don't know how we'd eat here in the Toenes house! Now, you tell your Mama there's no hurry to pay off this bill—just whenever her business picks up!"

Alyce tightened her grip on the basket's handle and stared at her feet. She didn't want Mercedes to see the tears of gratitude welling in her eyes. She signed the receipt for the groceries and hurried out the little store as Mercedes filed the slip of paper into a small metal box next to the cash register. Whenever Miss Alice received payment for a dressmaking job, she would make a small payment on the grocery bill. It took five years, long after Alyce had married and moved to west Mobile, before Miss Alice was able to reduce the Toenes grocery bill to zero.

But during that July of 1930, still only seventeen years-old, Alyce Hicks saw her young life blooming beyond her dreams. She had a job with a regular paycheck. Because the dressmaking business was slow, Miss Alice had time to fashion new dresses for Alyce to wear to dances and parties. From her salary Alyce saved enough to buy two pairs of high-heel pumps and two pairs of silk stockings. She had dates, lots of them. And she had a boyfriend.

His name was Dale Simpson. And he wasn't a boy. He was a tall, handsome man of twenty-one who worked as a bank-clerk at Merchants National Bank. He had a car, a rarity for a young man in Alyce's neighborhood. He lived with his family in more fashionable west Mobile. And he liked to buy gifts for Alyce.

"He's crazy, Peg!" Alyce chuckled as she extended her left hand for her friend to examine the ring.

"My God!" Peg Camilleri grabbed the hand to examine the small garnet. "Alyce Hicks, you're engaged and you're only *seventeen*!"

"I am *not* engaged!" Alyce threw her head back and laughed uproariously. "It's not a *diamond*!"

"It's a ring! And it's on your *ring*-finger on your *left* hand!"

"I can't help it if he likes to buy me presents," Alyce widened her eyes with delight.

"Well, when you get tired of him, you just send him over to my house!"

That night Alyce had a date with Dale to see a Clark Gable movie at the Saenger, only ten blocks from her house in downtown Mobile. Dale parked his car in front of the Hicks house on Bayou, and the young couple walked to the theater. After the movie they were walking down Dauphin Street towards Alyce's house when she stopped in front of a jewelry store to admire a pair of silver earrings set with red garnet stones.

"They match your ring. Do you want them?" Dale slid his arm around her shoulder as they both pressed noses against the glass window.

"No!" she pretended to be annoyed. "Because if I say 'yes', you'll have the jewelry store deliver the darn earrings to the Mobile Chemical Company—by special messenger—and all gift-wrapped!"

"So, what's wrong with that? I've got a good job at the bank!"

"I have enough problem, as it is, explaining that this thing *here*," she held up her hand with the red garnet ring under the street-lamp, "is *not* an engagement ring!"

"It's not?" he pretended to be shocked.

"I'm only *seventeen*! I'm not ready to get engaged, and I'm sure as heck not ready to get married! . . . I just want to have *fun*!"

"Then you need to meet Rappy Perez," he pulled her away from the showroom window and guided her down the street towards her house.

"Rappy?! . . . What kind of name is *that*?"

"If you want 'fun', he's a *lot* of fun! And one of the nicest fellows you'll ever meet."

"Does he have a job? I don't want to meet any fellows without a job."

"He works at the bank . . . with me! I'll introduce you to him . . . someday soon."

The earrings were not delivered the next day to Alyce's office. But when she arrived home at 5:30, she found a small gift-wrapped package sitting on the dining room table next to the grocery list.

♪ ♪ ♪

Alyce met her future husband in late August, 1930 at a Cavaliers' dance at St. Mary's parish hall. The Cavaliers were an organization of Catholic high school boys who had formed a social fraternity to rival the snobby Greek fraternities at high schools in Mobile. Now that she had a steady boyfriend, Dale, to take her to dances all over Mobile, Alyce no longer needed her brother's college friends to cut-in on each other to keep her dancing all night long. There were other boys waiting in the stag-line—ranging from high school boys to young bachelors as old as twenty-nine. Alyce Hicks had become popular.

It was during the first dance-number as Dale was guiding her through a foxtrot near the wall of the old wooden building that Alyce saw the short young man standing with the other stags, his hands shoved deep in his trouser pockets, his double-breasted jacket open in the heat of a sultry August night, but his necktie was snug around his slender throat. His eye caught Alyce's as Dale whirled her towards the stag-line. They stopped in front of the young man who was smoothing his black hair while staring at the pretty girl with the dark brown bob

14

and the coffee-colored eyes. Dale gave Rappy a hearty greeting as if he hadn't eaten lunch with him earlier that day at the bank.

"This is the guy I was telling you about!" Dale turned to Alyce.

"Hey," Alyce said sheepishly. She definitely found the young man cute but didn't like him staring a hole through her.

"This is Rappy Perez!" Dale enthused. "Why don't you two finish this dance while I go get some punch? . . . This guy *loves* to dance!"

"Now, Dale, don't you run off and find some pretty girl and forget to take me home!" Alyce tried to reduce tension by chastising her date, but he was already making his way through the crowd of dancing couples.

"You're a lot prettier than Dale described," Rappy continued to stare. At 5'6" he wasn't that much taller than Alyce—his dark brown eyes locked onto hers.

"You mean he didn't say I was as pretty as Norma Shearer?" Alyce fell into sassy banter, the only way she knew how to flirt.

"Let's go sit down," he gestured toward the row of folding chairs against the wall.

"Don't you want to dance with me?" she pretended to be miffed.

"We've got the whole night to dance—let's sit down for a minute. Later on you won't find an empty chair in the whole place!" he slid his hand under her elbow and led her to a pair of wooden folding chairs in the corner.

"I'd rather dance," she protested but she was eager to find out who this boy really was and why Dale said she should meet him.

"These chairs are hard as hickory!" he squirmed, stretched out his short legs, and crossed them at the ankles.

"Then let's go dance," she tested him to see if he really wanted to be alone with her.

Sitting in the corner of the dance hall they discovered how many people they both knew in Mobile's Catholic community. She learned that Rappy had graduated two years before her brother from McGill Institute, that the two boys had known each other to speak to on a friendly basis but nothing more. She and Rappy chatted about everything. They were so enthralled with each other that they never thought to get up and dance. They just talked and talked.

When Dale finally reappeared, Alyce realized that the band had started playing its signature last number, "Good Night, You Cutie." She took Dale's hand as he offered it for the final dance, rose from the chair, and let him guide her across the floor as she gazed back at Rappy still sitting in the folding chair.

I danced only two numbers the whole night! The first and the last! And both with Dale, which is as it should be! After all, he's my date!

For me, that's just unheard of! I'm only seventeen! And I love to dance! Who'd have ever thought I'd spend a whole evening in a corner talking to a boy I'd just met?! With that Rappy Perez?

Dale said Rappy loves to dance. Well, I love to dance. But we spent three hours sitting on hard wooden chairs . . . just talking.

♪♪♪♪

The following Saturday night Alyce waited in the living room for Dale to show up for the Cavalier Dance. Grandma Fanane sat next to the living room window so she could peer out to the street, one of her few enjoyments since she suffered a stroke when Alyce had barely turned thirteen. Partially paralyzed on her left side, Mary Frances Fanane was able to crochet with her right hand, the strand of crochet thread pressed against her side by her useless left arm. With her one hand, she crocheted baby clothes—tiny sweaters and caps—to sell to neighbors and add a few dollars to the household.

Alyce had her back to the window when she heard a car's engine turn off. Thinking it would be Dale pulling up to the curb, she glanced out the window to find that it was Herman Toenes parking across the street in front of his family's grocery store. She rose from the worn Victorian brocade sofa, stretched like a kitten, and smoothed the organdy flared skirt on her aquamarine party dress her mother had finished sewing that very afternoon.

"It's still light—I think I'll wait for Dale on the front porch," she eased toward the front door, pausing to test her grandmother's reaction.

"No you won't!" Grandma Fanane looked up from her crochet project. "You ain't gonna wait for a boy on the front porch and let the whole neighborhood think you're *fast!*"

"Grandma! Nobody's gonna think I'm fast just cuz I'm sitting in a swing all by myself waiting for a boy to take me to a dance! . . . After all, this is *1930!*"

Before her grandmother could reply, they heard a car engine turn off. Seconds later a car-door slammed shut, and Dale Simpson bounded up the wooden steps and onto the front porch.

"You ought to be waiting in your bedroom so I have to open the door to let him in—or, better yet, your brother lets him in. When *you* open the door for your gentleman-caller, it looks like you're too eager. Girls today just don't care if they appear 'fast'!" Grandma Fanane pointed her crochet needle at Alyce.

But Alyce had already opened the door before Dale could ring the bell.

When they got to the curb, the door of the car swung open and Rappy Perez jumped out of the front seat. She realized her mouth had flown open, but she avoided coming to a dead halt. She slid gracefully onto the front seat and grinned all the way to the Cavalier Hall as she nestled between the two young men from the Merchants National Bank.

She danced the first number with Dale. After all, he *was* her date, and she was relieved that Rappy didn't cut-in on them. He sat on a folding chair in the corner until the first number was over. Then he sprang to his feet and cut-in on Dale just as the second number began. All night long, Rappy continued to cut-in on her partners. And if another boy tried to cut-in on Rappy, he whirled her away and pretended he hadn't felt the hand tapping on his shoulder.

She refused to sit with him in a corner and talk as she had done the previous Saturday. And when the band took their break, she made sure she was dancing with Dale so he'd be the one to buy her a Coca-Cola. She wasn't going to let that Perez boy monopolize her again the whole evening. After all, she was merely seventeen. She came to the Cavalier Hall to dance. To dance with lots of boys.

As they were leaving the Cavalier Hall at 11:00 p.m., Alyce whispered to Dale to drop off Rappy before they got to her house. She had something important to tell Dale—she didn't want Rappy waiting in the car while she and Dale talked on the front porch at Bayou and Savannah.

On her verandah Alyce sat in one of the green wicker rocking chairs so that Dale couldn't snuggle up close to her as he liked to do on the swing.

"It's *Rappy*, isn't it?" Dale whispered. He leaned against a column opposite her rocker. He had his hands stuffed deep into his trouser pockets yet he was anything but relaxed.

"No," she sighed in exasperation, her voice barely a whisper. "I just never should've accepted this ring—I'm only seventeen!"

"It's not an engagement ring! It's just *friendship*! Hell, I like to buy you things!" his voice became hoarse as he tried to whisper and not wake up the Hicks family.

"Don't cuss!" she snapped. "And I don't care what it is! I don't want to wear your ring or anybody else's! I want to . . . to date other boys!"

"You want to *play the field*? . . . Swell! You date anybody you want—I don't care—but why can't you date other fellows and still wear that ring?" he had taken his hands out of his pockets and was gesticulating wildly.

"*Because*," she felt her face turning hot from rising anger, "I don't *want* to!"

"That's not a good reason!" he held out both hands, palms up, as if he were begging.

"Well, it's *my* reason!" she jumped from the rocker and shoved the red garnet ring into his open palm. She dashed for the front door hoping he wouldn't try to follow.

"Fine!" he snapped. "And just see if I care!"

She glanced over her shoulder just in time to see him wind up like a baseball pitcher and throw the ring over his car and into the street. She heard the silver ring bounce off the hood of Herman Toenes's parked car before it landed in the dirt road.

Twenty minutes later as she rolled her head on her pillow in hopes of sorting out what had just happened on the front verandah, she told herself that she had done the right thing. She was too young to be wearing some boy's ring—especially if the 'boy' was a twenty-one year-old man who had a good job at the Merchants National Bank. Giving the ring back to Dale had nothing to do with Rappy Perez.

Sure, Rappy's cute. And although he's the worst dancer I've ever tried to follow, he does love to dance—even if 'dancing' to Rappy means nothing more than whirling around the floor with no consideration for the music's tempo.

And, he's loads of fun with a great personality.

Of course I'd like to date him. . . . I mean, Dale's right that there's no law against dating other boys and still wearing Dale's ring.

But I can't let Dale think he has a special place in my heart. I wanna meet lots of boys so that when I finally get married, I'll be certain I've found the right fellow!

Maybe I should throw on a bathrobe and run out there and look for that ring! Nobody should be throwing jewelry in the streets—especially in these hard times when Bubber says the country's in a Great Depression.

I just can't forget those lines for the soup kitchen outside St. Joseph's Church when we went to Mass last Sunday. Mama sent me home after Mass to help Grandma Fanane start Sunday dinner, but Mama stayed to help serve all those people lined up at the Church rectory. There were whole families! Men with their wives and small children—hoping for a

19

Sunday meal with a chunk of stew-meat or a chicken neck in the bowl, not just the vegetable soup they get served during the week.

But she didn't dash to the street to look for the garnet ring. She had tried returning the ring to Dale but he, being the craziest boy she'd ever dated, decided to throw it in the street. She wasn't responsible. Still, she hated the thought of a nice piece of jewelry getting washed down the drain in the next heavy rain.

Four weeks later the ring reappeared. Alyce was at a Knights of Columbus dance with John Quigley when the band took their midway break. Monica Bridges, who was now dating Dale Simpson, bragged to Alyce about all the expensive gifts that Dale had given her. Having just taken a big swig of Coca-Cola, Alyce almost choked when Monica held up her right hand to show off her new "friendship" ring. It was the red garnet.

CHAPTER **2**

DURING THE AUTUMN of 1930 the Great Depression deepened while Mobile's unemployment grew and bread-lines lengthened. As Christmas approached, dusk came earlier. In fact, the sky darkened about the same time Alyce buttoned her overcoat and tied the head-scarf under her chin to leave the Mobile Chemical Company after her workday. As she made her way south on Bayou Street towards Savannah, she realized that the winter dreariness sharpened her awareness of the deepening Depression. She walked faster to ward off the bleakness—not just the gloom of the December cold but the depressing economy.

As a fulltime student at Spring Hill College, Alyce's brother was not expected to contribute to the household. Both Alyce and her mother were grateful that Bubber supported himself with his full academic scholarship to SHC and his part-time job at Smith's Bakery where he boxed pies at dawn each morning before classes.

I'm happy for Bubber. And, am I ever grateful for my job at Mobile Chemical! It's not getting any more interesting or challenging, and I'm never gonna advance. And, Lord knows when I'll ever get a raise—certainly not till this Depression's over. But it's a JOB!

I'm so thankful I can give Mama half my paycheck to take

some pressure off her dressmaking business. It's been sink-
ing right along with everybody else's business—except Toenes
grocery. Now, their problem is folks can't pay their bill.

My weekly contribution means Mama can afford a few extras
this year for Christmas dinner. No doubt, Aunt Celeste'll show up
with her Charlotte Rousse. I'm putting money aside each week to
buy some cranberries. They're so pricey this year!

Bustling around the tiny office at Mobile Chemical with only one other employee, Alyce got through the day wondering which boy might drop by Bayou and Savannah that night after supper to sit on the living-room sofa and listen to dance bands on the radio. Few boys could afford to take her to picture-show at the Saenger anymore, especially during the week. And she looked forward to the weekly meeting with her high school girlfriends.

Every Saturday she met with members of the Coquette Club, mainly former classmates from the Convent of Mercy, but also a few girls from Bishop Toolen High. After working the usual half day on that Saturday of Christmas week, she rushed across town to meet the girls for lunch at the Dew Drop Inn on the southwest corner of Government and Ann. She tried not to mention her job because so many of her friends were still looking for a job, *any* job. But it was difficult to ignore the reason why Alyce was the last to arrive at the Dew Drop. After leaving work at noon she had to walk twelve blocks southwest through the downtown business center to catch a streetcar for another twelve blocks west to the midtown restaurant.

"We're so poor at my house that I can't afford these Dew Drop hotdogs much longer," Girlie Callahan gazed around the six tables pushed together, looking for a reaction.

"Me either!" Kitty Doyle gave a sigh of relief. "I'm so glad you brought up the subject of money, Girlie. We've got to find a solution."

"I never thought I'd have to admit that I can't afford a nickel hot-dog," Modeste gave a sarcastic snort.

"Solution!" Monica held up her hands to stop the chatter. "We meet at our house cuz we've got that great big living room. Each girl brings her own sandwich from home, and Frieda and I provide some kind of punch!"

"Great idea!" everyone agreed.

"What I need is a job!" Girlie reached for the catsup bottle.

"I'd sell lipstick over the counter at Woolworth's," Monica complained as she spread mustard on her hot dog, "if they'd just *hire* me!"

"A lot of good that Classical Course did us in high school!" Frieda Bridges chuckled ruefully. "Four years of Latin, two years of Spanish, and those grueling Math courses! All that time I should've been taking Typing and Shorthand!"

"Well," Alyce stopped munching on her hot dog to commiserate. "I took that Classical Course just like y'all because my brother told me I *needed* to. You know, Bubber's the brain in our family, so I did what he told me. I rarely made above a "C" in anything, but it was enough to graduate, so maybe Bubber was right."

"Bubber was wrong!" Kitty Doyle sneered. "You didn't need any Latin and Algebra—you *needed* Typing and Shorthand!"

"So, Alyce, how did you get your secretarial job at that chemical company?" Monica ignored Kitty's interruption.

"My Aunt Katie Fanane teaches Typing and Shorthand—in her house on Reed Avenue," Alyce continued. "I took an intensive course with her right after graduation with five other girls for six weeks."

"You can't learn typing and shorthand in six weeks!"

"I'm up to forty words-per-minute! Mr. Geary never dictates cuz he's rarely in the office. He owns a realty agency across town that keeps him busy. It's just me, a colored man who cleans up and runs errands, and this salesman who's out calling on businesses to buy this powdered chemical that makes sweeping floors easier. Now when the *salesman* dictates a letter—which isn't more than once a week—I make him talk slow so I can use my own version of shorthand!" Alyce smiled at her good fortune. "Most of

23

the time I'm filing invoices, sharpening pencils, and answering the phone!"

"Well, your Aunt Katie explains how you learned to type but it *doesn't* explain how you got the job!" Monica had become impatient.

"My mother sews for his wife."

"*Whose* wife?"

"Mr. Geary's! . . . My boss. Mama's been sewing for his wife for *years*, so when he needed a new secretary, *Mrs.* Geary told her husband I needed a job," Alyce took another bite of her hot dog.

"And *you* took four years of Latin," murmured Kitty Doyle, "same as me. But who knew the country was headed for economic disaster?"

"Certainly not President Hoover!" Monica said with bitterness.

After the Saturday lunch Alyce jumped on the streetcar and sailed down Government Street where she got off at Bayou and hurried south six blocks to her house. Because she had a date that night, she needed to shampoo her hair and sit on the back porch in the afternoon sun, still warm enough in December on the Gulf Coast to dry her stylish bob.

In the kitchen she grabbed the grocery list off the table and dashed across the street to Toenes Grocery. Fourteen months had passed since the stock market crashed and threw the country into chaos. Now the economic depression was felt in every house in her neighborhood. No longer did she feel embarrassed about charging groceries at the Toenes Grocery. Whenever one of the Toenes boys needed sleeves shortened on a new dress shirt, he brought it to Miss Alice who did the sewing job on credit. And when Mercedes, four years older than Alyce, needed a new gown for the October Harvest Moon ball, Miss Alice created it with the same understanding that Mercedes offered for the Hicks grocery bill: "You can pay for it when you get the money."

It was 6:50 exactly when Alyce appeared in the front parlor where

Grandma Fanane sat crocheting in her rocker. The old lady faced a wood-fire smoldering in the fireplace used to heat the drafty room with twelve-foot ceilings.

"He's picking you up at seven, I suppose," Grandma didn't look up but she sniffed loudly to indicate Alyce had doused on too much White Oleander perfume.

"Yes, m'am," she smoothed the skirt of her new party dress. Then she turned slightly and glanced over her shoulder into the full-length mirror next to the front door to make sure the seams in her silk stockings were straight.

"I can always tell what time he's picking you up. You prance in here exactly ten minutes before he's due to show up."

"A girl should be on time," Alyce flounced herself on the brocade sofa.

"But a proper *lady* should wait in her bedroom until somebody knocks on her door to tell her the gentleman-caller has arrived and is waiting in the front parlor," the old lady pointed her crochet needle in disapproval.

"Don't worry, Grandma, I'm not *fast!*"

"But *he* may be! . . . After all, his daddy wasn't born here, you know, and those foreigners have different ideas about manners and such than *we* do!" she scowled at the tiny pink cap in her lap.

"You mean *Rappy's* daddy? . . . Mr. Perez's been living here in Mobile since he was *eight* years old! Rappy was *born* here! His grandfather's a doctor, a *medical* doctor!"

"Spanish people are just different than us, don't you think?"

"Besides, I don't have a date with Rappy tonight—I'm going out with John!"

"Oh!" the grandmother dropped her crocheting and looked up in delight. "You mean that John Quigley? . . . He's such a nice young man!"

"You think so?" Alyce enjoyed baiting her grandmother when she could imagine what the old lady was thinking. "Is that because he's so good-looking? Or because his family owns Mobile Coal and Ice?!"

"That's two things folks always need—ice in the summer and coal in the winter! What do you think your brother shovels into that pot-bellied stove in the dining room? . . . It ain't wood!"

"And it helps that John's tall and blond, right?" Alyce grinned at her grandmother.

"Well," she returned to her crocheting, "rich and handsome ain't a bad combination!"

"And *tall*," Alyce teased. "Don't forget how tall John is!"

"Well, Alyce, you could be happy with a rich tall man just as well as a short man from a family that's . . . that's *not* so rich, don't you think?"

"You want me to marry John Quigley, Grandma?"

"I just want you to be happy, honey, with whoever you marry."

"And what if that *whoever* is Rappy Perez?"

"That would be . . . all right!" she said half-heartedly. "As long as he don't lose that job at the bank. In these bad times, nobody knows if their job is safe anymore. But now, if a boy's family *owns* a company that sells coal and ice—then that boy doesn't have *anything* to worry about!"

"Well, Rappy's still got his job a year after the stock market crash. That says something, doesn't it?" Alyce had become serious.

"He's small, but his muscles are hard," the old lady mused.

"What's that got to do with anything?" Alyce laughed.

"If he loses that bank job, he'll be able to do manual labor."

"They like him at the bank. The only way he'll lose his job is if the Merchants National Bank fails . . . or if he can't play shortstop anymore."

"Especially the thighs and the back. Your grandfather always said *those* are the muscles a man needs to lift things. And young Mr. Perez's thigh and back muscles appear to be strong, if you've taken the time to notice," the old lady murmured.

"*I've* noticed the thighs and back, Grandma . . . and a lot more."

"Now, don't you go entertaining impure thoughts!" she shook her crochet needle again in Alyce's direction.

At the sound of a car pulling up to the curb, the two women abruptly stopped talking. A car door slammed. The slow, heavy foot-steps of a big man crept across the front porch. Before the doorbell could chime, Alyce sprang from the sofa, grabbed her winter coat and threw open the door for the young man who would take her to another KOC dance where she hoped she'd run into Rappy Perez.

ↄↄↄↄↄ

The Quigley family was well off, especially for Catholics of Irish descent. Grandma Fanane was correct—everybody needed coal in the winter and ice in the summer. And during that winter of 1931 when the economic chaos had taken on the label of the 'Great Depression', nobody stopped buying coal. Newer houses in west Mobile were built to burn natural gas for heating, but in the south part of town where the Hicks family lived on the corner of Bayou and Savannah, everybody still used coal.

And ice. The iceman came everyday to deliver a block of ice for a nickel. The cubic-foot block sat in the tin-lined icebox to keep perish-able foods from spoiling, the ice slowly melting into water collected in a tray at the bottom of the box until the iceman appeared the next day with another block of ice. The modern refrigerator—whether electric or gas—had not been on the market long enough for the price to fall to the affordability of working-class folks.

The Quigley family lived in west Mobile—a neighborhood called Spring Hill where businessmen built spacious new homes after achieving financial success. Locating his family to Spring Hill an-nounced that the entrepreneur had arrived at some level of Mobile society—if not by blood-line, at least by 'new money'. Because it was young John's grandfather who had made the first Quigley fortune in coal and ice, the family had been wealthy enough since 1900 to own a summer house across Mobile Bay on the prized eastern shore.

During the summer of 1931, a year after Alyce's high school gradu-ation, John Quigley finally asked Alyce to meet his family. Grandma Fanane was so thrilled at the prospect of Alyce marrying into the wealthy

Quigley family that she managed to get out of her rocker and limp to the front door to greet John when he arrived for the important day.

While rushing down the hallway to the front door, Alyce stuffed her bathing-suit into a beach-towel, rolled them up, and tucked them under her arm. When she saw her grandmother leaning against the doorjamb, beaming like a Jewish matchmaker, Alyce became furious—but she kissed the old lady on the cheek, greeted John with a barely audible "Hey!" . . . and dashed for the royal-blue Oldsmobile convertible.

Upon arriving at the Fairhope home, John stopped the car behind the Quigley house under the shade of giant pine trees. Alyce remained on the front seat, as always, waiting for him to open the door for her.

"Stay in the car a minute—I want you to be surprised the first time you see my boat!" he jumped from the Oldsmobile, disappeared around the corner of the house, and ran towards the shoreline.

Alyce sat in the convertible and took deep breaths to calm herself. She was always a nervous wreck when she met a boy's family, especially the mother. When the family was from her neighborhood—or anywhere east of Broad Street—she could hold her own, but the Quigleys lived in Spring Hill. They were rich. And here she was sitting in an Oldsmobile convertible—a new 1931 model—at their *second* home on Mobile Bay where the son was parading out his speedboat to show off. And the mother would probably appear at lunch on the wharf wearing a diamond necklace at noon. Monica Bridges' mother says a lady never wears diamonds before sunset. Alyce closed her eyes and wondered if John Quigley was worth the aggravation.

"Okay!" John's voice woke her from her reverie. "Let's go see the new boat!"

Alyce stood on the wharf and gazed at the 18-foot wooden speedboat docked below her. It was a Stauter-built boat, every wooden rib on the floor handmade, varnished to a gleam, and laid with care by Lawrence Stauter himself. A beautiful vessel with a marine-green hull, the top half of the boat was painted white.

She stood dumbfounded. Painted in black on the side of the boat's bow, a single name in bold letters sent a shiver down her spine and made her face turn crimson with rage:

Felicia

"Is *that* the surprise? . . . You named your boat 'Felicia'?"

"I named it after *you*!" John's face beamed with manly pride.

"My name's *Alyce*!"

"But Felicia's your middle name, isn't it?" he look bewildered.

"I hate that name!" she clutched the rolled-up towel with both her hands and kneaded it like a mound of bread-dough.

"I kinda like it," he said sheepishly. "It means 'happiness' . . . in Latin."

"I took four years of Latin! . . . I know what it means! But I still hate it! Why didn't you name it '*Alyce*'?" she yelled at the boy, not caring if his mother in the house and the rest of the family heard her. His stupidity needed to be revealed to the whole eastern shore.

"I don't know—I just thought that—"

"Let's go swimming!" she turned in fury and sashayed across the wharf to the overhead pavilion where she could change into her swimsuit in the bath house, leaving the poor boy with his mouth open.

A lunch of cold roast-beef and tomato aspic was served by a colored woman at the end of the wharf. John's mother wore three strands of delicate pearls with her yellow organdy sundress. Recalling Grandma Fanane's remark that John's mother had grown up not far from the Fanane house at Bayou and Savannah, Alyce concluded the mother had married into money and was still dressing to impress. John's father was a gentleman of the old school who had been rich all his life and knew how to put Alyce at ease as she struggled to keep the wind from blowing her napkin off her lap.

John and Alyce spent the whole afternoon speeding up and down the eastern shore in the boat named 'Felicia'. Behind the boat John pulled a new surfboard, the most fashionable toy for water recreation available in the 1930s before water-skis appeared on the scene. The surfboard was a flat piece of ¾ inch-thick plywood, about 3x5 feet, pulled behind the boat with a tow rope. The rider held onto a rope at the front of the board. He could lie flat on his stomach on the board, or he could show off by standing up and waving to the spectators as the boat sped past the wharf.

Alyce rode the board most of the afternoon so she wouldn't have to sit in the boat with John—she was still mad at him for giving the boat that awful name. When it was his turn to ride the surfboard, she sat in the front of the boat next to the driver, John's sixteen year-old brother, Billy, who appeared to have more sense than his older brother. Each time the boat made a full circle to turn around at Point Clear, Alyce strained to see if she recognized anyone waving from the wharf at the Grand Hotel. If she happened to be on the surfboard as the boat made the turn at the Grand, she managed to stand up on the surfboard, hold the rope with one hand, and wave to the folks on the wharf. For a moment she was a bathing beauty from an MGM movie filmed in Palm Beach.

On the way back to Mobile late that afternoon as the sun was setting across the bay in the west, John drove with the top down on the convertible. Sensing Alyce was seething about 'Felicia', he realized they wouldn't have to talk if the wind was rushing through their ears.

Clearly John likes me . . . a lot!

After all, he named his boat after me. I can hardly imagine any of my other suitors doing such. None of them even own a boat. We're in a Great Depression!

But John chose the wrong name. I could never marry a man who would be so presumptuous as to name a boat after me without first asking permission. And if I did give him permission, he'd need to have enough sense to choose my first name, not that middle name I detest.

John Quigley's just not husband material. But I'll still date him, if nothing else to keep Grandma Fanane quiet. As long as I date John, I won't have to put up with Grandma nagging me about Rappy Perez being so much shorter than John and from a family not nearly as rich as the Quigleys. Besides, John IS a gentleman and he does show me a good time. I'll continue playing the field—I'm not ready to go steady with anybody yet, not even my favorite gentleman-caller, Rappy Perez.

⤳⤳⤳⤳

Monica Bridges decided that the Coquette Club needed to become a Greek sorority. Although Alyce had no idea what a Greek sorority was, she agreed to go along with the crowd as long as it didn't involve anything scandalous or sinful.

"We're Catholics, you know!" she gave Monica a sidelong glance from the sofa in the Bridges living room. "Aren't there any *Latin* sororities we can join?"

"Yeah," Kitty Doyle lifted the waxed paper from around her egg salad sandwich, "I mean, all of us took four years of Latin!"

"Not that we remember a damn *word* of Latin—we've been out of school for over a year," Modeste Friedhoff guffawed, "but we sure as hell don't know any *Greek*!"

"It has to be Greek!" Monica rolled her eyes in exasperation. "And we're gonna do this *right*! . . . Everything has to be legal!"

Doing it 'right' meant going to the Mobile County Courthouse and filing a charter to become a social club. Alyce didn't dare ask for time off from work to accompany the Bridges girls to the courthouse, but she felt free to extend her coffee-break when Monica and Frieda bounded up the stairs at Mobile Chemical to show Alyce a receipt for the official document they had just filed at the courthouse.

Alpha Delta Kappa . . . the new official name of the Coquette Club.

The founding chapter was in Mobile, Alabama. By the time Alyce married three years later, Alpha Delta Kappa had expanded with chapters in Montgomery and Pensacola where some of the Mobile members

31

had cousins they trusted to manage a chapter. Evidently nobody had cousins they trusted in Mississippi because no chapters were founded in that state, but several Mobile members boasted cousins and friends in New Orleans where the fourth chapter was founded. And for reasons unknown, a fifth chapter was founded in Bogalusa, Louisiana.

The first Alpha Delta Kappa president in the founding chapter, by unanimous acclamation, was Alyce Hicks.

"All right," Alyce folded her hands in her lap and gazed around the spacious living room of the Bridges home, "I'll be president on one condition!"

"Can't imagine what *that* could be!" Modeste muttered under her breath.

"We don't *blackball*!" Alyce slapped the arm of the overstuffed chair she was sitting in.

"What's a black ball?" Kitty Doyle's eyes widened.

"The fraternities at Spring Hill College use the black ball," Alyce explained. "Members vote on a new boy by dropping a marble into a box—either a white one or a black one. Bubber says that if a boy gets just one black marble in that box, he can't be offered a bid to join. And the member who dropped the black marble into the box doesn't have to identify himself. So nobody knows who blackballed the candidate, much less why the member doesn't want the new boy to get a bid. . . . We're not gonna do that!"

"Right!" Monica slapped the arm of the sofa where she was sitting at the end. "If you don't want to give a bid to a new girl, then you have to say *why* in front of the whole chapter!"

"I agree!" Frieda cheered. "You can't keep a girl out unless you have a good reason."

"Well," Modeste cocked her head as if she wanted to start trouble, "can one single vote keep a new girl from joining . . . keep her *out*?"

All heads turned to Alyce.

"Of course!" she said emphatically. "We don't want a girl to join if a member has a good reason to keep her out—something we need to know about her *reputation* or her daddy's reputation—because then that member might cause the new girl to feel unwelcome. Or the member might resent the rest of us for letting the girl join."

"But the vote can't be secret, right?" Monica said.

"The member has to speak up and say why she doesn't want the girl to join!"

"But if we can't convince the member to change her mind, then the girl doesn't get a bid, and—"

"And she's not allowed to join! . . . Everybody agree to that?"

"Agreed!" the voices echoed throughout the Bridges' home.

The new rule about giving out bids was put to the test at the next meeting. Alyce had put up for membership the name of one of her best friends and when Frieda, the membership chairman, came to the name on the list, Modeste raised her hand in objection.

"Peg Camilleri," Frieda stared at the list. "What could you possibly have against Peg?"

"She's a *guinea*," Modeste said softly, apologizing for the truth.

"A *what*?" Kitty asked in bewilderment.

"A wop . . . *day*-go," Modeste glanced around the room at all twenty girls in hopes someone would help her resolve the dilemma.

"That means *Eye-talian*, Kitty!" Monica was losing patience.

"Peg Camilleri is Italian?" Kitty seemed incredulous. "She's as blonde as *me*!"

"Not all guineas are dark," Modeste gazed apologetically at Alyce who sat in the overstuffed chair trying to hold back the tears welling in her eyes.

"Peg Camilleri is one of my best friends," Alyce finally said, trying to disguise the lump in her throat, "and so are you, Modeste. I just can't believe that you would—"

"It's not *me*, Alyce! . . . But my daddy said last night that if we want to keep our reputation clean, we shouldn't let in guineas and spicks. I *like* Peg—I really do! I'm just telling you what my daddy said!"

"What about me, Modeste?" Kitty was on her feet. "I'm a *mick*!"

"Modeste, what kind of name is 'Friedhoff'?" Alyce asked so softly that she could barely be heard.

"German," Modeste glanced around the room wondering where Alyce was headed.

"When I first met you in the eighth grade, my mama thought 'Friedhoff' was Jewish, but she let me play with you anyway because she said you're a nice girl. . . . And then we found out your family's Catholic. But before we found out, my grandma said it didn't matter if you were Jewish because you were so funny!"

"Peg Camilleri's funny!" Frieda tried to break the tension in the room. "*Nobody* can tell a dirty joke like Peg Camilleri!"

"I can't tell dirty jokes at all—I can never remember the punch line!" Alyce gave a forced laugh and glanced around the room to see if she had been successful in reducing the tension.

"So what about Peg Camilleri?" Frieda stared at her list of prospective new members.

"We can't give her a bid," Alyce pronounced matter-of-factly. "A member has dissented and the member gave her reason. Who's the next name?"

"Wait a minute!" Modeste raised her hand in frustration. "It's not *me*! . . . My daddy was just saying that we need to be careful about who we let *in*!"

"Does that mean you're withdrawing your objection to Peg Camilleri?" Alyce gazed at her feet so as not to confront Modeste.

"I told you! . . . I *like* Peg! I want to give her a bid!"

"Anyone object to giving a bid to Peg Camilleri?" Alyce slowly scanned the circle of girls scattered on ottomans and on the oriental rug, looking for hands raised, but she found none.

"Good! . . . Next name, Frieda?" Alyce glanced at Modeste and gave her a warm smile.

⌇⌇⌇

In December of the next year, 1932, the Alpha Delta Kappas decided to host their First Annual Winter Ball. Because the Depression had finally hit Mobile hard in the belly, the girls were able to negotiate with the Battle House Hotel for a bargain price to rent their

Grand Ballroom. The historic hotel, which had opened before the Civil War in downtown Mobile, was their first choice. When the Ball Committee—consisting of Monica Bridges, Modeste Friedhoff, and Alyce Hicks—finished haggling with the general manager of the Battle House, Mr. Bragg Counts, he was so frazzled he was ready to give them the main ballroom for free, just to get them out of his office.

Alyce couldn't believe that a bunch of Catholic girls had managed to reserve the Grand Ballroom of the Battle House for the second Saturday in December. She asked her mother to add a chapel-length train to her flowing gown of white *peau de soie* to give a more cinematic effect when she descended the burgundy-carpeted main staircase. As president of the sorority, she had the honor of leading the Grand March. She would descend the staircase on the arm of her escort—he, like all the escorts, wearing white tie and tails—and they would stand in the center of the Grand Ballroom under that massive chandelier, five tiers of crystal dripping over the parquet floor as the other young couples descended the staircase and stood in a semicircle on either side of them.

But who would she ask to be her escort? If she asked Rappy Perez, her grandmother might have another stroke. Of course, the tall and slender John Quigley would look more elegant in the formal tails, but he couldn't dance any better than Rappy. Yet John never drank bootleg whiskey so there was no risk of him getting tipsy and running off to dance with all the other girls all night long.

It was the last Saturday in November when Mr. Counts called from the Battle House with a request for Alyce to change the date of the ADK Ball. She was sitting on the back porch letting her hair dry in the afternoon autumn sunshine—she had a date that night with Rappy—when her brother called her to the phone. In an instant the question of choosing an escort became secondary.

"But, Mr. Counts, we gave you a deposit!" Alyce wished Modeste Friedhoff was dealing with the manager on the phone instead of her.

"Well, Miss Hicks, it seems that another organization needs the ballroom for that second Saturday—they can't schedule another night, only that particular Saturday."

"Our invitations are in the mail—they're *engraved* and cost a small fortune!"

"I realize you signed a contract and you have a legal right to that date, but it really would help me out if you could change to another date."

"Who's this *other* organization?"

"It's the Delta Sigma Fraternity."

A huge lump formed in Alyce's throat. The Deltas were Mobile's rich boys. She felt doomed. How could the ADKs compete with the sons of Mobile's 'old money'?

"Tell them," she regained her voice, "that they have to find another ballroom."

"Would you like to talk to the president of the fraternity, Miss Hicks?"

"No, sir! . . . I would not!"

"He's sitting right here in my office, and I'd appreciate you explaining the situation, and perhaps you could—"

"We have a contract, Mr. Counts!"

"But, Miss Hicks," the manager whispered because he was embarrassed to admit that he had caved into the snobbery of Mobile society, "you don't know who this boy's father is—*and* his mother!"

"I don't care if he's the next King of Carnival! *We* have that date!"

"He says he's coming to your house right now to talk with you."

"No, sir! He's not!"

"Thank you, Miss Hicks. I'll let you and the Deltas work this out," and the manager hung up.

By the time the Deltas arrived at Bayou and Savannah, Alyce had rounded up Modeste and Monica to stand by her. Rather, they were *sitting by her* in the swing on the front porch, the three girls squeezed into the swing as it swayed back and forth in the setting sunlight as if they hadn't a care in the world.

The sleek maroon Chrysler pulled up to the curb and two well-dressed young men started up the front walk. Sensing they weren't welcome, they hung at the bottom step and called out to the three girls in the swing.

"Y'all must be from that new sorority, huh?" the shorter boy spoke cheerily but didn't bother to introduce himself, as if he expected to be recognized on sight due to his family's social status.

Alyce rose from the swing and, determined not to be intimidated by the rich boys, slowly edged to the top step. She fluffed her still-damp hair and leaned on the railing. When she saw the other boy, the tall blonde one, she almost lost her breath. At first she thought it was John Quigley, but she realized it was his brother Billy, the high school senior she had sat next to in the boat when he was pulling his brother on the surfboard last summer.

"Billy? . . . Billy Quigley?" Alyce started down the steps. "Are *you* the Delta's Ball Chairman? . . . It just never occurred to me that—"

"Alyce," the young boy didn't bother to introduce his companion, "Mr. Counts sent us over here—me and the Delta president here—to see if we could get you to change your mind."

"Y'all ain't getting our date!" Modeste stood at the porch railing—Monica at her side—launching a surly attack.

"Well," the young Quigley became more nervous as he realized he was up against three older girls, not just Alyce Hicks who dated his brother and who should have been a pushover.

"I know *you*!" the shorter boy pointed rudely at Alyce.

"I have no idea who you are!"

"I danced with you at one of the *Catholic* dances!" he chuckled as if he had used a curse word.

"I don't remember your face, much less you asking to dance with me!" she wasn't about to let him get away with arrogance on her front steps.

"I didn't *ask*! . . . I *cut-in* on Billy's brother!" the young man slid his thumbs through his belt-loops and kicked the bottom step.

"Lots of boys cut-in on Alyce," Modeste sassed from the porch railing. "That don't mean she's gonna remember you. . . . And you're not getting that second Saturday."

"Tell you what, ladies, y'all let us have that second Saturday, and I'll make sure y'all get invited to the King's luncheon this Mardi Gras."

"Since *when*," Modeste brayed, "did the Carnival Association start picking a teenager to be King of Carnival?"

"It's my brother—he's king this year. Actually, he's my second brother to be chosen king, which means that I'll probably be king in five or six years . . . so, what do you say, ladies? You wanna do a favor for King Biff here and let us have that date?" he cocked his head as if his future as king of Mardi Gras assured that he'd get his way with the ADK girls.

But the three girls stood their ground. After another five minutes of useless swaggering, the teenaged president of the Deltas caved in. He grabbed a mortified Billy Quigley by the elbow and pushed him into the Chrysler.

That night Alyce was running late for her date. Scurrying around her bedroom searching for a mate to her silk stocking, she relaxed a bit knowing that Rappy was rarely on time for a date. Every Saturday night he had to borrow a car, and he rarely showed up in the same vehicle. Because she had been hassled by those Deltas appearing in the front yard, this would be the one night—to Grandma's delight—when Alyce's mother or brother would knock on her bedroom door to tell her the date was waiting in the living room.

"You've got a visitor," the deep voice of Bubber, her brother, came from the hallway as he knocked on her door.

"I can't believe Rappy Perez is actually early!" she yelled through the door as she snapped the garter against her thigh.

"It isn't *Rappy!*" her brother replied ominously from the other side of the door.

Five minutes later, minus jewelry and with her hair not brushed, Alyce dragged the tall, broad-shouldered John Quigley from the front parlor down the long hallway to the kitchen where she shoved him into a chair at the table.

"Now you sit there and tell me what you're doing here unannounced on a Saturday night!" she stood with her hands on her hips.

He was so tall that sitting in the chair he was eye-to-eye with Alyce standing over him.

"I'm sorry, Alyce, really I am. But my mama wouldn't leave me alone until I came over here to plead the case for the Deltas getting that Battle House ballroom," he stared at his huge feet, afraid to face her.

"The Deltas! . . . Did it ever occur to you that I might have a date tonight?"

"I know!" he glanced up and gave her a pitiful look, "but I've got to get my mama off my back. Can't you girls move your ball to another date?"

"Why are you worrying about the Deltas and their stupid ball? Is it because of your little brother?"

"*I'm* a Delta! . . . I've been inactive for a couple of years cuz I don't like all that hard drinking and fooling around with those kind of women who—well, *those* kind of women! But my mama told me to use my influence with you to see if you'd think about—"

"Your *influence?* . . . What makes you think you've got any influence with me?"

"Okay," he folded his hands on the kitchen table, "I realize you're mad as a wet hen for me coming in here to get you to change your mind—and I don't blame you for being sore—but tell me this! . . . Are you going to marry me?"

"What?!" she glanced at the clock over the kitchen stove. "I have a date coming to pick me up at seven—and by that clock on the wall, it's already ten minutes *past*—and you're asking me to marry you?"

"We've been dating for two years, Alyce, and I need to know your intentions. If you're not planning to marry me, just let me know. You see, there's this *other* girl who wants to marry me. You're my first choice, Alyce, that's for sure. But if you don't want me, I'll marry the other girl."

"No," she snapped without hesitation. "I don't want to marry you. I'm marrying Rappy Perez."

"When did he propose?"

"He hasn't! . . . But if he doesn't, I'll just propose to *him*! . . . Now, get out of this house before Rappy gets here and finds you hiding in the kitchen!" she grabbed him by the elbow, dragged him across the linoleum, and pushed him out the back door.

On the second Saturday of December, as scheduled, Alyce led the First Annual ADK Winter Ball with Rappy Perez . . . in the Grand Ballroom of the Battle House Hotel.

In January, Rappy proposed marriage to Alyce.

On Valentine's Day John Quigley gave a diamond engagement ring to The Other Girl.

And six years later Biff, the snotty president of the Deltas who lost the Battle House ballroom to the ADK's, became King of Carnival.

CHAPTER **3**

A MONTH AFTER Alyce led the ADK ball with Rappy, he asked her to marry him. He surprised her on the verandah at Bayou and Savannah where they cuddled on the swing to ward off the cold as they listened to the Dorsey Brothers on the radio. She had seen the marriage proposal coming because he hadn't taken her to the picture-show in three months, a sure sign he was saving his money for something.

"Before I can say 'yes', you need to talk to somebody, don't you?" she rested her feet flat on the porch floor to keep the swing from swaying.

"Talk to somebody? . . . *Why*?" he wrinkled his forehead as if the thought had never occurred to him.

"To ask for my hand!"

"I don't want your *hand*! Your hands are always cold!" he grinned and squeezed both her hands through the woolen gloves she was wearing.

"Aren't you gonna do this thing *right*?" she tried to sound indignant.

"Well, you don't have a daddy, so who do I talk to?"

"Bubber, I guess," she softened. "He's the man around here."

"He's two years younger than me! You want me to ask your brother if I can marry his little sister?"

"Well, I don't know what you should do! What about my Uncle Manny?"

41

"Relax, Hickory," he leaned back in the swing, clasped his hands behind his head and chuckled. "I talked with your mother last night."

"You talked with Mama? And you didn't tell me you were gonna do it?" she socked him in his shoulder with her fist. "What did she say?"

"She asked me how much money I make at the bank, so I told her. Then she said I could marry you if you wanted to marry *me*," his eyes twinkled with devilment.

"I don't know," she became coy.

"Hickory, will you marry me?" he took her hand and, tongue-in-cheek, spoke as if he were reading lines from a Gary Cooper movie script.

"I hope you didn't buy a diamond ring! You don't have money for that! I can do without a ring, you know!" she gave a deadpan stare into his dark eyes.

"I can't *buy* you a ring—I'm lucky to still have a job—but will this ring do?" he held up diamond ring which she recognized instantly.

"That's Mama's engagement ring!" Alyce felt her eyes fill with tears.

"She gave it to me last night," he slipped it on her finger.

"I haven't said 'yes'," she spoke softly to show she was serious.

"You're not kidding, are you?" he dropped her hand.

"I love you, Rappy, but I've got to be sure you're the one I should spend my life with."

"*Should*? . . . Don't you *want* to spend your life with me?"

"I'll let you know Tuesday at lunch. I need a couple of days to talk to Mama and . . . and somebody else."

♪♪♪

Twenty minutes later Alyce was sitting at the dining room table next to the pot-bellied coal stove. Her mother, Miss Alice, was busy at her sewing machine in the corner of the dining room where a lamp had been installed on the wall over the machine. In the summer Miss

Alice worked in her bedroom where the tall French windows opened to the side verandah to permit the bay breeze to waft through the rambling cottage, but during the winter she moved her sewing machine into the dining room to work close to the major source of heat for the entire house.

Grandma Fanane sat in her rocker in the living room facing the fireplace where she was warming her feet. With her one good hand, she sewed buttonholes in a purple satin costume for a Mardi Gras crewe that would be parading through Mobile's downtown streets in less than two months.

"Which Mardi Gras society?" Alyce took a wax pear from the glass bowl in the center of the table and turned it over and over as if she were looking for flaws.

"The Crewe of Columbus, who else?" Miss Alice didn't look up—she ripped open a seam in disgust with a Gillette double-edged razor blade.

"Rappy said he talked to you last night," she continued playing with the wax pear.

"He did," she lined up the two pieces of purple satin to sew them again.

"What did you tell him?" she stared at the back of her mother's graying head.

"He didn't say what I told him?"

"Well, yes m'am, but I wanna hear it from *you*," she knew her mother loved her but, considering what happened to her mother's marriage at such a tender age, these kinds of conversations about love and commitment were difficult for both of them.

"I *told* him," Miss Alice turned and faced Alyce, the razor blade poised in her right hand, "that it was fine with me if you married him—assuming he told me the truth about how much he makes at that bank—but it was up to you."

"Yes, m'am, that's what he said."

Miss Alice returned to the purple satin and passed it through the sewing machine. For a few minutes she worked on the machine. The belt turned the wheel with a piercing whir, and then stopped to a dead halt which only emphasized the silence between the two women. Finally, Miss Alice dropped the costume in her lap, turned in her chair and faced Alyce.

"You're not gonna accept his proposal?" the older woman stroked the satin fabric as she gazed at her daughter fretting at the head of the dining room table.

"I want to! . . . It's just that—I mean, how do I know he's the right one?" she searched her mother's blue eyes for support.

"You don't know for sure, I spoz. . . . You just have to trust in the Lord."

"So how do I know if this is God's Will?"

"Pray, Alyce. Ask Him for a sign."

♪♪♪♪

"Mama says I should ask God for a sign," Alyce sat opposite Sister Mary Consuela in the front parlor of the Convent of Mercy. She pulled at the fingertips of her brown cotton gloves to remove them so that she could eat the deviled ham sandwich she had brought from home. She felt awkward eating in front of her former high school principal, but she had given up her lunch hour to seek advice.

"I think you've already received your sign," the middle-aged nun adjusted her veil and sipped her hot tea, envying Alyce nibbling on the sandwich and resenting her Order's rule that a nun never eats in front of anyone but another sister.

"Well," Alyce joked, "I didn't see any halo around Rappy's head when he proposed!"

"But he did propose! And he already had a ring to slip on your finger!"

"Is that a sign from God?"

"You've got a Catholic boy from a good Catholic family who wants to marry you in a Catholic church! What girl could ask for more than that?"

"But is that a *sign*?"

"Who knows? . . . Does this young man have a job?"

"A *good* job . . . at Merchants National Bank!"

"In *these* hard times *that* could be a sign—the man has a job!"

"I guess I was thinking of something more spiritual, you know, something supernatural."

"Like an Angel of God appearing at the foot of your bed with a trumpet? And he announces that God the Father wants you to marry this Perez young man?"

"Sister, I have *prayed* to the Blessed Mother over this!"

"Alyce, right outside that backdoor," the nun pointed toward the kitchen, "we feed over 100 unemployed men—*and* women—everyday! Some of them have toddlers in their arms and puny children riding piggy-back. And *you're* worrying about which man to marry!"

"I don't think I have to worry about John Quigley anymore. He's already asked that other girl to marry him!" she had a half-smile on her face.

"Isn't he the one you chased off last month? . . . If he's already asked that other girl so soon, then that's another sign from God, wouldn't you say? . . . *St. Peter*, Alyce! How many signs do you need?"

"I just want to do God's Will," she gazed at the statue of the Virgin Mary standing on a pedestal in the corner of the parlor.

"You know, Alyce, in your senior year, we thought you might go off to join our order, the Religious Sisters of Mercy. . . . Do you remember what you said the day before graduation when I asked for your final decision?"

"I said I didn't think the Lord wanted me."

"And," the stern nun adjusted her veil, "what did I say to *that*?"

"You said, 'Don't you mean that *you* don't want the Lord?'"

"Alyce, you would've made a fine Sister of Mercy!"

"But Sister, I just think I can do more good out there in the world!"

"That sounds pious, Alyce, but what's the real reason?"

"I guess I like to dance too much," Alyce winked, reveling in a mysterious side that not even her mentor had discovered.

The wedding was set for June 6, 1933.

On the first Friday of January Alyce met Rappy during lunch hour to pick out furniture for their house. They had already put down a deposit to rent a two-bedroom cottage in west Mobile. The house, near the corner of Mohawk and Old Government, was currently occupied but the tenants were moving out on May 31, just in time for the Perez newlyweds to settle in.

The 1920s cottage was only two blocks from the Loop, the busy intersection of Government Street where four different roads converged, wide enough for the streetcar to loop around and head back to downtown. The Loop neighborhood boasted grocery stores, drug stores, and a sheltered bus-stop which meant Rappy could easily take the streetcar to work and not need a car. Buying a car was totally out of the question.

The house was perfect, except for the railroad track behind it. The Louisville & Nashville freight trains traveled north and south on this line, plus a few passenger trains to Birmingham, but mostly the trains passing behind the little house carried freight—and bums from the North arriving in the warm Gulf climate to look for work picking fruits and vegetables in the early growing season.

Alyce felt they could get by for a couple of years with only the essentials—a bed, a sofa, table and chairs in the dining room, a stove and icebox—and 'make-do' with homemade shelves for their clothes and the dishes in the kitchen. But Rappy insisted on a traditional dowry for his bride. He wanted new furniture for the entire house—except the spare bedroom. Every room would have a matching set of furniture, including night-tables in the bedroom and lamp-tables in the living room. The dining room would have a table with six chairs, a sideboard, and a china closet to hold their wedding china. Realizing that friends and family couldn't afford expensive wedding gifts in the middle of the Great Depression, Alyce planned to register an inexpensive china pattern at Goldstein's and the other jewelry stores in town.

"You *know* we can't afford a whole household of furniture," Alyce pulled her winter coat around her neck as they stood outside the Adam Glass store where the January wind whipped down Royal Street.

"Don't fret, Hickory!" Rappy took her by the elbow and guided her through the revolving doors. "You're gonna learn all about 'layaway'!"

Inside the store Alyce went from one showroom display to another, dizzy with the huge selection of furniture. With her brown woolen gloves still covering her hands, she held them together as if she were praying, hoping that this was indeed God's Will. Her fiancée still held her elbow as he guided her from display to display, his face beaming in pride that, despite the Great Depression, he could provide an entire house of furniture, every stick matching, for his adorable Hickory. The solution to their financial problem was the capitalist innovation of 'Layaway—easy terms available'.

"I've never been inside Adam Glass before—Mama and I looked inside the window lots of times on the way home from Mardi Gras parades. I had no idea it was so . . . so immense!"

"You like this one? . . . What about that walnut set over there?" he was pointing all over the store, not giving her time to respond.

By the time lunch hour was over—before arriving at Adam Glass they had grabbed an egg-salad sandwich from Tanner's—they had picked out as much furniture as they could afford for $500. Alyce broke away from Rappy, who held her elbow the whole time they sauntered through the displays selecting whole rooms of furniture, and she followed the floor-salesman around the store as he tied "Sold" tags on all the sets she had selected.

The $500 purchased full sets of furniture for living room, dining room, bedroom, breakfast room, and kitchen. The breakfast suit included a small table and four chairs, plus a corner hutch. For the kitchen they bought a gas stove and an icebox.

"Why don't we just go ahead and buy one of those new refrigerators?" Rappy asked Alyce as the salesman seated at his desk wrote up the layaway papers.

"Oh, Rappy," she laughed, "we could never afford one of those."

"Actually," the red-headed young salesman didn't look up from his notepad, "we don't sell refrigerators—you'd have to go to an appliance store, and they *are* expensive! Right now the only folks who can afford a refrigerator are restaurants, big commercial refrigerators, and those—"

"Yeah," Rappy interrupted, "Romie's got two big ones at the Spic and Span."

"We do *not* need a refrigerator, Rappy!"

"But," the salesman continued, "in a few years I suspect the price of the household refrigerator will come down so it'll be affordable."

"We'll wait till then," Alyce glared at Rappy to end the discussion.

"But just look at that little icebox—it's barely waist-high!"

"It's just like your mother's! One side for shelves and the other for the block of ice."

"And just who's gonna empty the water out of that bottom tray every morning?" Rappy teased.

"*You* are! . . . The last thing you do before you run to catch the streetcar!"

"I'll leave a nickel tip on top of the icebox for the iceman to empty it when he brings the block," he chuckled.

"You leave a nickel on top of the icebox, and that iceman will never see it! I'll spend it on a Hershey bar! You know that!" . . . Go ahead! Leave the nickel! *I'll* make sure the tray's emptied."

♪♪♪

Once she had the diamond engagement ring on her finger—and the furniture on layaway—Alyce figured she and Rappy could take a break from the wedding preparations for a few weeks. Her mother was busy finishing costumes for the Crewe of Columbus parade in mid-February. Then, after a week's rest Miss Alice would start on her daughter's wedding gown, the bridesmaids' dresses, and new outfits for herself and Nellie Perez, the mother of the groom. But all that

48

could wait until February. Alyce saw no problems on the immediate horizon.

Unless you would call Romie being refused membership into the Knights of Columbus a problem. And it probably wouldn't have been a problem for Rappy and Alyce if Rappy had not decided to stand loyally next to his favorite brother and against the revered organization of Mobile's finest Catholic men.

Alyce stood by Romie also. She admired Rappy for supporting his younger brother. And years later, well into the 1940s, even after Romie died young during World War II and the KOC approached Rappy to join year after year, she respected her husband for refusing the bid every time. And in the 1960s when Rappy was tapped as a Knight of St. Gregory—the highest honor the Vatican can bestow on a Catholic layman—Alyce felt a sense of vindication that he was honored without ever joining the KOC.

Rappy's family was large. It was so big that Alyce blamed the number of children for the reason she had knocked over that glass of iced tea the first time she ate dinner at their Monterey Street home, just one block from the Little Sisters of the Poor. Her first invitation to the Perez household had been in January of 1932, a full year before she and Rappy had become officially engaged. She was seated in the center of a table designed to seat eight people comfortably —three on each side and one at each end—but eleven family members had squeezed around the table in a dining room so small that Alyce could barely move her elbows.

The two oldest boys—Louis and Julius—had left home a couple of years earlier to drift separately along the Gulf Coast from New Orleans to Pensacola, neither of them bothering to send money home to a household where their father, at age fifty-six, was out of work and the only paycheck arriving regularly was Rappy's.

The oldest son still living at home was Rappy. Below him were four younger brothers and two sisters, ranging in age from twenty-two down to the six year-old Mary Helen. A widowed aunt, or two, would occasionally be squeezed into the crowd at the Perez dining table.

The handsome and devilish Romie—named after his maternal grandfather, Jerome Leopold Callus, who was born on the island of Malta where his parents had fled during the Irish Potato Famine in 1849—was four years younger than Rappy. At nineteen Romie was already a successful entrepreneur with a small restaurant at the Loop, the 'Spic and Span', where he was becoming famous for a tasty hot-dog that rivaled the Dew Drop Inn's. Alyce was seated between Romie and young Mary Helen at her first Perez family dinner. Romie made a lasting impression on his future sister-in-law when he blamed himself after she knocked over her glass of iced tea.

"It was my elbow, Mama! I'm just a clumsy jerk!" protested Romie, who could never be described as clumsy, especially by the girls who lined up at Cavalier dances to glide across the floor in his arms. He devilishly raised his hands in mock-surrender to his mother.

Mrs. Perez jumped from her chair, napkin in hand to mop up the cold tea soaking through the tablecloth, all the while trying to impress upon Alyce that folks spilled iced-tea all the time at the Perez dining table.

"We need a bigger table," Mrs. Perez lifted Alyce's plate to soak up the iced tea so it wouldn't seep onto her lap. "That's what we need with all these folks! A table that seats at least twelve!"

During Prohibition Romie's little restaurant had a 'backroom'. No one called it a 'speakeasy', but that's what it was. For select customers who arrived at the 'Spic and Span' to drink bootleg liquor and play cards, they didn't bother with the front door. These customers parked behind the building where that same L&N railroad bordered Romie's property. When they knocked on the back door, they did indeed 'speak easily' as they whispered the secret password for admission.

"*Friend of Jerome Leopold Perez.*"

If the customer didn't know Romie's full name, he didn't get into the back room.

On any given night at the Spic and Span, it wasn't unusual to find in Romie's back room the county sheriff—from an old Mobile Catholic family—and a few prominent politicians as well as a handful of Catholic

50

priests. Some sat at the small bar and drank bootleg whiskey—Prohibition wouldn't be repealed until December of the next year, 1933—and some sat at tables with their shirtsleeves rolled to the elbows playing poker under a lazy fan that hung from the center of the ceiling.

Catholic priests were welcome at the back door of the Spic and Span. In 1932 many priests in Mobile were either Irish-American or directly off the boat from Ireland, recruited by Mobile's bishop, Thomas J. Toolen, a second-generation Irishman who recruited heavily from the old country. Because Romie came from a notable Catholic family—and his mother was second-generation Irish—the priests felt honored to patronize the Spic and Span. When a priest spent too much time in the back room at the poker table, Romie made sure that his barmaid drove the tipsy priest back to his church rectory.

But when Romie's name was brought up at the Knights of Columbus meeting as a prospective member, he was voted down. Word had been sent—via a prominent monsignor who regularly patronized Romie's backroom—that the Knights of Columbus could not offer membership to a practicing Catholic who openly broke federal law six days a week serving bootleg alcohol and then attended holy Mass on Sunday. The Knights of Columbus did not offer membership to known criminals.

Rappy was incensed. The following Sunday instead of attending Mass at St. Mary's with Alyce, he took her to Little Flower Church for the 11:00 Mass. After Mass the couple knocked on the door of the rectory where Rappy confronted the pastor, Father Eddie Kerns, a friend of both the Hicks and Perez families since Alyce and Rappy had been children. Father Kerns had already agreed to marry Rappy and Alyce in June.

"Father Kerns!" Rappy paced the parlor of the small rectory while Alyce sat on the sofa holding her purse on her lap, constantly picking at the veil from her hat which tickled her forehead.

"*You* drink beer at the Spic and Span!" Rappy pointed at the priest who was sitting in a straight-backed mahogany chair he had brought in from the dining room.

51

"Rappy, I don't have any influence in this thing," the Irish priest with heavy eyelids always wore a weary expression that made him appear to be half asleep at any hour of the day.

"Maybe Romie should stop serving alcohol to priests, huh, Father?"

"I'm not even a monsignor, Rappy."

"Well, if y'all don't let Romie in the KOC, you can forget about me!"

"Don't cut off your nose to spite your face, my boy. That KOC membership can help you with your career at the bank—and it looks good for your family. Think of your mother and daddy."

"I *am* thinking of them!"

"What do *you* think, Alyce?" the priest smiled at her on the sofa.

"I don't know, Father. I guess I go along with Rappy," she stared at her hands where she was smoothing the cotton fabric of her white gloves she hadn't removed.

"Back in Ireland, you know, a woman's allowed to have her own opinion, Alyce."

"Well, since I'm gonna marry Rappy in a couple of months, it's my duty to stand by him. But aside from *duty*, I think the KOC is wrong to keep Romie out. . . . I really like Romie—he's a good fellow."

"Rappy, you just need to think of your mother and daddy," the priest repeated in frustration.

"Father, how do you think Mama and Papa are gonna feel when they find out the *reason* you folks blackballed Romie? You deny him membership cuz he's breaking the law—but all you priests still drink his beer and sit in on the poker game! . . . They've got a name for that, Father, but I never went to college so I don't know what they call it!"

"*Hypocrisy*," the priest hissed under his breath as he leaned across the coffee table for his bootleg bottle of Carling's Canadian Ale.

♪♪♪

On the first Saturday in March, Rappy returned home for lunch after his half-day at work to find a bill from Adam Glass in the center of his luncheon plate.

"Papa, what's this?" he tried to sound respectful as he gazed at his father sitting at the head of the table in a three piece suit. A gold chain stretched across the older man's broad belly from the watch in the left vest pocket to a solid gold fob hidden in the right pocket.

"Your mother needs a new dinette suite," the older man sat with his hands folded over his stomach. "You'll have to pay for it, Rappy. You're the only one with a regular paycheck."

"Yes sir," he searched for words that wouldn't upset his father who expected blind obedience, "but I'm getting married in June   I've put a whole houseful of furniture on layaway, and—"

"I don't believe in layaway or any of that credit business. You'll have to pay for this dinette suite in full. . . . Maybe they'll agree to monthly installments."

Rappy stared at the bill. The mahogany dinette suite his father had bought cost half as much as the whole houseful of furniture he and Alyce had on layaway. He searched the room for support. He realized that the only siblings at the table were his two sisters and his youngest brother, Joe, an eighth grader too young to contribute anything to the household finances other than his paper-route tips. His mother had fled to the kitchen, too embarrassed to witness what she saw coming the minute her husband slid the Adam Glass bill onto Rappy's plate.

Nellie Perez was Rappy's champion. She was ever grateful that he handed her 95% of his salary every payday, actually placing the cash in her hand to keep his father from intercepting it. She made sure Rappy was well fed, that if there was an extra piece of stew-meat in the pot, Rappy would get it—even if it meant slipping it to him in the pantry where no one else would see them. Since Rappy didn't like iced-tea, his mother hand-squeezed a pint of lemonade for him at each meal. And every payday she tried to bake his favorite layer cake—her homemade coconut.

It was the twenty-four year-old Rappy who supported the house. Romie's restaurant was barely getting off the ground so he wasn't paying himself a salary yet. And Romie was only twenty years-old. Two younger boys were in high school, and Joe was still at St. Mary's parochial school. Margie had a secretarial job but what she contributed barely paid the milkman. Rappy was Nellie's savior. Knowing that Rappy had no defense against her husband's Spanish authoritarianism, she couldn't bear to enter the dining room. She served her plate and sat down alone at the kitchen table, but she couldn't eat a bite.

"Papa," Rappy tried to reason with his father, "this new dining suite you bought has only six chairs, just like this one we're sitting at!"

"We'll keep some of these old chairs to add to it," Papa tied a white cloth napkin around his neck to protect his vest.

"But the new table won't be any longer than this one!" Rappy tapped the walnut surface.

"It comes with two leaves, Rappy!" he slurped his soup and took a huge bite out of his dinner roll.

"Can't we get leaves made for *this* table? I bet Romie could do that! At Murphy High he took Woodworking his senior year!" Rappy sounded desperate.

"Don't talk back to me, son. Just do what you're told."

The next day, after Sunday Mass at St. Mary's, Alyce sat alone on the Perez front porch. Usually she helped Mrs. Perez in the kitchen for the one o'clock Sunday dinner, but she knew she didn't belong inside while Rappy was still trying to convince his father to cancel the new dining room suite. She tried to relax by pushing herself gently in the swing, but with Mary Helen, age six, buzzing across the porch on roller skates, it was impossible. With the skates clattering across the wooden porch floor, and the child chattering about how much she loved Sister Mary Dorothy, her first-grade teacher, it was difficult for Alyce to hear what was going on inside the house. The front door was wide open, but she had to strain to hear anything. From the dining room where Mrs. Perez was setting the table for Sunday dinner, Alyce heard only two voices—Rappy's rose with frustration yet mindful of respect, but his daddy's was firm and unyielding.

"Rappy shouldn't talk back to Papa," Mary Helen was obviously precocious. "My papa's always right! He lets me skate down the hallway. That's where I learned to skate, holding Papa's hand as he dragged me right down that hallway!"

"Your papa must love you a whole lot," Alyce said absently as she stared into the street. She had given up trying to hear what was going on in the dining room.

"Mama says I've got him wrapped around my little finger!"

"Really?" Alyce was afraid to reply to this child who apparently repeated everything she heard.

"Papa never yells at me like he does the boys—my brothers."

"Oh?"

"But I have to obey him, Mama says. I can't talk back. Nobody can talk back to Papa. You have to say 'yes, sir' and do exactly what he tells you. That's why Rappy has to pay that furniture bill to Adam Glass!"

"Well, maybe Rappy won't have to pay it," Alyce said gingerly.

"Mama says that when Papa wants something, he doesn't care if the country's in the middle of a Depression—he just buys what he wants and gives the bill to Rappy to pay. That's just how Papa is! . . . And *that's* why you have to postpone your wedding for a whole year!"

"*Postpone?* . . . Mary Helen, where did you hear that?" Alyce felt her breath stop.

"Cuz Mama says Papa will never give in, especially to Rappy!"

"*Oh*," Alyce was speechless. She felt hot tears running down her cheeks. She hurriedly wiped them away before the child could see them and dash into the house to blab that Alyce was crying on the front porch.

"Next year I'll be seven! . . . Will that be too old to be a flower-girl in your wedding?"

The child's chatter dissipated into the March breeze.

It's this Great Depression!
My Lord, Rappy's 24 years-old! But in his shoes I'd have

to do the same. If Mama dropped a bill in my lap, I'd have to pay it. I wouldn't be able to talk back. When children still live at home, they do what they're told, even if they're thirty years-old. It's called 'duty'.

Mama would never do such a thing, certainly not just three months before my wedding when Rappy and I are skipping our Saturday night picture-show and saving every dime we can get our hands on.

But Papa Perez did it.

Rappy and I need to get married SOON! I don't know how much longer we can resist each other. We love each other so much! It hurts! . . . Physically!

All right, Alyce! . . . Dry your eyes and accept it as God's Will!

Damn this depression!

When Rappy emerged from the house, he found Alyce sitting in the swing and gazing into Monterey Street where Mary Helen was demanding to be watched as she skated up and down the sidewalk. Alyce heard the screen-door slam behind Rappy but she didn't look up.

"There's nothing I can do," Rappy leaned against a porch column.

"I know," she muttered, still gazing into the street.

"You probably hate my papa."

"I'm not gonna let myself hate him."

"Well, you're gonna resent him until we get married . . . which might be next year."

"I won't let myself resent him."

"What are you? Some kind of *saint*?"

"Tomorrow," she turned and stared him in the face, "maybe tomorrow I can accept this as God's Will. But, I'm not about to let myself resent your daddy—I want to be close to him. You see, I never had a father so I hope he'll be one for me."

"I hope so too, Hickory, but Papa might not be the kind of father you're looking for."

ﻼﻼﻼ

The day after his inauguration in March, 1933, President Roosevelt closed all banks in the country while he pushed the Emergency Banking Bill through Congress. Until the 'bank holiday' ended on March 13, all financial transactions throughout the country were frozen, even cashing a check.

In Mobile, Alabama at the locally-owned Merchants National Bank, Rappy feared his job was in jeopardy. When the banks re-opened after eight days, he discovered he still had his job. But all the employees at his small bank had suffered a steep cut in salary. When he returned to work after the bank holiday, Rappy learned that his salary was slashed to $100 a month. Before the salary cut, Rappy had hoped he could find a way to pay off the bill for his father's dinette suite and continue the layaway payments on his own furniture at the same time. But with both bills staring him in the face on only $100 per month, he realized he and Alyce would have to postpone the wedding. They would need a year to pay off the dinette suite and to save money for the wedding expenses beyond their own furniture. They would marry in June of 1934, a whole year later than originally planned.

On March 14 when Alyce learned she would have to postpone her wedding for a year, she cried all night long—she sniveled through the next day at work and even after she got home and crawled in bed with the covers over her head. Miss Alice sat at the foot of the bed— a stoic Irish Catholic not given to comforting a grieving child with a hug—and tried to convince Alyce that this was God's Will.

"Maybe something good will come out of this," Miss Alice spoke matter-of-factly, sitting erect on the bed holding a folded brown paper bag on which she had sketched a preliminary design for Alyce's wedding gown. "If nothing else, it means I have all summer to work on your wedding dress between the orders for school uniforms."

"I *hate* this Depression!" Alyce whined from under the layers of quilts and blankets.

"You can't hide under there for a whole year waiting for your wedding!" her mother headed back to her sewing machine. "Come in here and help your grandmother cover buttons for these bridesmaids' dresses. You know how slippery satin is! It's hard to work with when you only have one hand!"

After work the next day Alyce met Rappy in front of Adam Glass to face the nice, redhead salesman with the bad news that they'd have to give up their furniture.

"I understand," the young man looked up from the piles of papers on his desk and gave a weak smile. "We heard that the Merchants bank cut everybody's salary. You're not the first customers to be back here for a refund. We're just glad the banks have opened up again."

"We don't want a refund," Rappy held his fedora at his chest with both hands.

"We want to keep the furniture on layaway and suspend the monthly payments until this time next year. . . . Then in March of next year, we'll start making the last three payments."

"And not make any payments for twelve months?"

"We had to postpone our wedding for a whole year," Alyce couldn't let Rappy handle this all by himself.

"Well, we can't do that, Miss Hicks. What we *can* do is refund the three monthly payments you've already made and—"

"I didn't think you refunded layaway payments if the customer defaulted," Rappy used his banking terminology.

"Usually we don't, but Mr. Glass told me yesterday—after the banks reopened—that if any bank employees defaulted on their lay-away, we can give them a refund."

"That's terrific! . . . But *why*?"

"It's the Depression, Mr. Perez! We want to keep our good customers until this thing is over and they can come back and stay with us. Mr. Glass says it's just 'good business'!"

"So next year we have to come back," Alyce frowned, "and pick out furniture all over again?"

"Tell you what, Miss Hicks!" the young man jumped from his chair and clapped his hands together with enthusiasm. "Instead of returning your furniture to the showroom floor, I'll just leave it in storage for a year. When you finish paying for it, you'll get the same furniture. And don't worry about dust and such—it's all covered with drop-cloths!"

"Hickory!" Rappy poked her in the ribs. "What're you waiting for? Kiss the boy!"

"Oh, you *are* a swell fellow!" she laughed as tears welled in her eyes.

"By the way," the salesman shouted across the showroom floor as Rappy and Alyce started through the revolving door leading to the street. "Will someone be home on Saturday afternoon? That's when they plan to deliver your daddy's new dining room suite."

"Yeah," Rappy stopped in his tracks as if he had been shot in the back. "Somebody'll be there."

"It's a *beaut!*" the salesman raved. "That's solid mahogany, you know! *Honduran* mahogany! Tell your daddy he's got good taste!"

They left Adam Glass and went straight to the Saenger to see Fay Wray in the new movie about the gorilla named "King Kong" climbing the Empire State Building.

"Rappy, we shouldn't be spending money like this," she whispered as he passed two silver coins to the woman in the box office window.

"Hickory! For the past year we saved every dime we could cuz we were getting married in June. Now, we've gotta wait a whole year, fifteen months to be exact, so why don't we blow a little money on a picture show? . . . We've got plenty of time to make up this twenty cents!"

"Damn this Depression!" she muttered under her breath so he couldn't hear her cuss.

Fawn River
South Mobile County, Alabama
January 21, 2012

THROUGHOUT THE MORNING my daughter dozed in her recliner as she watched television. After my grand-daughter helped her into her bedroom slippers, they entered the tiny elevator—the aluminum three-wheel walker tagging behind—and ascended to the upstairs level where my grand-daughter lives with her husband of fifty-three years. At age seventy-seven, despite several medical issues he comes downstairs often because he dotes on my daughter shamelessly.

After breakfast, the two women returned and emerged from the elevator. My daughter settled into her recliner and resumed watching her morning shows. My grand-daughter returned to her living quarters in the elevator to greet the visiting health-aide who later would bathe my daughter before she dressed for the birthday celebration.

"Did you really think Julius could be a father for you?" I asked after she was comfortable in her recliner.

"Julius? . . . I told Tommy he couldn't mention the specific *trouble* Julius got into! Tommy knows he can't put that in the book!" she glanced at me and returned to the TV screen.

"Not your *brother*-in-law! . . . I'm talking about your *father*-in-law! . . . Julius, *Senior*!"

"Everybody called him 'Papa'. . . . . . . What about him?" she searched the end-table for the remote control.

"You said you hoped he'd be a father for you."

"That was before Rappy and I married."

"And after?"

"I realized it was a silly dream," her face showed no expression. "So I gave up the idea."

"No, you didn't!"

"How do you know?

"I was there."

"Don't start that again," she gave a sigh of exasperation.

"I think you expected more from Papa Perez at your wedding . . . I mean, the reception."

"It wasn't a *reception*—just a breakfast for the wedding party and immediate families."

"Did you miss not having a father to walk you down the aisle?"

"How can you miss something you never had? . . . I told you—I never had a father!"

"Why can't you admit that it saddened you?"

"It was the middle of the *Great Depression*! . . . We were grateful to afford a church wedding and that small breakfast. I never had a father! I was just thankful I had an older brother to walk me down the aisle. And if there'd been no brother, I would've called on one of my many uncles. I had a bunch of uncles!"

"But your real father would've made it perfect, no?"

"Whose life is ever perfect?"

"I wish I could've been there for you."

"It was the Lord's Will."

CHAPTER **4**

FIFTEEN MONTHS AFTER postponing their original wedding date, Alyce and Rappy finally were married on June 7, 1934. Not a single photograph exists from their wedding. None were taken.

In the vestibule of St. Mary's Church on Lafayette and Old Shell Road the two flower girls stood next to the baptismal font as four ushers in white suits breezed past to escort guests to their seats. Betty Midgette, the bride's first cousin, was just one year younger than seven year-old Mary Helen, the groom's baby sister. At her waist Betty clutched a nosegay of blue and pink hydrangeas picked from her front yard and fashioned into a bouquet by her mother who had made a matching one for Mary Helen.

"My dress has much more detail than yours because it was made for Sissy's wedding!" Mary Helen boasted. "She's my cousin—her daddy has lots of money!"

"My mama had to finish my dress cuz Aunt Alice ran out of time!" Betty compared her simple powder-pink organdy dress with Mary Helen's, trimmed with yards of lace, tucks, and ruffles, all the hallmarks of an Alice Hicks original.

"Sissy had eight bridesmaids but Alyce only has two!" Mary Helen whispered as if it were shameful.

"My mama says nobody in Mobile has any money!"

"When do they take our picture?" Mary Helen searched the vestibule for a photographer.

"My brother Oliver has a camera!" Betty whispered. "But Mama don't let him take it to church!"

"Where's the photographer?" Mary Helen pulled on her mother's arm. Nellie Perez was talking with Miss Alice, praising her for creating Alyce's stunning wedding gown.

"What's a photographer?" Betty asked.

"A *photographer* is a man who takes pictures, silly!" Mary Helen put her hand on her hip. "Mama, when's the man gonna take my picture? . . . and Betty's too!"

"Hush, Mary Helen, there's not going to be any pictures!" Nellie smiled through her embarrassment, ignoring the candor of her precocious seven year-old.

"Sissy had lots of pictures, Betty!" Mary Helen whispered to her new friend. "They took my picture all by myself because I was the only flower girl! This is the dress I wore!"

"That's a real pretty dress—I bet Aunt Alice made that dress!" Betty showed no signs of envy.

"Mama," Mary Helen pulled on her mother's sleeve, "why didn't I get a new dress for Rappy's wedding, huh Mama?"

"Keep your voice down, Mary Helen! . . . I'm talking with Miss Alice."

"Now, Sissy's daddy has lots of money. He owns a big restaurant! But Alyce doesn't have a daddy to buy her a photographer!"

"I suppose," Miss Alice said as she overheard the child going on about the photographer, "that Rappy and Alyce could've gone to a studio and had their picture taken like Thomas and I did, just the two of them standing in front of a backdrop."

"Oh, Alice," Miss Nellie said. "I don't think Rappy could afford that."

"But the bride pays all the wedding expenses, Nellie! Maybe I could've found a studio that would let me pay for it monthly. I mean, it couldn't cost *that* much—not just one picture—could it? Even Thomas and I could afford *one* picture when we got married!"

"That was twenty-five years ago, Alice! People don't have their wedding photo taken at a studio anymore. The photographer takes all the pictures in the *church*—and at the reception."

"To tell you the truth, I was so busy finishing these dresses—not just Alyce's but yours and mine too—that I just never thought about any photographer—not that we could afford one!"

"Emile has a Kodak," Miss Nellie glanced at Alyce who had appeared at her side, "but he can't afford film for the silly thing. I just never thought about pictures either."

"We did," Alyce reached under her bridal veil and smoothed a spit-curl tickling her cheek, "Rappy and I had the photographer listed on the budget, but he was way at the bottom. When we started cutting expenses, he was the first to go."

"You didn't tell me that!" Miss Alice felt slighted that her daughter hadn't shared that detail.

"Mama, we knew from the start we didn't have money for extras so we just never gave a photographer a second thought! . . . Fifty years from now it won't matter."

"Well, I can't believe we won't have a single photograph of your dress I worked on so hard!"

"Stop worrying about it, Mama! It's God's Will!"

As the pipe organ crescendoed into a Bach fugue, Romie appeared at his mother's side, dashing in his summer white suit with white shoes. He offered Miss Nellie his arm and together they proceeded up the long aisle to mark the beginning of the wedding ceremony. Miss Alice whispered to her daughter to hold her shoulders up, took the arm of the other usher and followed Miss Nellie to the front pew on the opposite side of the aisle. The two flower girls followed—Mary Helen sashaying and Betty glancing around in delight that she had been chosen to participate in such a grown-up affair.

The two bridesmaids were Alyce's best friends. Peg Camilleri wore a sky-blue gown of *crepe de chine* with a cloche hat in pale pink. Alyce's cousin, Euphemia McHugh, served as Maid-of-Honor in the same colors, only reversed. She wore pink *crepe de chine* with the blue cloche. Like the flower girls, the bridesmaids carried nosegays of blue and pink hydrangeas from the Midgette's front yard.

When the organist began the wedding march, Alyce took her brother's arm who was dressed in white like the ushers. As they started up the aisle, she let out a deep breath, feeling relief that—despite her struggle against the Great Depression—her day had finally arrived.

> *Am I a happy bride? . . . Ecstatic.*
>
> *Did I make the right choice with Rappy Perez? . . . Absolutely!*
>
> *We'll have a great life together. Of course, we'll face setbacks like all married folks do. But as soon as this depression is over, everything's gonna be great!*
>
> *I'm so grateful I'm not marrying for convenience, or social position, or money. . . . I'm marrying for love.*
>
> *Bubber's walking too fast. I wonder what it would be like to have a father walk me down the aisle. Not that it matters whether it's a father or a brother, Rappy and I would still be married in the eyes of the Church. But still, holding the arm of my father would've been . . . nice.*
>
> *If I'm so happy, why do I feel a bit melancholy?*
>
> *Thank God this veil's got two layers of tulle covering my face. I wouldn't want all those guests in the pews to think I'm some silly bride crying on her wedding day just because she's so happy . . . or because she has no father to walk her down the aisle.*
>
> *I'm not sentimental!*

For the two hundred guests attending the wedding ceremony, there was no reception, not even punch in the parish hall. After the ceremony the newlyweds waited in the June heat on the church steps to receive good wishes from their guests. Wedding gifts were dropped off at the Hicks home at Bayou and Savannah.

Instead of a reception hosted by the bride's family—which Miss Alice couldn't afford—she arranged a breakfast for the wedding party and the immediate families. Manny Fanane, Miss Alice's youngest brother, and his wife Celeste hosted a wedding breakfast in their home on Grant Street.

"Alyce, this is our wedding present to you!" Aunt Celeste assured her husband's niece when she first suggested the idea six months prior to the wedding. "We'll take care of all the food and drinks!"

"But Aunt Celeste! . . . Can y'all afford such an expense?"

"Sure, honey! It looks like Manny and I aren't ever gonna have any children," she gazed out the window wistfully, "and Manny's always been crazy about you ever since your mama came back home before you were even born, and—"

"Are you gonna make all the food?"

"Of course! . . . You know how I love to do party food! But we have to keep it small—only the wedding party and immediate family."

"That won't be a problem! Most of Rappy's big family is *in* the wedding party—the two groomsmen and ushers and altar boys and flower girls. But I know we can't *all* fit around your table."

"I'll have a few bridge tables set up in the living room and the hallway and even the front porch!"

"Now that Prohibition's over, maybe Uncle Manny can afford some real whiskey for your bourbon balls."

"I've already put Romie in charge of whiskey and beer!"

At the wedding breakfast Alyce sat at the end of the table with Rappy at her side. The Perez boys sang and joked through the meal as each in turn rose to outdo the other with a witty wedding toast. At the far end of the table Rappy's daddy sampled everything that passed his plate, munching steadily and only occasionally looking up to give a wan smile when his wife elbowed him to acknowledge a toast.

Papa Perez sat at the head of the table, his wide girth straining against the spindly wooden arms of the captain's chair. He wore a brown three piece suit, his sturdy watch chain stretched across a broad stomach with a white cloth napkin hanging from his neck to protect his vest.

Alyce laughed heartily as Peg Camilleri whispered a risqué joke about an Irish Catholic couple on their wedding night, but she stole a glance at her new father-in-law popping two bourbon balls into his mouth.

"How can I get close to your father?" she whispered to Rappy.

"He's not close to anybody except Mama . . . and Mary Helen."

"Maybe he can be the father I never had."

"Lots of luck, Hickory!" he gave a sad chuckle.

"You don't understand, Rappy. . . . I never had a father."

"I never had a father," Alyce could be heard to state on many occasions in her life.

Everyone has a father. *Somewhere.*

Alyce's father had not abandoned his pregnant wife and two year-old son three years after marrying Alyce's mother. Thomas Hicks married Alice Fanane in November of 1909. A year later they welcomed a son, Thomas, Jr., in November of 1910. At that point, November appeared to be a lucky month for the growing Hicks family.

Then, in November of 1912 Alice found herself seven months pregnant with her second child when her young husband was rushed to the hospital with an inflamed appendix. By the time the doctors opened him up on the operating table, the appendix had burst and sent lethal infection throughout his abdominal cavity. With no penicillin, or any other antibiotic available in 1912, the doctors packed his abdominal cavity with sulfur and sewed him up. Within two hours he was dead at twenty-six. His widow was the same age.

Alice Fanane Hicks sat erect on a wooden bench in the dimly lit basement hallway of the Mobile County Hospital waiting for her husband's body to be released for burial. Her mother sat on one side with her hands folded in her lap clutching rosary beads. Alice's younger sister, Olivia, on the other side, fidgeted as they waited patiently for the doctor—up on the third floor where he was performing another appendectomy—to come down so he could sign the death certificate.

"The doctor said there ain't no need for an autopsy," muttered Alice's oldest brother, Danny, as he paced the corridor with his hands deep in his trouser pockets.

"Hush, Danny!" Mrs. Fanane whispered. "Don't talk about such as that!"

"That's one thing we can be grateful for," Alice stared ahead, one hand resting on her womb where a seven month-old baby was growing to full term. "They don't need to cut on him anymore."

"Seems like they could've saved him. I mean, we did get him here right after he started all that vomiting," Danny glanced into the morgue through the glass windows at the top of the swinging doors where two undertakers from the Magnolia Funeral Home lounged next to a marble slab holding the corpse of young Mr. Hicks under a draping white sheet.

"It seems like they could've stopped the poison," Olivia at age sixteen was bewildered by her first encounter with death since her father died when she was only five.

"Hush, Olivia!" her mother hissed, her patience wearing thin as she glanced again toward the stairs.

"It's the Lord's Will," Alice's blue eyes were vacant. "That's the only thing that's gonna get me through this—if I can just go to bed every night accepting that it's 'God's Will', and get up every morning remembering I got two babies to take care of."

"You're coming home and live with us on Bayou and Savannah," her mother wanted no argument.

"I don't have anything black to wear!" Alice erupted and bolted from the bench. She glanced down the gloomy hallway as if she were searching for a hidden door.

Olivia began sniveling then let out a howl. She buried her face in her mother's shoulder and sobbed.

Alice started for the stairs to the first floor.

"We have to wait for the doctor!" her mother yelled in desperation.

"I've got to make a black dress! I don't' have anything black . . . for the funeral, except that broadcloth shirtwaist I made last year, but those sleeves are only elbow-length! I have to have a dress with *long* sleeves—all the way to the wrist!" her eyes had become wide with terror as she slowly turned in a lazy circle in the middle of the long hallway. Then she fell to her knees. She threw her head back, and with both hands grabbed her swollen belly. She moaned with inconsolable grief, "Oh, God! Why did you *take* him from me?"

ↄↄↄ

When her husband died at age twenty-six, Alice Hicks—seven months pregnant—took her two-year old son, Thomas Jr., and went home to her mother's house on the corner of Bayou and Savannah. In 1912 the neighborhood was working class with a large population of Irish Catholics. Thomas Hicks' family was Irish on both sides—the same as Alice's family. Her mother was Mary Frances Doyle before she married Daniel Fanane whose parents were born in County Cork, Ireland.

During those last two months of pregnancy, Alice Hicks settled herself and her toddler into her mother's cozy Victorian bungalow with the wraparound verandah and let the entire neighborhood know that she planned to support herself as a dressmaker as soon as she recovered from the impending childbirth—and from the two weeks of 'lying-in' after the delivery.

As a young girl Alice Hicks learned to sew from her mother and her grandmother. By the time she was a teenager, everyone recognized that Alice had an extraordinary talent not only for sewing but also for designing dresses, from the simple white graduation frock to elaborate beaded gowns for rich ladies attending Mardi Gras balls. In 1902 at age sixteen she designed and crafted her high school graduation gown, a white organdy creation in the Edwardian style of leg-of-mutton sleeves festooned with rows of inset lace, a bodice full of tiny tucks from neckline to waistline, and a sweeping train modeled on a photo she saw in the *Mobile Press Register* of Queen Alexandra at-

70

tending a British state dinner to honor President Theodore Roosevelt.

In her graduation photo she is posed in front of a backdrop painted with a scene of an idyllic English meadow. She stands demurely, surrounded by lush ferns on shoulder-high marble stands, virginal in her white organdy glory on the brink of womanhood. A striking teenager of working-class Irish stock with chestnut hair she stares at the camera with piercing blue eyes. She expects a lifetime of marriage and children . . . and bliss.

On January 21, 1913 Alice Fanane Hicks delivered a baby girl.

The baby was named for the mother, Alice Felicia Hicks, because Thomas Hicks hoped his second child would be a girl and had mentioned—only a month before his unexpected death—that the infant should be named after his wife. But the day after giving birth, Alice made it clear that the baby would be called 'Alyce'. She insisted the stress is on the last syllable, pronounced 'al- LEES.'

"I don't want her to be called 'Little Alice' or anything like that," she adjusted the goose-down pillow behind her back so she could nurse the baby girl, "and besides, I've got a good friend who sews for Mr. DeCelle named 'Alyce,' so don't call this baby 'Alice', y'all hear?"

Exactly one week after delivering her second child, Alice appeared in the kitchen dressed in black from head to toe and declared her confinement had ended. She went straight to her White sewing machine set up in the dining room next to the pot-bellied stove and started on her first professional assignment—a Mardi Gras ball-gown for one of the Toenes girls across the street. As soon as Mardi Gras was over in late February she took orders to make Easter frocks for the children of society ladies who lived in the post-Civil War mansions on Government Street, west of Broad. Making her living as a dressmaker served two purposes for the young widow. Obviously it provided her with a steady income to support her two children. Her husband had left no pension from his job as a salesman at Frank Stoll Haberdashery.

But also the dressmaker career gave her a reason to stay indoors for a full year of mourning. A young Catholic widow of Irish descent in 1913 America was expected to follow the traditions and rituals of the old country. One tradition Alice embraced was not socializing outside the family home, except to attend family functions such as birthdays and funerals. Weddings, even for siblings, were off limits to a grieving widow for a full twelve months. The sewing machine was the anchor that kept Alice busy inside the house when she felt an urge to break with tradition and appear at a cousin's wedding.

Another custom required the widow to wear nothing but black for a full year, and Alice followed that dictum religiously. On the first anniversary of her husband's death in November of 1913, she started wearing dark grays and violet. By the fifth anniversary in 1917 she had phased out most of her black clothing and was wearing lighter grays and lavender.

Alice's son, Thomas Jr., had turned two just one week before his father died. For a while he was able to identify his 'Papa' in the wedding photograph on his mother's bedside table, but before another year passed, he was no longer able to envision his father's face without first studying the photo.

As Alyce grew up, the only image she had of her father was that same wedding photo where he stands in that same photographer's studio where her mother had posed as a high school graduate. The handsome groom lounges on the edge of a sofa arm while his bride stands erect holding a huge bouquet of white mums in front of a backdrop painted with that same English meadow scene. The couple is surrounded by ferns on the same white marble stands.

Alyce's earliest memory of life is walking to Magnolia Cemetery on Sunday mornings to visit her father's grave. She remembers toddling between her mother and her brother—Bubber was two years older—and holding their hands to keep from stumbling on the cobblestone street. The journey from their house was only six blocks, but at the time it seemed an eternity. Alyce was barely two-years old, just learning to talk. The weekly visits to the cemetery continued until she was a teenager as her mother, the loyal widow, ushered the two children to their father's grave every Sunday after Mass. Then they walked back home where Grandma Fanane was already busy in the kitchen laying out strips of homemade noodles to accompany the roast beef for Sunday dinner.

Alice Fanane Hicks never married again. After her young husband died in 1912 when she was only twenty-six, she became known in the neighborhood as 'Miss Alice.' Her neighbors knew her too well to call her 'Mrs. Hicks' but wanted to recognize her social status as a grieving widow despite her youth, so they addressed her as 'Miss Alice.' Only her three best friends from childhood called her 'Alice.'

Jimmy Cain seriously courted Miss Alice. As a close friend to Thomas Hicks, he had been a groomsman in the wedding. In 1914 he owned one of the few automobiles visiting the working class neighborhood, and he flaunted it in his campaign to win the young widow Hicks when he showed up at the corner of Bayou and Savannah. As soon as Miss Alice finished her second year of mourning—November of 1914—the dashing Cain made his move. Nearly every Sunday afternoon Jimmy showed up, unannounced—the Fanane house didn't have a telephone yet—to take the widow Hicks and her two small children for a spin in his luxurious automobile, a 1913 maroon Oldsmobile convertible.

Jimmy Cain's courtship lasted two years until Mr. Cain, a bachelor at thirty-one, finally realized that Alice Hicks remained devoted to the memory of her dead husband and was not about to marry a second time—at least not in the foreseeable future. But the whole family—the toddler Alyce, her brother, her mother, and even Grandma Fanane—enjoyed the Sunday afternoon spins in Mr. Cain's Oldsmobile.

Alyce had just turned four when Jimmy Cain finally abandoned his courtship of her mother. When she was told that Mr. Jimmy wouldn't be taking her for a ride anymore on Sunday afternoons, she felt confused. Whenever she heard her playmates in the neighborhood refer to their 'daddies', she wondered if Mr. Jimmy could be her daddy. As her little friends stood on the curb on Sunday afternoons waving goodbye to Alyce, they assumed she was riding off with her daddy who lived in another neighborhood and visited only on Sundays. Alyce hung out the side of the fancy convertible and waved back. She never told her playmates that Mr. Jimmy wasn't her daddy—she didn't know if he was or not. She only knew that he had a bigger and shinier car than anyone who drove through the neighborhood, and he dressed much fancier than any man she had ever seen.

Many years later Alyce learned from her mother that Jimmy Cain's wardrobe was one reason he was ruled out as a serious contender for Miss Alice's hand. In photos of Jimmy sitting on the front steps with the Hicks family, his straw boater is jauntily sliding over his right eyebrow. As the quintessential dandy, he couldn't have been within Alyce's vision of what a daddy should look like. He didn't look a thing like her playmates' daddies. Jimmy was too slim. His watch-chain draped across a flat stomach, not a potbelly. And he didn't smell like any of her male relatives who visited the house, or of her playmates' daddies who smelled of sweat and beer.

By the time she was five Alyce discovered that she was a favorite of Uncle Manny, her mother's younger brother who lived with the extended Fanane family on the corner of Bayou and Savannah, and of a man named Uncle Ed who visited regularly with his wife and two little girls. In addition there was a young sailor named Joe Midgette who courted her Aunt Olivia at the house, who always brought Alyce a present when his ship docked at the foot of Government Street. Joe Midgette was ten years younger than Jimmy Cain but, as a merchant marine sailor, his hands were calloused and he smelled of sweat when he got off work, not Bay Rum after-shave lotion as did Jimmy Cain. Although Joe Midgette's Model "A" Ford wasn't as sleek as the Oldsmobile, Alyce and Bubber discovered it raced just as fast down Broad Street when Joe entered their lives during the latter years of World War I.

Whether Alyce realized it or not, her search for a father had begun in earnest.

Grandma Fanane, herself a widow for over fifteen years, had

74

borne seven children to Daniel Fanane. When he died unexpectedly at the turn of the century, she still had three school-aged children at home. And when Alice Hicks returned to the Fanane home in 1913, she had to share a bedroom with her younger sister, Olivia, now a sixteen year-old in love with Joe Midgette. The two year-old Thomas Jr. slept in a child's cot in a bedroom with his uncle Emmanuel, known to the family as 'Manny'.

Ed McHugh was a successful realtor married to Agnes Fanane, the older sister to Alice. Uncle Ed had his own real estate agency which flourished during the Roaring Twenties and a spacious new house in Monterey Place in west Mobile. With three children of his own—two were girls—he had the job of shopping because Aunt Aggie didn't drive. The older girl was named 'Euphemia' but, for obvious reasons, Euphemia was known in the family as 'Sister'. Whenever Uncle Ed bought gifts for his girls, he bought an identical gift for Alyce, especially if he was buying a surprise for Sister who was six months older than Alyce. If Sister received a baby-doll from her daddy, Alyce would receive the same baby-doll. Until she was seven, Alyce thought that Uncle Ed's treating her equal to her cousin, Sister, meant that he might be her daddy.

With so many men doting on Alyce—her Uncle Manny who slept in the bedroom across the hall until he left home to marry Celeste when Alyce was six, plus Mr. Joe and Uncle Ed who both presented her with presents when she greeted them on the top step of the verandah—Alyce wondered which one she should consider her daddy. She had no idea how a little girl picks a daddy, but she prayed every night that God would send her a sign, maybe send an angel with fluffy white wings and a golden halo to whisper in her ear which one was her real daddy.

♪♪♪

Alyce's pre-school years on Bayou and Savannah were pleasant. The household wasn't well-off, but there was plenty to eat because until 1919 there were three adults contributing cash to the Fanane household. Both Olivia and Manny handed their mother most of their paychecks once a week, and Miss Alice contributed all of her modest commissions from her dressmaking business. There was enough money to shop at Toenes Grocery across the street, and from March through October Alice helped her mother maintain a lush vegetable garden in the backyard which provided okra, tomatoes, peas, beans and potatoes. Nobody went hungry.

The first crisis to hit the young Hicks family after Miss Alice returned to her mother's home came with the Spanish Flu pandemic in 1918. By November of that year—two months before Alyce celebrated her sixth birthday—everybody in Mobile knew of someone who had died from the dreaded flu. Hardly any house had escaped at least one member coming down with a case of the flu.

On the first Sunday of November, Miss Alice sat with her mother at the dining room table reading aloud from the *Mobile Press Register* where she searched for weekly statistics of Mobile's flu cases . . . and deaths.

"It says here," Miss Alice shook the newspaper to make the pages lie flat on the table, "that last week alone there were 26,000 cases in the state of Alabama."

"In the *state*? . . . That don't mean anything to me," Grandma Fanane unrolled a skein of crochet yarn as she warmed her feet next to the potbellied stove. "What's it say about *Mobile*?"

"And 135 people died from the flu in Birmingham during the last week of October," Miss Alice murmured.

"Birmingham ain't Mobile, Alice! . . . Stop tormenting me!"

"If it gets any worse here I suspect they'll close down the schools, wouldn't you think so?"

"Until they do, Alice, you make sure Thomas wears that mask—even if he throws a fit!"

"Well, at least Alyce hasn't started school yet," Miss Alice continued to scan the paper for statistics on Mobile's flu cases.

"I told you about Wilson, didn't I?" Grandma Fanane didn't look up from her crocheting.

"Yes, M'am—and that's right worrisome because Wilson was only thirty years-old, not like he was a baby or an old person too weak to fight off the flu bug."

"We need to go next door and take them a cake or something."

"When're they having the funeral?"

"They buried him right away—it wasn't even announced in the paper."

"Why didn't you *tell* me? We should've gone to the funeral—his Mama and Daddy are our next-door neighbors!"

"I didn't tell you, Alice, so you wouldn't argue about going! I'm not about to let you attend any funeral where the dead person's still full of flu germs! You're not bringing that bug home to infect these children—or any of the rest of us in this house, including *me!*"

Before Christmas arrived, everyone in the Fanane household had come down with the Spanish Flu. Everyone except Alyce. Luckily Miss Alice and her mother weren't confined to bed during the same week—neither woman suffered a severe case—so that someone was well enough to nurse Olivia, Manny, and young Thomas who also suffered fairly mild cases.

To keep Alyce from being infected, she was restricted for two weeks to the front porch to play with her baby dolls and the marmalade housecat. The upside was that she got to entertain Mr. Joe Midgette when he came by to check on Olivia, his fiancée, who was bedridden for a full week. Because he didn't risk entering the house where he might contact the virus, Mr. Joe sat in the porch swing and answered Alyce's many questions regarding her duties as a flower girl to Olivia in the upcoming wedding. Joe had convinced Olivia to marry him on Alyce's next birthday, January 21, 1919.

CHAPTER 5

ALYCE'S CHILDHOOD WAS relatively carefree . . . at home.

But when she arrived at St. Joseph's School in September 1919 at the age of six, she encountered a problem that would follow her until she left St. Joseph's. Her beloved brother was the teacher's pet for every nun who taught him. And being only two years younger than Bubber, Alyce followed behind him into the same classroom where the same nun had been waiting patiently for fifteen months to see if Thomas Hicks' little sister was as smart as her brother.

It wasn't until the third grade that Alyce became aware that she was being compared to Bubber. Her first grade teacher had never taught Bubber. The second grade teacher, Sister Mary Elizabeth, was a young nun sensitive enough not to compare any student with an older sibling, at least not to the child's face. Besides, although she had taught Bubber two years before—and was aware that he was a superior student to his little sister—the nun actually favored Alyce's spunk and spirit to the more sober Thomas E. Hicks, Jr. But in the third grade Alyce encountered a blatant comparison she couldn't ignore, a curse that followed her until she left St. Joseph's School after her sophomore year and transferred to the all-girls Convent of Mercy.

"You're not as smart as your brother, are you Missy?" Sister Mary Declan said matter-of-factly as she stared at the Arithmetic test paper with red ink all over it.

"Mama says Bubber's the brain in the family," Alyce assumed her explanation would let her off the hook.

"Well, *Missy*," the red-faced Irish nun—with jowls protruding from her white-starched wimple—continued to study the test paper, never glancing at the eight year-old child during the entire dressing-down, "it appears that you've just written down any number that popped into your head!"

"Yes, Sister," she knew better than to argue with a holy sister who considered herself a Bride of Christ.

"How can 3 + 3 equal 9? . . . *Nine?* . . . I mean, the good Lord gave you two hands full of fingers to count on! If you count three fingers on one hand and three fingers on the other, you'll come up with the correct answer!"

"But, Sister, you told us we can't count on our fingers!"

"It appears that some little girls *need* to count on their fingers!"

"Yes, Sister."

"Saints preserve us, child! You'll never be the student your dear brother is!"

Alyce made up her mind—right then and there—that when *she* had children, she'd try like heck not to compare them to each other, especially not to compare their *brains*. But she comforted herself with the certainty that at least one person in her family was smart enough to please the holy sisters at St. Joseph's School. Jesus was married to all of them.

As she grew older, Alyce sensed that Bubber was favored outside of school as well as in St. Joseph's. Great things were expected of her brother. Was it merely because he was a boy? Or, was he actually a special person?

After Alyce's brother turned eight and their Uncle Manny left Bayou and Savannah to get married, Bubber was the only male in the house. Because both his grandmother and mother counted on him to one day enter the working world and bring home a handsome paycheck, they catered to him—each in her own way. Alyce was taught that Bubber would be a breadwinner someday—maybe as early as fourteen if he chose not to attend high school and took a job fulltime, which was typical of teenage boys in the Irish Catholic neighborhoods. On the other hand, he might win a scholarship to McGill Institute, the all-boys Catholic high school. After all, everybody said Bubber was the brains in the family, so Alyce made sure he wasn't disturbed when he was doing his homework.

And after breakfast on school mornings she carried his dishes to the sink so he could have a few minutes to check the headlines of the *Mobile Press Register* to impress the nun in Social Studies class. Then he took Alyce's hand and guided her across the eleven blocks to St. Joseph's School. At home she waited on Bubber with no resentment but with a wary acceptance that God's Will required girls to get married one day and have babies.

She took comfort that somewhere in Mobile a younger sister was doing what she could to make life comfortable for an older brother who one day would 'go to work' to support Alyce at home with her babies.

♪♪♪

In November of 1922 Alice Hicks had a memorial Mass said on the 10th anniversary of her husband's death. With eleven year-old Thomas on her right and nine year-old Alyce on her left, she knelt at the altar rail of St. Joseph's Church to receive Holy Communion and pray for the soul of her dead husband. After ten years of traditional mourning, Miss Alice at age thirty-six had brightened up her wardrobe with a few blouses of lavender, mauve, and pale blues. She especially liked the shade called "Alice-blue", named after President Theodore Roosevelt's famous daughter who had become America's fashion trendsetter.

But Miss Alice still chose mid-calf skirts of charcoal-grey, navy, or midnight-black draped over black cotton stockings. The year after her husband died in 1912, Alice Hicks bought a jet-black winter coat to the ankles. During the ten years since her husband's death, Miss Alice found it necessary to replace her coat once. She bought another black overcoat identical to the old one.

81

In March of 1923, when Miss Alice decided it was time to replace the second overcoat, now shabby after five winters, she checked the newspaper advertisements on winter clothes marked down after the Mardi Gras holidays. The best buys were at Hammel's, the large department store located next door to Adam Glass.

"Mama, it's time you bought a *pretty* coat!" at age ten Alyce was becoming fashion conscious of what her friends' mothers were wearing. "You always wear *black* coats!"

"Well," Miss Alice fingered the coats on the rack as she sauntered down the aisle, "*black* can be pretty, can't it?"

"But you're only *thirty-five*, Mama, and Papa's been dead for ten years!"

"Thirty-six, Alyce, thirty-six!"

"I like *this* one!" Alyce grabbed the sleeve of a rich maroon wool.

"My stars, Alyce! That coat's as red as Jimmy Cain's Oldsmobile convertible!"

"Please, Mama! Don't buy another black coat."

And she didn't. The price-tag dangling from the collar button identified the coat's color as 'forest-green'. Hanging next to a black wool coat in the same style, it did indeed appear a dark green. But when Miss Alice slipped into the new green overcoat and emerged from the store onto Royal Street into the bright March sun, it appeared that she had bought another black coat.

"It's *black*!" Alyce moaned as she halted in front of Adam Glass clutching the large brown shopping bag holding the older coat.

"You saw the tag, Alyce! It's green . . . forest *green*!"

"Mama, if that's forest-green, then that's the *darkest* forest in the whole wide world!"

"Well," Miss Alice ran her hand across the dark wool fabric, "it looked green when we held it up next to the black one!"

"Next time, Mama, *next* time I get to pick out your winter coat!"

"We don't have to wait till next time! We'll just march right back in there and exchange this thing for that red one you like!"

"*Maroon*, Mama! . . . Papa's been dead ten years! Surely, he wouldn't mind if you wore *maroon*, would he?"

"I don't imagine he would, Alyce," Miss Alice gazed absently into the distance as she guided the child toward the revolving doors. "I don't imagine he would."

♪♪♪

In the early 1920s Miss Alice realized she needed a steady income to support her children as they approached their teenage years. Her dressmaking business provided enough income to get by, but at the end of the month she had little money left for 'extras'. She could always find time—even if it meant staying up after midnight—to fashion a party frock for Alyce to attend a classmate's birthday party, but shoes, gloves, and hats were another thing. She could purchase those only at a department store. And tailoring a white dress shirt for the growing Thomas now entering adolescence just took too much time to make it look 'store-bought' and not homemade. More cash was needed.

With no effort at all Miss Alice landed a sewing job in the costume shop of Edmund C. DeCelle, Mobile's premier Mardi Gras designer. In his late thirties, the same age as Miss Alice, the native New Yorker had emerged as *the* master of Mobile's Mardi Gras design spectrum. Starting in the summer his staff fashioned costumes for members of several crewes to wear on their floats.

In addition, DeCelle designed floats for several crewes each year as well as the scenery for the tableau to open the ball at 9:00 p.m. right after the parade ended. DeCelle was so much in demand that he secured the prize commission coveted by all Mobile designers—creating the costumes and floats for the Order of Myths crewe, the oldest parading society in Mobile which traced their first parade back to 1868. The OOMs boasted the honor of hosting their parade and ball as the culminating events of Fat Tuesday every year.

With three other seamstresses in the workshop creating costumes of satin and sequins, Miss Alice found the work routine and pleasant.

She would rather have been home creating her own designs instead of sewing twenty identical *Blackbeard* costumes for Float #1 while a colleague made twenty identical *Jean Lafitte* costumes for Float #2 and then finished eight more floats to complete the "Famous Pirates" theme, but Mr. DeCelle paid his ladies well. As the deadlines for the first Mardi Gras parades appeared on the horizon, the women usually found themselves behind schedule.

By the age of twelve Alyce discovered that after school she looked forward to walking the six blocks from home to Mr. DeCelle's workshop on Broad Street to help her mother meet a deadline. It was in that workshop that Alyce learned to sew on a button so it wouldn't fall off as a masker hooped and hollered atop a float—and she learned how to make buttonholes by hand, as well as applying sequins and other 'handwork'. She realized she'd never attain the artistry of her mother, but what Alyce learned in Edmond DeCelle's costume shop would serve her well years later when she found herself mending hand-me-downs she passed from one of her children to the next in line.

Making Mardi Gras costumes was seasonal work—taking up only seven months of the year—beginning in July when Mr. DeCelle laid out his designs on the huge worktable in the center of the workshop and ending in February after the OOMs paraded and Lent began the next morning on Ash Wednesday. In March Miss Alice was set free to devote time to her own designs, that of creating fairy tale weddings for rich Spring Hill girls who, during the financial bonanza of the Roaring Twenties, could afford such extravaganzas with as many bridesmaids as they wanted.

Although Edmond DeCelle was in demand by every mystic society in Mobile, he could handle only 3-4 accounts a year. That left the remaining crewes searching for lesser known designers to create their floats and sew their costumes. As Miss Alice sat at her sewing machine in DeCelle's workshop, she kept her ears pricked as Mr. DeCelle turned down requests from young businessmen pleading with him to create costumes for their crewes, often a crewe which had just incorporated and was late in securing a designer. Because the DeCelle sewing-ladies kept hours from only 10-4, Miss Alice figured that she could earn extra money moonlighting at home if she could find a new mystic society desperate for a costume-maker, a crewe that didn't demand the DeCelle reputation, one that couldn't afford any of Mobile's recognized designers.

She found one. But she didn't discover the desperate crewe while eavesdropping on her boss's conversations in his workshop. Rather, the news was delivered at her dining table by Father Eddie Kerns.

Father Kerns, stationed at the Cathedral of the Immaculate Conception, took care of the Catholic Missions across the bay in rural Baldwin County. In addition, he had become a 'Father Flanagan' for Catholic boys living in downtown Mobile. With a Model-T Ford at his disposal, Kerns carted boys all over town, taking them to football practice and picnics at the Pumping Station's swimming hole. He particularly looked after boys who didn't have a father in the house, such as Thomas Hicks, Jr.

Because Father Kerns needed an altar boy to serve him at Mass over-the-bay every Sunday, Tommy Hicks became his regular acolyte. It was on one of these mission outings to Daphne when the Model-T broke down and priest and acolyte had to spend the night in the Gallagher home in Daphne that the fourteen year-old Tommy Hicks first met the twelve year-old Emma Gallagher who twenty years later— after Tommy had survived World War II fighting in the Philippines and after Emma had spent seven years as a cloistered nun at the Visitation Convent—would become his wife.

"It's the Knights of Columbus, Alice," Father Kerns sat at the head of the Hicks table at Sunday dinner with a white napkin tucked in his Roman collar to protect his chest from the roast beef gravy.

"I heard they're forming a mystic society, Father," Miss Alice volunteered gingerly as she sliced into the rarest section of the roast.

"They can't afford a professional . . . you know, whatever they call the man who—"

"*Costumer!*" Miss Alice said impatiently, anticipating what the priest would say next. "They can't afford a professional costumer like Mr. DeCelle, right?"

"Certainly not Mr. DeCelle!"

"I can make their costumes . . . at night!"

"They need more than a dressmaker, Alice, they need someone to make the drawings of what they should look like, you know, to—"

"To *design* the costumes! . . . I can do that too!" Miss Alice said confidently as she sat back in the dining-room chair, pushed her plate aside, and fingered the white tablecloth.

"Mama helps Mr. DeCelle with all his designs. I've seen her!" the nine-year-old Alyce beamed proudly.

"Hush, Alyce!" Grandma Fanane admonished. "The grownups are trying to talk!"

"But I've seen her! . . . Mr. DeCelle doesn't ask Mrs. Schexnayder for ideas—or that other lady in the corner—he only asks *Mama* if she can make the drawing look better! . . . '*Make it come to life!*' . . . That's what Mr. DeCelle says all the time! He says, 'Here, Mrs. Hicks! Make this come to life!' . . . Let Mama do it!"

꙳꙳꙳

In July of 1922 three members from the newly-formed *Crewe of Columbus* arrived at Bayou and Savannah and signed a contract with Miss Alice to "design, sew, and deliver" one-hundred costumes for their parade the following February during the 1923 Mardi Gras season. Miss Alice signed the contract without hesitation because she had no doubt that she could whip out one-hundred costumes in six months time.

To make sure she met her deadline she needed help. She bought a second White sewing machine to hire an assistant. Several of her seamstress friends had part-time experience with Mr. DeCelle but now, with small children to care for, they couldn't be away from home all day at DeCelle's workshop. They could easily spend two hours a morning at the new White machine next to Miss Alice while their children played in the front parlor.

Miss Alice's sister, Agnes McHugh, was glad to help a couple of days a week. In addition, Miss Alice could count on her mother to do handwork and make buttonholes down the back of the costume-shirt because zippers in 1922 had not been perfected to withstand the acrobatics of a masker frolicking atop a Mardi Gras float.

Even the nine year-old Alyce was eager to help, learning from her Grandma Fanane how to sew a double-string of sequins down the outside seam of a pants-leg.

This family project at Bayou and Savannah guaranteed the contract would be fulfilled in time for the Crewe of Columbus parade in February.

The Crewe of Columbus was composed of Catholic men who also belonged to the Mobile council of the Knights of Columbus. In the early 1920s a group of KOC members decided to form a Mardi Gras society for Catholic men. Their plan was not to discriminate against non-Catholics so much as to provide fellowship for Catholic KOC members who wanted to revel in the Mardi Gras merriment. They wanted to have fun.

But from the start these founding members should have realized that trouble would follow if they formed a parading society in a city with a growing population of working class non-Catholics moving in from rural Alabama—from counties which were heavily Protestant, especially fundamentalist. When the parents of these rural sharecroppers moved into Mobile during Reconstruction, they brought the Ku Klux Klan with them.

The Knights of Columbus is the world's largest Catholic fraternal service organization. Founded in the United States in 1882, it's named in honor of Christopher Columbus and describes itself as being dedicated to the principles of Charity, Fraternity, and Patriotism. But by 1922 rural rednecks living in Mobile's working-class neighborhoods south of downtown didn't believe KOC members were Patriotic to their *country*. These non-Catholic former sharecroppers feared that KOC allegiance was to the Vatican, to "that Pope in Rome!"

In late 19th century America, Catholics were either barred from many popular fraternal organizations or their bishops issued edicts forbidding Catholics from joining the Masons and other similar fraternal groups. The Knights of Columbus provided an alternative for Catholics, but because the KOC had its own secret rituals, the members were suspected of all kinds of outrageous behavior, including laying the groundwork for the Pope to arrive from Rome and set up a government of Catholic bishops to overthrow the United States of America.

The Ku Klux Klan's first movement reached a zenith in the South during Reconstruction immediately after the Civil War, but it was diminished severely by rigid federal laws and aggressive prosecution. When the Great Migration occurred in the early twentieth century with thousands of southern Blacks moving to the North, the second Klan movement was founded in 1915. This new Klan momentum reached its peak in the 1920s when urban Klan members were emboldened to attack targets they felt were a threat to White Supremacy and the American way of life—targets such as Communism, labor unions, Jews, and Catholics, as well as the original target of the freed black slave.

So, when nine year-old Alyce glanced out the front window in November, 1922 and saw the monstrous cross burning on the corner of Bayou and Savannah, nobody in the neighborhood should have been surprised that Miss Alice had been targeted by the KKK.

But they *were* surprised. It hadn't dawned on anyone—not Miss Alice, not her family, not Mr. DeCelle, not any of the neighbors—that a stack of unfinished Mardi Gras costumes could be the reason a 15-foot wooden cross soaked in creosote and kerosene was ablaze on the Hicks' front lawn.

"My stars!" Miss Alice gasped. She stood behind Alyce as both stared out the front window. As she struggled to catch her breath, she pulled her daughter close to her chest.

Then she sprang to action. She flew into the hallway to call the fire department. The cross on the lawn was so tall that if it fell, it would land on the front verandah causing the entire wooden house to burst into flames.

Fire department. No telephone in the house. The Toenes Grocery has a phone. I use it for emergencies. This is an emergency. Fire Department. Toenes Grocery. Phone.

She snatched her coat from the hall clothes-rack, threw open the front door, and ran smack into Herman Toenes, the twenty year-old neighbor from across the street.

"Don't go out there, Miss Alice!" he grabbed her shoulders and shoved her back into the hall.

"It'll burn the house down!" she tried to appear calm, straining to get past him.

"Don't let 'em see you upset! Don't give 'em the satisfaction!"

"But I have to call the fire department! We don't have a phone!"

"I've already called the fire department!" the young neighbor was guiding her into the dining room where Grandma Fanane was sitting by the potbellied stove and Alyce was standing close by holding the old lady's hand.

Miss Alice gazed out the window at the gigantic cross blazing into the dark November night. The smell of creosote and kerosene had seeped into the front parlor where she stood with Herman Toenes at her side. Bits of burning wood and viscous creosote were dripping onto the grass lawn as neighbors raced to throw buckets of water onto the oily flames.

"Where's *Thomas*?" Miss Alice turned in panic and shouted towards her mother next to the stove.

"Miss Alice, he's *okay*!" Herman pointed at a group of teenaged boys scurrying across the lawn, struggling with pails of sloshing water.

"My stars! . . . He'll get burned out there!"

"The boy's *twelve*, Miss Alice! . . . Let him help put out the fire! He's learning to be a man out there!"

At dawn the next morning when Alyce cracked open the front door to leave for school, she was hit by a wave of stench. Acrid smells of creosote and kerosene wafted across the front porch. The charred remains of the giant cross lay on the front lawn where the neighborhood fire brigade had pulled it down after extinguishing it the night before.

She would have to walk to school alone. Bubber was allowed to sleep late. After the firemen left and all the neighbors drifted home, Bubber and his mother sat up until midnight to make sure the charred wooden beams didn't ignite again. Bubber could afford to miss a day of school.

Closing the front door behind her, Alyce glanced over her shoulder and noticed her mother at the sewing machine next to the potbellied stove. Miss Alice was already back at work on the Crewe of Columbus costumes. She had a deadline, and she intended to meet it.

>))).

The following summer Alyce experienced the loss of her third surrogate father. Of course, she had not really 'lost' the first two—Uncle Manny and Joe Midgette—because after their weddings, they continued to visit Bayou and Savannah with their young wives at least once a week, usually on Sunday afternoons.

Bubber was delighted when, at age eight, he helped Uncle Manny carry his suitcases to the front door as Manny moved out to marry a perky young woman that Bubber and Alyce were told to call 'Aunt Celeste.' Now Bubber would have a bedroom all to himself. But Alyce saw Uncle Manny's moving out as a sign that one of her 'daddies' was leaving her.

With Joe Midgette, the situation was different. When he married Aunt Olivia in January, 1919—only a few months before Manny moved out—Alyce didn't feel much of a change. Joe had never lived in the Hicks home. Every Sunday when he was in port, he visited Bayou and Savannah with his wife, Olivia. The main difference for Alyce was after Olivia married on Alyce's sixth birthday, she realized that "Lee-Lee" wouldn't be there any longer to shower attention on her, to kiss away the boo-boos when she fell out of the chinaberry tree.

Six years later Alyce was totally unprepared for the disappearance of her third surrogate-daddy, Uncle Ed McHugh. It was June of 1924 and Alyce was eleven, having just finished the 5th grade at St. Joseph's School. For several weeks she had heard hushed talk about Edwin and 'the cure', and moving to 'Monterey Place' . . . 'Texas' . . . 'consumption'.

Then on the second Saturday of June Alyce awoke and walked into the kitchen to find her mother and her grandmother packing food into cardboard boxes. Alyce and Bubber were told to pack all their summer clothes into their suitcases. The whole family was going to live with their McHugh cousins in Monterey Place until Uncle Ed and Aunt Aggie returned from Texas.

"When did they go to Texas?" Bubber glanced at Alyce on the chance that she had known all along what was going on.

"They haven't gone yet," Miss Alice sealed closed a cardboard box of tinned milk.

"We're gonna live at the McHugh's?" Alyce beamed at the idea of spending her summer with her favorite cousins.

"Uncle Ed has a sickness. It's called consumption, and he can't get well here in Mobile with all this rain, so he's going to the Texas desert where it's dry."

"Will he get well in Texas?" suddenly Alyce realized there was a possibility of death. Uncle Ed could end up dead, like her real father, the one in the wedding photograph.

"If it's God's Will, Alyce!" Miss Alice tried to hide her worry. "He'll get well if it's God's Will! . . . Now, go pack your clothes like I told you!"

Miss Alice moved her two children and her mother into her sister's house in west Mobile so that Agnes could accompany her husband on the train to El Paso where Edwin would 'take the cure' for tuberculosis. Recalling what a strong emotional support her older sister had provided when Thomas Hicks died some twelve years ago, Miss Alice readily offered to care for the four McHugh children—plus her own two, as well as her invalid mother—in the spacious new house in Monterey Place.

The night before Uncle Ed and Aunt Aggie left on the L&N train for New Orleans and points west, Alyce lay awake and eavesdropped on the adults talking at the dining room table. Because it was a hot June night, all the doors in the house were thrown open—it was easy to hear what Miss Alice and her sister were discussing with Uncle Ed. Alyce lay motionless in a double bed next to her favorite cousin, Sister, who was known to be a heavy sleeper.

"I've decided to lend Pike that money," Miss Alice's voice drifted across the hall and into the front bedroom where Alyce lay.

"*What* money?" Aggie set down her glass of lemonade.

"Thomas left me some life insurance money. I haven't touched it since he died."

"My stars!" Aggie widened her eyes in disbelief. "You mean to say you've been sitting on life insurance money for twelve years while you scrimp and save . . . and work your fingers to the bone sewing all those bridesmaid dresses and school uniforms and Mardi Gras costumes and—"

"I'm not touching that life insurance money! It's earmarked to send Bubber to college . . . and for a fancy wedding reception at the Battle House when Alyce gets married," Alice sipped her iced-tea and turned her attention to her brother-in-law.

"Two-thousand dollars is a lot of money, Alice!" Uncle Ed's voice was hoarse.

"Two-thousand dollars! . . . Thomas Hicks left you *two-thousand dollars?*" Aggie covered her mouth when she realized she was shouting loud enough to awaken the children sleeping in the next room.

"I don't need it now," Alice ignored Aggie, continuing to address Ed. "Pike'll pay it back in five years, he said, and that'll be time enough for Thomas to start college. Until then I don't need it!"

"You don't need it, but Tommy Hicks left that life insurance money for his wife and children—*not* for his best friend!"

"If it'll help Pike start a business, then I can lend it to him. After all, Gracie's one of *my* best friends!"

"Don't let friendship influence your decision, Alice."

"Edwin, if my husband was alive, *he'd* lend the money to Pike. Like you say, they were best friends! They worked side-by-side at Frank Stoll Haberdashery!"

"And another thing, Alice, we don't know if Mobile *needs* another haberdashery! Who knows if Pike Garrett is smart enough to make *money* in a haberdashery!"

"Times are good, Edwin! You tell me that all the time!"

"Times are good *now*, Alice. My real estate business is booming, but we never know how long this stock market can go up. Pike says he'll pay back the loan in five years—which would be 1929—but we have no idea what might happen to the economy in these five years between now and 1929!"

"Well, the money's not doing anybody any good sitting in a bank! If it'll help Pike go out on his own, then I'm gonna lend it to him."

"Make sure, Alice, that he signs some sort of loan agreement."

ﺝﺝﺝ

In late August of 1924, barely three months after she had taken her husband to the west Texas desert for the tuberculosis cure, Agnes Fanane McHugh returned on the L&N train with her husband's corpse. He was buried in the Magnolia Cemetery—in the McHugh family plot close to the grave where Thomas E. Hicks, Sr. had been buried twelve years earlier.

Miss Alice left Monterey Place with her two children and her mother and moved back to Bayou and Savannah just in time for the school year to begin. At age fourteen Thomas Jr was beginning high school at McGill Institute, the all-boys Catholic school in downtown Mobile built with money from the wealthy McGill brothers. Most of the other Catholic boys of his age in the neighborhood were opting instead for a fulltime job. Pike Garrett said he'd offer Thomas a fulltime job as a salesclerk in his new haberdashery, but Miss Alice was listening to advice from nuns and priests who saw an academic future for the bright Thomas.

"I bet we can get him a scholarship to Spring Hill College!" the energetic Father Kerns promised. "But first he's got to perform well in high school at McGill!"

Alyce, soon to be age twelve, was dreading the new school year with a nun who had taught Bubber two years before. But on the brink of puberty and starting to notice boys, she looked forward to getting back to her friends at St. Joseph's. The summer spent in the McHugh house with her cousins had been great fun, but she had been jolted by Uncle Ed's death. Everyone had told her he would be cured. He was going to Texas to 'take the cure'.

But there was no *cure*. Like Alyce's father, Uncle Ed had died of a disease. He could no longer serve as a daddy for her. She would have to find someone else.

♩♩♩♩

One year later Alyce finished the 7th grade and was thrilled to begin high school at St. Joseph's. As late as the 1920s the Diocese of Mobile required a student to complete only seven years of elementary school so that the student entered her freshman year of high school at age thirteen.

Each parochial school in the diocese had its own high school—following the seventh grade—so Alyce entered her freshman year in St. Joseph's high school program in 1926, but two years later the parochial schools stopped their K-11 curriculum and limited their classes to K-7. Alyce was forced to transfer to another high school for her last two years.

Catholic boys finishing the 7th grade would start their freshman year at McGill Institute, a Catholic high school operated by the Brothers of the Sacred Heart. It was founded with an endowment from Arthur and Felix McGill, two wealthy brothers who left an estate to provide free education for any Catholic boy willing to pursue a high school education rather than join the workforce at age thirteen.

Catholic girls entering high school had three options. In 1928 the diocese opened a new Catholic school for girls, Bishop Toolen High, operated by the Sisters of Loretta at the Foot of the Cross. The new school on Lafayette Street in midtown Mobile offered free tuition for any Catholic girl. The second choice was the Convent of Mercy, a day-school with only 120 girls in the high school and tuition fees of $3.00 per month. 'The Convent', by necessity, drew girls from families in a higher income bracket. Most Catholics in Alyce's working class neighborhood considered 'the Convent' to be an elitist school, so when St. Joseph's closed its high school, Alyce felt certain her mother would enroll her at Bishop Toolen High with her friends from St. Joseph's.

The Convent of Mercy was located on Bayou Street and Springhill Avenue, right across the street from St. Joseph's School where Alyce was finishing her 7th grade. The nuns operating COM were from the same religious order, the Sisters of Mercy, as the nuns teaching at St. Joseph's. Realizing she was leaving that neighborhood for Bishop Toolen High in west Mobile, Alyce felt a twinge of sadness that she would no longer see Sr. Mary Consuela, St. Joseph's principal who also acted as Vocation Counselor to high school girls deciding whether to join the workforce as a salesclerk or secretary in downtown Mobile, or an early marriage right after graduation, or a religious vocation as a Sister of Mercy.

"Now, Alyce," Sister Mary Consuela sat at her desk in her classroom and folded her hands in earnest on the green blotter in front of her, "I don't think we should even *think* about a religious vocation until you finish high school."

"Sister!" Alyce almost jumped out of the student desk. She and the nun sat in the front of the empty classroom during Little Recess. "You never mentioned a *vocation* before today! And I know *I've* never mentioned it! You're not trying to send me off to Mount Saint Agnes this summer, are you?"

"You're only fifteen, Alyce! Rarely do we take a girl before high school graduation unless she's extremely mature! You still have some growing up to do."

"But, Sister! I don't think I want to become a nun even *after* high school! I mean, I've prayed about it and all—especially during that Lent retreat—but God hasn't sent me *any* kind of sign!"

95

"Then pray to the Blessed Mother! She's the patroness of our order. If she wants you to be a Religious Sister of Mercy, she'll send you a clear sign."

"Oh, Sister! Please don't tell me that!"

"Relax, Alyce, we've got two more years to think about this. Meanwhile, we have to get you transferred to our high school across the street at the Convent. We can't let you fall into the hands of those Sisters of Loretta!"

"Mama could never afford the Convent's tuition. We're not rich, you know."

"I'm working on a scholarship for you."

"*A scholarship?*" Alyce guffawed. "Sister Consuela, have you seen my grades?"

"Not an academic scholarship, of course, but maybe something sponsored by the Sodality of the Blessed Virgin Mary. Tell Miss Alice to call me this weekend. I think we can help you."

"If I transfer to the Convent, will I have to go off after graduation to become a Sister of Mercy?"

"Alyce! You know we'd never demand that of you!"

"Because if that's so, I'll probably forget to tell Mama to call you."

But Alyce did indeed tell her mother to call Sister Mary Consuela. The persuasive nun convinced Miss Alice that a teenage girl of Alyce's character was an asset to the Convent of Mercy.

"Not just me, Miss Alice—all the sisters want Alyce to study at the Convent. Besides, she could still walk to school like she's been doing the past nine years. If you send her to Bishop Toolen High, she'll have to walk over here *anyway* to catch the streetcar. She'll have to wait across the street in front of St. Joseph's, and then take the Springhill Avenue car clear out to Lafayette Street! . . . Now, Miss Alice, does that make any sense?"

"It's the money, Sister Mary Consuela! That new Bishop Toolen school is free! Now, I *know* how much the Convent costs, and I just can't afford it," Miss Alice leaned against the wall next to the cash register at the Toenes Grocery where she was borrowing their phone.

"Don't worry about the money, Miss Alice! You've done a lot of sewing for our sisters, not to mention our scholarship girls who could never afford their own seamstress."

"But, Sister, I *am* worried about money! I don't have enough for your tuition fees!"

"I'm making a private novena to the Blessed Mother—she'll find the money."

"Well, you know I'd much rather Alyce study with you sisters—I don't know anything about those nuns at that new high school. . . . I hear they're from some state way up North! . . . Kentucky, so they tell me."

"Just make sure you register Alyce before August 15. It's a Holy Day of Obligation so you can't forget the deadline—the Assumption of Our Lady—and make sure Alyce turns up for the first day of school!"

"The day after Labor Day, right?"

"Meanwhile, I'll find some second-hand books so she can continue her Latin and classical studies."

"Well, I can probably afford *some* of the tuition each month, maybe a quarter of it, so when do I pay the first installment?"

"You don't pay anything until I send you a bill, Miss Alice. You understand that?"

"Yes, Sister, I'll wait for the first bill."

The first bill didn't arrive at Bayou and Savannah before Labor Day. Alyce entered the Convent of Mercy in September of 1928. When Alyce was graduated in June of 1930, Miss Alice was still waiting for that first bill. Alyce had completed her high school education at the exclusive day-school on the Blessed Mother's dime.

Fawn River
South Mobile County, Alabama
January 21, 2012

AFTER MY DAUGHTER was bathed and dressed by the visiting health-aide, she returned to her recliner to doze a bit before lunch.

"Pike Garrett never repaid that $2,000, did he?" I sat on the sofa so I wouldn't obstruct her view of the TV screen.

"His son paid it back after Mr. Pike died."

"Your mother never told you about the loan, did she?"

"I didn't know a thing about the loan, and neither did Bubber. We were both shocked when Mr. Pike's son—who was my age—showed up in 1964 with two checks of $1,000 each to pay off his father's debt. Mr. Pike had died just the month before."

"Guilt money."

"Evidently Mr. Pike instructed the executor of his will to pay back Mama that $2,000, but she died a year before he did."

"So Pike's son paid it off to you and your brother."

"I was glad to get it—I spent it on prom gowns and graduation stuff for Snookums and Cathy."

"I spoz $1,000 was a tidy little sum in 1964," I was searching for signs of resentment against Pike Garrett.

"It *was*, indeed, but the older children—especially Little Rappy who was doing great with Connecticut Mutual at the time—were outraged that Mr. Pike hadn't paid any interest on the loan."

"Your mama had made it a personal loan, you realize. . . . No interest due on personal loans, usually."

"Yeah, but I'm sure she didn't expect him to take forty years to pay it back!"

"You never knew your mama got $2,000 in life insurance proceeds when I died?"

"I imagine that was a lot of money in 1912," she hit the 'mute' button on the remote and gave me her full attention.

"It was a *lot* of money in 1912," I emphasized, "and it was still a lot of money in 1924 when your mama gave it to Pike."

"She *loaned* it to him!"

"In essence she *gave* it to him because Pike had no chance of success as a haberdasher. He was a terrible businessman."

"But he worked with you at Frank Stoll Haberdashery, didn't he?"

"Indeed he did. And we were good friends. He was a fine salesman—knew his gloves and spats well—but he knew nothing of running a business."

"I wonder how much that money would've grown to over forty years if it had been invested in a savings account at Rappy's bank," she stared wistfully through the window towards the marsh.

"Your mama could've opened her own business with that $2,000 after you started the first grade. She could've rivaled Edmund DeCelle with her own costume shop, four new sewing machines and four good seamstresses to free her up to design the Mardi Gras costumes."

"That money sat in a bank from 1912 till 1924 earning interest. What happened to the interest?" her voice was taking on an edge.

"Pike got that too when she gave him the original $2,000."

"I was only eleven in 1924."

"That would've been the perfect time for her to begin her costume business—you and Bubber were old enough to take care of yourselves after school."

"It's just like Mama to give a friend a big inheritance and never say anything about him paying it back."

"He went bankrupt when his haberdashery failed in its third year."

"That's probably when Miss Gracie stopped coming to visit us on Bayou and Savannah," she gazed at me as if she had just solved a mystery.

"You see," I leaned back on the sofa, "before you were born, I had started saving money to go into business with Pike Garrett. He was going to invest with me in your mother's business. I had planned to set her up in her own costume business, but she and I decided we'd wait till after you started school, which would've been about 1920. We figured she could get the business off the ground with $600 in start-up costs. That would've given Pike and me six years to save $300 each."

"So, Mama could've had her own costume shop if she hadn't given that money to Mr. Pike," her voice was monotone as she stared at me.

"Pike had good intentions, I imagine. He was just inept."

"Sister Consuela always said that the road to hell is paved with good intentions."

Mohawk Street

CHAPTER **6**

WHEN THEY RETURNED from their honeymoon in June, Alyce and Rappy settled into their bungalow on Mohawk Street. The economic disaster triggered by the Crash of '29 was now referred to in the *Mobile Press Register* as 'The Great Depression'. It was felt in every corner of America—it was worldwide.

Upon moving to Mohawk Street, Rappy was earning only $100 per month as a bank clerk. During the year leading up to their wedding, he and Alyce saved enough to pay for the furniture in storage at Adam Glass warehouse while paying off Papa Perez's mahogany dinette suite at the same time. And somehow they managed to save extra for a 3-day honeymoon in New Orleans. Because the Depression had wrecked the tourist industry in New Orleans, room prices had crashed. The newlyweds were able to afford the Jung Hotel in the French Quarter. Hotels all over the Quarter were barely half-full during the tourist season. And for just a few dollars, the couple indulged in a gourmet meal at Arnaud's restaurant, one of the most famous in the Quarter where Rappy passed up the fancy Oysters Bienville and started the meal with a dozen oysters on the half-shell.

But when they returned to Mobile and began married life on Mohawk Street they put themselves on a serious budget. Alyce's job at the Mobile Chemical Company no longer seemed plausible. Living in west Mobile, she wouldn't be able to walk to work as she did from

Bayou and Savannah. Part of her $6 per week salary would have to be spent on carfare to ride the streetcar from the Loop all the way downtown to Bienville Square. And when she got home from work, she would need a couple of hours to fix a home-cooked meal for her husband and herself. Hiring a cook was out of the question. They couldn't even afford 50 cents a week for a maid to clean the house if Alyce continued to work.

Besides, both Rappy and Alyce expected that she would become pregnant right away. It was decided that she would stay home and keep house. In this way Alyce could avoid the stress of working in an office all day long and then rushing home to cook dinner from scratch. Instead, she would provide Rappy with a well-kept house while she waited to become pregnant.

Rappy received his $100 in two paychecks—on the first day of the month and again on the 15th. After paying the rent, utilities, and insurance premiums, the young couple put aside money for groceries and carfare for Rappy's ride to work. Because he didn't own a car to take turns in a carpool, he contributed $1.25 a week for gasoline expenses. That left $2.50 for entertainment for two weeks until the next paycheck. If money ran low before payday, they walked to a neighborhood movie instead of taking the streetcar downtown to see a first-run Gary Cooper feature at the air-conditioned Saenger. And if they ran out of money before payday, they stayed home on the weekend, made popcorn, and listened to Jack Benny on the radio—or, better yet, they had friends over from the Cavalier Club, their crowd who had partied together since high school.

"But how can I complain?" Alyce mused as she walked through the little two-bedroom house waiting for Rappy to come home with his paycheck on the last Saturday in June. "We've got a houseful of furniture. My kitchen has a gas stove. I've got an icebox and two sets of dishes. For company I can use the wedding china—I can't believe all those people sent wedding presents even though they knew they wouldn't get to attend a reception! . . . I'm so lucky—so many people in this country are just hungry!"

She stood in the doorway of the empty spare bedroom. Soon she would furnish it with a crib, a bassinet, a rocking chair from Grandma Fanane's attic—the 'bedroom rocker' with no arms so she could cradle the baby comfortably as she rocked him to sleep. When she became pregnant—the minute the doctor confirmed it—she would head to Adam Glass and ask the nice redhead salesman to put the baby furniture on layaway so they could have six months to pay for it. But first God had to agree to a pregnancy. She asked the Blessed Mother to take care of it. Surely the Lord would understand his own Mother interceding for another woman anxious to become a mother.

She wasn't about to refer to the second bedroom as 'the baby's room'. That would bring bad luck, like a curse. She called it 'the spare room.'

♪♪♪♫

For newlyweds in the 1930s like Rappy and Alyce, entertainment had to be inexpensive. If they had no cash for a picture show—the cheapest good-time for young people wanting to 'go out'—then they visited friends. In the summer they lounged on front porches to escape the heat because no homes were air-conditioned. In the winter they gathered around a kitchen stove with hot chocolate and coffee to dream of a brighter future for America.

Alyce and Rappy were the first in their crowd of friends to marry. Some, even older, were still struggling to save enough money to afford a modest wedding and furniture for a rented house. So it was only reasonable that the little house on Mohawk Street would become the focal point for the crowd who had grown up together in Mobile's Catholic neighborhoods.

Nobody had money for nightclubs. Even a hotdog at Romie's New Spic restaurant was an extravagance. Entertainment had to be cheap or, even better, free. The crowd didn't think twice about walking three miles to a high school football game on Saturday night, especially when one of Rappy's younger brothers was quarterbacking. And after the game the whole gang descended on Mohawk Street where

Alyce and Peg Camilleri made waffles until midnight for ten couples or more.

"This is a terrific idea, Peg!" Alyce ladled the batter onto the hot grill.

"Yeah! Waffles are nice and cheap—just flour, milk and eggs!" Peg cracked two eggs against each other and started another bowl of batter.

"I never realized I'd get so much use out of this waffle iron!"

"Every time I pick up an egg, Alyce, I remember the time at that Belle Fountain houseparty when you slept with the eggs in your bed!"

"You're never gonna let me live that down, are you, Peg!"

"I never blamed you. The boys were staying up all night making those nasty cocktails with gin and raw eggs!"

"And *orange juice*! . . . If I hadn't hidden the eggs, Peg, there wouldn't have been any for breakfast!"

"Was that the weekend the boys decided to call themselves the '*IFTs*'?"

"No, Peg, it was at that Gulf Shores houseparty when Goober got tight and walked clear across the room to rub Sue Ellen's thigh."

"That was a horrible introduction to our crowd for poor Sue Ellen, wasn't it?"

"Her first date with Goober, but she was a good sport about it."

"Alyce, have you ever told your mama what '*IFT*' stands for?"

"Goodness, no! . . . Mama'd have a fit!"

"I told my mama—she laughed uproariously!"

"But, Peg, your mama's much more modern than mine! I could never use the word 'thigh' in the same sentence with '*feel*' in front of Mama."

"Not '*feel*', Alyce! . . . It's '*I Felt a Thigh*!'"

While Alyce and Peg were in the kitchen making waffles, the other young couples were scattered throughout the front of the house listening to Benny Goodman's orchestra on the radio. Some were perched on the front porch where the air was still warm enough in October to sit on the steps, re-hash the football game, and drink beer.

The beer was homemade—community property of the entire gang of buddies—brewed and stored in Alyce and Rappy's spare room.

The federal prohibition of alcohol had been repealed two years earlier but Rappy and his friends—who had learned to make moonshine in their teens when alcohol was first made illegal—continued to brew their own beer after Prohibition's repeal rather than buy a case of Budweiser at the store. The young bucks—most in their mid twenties—realized they were breaking the law, but they took the risk. They figured that the Feds were too busy chasing big-time bank robbers like John Dillinger than worrying about twelve cases of home brew fermenting in a bedroom in west Mobile, Alabama.

Sunday morning after she dressed for Mass, Alyce emerged from the bedroom wearing a new cocoa-brown frock Miss Alice had finished the week before. She was wearing beige suede high-heels, a four year-old brown felt hat refurbished with a new veil, and in her hands she carried a new fawn leather clutch-purse and a pair of beige cotton gloves. She posed before the full-length mirror at the end of the hall and saw a stylish twenty-two year-old woman who appeared the essence of middle-class respectability.

Then she glanced into the spare room and realized she certainly did not feel respectable. She considered herself a criminal.

The spare room was no longer empty, no longer a bedroom waiting for the arrival of a baby's crib. It had been converted into a storage room filled with wooden crates of beer bottles. A few bottles hissed from the gas trying to escape. Occasionally a bottle exploded and blew bits of broken glass against the walls and the window shades which were always drawn down. Alyce resisted an urge to raise the shades and let some sunlight into the room.

"Do we need to confess this?" she turned to her husband as he came out of the bedroom knotting his necktie.

"What are you talking about?" he was genuinely perplexed.

"We're breaking the law, Rappy! Isn't that a sin?"

"Aw, Hickory! How can it be a sin? . . . If it's not a sin against God to *drink* beer, how can it be a sin to make it?"

"Then, why's making beer against the law?"

"It's not against the law *anymore*, Hickory! . . . Mr. Schlitz makes beer! Mr. Budweiser makes beer! Mr. Pabst!"

"That's *commercial* beer, Rappy! Why's it against the law for us to make beer in our own house?"

"Because the government can't collect tax on it! When we buy it at the store, they tax the store for each bottle they sell. In our spare room they can't tax us. It's all about taxes!"

"So, is it a sin?"

"Hell, no!"

"Stop cussing! . . . Still, I'm gonna talk to a priest about this."

"Talk to an *Irish* priest—no Irish priest would dare call moonshine a sin!"

The next morning Alyce was washing the breakfast dishes right after Rappy had left for work when she heard a gunshot.

Maybe it's just a car backfiring! Or a tire blowing out!

No, I'm sure it's a gunshot!

The police have the house surrounded! If I open the front door I'll find the Feds in double-breasted suits with Tommy-guns cradled in their arms! . . . In the newsreels they're called 'G-men'!

They've come for that damn beer in the spare room!

No use calling Rappy—he hasn't had time to get to his desk at the bank. I could call Romie at the Spic and Span! Romie'll know what to do!

She was hurrying down the hall towards the telephone table when she spotted a stream of sudsy liquid oozing from under the spare room door. She realized the explosion hadn't been a gunshot. It was another beer bottle. She promised herself that the next time a bottle exploded, she wouldn't panic. She had to keep in mind at all times that she was guarding a roomful of moonshine. She had to forget about Eliot Ness.

A second explosion. She opened the door to clean up the spare room—the third time that month.

A raid by J. Edgar Hoover's G-men wasn't Alyce's only worry when she was home alone on Mohawk Street. There was the problem of the L&N railroad running behind the house. The train of freight cars slowed to a crawl every morning just before arriving at Government Street where it intersected with three other streets all coming to a point at the Loop.

When she heard the train slowing down between 10 and 11, she ran to the kitchen and peeked out the window. As soon as the caboose passed, she would see a handful of transients dusting themselves off after jumping from the moving train into the ditch bordering the train track.

"Six! I don't have enough bread to make that many sandwiches! Maybe some of 'em will pass me by this time," Alyce hid behind the curtain.

And some did pass by her house. They followed the track towards the Loop intersection. But inevitably at least one transient would leap the ditch and head straight for Alyce's kitchen door.

It was her mother-in-law, Nellie Perez, also living close to a railroad track who urged Alyce to feed any transient who knocked on her kitchen door.

"Some of 'em are bums, that's for sure, Alyce. But some of 'em are businessmen who lost their jobs, their house, their family—lost *everything*!" Nellie telephoned Alyce several times a week to make sure she was safe in a house so close to the railroad track.

"So how can I tell which are bums and which are businessmen?" Alyce asked.

"The businessman usually wears a suit—the only clothes he still owns—a pretty dirty suit he holds onto cuz he still has hopes of finding an office job. The truth is he's gonna end up out there in Grand Bay picking watermelons!"

"So I should feed only the ones in a business suit?"

"Alyce, you feed anybody who knocks on your door! They're all hungry after riding those freight cars for a whole week!"

"Feed the bums too?"

"The Lord would feed 'em, wouldn't He? . . . Didn't Jesus feed those 5,000 folks when they were all hungry? I bet a lot of *them* were bums! . . . But, Alyce, don't let 'em *inside* your house!"

Alyce rescued every scrap of food left on her plate—and Rappy's plate—after their evening dinner. She saved the scraps in the icebox and the next day she heated them up in a frying pan with a little lard before ten in the morning. When she slid the contents onto a plate, it looked like some kind of mystery-stew, but she never had a hungry man complain.

If a man appeared on her back step in a business suit, she couldn't help but say a prayer of gratitude that her husband still had a reason to put on his business suit every morning. If she had a can of potted meat, she made a sandwich for the transient—assuming she had extra slices of bread after making Rappy's brown-bag lunch that morning.

One chilly November morning an older man in a shabby suit—double-breasted navy blue—knocked on the kitchen door after the train passed behind the house. When Alyce opened the door and turned for the icebox, the man followed her into the kitchen and sat down at the breakfast table. She knew she had to get him out of the house—she certainly couldn't allow a stranger to sit at her kitchen table, no matter how hungry he was. But this was an old man, easily sixty. He had a solid white mustache that curled down over his top lip. His thick eyebrows were equally white, as well as the tufts of hair that stuck out over his ears under the dusty brown fedora.

All she had to offer him was a bowl of cold grits with milk. He couldn't wait for her to heat the milk in a saucepan—he picked up a soup-spoon and attacked the grits. At that moment the phone rang in the hallway and she dashed to answer it, leaving the old man at her kitchen table.

"Hickory?" Rappy's voice on the telephone sounded concerned. "You shouldn't stay there alone today—there might be another bank holiday, and—"

"Are y'all closing the bank?"

"That's the rumor, but nobody's telling us for sure."

112

"So why can't I stay here?"

"There might be trouble in the streets with the labor unions protesting and all that!"

"But that'll happen downtown!"

"Yeah, Hickory, but all kind of folks might be getting off that train behind the house."

Alyce gasped. Her husband was warning her of union agitation against the banks, and she had a transient at her kitchen table, an old man who'd jumped off a freight train less than twenty minutes ago.

"I called Romie," Rappy continued. "He's sending a boy in a truck to pick you up. You wait at the Spic and Span and I'll meet you there after work . . . or sooner if they close us down today."

"Okay," she said absentmindedly. Without telling Rappy that she had a stranger seated at the kitchen table, she hung up.

She stood next to the telephone table in the hallway, wondering how to get the stranger out the door when the phone rang again. It was her mother-in-law.

"Get out of the house!" Nellie Perez was excited at the other end of the line. "You have to get out of that house *now*!"

"Yes M'am, but what's wrong?"

"The Communists are coming!"

"Grandma, what are you talking about?"

"It's on the radio, Alyce! . . . The unions are gonna march in the streets cuz they're mad at the banks—and everybody knows the unions are full of Communists!"

"Yes M'am, but I don't even know what a Communist is!"

"It's something to do with Russia! And I didn't even know we had Russians living here in Mobile. The radio says these agitators are coming down from the North on those freight trains!"

"To march in the streets?"

"You need to get out of there—you live next to that railroad track, and no telling who might be jumping off the trains today!"

"Yes M'am. . . . Romie's sent a boy in his truck—I'm going to the Spic and Span to meet Rappy—so everything's okay."

Five minutes later Romie's bartender knocked on the front door as Alyce ushered the old man out the back door. The stranger tipped his hat like a gentleman and thanked her profusely as if she had served him a Porterhouse steak. When she arrived at Romie's restaurant, Rappy was waiting for her at a corner table. She didn't tell him about the old man eating cold grits at the kitchen table. And she never told her mother-in-law either.

The following spring when Rappy decided to wash down the wood siding of the house, Alyce discovered why so many transients had been knocking on the kitchen door to be fed. On the rear of the house, at the corner closest to the railroad track, someone had made a mark on the white siding with a lump of coal. The modified "X" symbol had become a universal sign—all across America—to anyone jumping off a freight train that the woman living in that house wouldn't turn away a hungry man.

♪♪♪♪

When Alyce and Rappy celebrated their first wedding anniversary on June 7, 1935, she had not yet become pregnant. A year later on their second anniversary, she still wasn't pregnant.

"Why doesn't God let me have a baby?!" Alyce leaned back in the swing on the front porch at Bayou and Savannah, lazily pushing herself back and forth as she gazed across the street at customers entering and leaving the Toenes Grocery store.

"You don't need to give up, Alyce—you've only been married two years," Miss Alice sat in a rocking chair taking a break from her sewing machine where she had been working on a wedding project of nine bridesmaids. In her lap lay a huge picture-frame hat half-covered with salmon-pink tulle.

"But *you* got pregnant right after your wedding!"

"Three months after, to be exact, but I had regular periods—you don't!"

"What's that got to do with it?"

"Maybe nothing—I don't know. I'm just looking for a reason."

"Please don't tell me it's God's Will!" Alyce let out a sarcastic chuckle.

"Well, I guess this *is* God's Will."

"*Everything's* God's Will, Mama!"

"Indeed it is," Miss Alice stroked the tulle fabric covering the hat in her lap, "but that don't mean you have to give up! . . . Who're you praying to, anyway?"

"I'm praying to *God*—and the Blessed Mother!" Alyce had become impatient. "Who else should I pray to?"

"St. Gerard is the Patron Saint of Mothers."

"Well, I'm not a mother yet," Alyce realized that her eyes were brimming with tears.

"It can't hurt."

"Who's the Patron Saint of Getting-Pregnant?" she tried to laugh so her mother wouldn't notice the tears about to stream down her cheeks.

'You'll have to ask a priest—or the nuns. . . . Get the holy sisters on the job—they'll know who to pray to!"

The nuns at St. Mary's School remembered Rappy as one of their favorites when he was a student in elementary school. Whenever Alyce and Rappy attended Sunday Mass at St. Mary's Church, his former teachers always asked when the young couple would be starting a family. When Alyce finally confided in Sister Mary Teresita that she was having a hard time getting pregnant, the tiny Irish nun promised she'd storm heaven with a special prayer—and that she'd have all the nuns at St. Mary's and the Convent of Mercy pray for a Perez baby.

The nuns never told Alyce exactly whom they were beseeching in heaven, but whoever it was, it worked. At the end of that summer of 1936 Alyce became pregnant for the first time. Unlike her sister-in-law, Margie—who couldn't go shopping in her early months of pregnancy for fear of throwing up on the curb—Alyce never suffered the usual morning sickness. It was an uneventful pregnancy.

It was in the sixth month of pregnancy when Alyce was beginning to 'show' that Rappy realized they had to buy a car. He would need transportation to take his wife to the hospital when it came time to deliver the baby. He didn't want to call Romie in the middle of the night to borrow his car and he certainly couldn't take Alyce to the hospital on the streetcar. Because he finally had received a small raise in his bank salary, Rappy was saving money for the hospital bill. But he wasn't able to afford a down payment on a car. Alyce added an automobile to her list of nightly petitions to the Blessed Mother.

A few months later Emile, one of Rappy's younger brothers, found himself unable to make payments on his 1936 black Plymouth. Rappy took over the payments to have a car just in time for the birth of their first child. It was a boy—born on May 5, 1937. Alyce named the boy after her husband, Alfred Leonard Perez, Jr. Because her husband had been known throughout his life as only 'Rappy', she realized that her son would grow up as 'Rappy, Jr.' . . . or Little Rappy—and he did.

A year later Alyce gave birth to her first daughter, named Mary Hicks Perez in honor of the Blessed Mother. Before the baby girl left the hospital, her daddy was calling her 'Mickey' because he remembered a favorite Irish ballad from his childhood with the lyrics of "Mickey, pretty Mickey!"

Two years later another baby girl arrived for the growing Perez family. Shirley Anne was born in July of 1940.

A month after the baby's birth Miss Alice showed up at Mohawk Street on the Sunday morning scheduled for Shirley's christening. In her arms she carried the heirloom baptismal gown that her mother, Grandma Fanane, had created for her firstborn, Daniel, in 1881. Alyce sat in Grandma Fanane's bedroom rocker with no arms breastfeeding the infant.

"I'm glad you're still nursing," Miss Alice said as she laid the three-foot long embroidered gown on Little Rappy's bed.

"I'm almost through," Alyce glanced at her wrist watch.

"I mean that I'm glad you're nursing *Shirley Anne*—that you can find time to nurse a new baby when you have these other two to take care of," Miss Alice sat on the edge of the bed and pulled at her white gloves.

"I can always find time to nurse, Mama. It's important for the baby. I don't want to give her a bottle as long as I've got milk. Besides, I do enjoy it. It makes me feel close to the baby."

Miss Alice sat silent and gazed at her daughter who had managed to escape the working-class economy of Bayou and Savannah centered in a blue-collar neighborhood.

"You're a lucky girl, Alyce" the older woman's blue eyes misted a bit.

"I *am*, Mama. Somehow we made it through the Depression. And Rappy's still got his job, and each of the past three years he's gotten some kind of raise. Usually a small raise but still a raise! We can afford to rent our own house out here near the Loop where it's better to raise children, and—"

"And all of your children are healthy—none of 'em deformed or anything.

"Yessum. All healthy . . . and normal.

"And you've got a good husband to provide for you. He wears a white dress-shirt to work every morning. We can't forget *him*!"

"No m'am, we can't forget him," Alyce laughed and handed the infant to her mother.

"Now, where in the world did you find that name, *'Shirley'*?" Miss Alice laid the infant on Little Rappy's bed next to the baptismal gown.

"I just like it," Alyce said.

"Well, it *is* a pretty name! . . . And how about the middle name, 'Anne'?"

"The mother of the Blessed Mother! *St. Anne*! I prayed to her before I finally got pregnant the first time with Little Rappy—and I promised I'd name a baby after her one day! First I had to name a baby 'Mary' for the Blessed Mother!"

"Don't make any more promises for a while. You need a break from babies."

"It's those nuns at St. Mary's!" Alyce laughed. "I had them praying for a baby before Little Rappy came along!"

"My stars! That was four years ago! Tell them to stop praying!"

"I can't find most of 'em! . . . They've been transferred to schools all over the country!"

"Well, you'd better find out where each one went so you can write and tell her to stop the prayers! Otherwise you'll end up with more than a dozen children!"

Laurel Street

CHAPTER **7**

EVERY AMERICAN COULD tell you exactly where he was the moment he heard that the Japanese had bombed Pearl Harbor. Alyce was stooping down to light the gas stove in the center hall of the new house on Laurel Street. Her first thoughts were of Rappy's three younger brothers under age thirty. Emile, Charles, and Joe would certainly be drafted into the army. For several months she had read predictions in the *Mobile Press Register* that the USA would have to help England and France fight the Germans and Italians in Europe.

"If we have to fight that war in Europe and another one in the Pacific," Alyce said to her mother who was leaning over the Zenith console radio in the living room corner, "then you *know* they're gonna have to draft a million men!"

"Well," Miss Alice turned up the volume on the radio, "maybe it'll turn out like that last war in 1917. By the time our boys got to France to help out, the war was almost over!"

"What about Bubber, Mama? He's over thirty, but he's still single. Will they take him just cuz he's not married?"

"Maybe, but I don't think they'll take Rappy, not right away—not with a wife and three children to support!"

"And Romie's got those two little girls," Alyce leaned over and picked up Shirley, the seventeen month-old toddler who was wandering too close to the gas stove, "so they probably won't take him either."

Alyce and Rappy had been living in their house on Laurel Street for only ten months when the United States entered World War II. The fact that they were able to obtain a mortgage on the fifteen year-old house near the Loop had been a miracle. When the previous owner of the house at 1706 Laurel Street defaulted on his mortgage held by the Merchants National Bank, the head of the mortgage department approached Rappy about assuming the mortgage. No money down— just take over monthly payments of $30.05 on the three bedroom house in a 1920s residential neighborhood near the Loop.

Because Grandma Fanane had recently died, her five children decided to sell the Fanane family home on Bayou and Savannah. Miss Alice and Bubber needed a place to live. With three bedrooms, the Laurel Street house was perfect. Rappy and Alyce took one of the smaller bedrooms while Bubber slept in a small room with Rappy Jr., now four years-old. The largest bedroom was reserved for Miss Alice, who needed space for her sewing machine and a work table to cut fabric for ball gowns, plus a bed for the two girls, Mickey and Shirley.

"Should we take over this mortgage, Hickory?" Rappy had been staring for half-an-hour at the paperwork scattered on the kitchen table at the rented house on Mohawk.

"It's God's Will, Rappy!"

"You always say that, Hickory! How do you know when it's *God's* Will?"

"When it falls into your lap! . . . We didn't set out to buy a house! This man defaulted on his mortgage, the bank repossessed the house, and the bank officers approached you to take over the payments! . . . Isn't that how it happened?"

"That's exactly how it happened," Rappy smiled at her tenacity.

"So God dropped it in your lap!"

"God and Mr. McRae."

"Sometimes God works through bank presidents."

The weekend after Pearl Harbor was attacked Alyce and Rappy enjoyed a welcomed night out at Romie's 'New Spic Supper Club' located on Holcombe Avenue in west Mobile. They sat at a table near the door, far from the bandstand where a honey-smooth Glenn Miller sound emerged from a fifteen-piece band specializing in the jitterbug and swing dancing.

"It's great to have Mama living with us," Alyce sipped her high-ball, a tall glass of Coca-Cola spiked with a half-jigger of bourbon which would last her all evening. "She said she'd baby-sit any night we want to go out."

"But we don't want to take advantage of her, Hickory."

"I don't plan to, Rappy! But she doesn't mind taking care of the children on a Saturday night—especially if we don't leave home before they're asleep!"

Alyce loved a night out. Seven years into marriage, her daily routine was that of a typical housewife in 1940s America. Despite not being able to get pregnant for more than two years after her wedding, she now found herself with three healthy children and a three bedroom house. Never in her dreams had she imagined that she and Rappy could save enough money for a down-payment on their own house. But they hadn't needed a down-payment—thanks to Rappy's job at a bank which held mortgages on residential homes.

They were slightly crowded in the house—but the advantages were several. Alyce was delighted to have enough space for her brother to share a room with the Rappy, Jr. The two little girls were small enough to sleep together in a single bed next to their Grandma's bed in the largest bedroom. The greatest advantage for Alyce was having her mother live with her. Despite Miss Alice's busy schedule with wedding dress orders and school uniforms, she found time to help Alyce with the housework.

The worst chore was laundry. Operating the aging wringer-washer meant feeding each piece of wet laundry through the wringer, one garment at a time, a tedious process when there were diapers and children's clothes to wash during the week. The laundry operation was performed in a shed behind the garage. In January a frosty breeze blew through the open shed and chapped the wet hands of the two women—in August the Gulf Coast humidity was muggy, stifling, and still. But Alyce found that laundry days, twice a week, passed quickly when her mother could take the time to help.

In July and August, when Miss Alice was busy at her sewing machine turning out Catholic school uniforms for a September deadline, Alyce did the laundry alone—always hurrying to get the wet clothes on the line between 'scattered thundershowers' for which the Alabama Gulf Coast is famous. Often, as she trudged across the backyard to the laundry shed with an armful of dirty clothes, she noticed Little Rappy following two steps behind. Barely five years old, he delighted in helping his mama operate the defiant wringer washing machine. On more than one occasion she had to depend on the child to unwind the crank and free her hand caught in the wringer when she was working too fast to finish before the next rainstorm.

What in the world will I do if I have any more boys?

It'd be unfair to compare them to Little Rappy. But I'm afraid I'd end up doing just that!

That would be terrible! I know how I hated being compared to Bubber! I never compare my two little girls with Little Rappy . . . or with each other! They're so different.

But two boys in the family might be a problem for me.

Maybe the rest of my babies will all be girls. Then I can dote on this cute little boy with no worry of showing favoritism.

Saturday night at Romie's New Spic Supper Club was a respite from household chores. She loved sitting at a corner table with Rappy eating the New Spic's famous hotdog as Romie maneuvered his way through the tables making sure every diner was satisfied. For sure, Romie was a born *restaurateur*. Rappy, especially, felt proud watching Romie check on each table to make sure his customers developed a loyalty to return every Saturday night for good food and live music.

124

Romie worked the room like a county sheriff running for re-election.

"Is everything okay? . . . Your waitress treating you all right? . . . Can I get you something else?"

Only the week before, while Rappy was in Romie's office going over the books, Alyce witnessed a scene at a table of eight customers which convinced her that Romie would one day own a five-star restaurant. A patron had complained to the waitress that his Porterhouse steak was too rare. He sent it back to the kitchen to cook longer. When it was time for the waitress to return the steak to the table, Romie carried the serving tray himself and delivered the steak to the dissatisfied customer. Romie waited at the head of the table as the diner tasted the steak and pronounced it cooked to his satisfaction.

"Is it okay?" Romie leaned towards the man sitting at the head of a table for eight located next to the parquet dance floor.

"Perfect, Mr. Perez! Medium-well, just as I like it!" the customer beamed at the personal attention he was receiving from the supper club's owner.

"Call me 'Romie'! . . . And I want you to know that this is on the house," he made a sweeping gesture with his hand that took in the whole table.

"My steak's on the house?"

"This whole table's on the house! Tonight you're my guests!"

Later when Rappy emerged from the office where he had completed the weekly bookkeeping for his brother, he chided Romie for such grandiose generosity.

"The books say you're making plenty of money, Romie, especially the liquor receipts—but you just can't treat eight people to a free meal!"

"They'll be back!" Romie was seated next to Alyce, but his eyes continually searched the room on the lookout for another disgruntled customer.

"What're you trying to do? . . . Buy loyalty?"

"After tonight, that table won't dare go to another club!"

"Besides, Rappy," Alyce sipped her bourbon-and-Coke, "there're eight people at that table who got a free steak dinner, and if each one of them tells their family and friends how great Romie treated them, he might get 100 new customers from that *one* table!"

"You tell him, Hickory!" Romie gently slapped Alyce on the back as he sprang from the chair to continue working the room.

After they finished their dinner Alyce and Rappy took to the dance floor with the other young couples dancing to swing music from the New Spic's live band. Alyce pressed her cheek against her husband's as they glided across the floor to "String of Pearls." She relished her night away from Laurel Street with its demands of cooking, laundry, and caring for three children under the age of five. For a few hours she and Rappy could dance and laugh with the *IFT* crowd, knowing that her children were safe at home with their Grandma Hicks.

When the band went on break, Rappy guided Alyce by the arm back to their corner table where a Brandy Alexander waited for her.

"I know you're not much of a drinker," Romie had once told her, "but Rappy says you're crazy for Hershey's milk chocolate, so you're gonna love this Brandy Alexander!'

Rappy raised his mug of draft beer—Alyce raised her Brandy Alexander—as they prepared to make a toast.

"Well, Hickory, what do we toast?"

"President Roosevelt! . . . If we're going to war, he needs our prayers!"

"To *war*!" Rappy raised his mug so high that beer sloshed over the rim onto his hand.

Alyce felt a shiver run down her spine. She saw in her husband's eyes that 'war' meant *adventure*. To her the new war meant that thousands of young men would be sent overseas, many never to return. Her brother, Bubber, was at risk. Rappy's three youngest brothers would surely be called up. But being over thirty—married and with children—both Rappy and Romie wouldn't be called up to fight. Certainly not.

Still, to make sure, she made a mental note to add another decade of the rosary to her night prayers.

One year later Alyce found herself pregnant for the fourth time. As always, she had an easy pregnancy, no morning-sickness at all. Her third child, Shirley, was now two years-old, so she didn't feel she was having her children too close together. By the time the new baby arrived in late July, Shirley would have turned three.

"Well, just how many children do you plan to have?" the next-door neighbor, Mrs. Cooke, asked her question bluntly as Alyce emerged from the shed with a bucket of wet laundry on her way to the clothesline.

"As many as the Lord sends me," Alyce laughed.

"Well, I know you're a Catholic like me, so you think you can't do anything to stop so many babies, but you know, there *are* ways to prevent getting pregnant!" the older woman—tall and cumbersome in her large frame with padded hips—shook her finger at Alyce as if she were admonishing a child.

"Well, *you* had four children, didn't you, Mrs. Cooke?" Alyce made certain she showed respect to her neighbor, a good-hearted, yet opinionated, woman in her fifties.

"Five, actually—one died in the delivery room. But my husband, you know, is a non-Catholic so when he said he didn't want any more children, I had to find a way to make sure I didn't get pregnant. That's real important when you're married to a railroad man who might be gone 3-4 days in a row and comes home looking for his . . . for his *romance!*"

"Well, Rappy doesn't travel with his job, so we don't have *that* problem!" Alyce laughed but she felt uncomfortable whenever someone brought up the subject of preventing pregnancy.

"You better hope he don't get drafted into the army and leave you here with all those children and your mama to take care of!"

"Rappy's thirty-four! They're not gonna draft a man that old with four children!" Alyce started hanging the wet garments on the clothesline.

"You don't know what they're gonna do! Already they're rationing gasoline and coffee, and sugar! I heard they need schoolteachers so bad—so many men have been drafted—they're putting women in front of the classroom with *no* teaching certificate and *no* college degree! I plan to look into that myself!"

"Just make sure they put you in a school close by," Alyce shouted over her shoulder as she worked her way down the clothesline, "so you can walk to work and not have to use up your gas coupons!"

As soon as rationing started in May, 1942—just five months after Pearl Harbor—gasoline coupons became a treasure. President Roosevelt's administration had hoped they could rely on voluntary conservation of gasoline—every American realized that military tanks and jeeps ran on gasoline, not to mention the thousands of bomber and fighter planes burning fuel made from petroleum—but by the spring of 1942 it was apparent that gasoline had to be rationed to force the public to cut back on driving.

The Office of Price Administration was born—with offices all over the United States.

Since Alyce would drive the car while Rappy was at work, she went with him to register the seven year-old Plymouth for a ration sticker placed on the windshield inside the car. The young Perez family qualified for an 'A' sticker which allowed four gallons of fuel per week. That class of sticker was issued to owners whose vehicle use for the war effort was nonessential.

Consequently the Plymouth was driven rarely during the week—only once to the grocery store and to St. Mary's Church for Sunday Mass. Later that afternoon the whole family drove out to see Rappy's parents who lived near the New Spic after they dropped off Miss Alice to spend Sunday afternoon with one of her brothers or sisters.

Romie would have loved to finagle a 'T' sticker for truckers which allowed for unlimited amounts of fuel, but he wasn't able to sweet-talk the female bureaucrat at the OPA office. But because Romie still had his Spic and Span hamburger restaurant on Williams Street, as well as his new supper club on Holcombe Avenue, he maintained a fleet of vehicles whereby each qualified for gasoline coupons of four gallons per week. At the end of the month he usually had coupons left over which he didn't need. Rather than have them expire worthless at the end of each month, he was delighted to give them to Alyce. Consequently, she rarely had to get on the phone and find someone willing to trade gasoline coupons for coffee coupons.

By spring of 1943—when Alyce was six months pregnant with her fourth child—the mad dashes to the GM&O train station began. It seemed like every few days the telephone rang to say that some soldier was arriving on the train that afternoon for a 24-hour furlough. Usually the caller was Rappy's mother, Nellie Perez, who had three sons in the armed forces and who knew which of her many nephews were overseas in Europe or the South Pacific. On any given day Nellie knew which boys were in boot camp and which were arriving home on a three-day pass before being shipped out to battle. Nellie expected the whole family to drop what they were doing and find a way to the station platform to mob the young soldier when he stepped off the train.

Alyce loved the excitement of the GM&O train station. When her mother-in-law called, Alyce dropped what she was doing and, urged by Miss Alice whose son was serving in the Philippines, dashed out the front door to wait for a car at the curb. She never knew who would be speeding down Laurel Street to pick her up. Usually it was Romie's wife, Cleo, at the wheel of a vehicle from the New Spic, but sometimes it was Romie himself or one of his dishwashers. Whichever, Alyce tried to make sure that when she climbed into the car with 7-8 other people that she was sitting on someone's lap and not squeezed against the door where her pregnant belly would be jostled during the fifteen minute ride downtown.

Baby #4 wasn't due until August 13, Rappy's birthday, but the baby came two weeks early. The new baby had two bachelor uncles currently in harm's way—Rappy's youngest brother Joe was stationed at a Pensacola naval base waiting to be shipped overseas any day, and Alyce's brother, Tommy, was somewhere in the Philippines. Alyce and Rappy had decided a month before the baby arrived to name him after the two bachelor uncles. If either of the young soldiers died in the war, he would have a nephew carrying his name.

So, on July 30, 1943 when Alyce gave birth to her fourth child and it turned out to be a boy, the decision had already been made to name him Thomas Joseph Perez.

At midnight the labor pains started so suddenly that, unlike the deliveries of her other children, Alyce didn't have time to call her mother-in-law to tell her she was on her way to the hospital. After Miss Alice got her daughter out the front door and into the waiting car with Rappy at the wheel, she returned to bed for a few hours sleep—expecting to call Miss Nellie in the morning while she waited for Rappy's phonecall to say that the baby had arrived. But by the time Miss Alice had risen and finished giving the three grandchildren their cornflakes, the phone rang at 7:15 when Rappy announced, "Tommy's here!"

Miss Alice was delighted that Alyce's fourth child had been born a boy. Now the family boasted two girls and two boys.

As soon as Rappy hung up, Miss Alice tried to call Rappy's mother, Miss Nellie, but her line was busy. Instead, she called Rappy's sister, Margie, who was known affectionately as the Family Alarmist.

"Tommy's here!" Miss Alice repeated Rappy's perky announcement without thinking that Margie could interpret the message to mean that Alyce's *brother* had arrived from the Philippines because his sister was dying in childbirth.

"Which hospital?" Margie gasped in shock.

"The Allen Memorial."

"I'll be right there!" Margie sobbed and hung up quickly.

Immediately Margie dialed her mother, Miss Nellie, to get the entire family to the hospital to support Rappy as Alyce died in childbirth.

"That baby's not due for another month!" Margie shouted over the phone to her mother who was hard-of-hearing. "The army brought Tommy home from the Philippines because his sister's dying in labor. I just hope he gets here in time! I'm on the way to the hospital but I don't have enough gas coupons to drive all the way out there to pick you up, Mama! Call Romie and have him send one of his dishwashers to pick you up! Get on the phone and call Cleo and Moon and—just call everybody! I'll pick up anybody who's on my way to the Allen Memorial! Tell 'em Alyce's dying in labor!"

Forty minutes later Rappy glanced up from the sofa in the Delivery waiting room where he was reading the newspaper to find an hysterical Margie barging through the swinging doors. Behind her trailed a mob of relatives—four sisters-in-law and Romie—all rushing towards Rappy with grief-stricken faces. In the forefront of the crowd was Rappy's mother who hurried toward him shaking her head in fateful acceptance of Alyce's imagined death.

"I told her not to ride to the train station in a car full of people packed like sardines! It just takes one time when you're on the bottom for the baby to get squashed!" Miss Nellie sighed dolefully as she put her hand on Rappy's shoulder. "And why aren't you in there with her? Does this mean she's already dead?"

♪♪♪♪

Rappy was drafted into the army in December of 1943—just five months after the birth of his fourth child.

He was 35 years old.

"It's my duty to go," he held Alyce in his arms as they lay in the midnight-dark bedroom trying to drift off to sleep, only hours after he had received the notice in the mail that he was to report for boot camp early in 1944.

"If the country really needs you," Alyce sighed, "it's your duty. But aren't there plenty of twenty year-olds left to draft?"

"Apparently not, if they're drafting me and Hank Sorrentino—and a couple of other guys at the bank who're well past thirty."

"Peg says Mr. McRae can get y'all out of it."

"Out of it?"

"Mr. McRae's on the draft board, isn't he? . . . Why can't he get an exemption for you and Hank?"

131

"You mean *pull strings?*"

"Whatever it takes," Alyce turned on her side and faced the bedroom wall.

"Now, Hickory, that wouldn't be fair, would it?"

"You've got four children and a mother-in-law to support. I don't see anything wrong with pulling strings," she tried not to sound petulant.

"Well, Peg may have told you that Mr. McRae can pull strings, but I can't imagine Hank Sorrentino staying home in time of war. No sir-ree! Not Sorrentino!"

"You need to talk with Mr. McRae just to see what he says. Surely he doesn't want all his employees going off to war—he needs men to run his bank. If Mr. McRae can do something about it, then we'll know it's God Will for you to stay home. And if he can't do anything, then it's God's Will that you do your duty!"

"And you're always preaching *duty*, Hickory."

"I can accept that it's your duty to go off—and *my* duty to support you by taking care of the home-front while you're away—but you need to first talk with Mr. McRae and let *God* decide. Without talking to Mr. McRae, you're giving God only one option!"

Rappy never sought out Mr. McRae, but the bank president approached Hank Sorrentino, a graduate of Spring Hill College and on the fast track to becoming a bank officer. McRae felt he couldn't spare Sorrentino and had his draft notice revoked so that Hank never had to serve in World War II.

When Mr. McRae approached Rappy about getting his draft notice revoked, Rappy politely refused.

"Peg says Hank doesn't have to go," Alyce broached the subject timidly. "Did you talk with Mr. McRae?"

"Yeah, I talked with him," Rappy's answer was terse.

"Hank got the news three days ago—so when did *you* talk with McRae?"

"About the same time," he rolled in the bed and faced the wall.

"So? . . . What'd he say?" she sat up in bed.

132

"He offered to get me an exemption," Rappy said quietly.

"And you refused," her voice was full of pain, barely audible.

"I could tell he wouldn't respect me if I took his offer."

"What're you talking about?"

"He spoke of duty and honor—you see, he served in the first war. It was only the last few weeks in France, but still he arrived with our troops . . . to do his duty."

"Why'd you wait three days to tell me?" she felt a hot tear run down her cheek.

"I knew you wouldn't understand."

"You're going against the Will of God!" her voice was angry but controlled.

"You don't know that, Hickory," he tried not to irritate her further.

"God offered you an exemption and you turned it down!"

"*J. Finley McRae* offered me an exemption!" Rappy's voice was stronger and louder.

"McRae is an *instrument* of God's Will!"

"If I took that exemption, I'd never be able to live with myself . . . ever!"

"Well," she lay back on her pillow, "I never had a father so I don't know how a man's mind really works. You're a man so I guess you know what's best."

"You're tough, Hickory. You and your mama will do fine while I'm away.

"If you're gonna go through with this, I just hope you serve your country with pride . . . and honor!"

༉༉༉

In February of 1944, Rappy reported to boot camp at Fort Leonard Wood near St. Louis, Missouri. The younger men in the barracks—by the end of 1943 most draftees were boys still in their teens—quickly gave Rappy a nickname. As he was the oldest in his unit, the boys called him 'Pappy'.

133

Back home in Mobile Alyce, with her mother's help, was doing her best to hold down the home-front. She considered taking a Rosie-the-Riveter job at Brookley Field which was gearing up for a project to repair B-29 bombers and P-51s to send them back to the battlefront. She even considered learning to weld so she could take a job in one of the several shipyards where the US Navy was building boats as fast as they could.

Brookley Field's over five miles from Laurel Street! And the shipyards are scattered all along the coast. Why, I'd spend every weekend trading coffee coupons for gasoline coupons to get back and forth to work.

I've got Little Rappy in the first grade and Mickey in kindergarten. Mama can keep Shirley and Tommy at home while she sews, but she can't help out with the carpool cuz she doesn't drive. Kindergarten lets out at noon. And St. Mary's School's out at three. Those children need at least one parent here when they get home after school.

Besides, I can't rush off to work at 7:15 every morning and leave Mama to care for four children under seven. Tommy's only eight months-old. Mama'd never make any money from her sewing if she were tied down all day with a toddler crawling under her feet.

Alyce's fear of losing the house were put to rest when Mr. J. Finley McRae announced that the Merchants National Bank would supplement a soldier's army pay so his monthly income would remain the same as if he were still working at the bank. Still, she wanted to contribute to the war effort so she kept alert for any job that wouldn't take her away from her children all day.

She never took advantage of black-market goods, but she did trade ration coupons with neighbors and the many members of Rappy's family. Neither Alyce nor her mother drank coffee so she traded coffee coupons for gasoline and sugar (the latter which remained rationed two years after the war until 1947).

"Why do they call it *Victory Speed?*" Miss Alice looked up from her sewing machine where she was swallowed in fifteen yards of white organdy, the beginning of a prom dress for Mary Helen, Rappy's baby sister who was graduating that spring from the Convent of Mercy.

"Because if we drive only 35 miles an hour, we can save more gasoline and rubber to win the war—and we'll have *victory* over the Germans and Japanese," Alyce was holding Tommy on her lap trying to teach him to drink apple juice out of a cup instead of a baby bottle.

"You'd think we'd have plenty of gasoline in Texas alone!"

"That might be true, Mama. I heard Walter Winchell on the radio say that the main idea is to conserve *rubber*, not gasoline!"

"So that's why Arnold's Shoe Store stopped carrying rubber galoshes! There isn't a store in town selling galoshes this year!"

"And that's why that woman from the OPA knocked on the front door last week and asked if we had any spare automobile tires in the garage!"

"Just imagine!"

"When Rappy and I applied to the local OPA for that windshield sticker to qualify for gas coupons at the beginning of the war, he had to sign something certifying that we didn't own more than five tires."

"What's the OPA?"

"*The Office of Price Administration* . . . They can deny mileage rations to anyone owning passenger tires not in use."

"You mean to say, Alyce, that the government's rationing gasoline so folks don't wear out the rubber tires driving too much?"

"Uncle Joe says the Japanese took control of the rubber plantations in Southeast Asia."

"What about that tire hanging from the pecan tree in the back yard? That tire Rappy made into a swing for the children?"

"That old tire's missing an inner tube—it wouldn't be of any use to the army."

"This rationing, Alyce, is a bit tedious, but we can't complain."

135

"I'm just glad you're here living with us, Mama. That's a big help for me."

"We can only do the best we can. Everybody knows we're all in the same boat."

"That's another big help!"

CHAPTER **8**

IN MARCH OF 1944 Alyce boarded a train to St. Louis for a weekend with Rappy who was midway through boot camp. As the train traveled north through Mississippi, it stopped along the way to pick up passengers, including an attractive blonde who introduced herself as Evelyn Moses when she plopped herself next to Alyce in the second-class section. After chatting for ten minutes, the vivacious young woman identified herself as the wife of Clark Moses, Rappy's bunkmate, whom Rappy had mentioned in his letters home.

"What a coincidence that our husbands are bunkmates and that you and I just happen to be sitting next to each other on our way to Leonard Wood!" Evelyn was a slender chatterbox in her mid-twenties and full of nervous energy.

"Rappy often talks about your husband in his letters," Alyce shifted the hatbox she had been carrying in her lap since the train left Mobile six hours earlier.

"We've only been married six months, and I sure as hell don't intend to get pregnant this weekend—not with him about to ship out overseas as soon as this boot camp is over in April—you got any children?"

"Four," Alyce smiled, "and I don't want to get pregnant this weekend either."

"I brought along some stuff that's supposed to keep you from getting pregnant. . . . Are you taking any precautions?"

"I'm praying I don't get pregnant! I don't want to deliver another baby while Rappy's overseas, but if it's God's Will, then I'll have to accept it."

"Clark said you folks was Catholics, but still there *are* precautions you can take," Evelyn was digging in her purse for a pack of cigarettes.

"Well, if you're talking about the rhythm method, it doesn't work for me cuz my periods aren't regular."

"Then you might talk to one of your preachers about taking other precautions. Surely it can't be God's Will for you to get pregnant when you already got four children and your husband's about to ship out to those Pacific islands where he might get killed by those dirty Japs and the new baby never gets to see his daddy, now is it?"

Clutching the Lucky Strikes in her hand, Evelyn sprang from her seat and headed towards the smoking car, leaving Alyce to ponder how she would handle another baby without Rappy if God intended for her to get pregnant the coming weekend in Missouri.

After Rappy and Clark met their wives at the St. Louis train station, the four spent most of the weekend together, even staying at the same hotel. They dined on sirloin steaks in 4-star restaurants and took in all the tourist sites, including the zoo. At night in bed, Rappy propped himself on his elbow and asked endless questions about the four children back in Mobile. Three weeks away from his children, he wanted to know how each was progressing, especially the youngest, Tommy who at eight months was pulling up on chairs and getting ready to walk.

In addition to the updates on the children, the three nights in St. Louis were filled with lovemaking—a second honeymoon for Rappy and Alyce—two months shy of their tenth wedding anniversary.

Upon completing his basic training at Fort Leonard Wood, Rappy arrived April Fool's Day on the platform at the GM&O train station where he was mobbed by his huge family, Alyce's numerous cousins, most of the neighbors on Laurel Street, and some *IFT* wives who recently had seen their own husbands shipped off to England. Rappy returned for a brief leave before shipping out to the South Pacific—just two months before what would become 'D-Day' when the American troops gathering in England would land in Normandy to liberate France.

As soon as Rappy walked into the house at 1706 Laurel Street, he pulled from his breast pocket an official War Department brochure. Still in his uniform with his duffel bag resting at his feet, he silently handed the brochure to Alyce as his three oldest children clung to his legs.

Alyce assumed that the flimsy brochure contained his orders detailing exactly where he would report on the California coast *en route* to the South Pacific, destination classified. She sauntered into the kitchen—holding Tommy on her hip—and stood at the kitchen counter with her back to the rest of her family so she could read the brochure in the sunlight streaming through the window over the sink.

"I don't understand," she lied as she spun around with the toddler in her arms, the paper brochure fluttering in her right hand which trembled with fear and dread.

"It says I don't have to go," he glanced at her face nervously and then turned his attention to the three children at his knees—tousling the hair of each one in succession so as to avoid her searching eyes.

"Don't have to go *where*? . . . Overseas?"

"Anybody thirty-five and older doesn't have to report for duty . . . *overseas*! He can be stationed here stateside."

"Even if he's completed his boot camp?"

"It's a new order from President Roosevelt . . . well, from the War Department, actually, so . . . so I don't have to ship out."

Alyce turned quickly with the baby clutched to her chest and slowly returned to the kitchen sink. Her eyes were opened wide—as if she had witnessed a horror. She gazed absently out the window at Mrs. Cooke's blue hydrangeas. She could feel her eyes filling up with something hot, but she was too angry to turn around and let Rappy see the tears brimming. She defied herself from sobbing. Feeling the weight of the baby on her bosom as her chest heaved with short terrifying breaths, she stood motionless, too angry to blink and betray herself by letting the tears flow.

"I know what you're gonna do," she murmured finally, still gazing at the blur of blue hydrangeas.

"No, you don't!" he rasped from the dining room. He shook the three children from his legs and ambled to the kitchen door as if ashamed to be in the same room with her. "Because I don't know what I'm gonna do *myself*!"

♪♪♪

One week later Rappy shipped out for the South Pacific.

At the GM&O station Alyce stood at the front of Rappy's *bon voyage* mob waving her little American flag vigorously like the rest of the army wives laughing and crying from the platform as the troop train pulled out. Like Alyce, the other wives were dressed in their pastel Easter finery with sporty straw hats and white gloves. The difference was that the other army wives were ten years younger than Alyce— and not one of them had brought along four children. Alyce's three older children stood in front of her, each waving an American flag. Rappy Jr. at age seven was the only one old enough to realize that his daddy might end up in battle, eye-to-eye with the dreaded Japanese.

Alyce stood between her mother and Sister Mary Consuela, each of the older women supporting the new army wife by secretly sliding a hidden arm under her elbow while Alyce continued to wave her flag vigorously with one hand as she balanced Tommy on her hip with the other. When the troop train disappeared around the bend in the shipyard, Mary Helen and her mother rushed forward to grab Tommy from Alyce's arms in expectation that his mother would now collapse in grief and exhaustion.

"Let me have him!" Alyce tussled with Mary Helen to keep the toddler balanced on her hip.

"Let him go, Alyce!" Miss Alice was trying to push the child into Mary Helen's outstretched arms.

"I'm fine, Mama, I'm just fine!" the hot tears dammed up for a whole week were now gushing from Alyce's eyes.

"You're *not* fine! . . . Sister, tell her she's not fine!"

Mary Helen gave a yank and Tommy fell into her arms. Quickly she spun away with the toddler before his mother could grab him back.

Alyce slowly pivoted to catch a final glimpse of the red caboose rounding the bend. Then she collapsed into the arms of Sister Mary Consuela.

"You did fine, Alyce," the usually stern nun removed Alyce's navy blue straw hat whose veil had become tangled in one of her earbobs. The nun stroked Alyce's hair. "Yes, you did fine! And you were right about doing more good out here than behind the convent walls as a sister!"

Alyce laid her head on the shoulder of the taller woman, closed her eyes, and permitted her wet tears to slide across the heavily-starched white wimple round the nun's neck. With her eyes closed, she stretched out her arm for her mother and felt Miss Alice take her hand.

"We'll be okay, Mama! We can do this!"

"I'll be right by your side till Rappy comes home!" Miss Alice squeezed her hand.

What's wrong with my legs? They feel like rubber!

I'm sliding! . . . Something's scratching my face, something black, and dry. I smell Sr. Mary Consuela's perfumed soap.

Hands! . . . Why are all these hands pulling at me? Mama's hands, a man's hands—grabbing me. Somebody tell 'em I'm not gonna fall.

Voices shouting for water, for smelling salts, rosary beads.

Mary Helen's voice, shrill. Rappy's mother's voice, tired and thin.

The train conductor's shouting 'All aboard!' . . . There's Rappy jumping off the train. He's throwing aside his duffel bag. He's racing toward me with his arms open. He's shouting "I'm back, Hickory! I can't go off and leave you here alone with— . . . with . . . "

Five minutes later she came to in the back seat of Joe Midgette's Chevrolet with her mama holding a cold wet cloth on her neck, just in time to see Romie drive off with all four of her children in the back seat with Mary Helen, heading towards Laurel Street.

"All right, Alyce, let's get home and get supper going! Those children gonna be mighty hungry after all this excitement with these trains and all this hullabaloo!" Miss Alice was chirpy but had no intention of hurrying her daughter whose head was bent low over her knees.

"Yes, m'am," Alyce took the wet cloth from her mother's hand and threw it on the floor of the car.

"My stars, Alyce!" Miss Alice exclaimed. "I've never known you to faint in your whole life!"

"I'll never faint again—even if Rappy comes home in a coffin! That's a promise."

As Uncle Joe Midgette started the engine and maneuvered the car out of the GM&O parking lot, Alyce replaced her hat on her head, adjusted the veil, and slipped her hands into her white cotton gloves. She sat up straight and gently crossed her gloved hands on her knees as she had been taught by the nuns at the Convent of Mercy.

♪♪♪♪

Two weeks later on the first Saturday in May, Alyce prepared for her weekly Confession. Because she was running low on gas coupons and it was only the middle of the month, she jumped on the second-hand bicycle she had recently bought to save gasoline and pedaled the ten minutes to St. Mary's Church.

Kneeling on the cold marble ledge in front of the statue of the Infant of Prague, she lit a votive candle in thanksgiving that her period had arrived, although two weeks late. She felt great relief that she had not gotten pregnant in St. Louis—or during Rappy's 7-day furlough in Mobile before he shipped out.

I always said I'd take as many children as you send me, but it wouldn't be fair to have another baby until Rappy returns from war. That Moses woman was right—a baby shouldn't be born if his daddy dies in the war and the baby never gets to see him.

So I do thank You for not letting me get pregnant in St. Louis! . . . If Rappy comes back alive from the war, I'll take as many children as you send me—without a single complaint— even if Rappy never gets another raise at the bank.

And another thing . . . If You can find a yard-and-a-half of white organdy for Mickey's First Communion dress, we'd appreciate it—Mama and me.

Are you listening, Lord? . . . I'm not just talking to hear myself talk! . . . This is a prayer!

Although cotton fabric was not rationed by the Office of Price Administration, it somehow had become scarce due to the war effort because Miss Alice found only a few yards of white organdy on the black market when she searched in late April to begin the First Communion dress. And the little bit she found was priced at *three times* the cost she had paid for the same organdy to make Mary Helen's prom dress only two months before.

"Maybe you don't read the newspapers but President Roosevelt says you're not spoz to raise prices on *anything* until this war's over!" Miss Alice stood in the dining room of a Hannon Avenue neighbor whose long table was covered with three-yard remnants of everything from organdy to velvet to burlap.

"But that's the purpose of the black market, Missy! We can charge what the market allows! . . . So, does this mean you're gonna report me?" the stocky woman with dyed orange frizzy hair was in her mid-fifties. She smiled defiantly, then took a drag off her Camel and blew smoke across the table over Miss Alice's head.

"I'm not reporting you or *anybody*," Miss Alice gently fingered the organdy as she ignored the cigarette smoke settling into her hair.

"Well, ain't you sweet!" the woman chuckled sarcastically.

"My son's in the Philippine Islands so I support the war effort, whether President Roosevelt asks me to or not. Don't you have some-body overseas—in harm's way? Maybe a nephew or a cousin? . . . I mean, everybody's got *somebody* overseas!"

"My son's in England. They ain't doing nothing there but sitting around at an air base. He told me not to tell nobody but he thinks they're getting ready to go to France," the woman spoke noncha-lantly, as if her son was heading for an afternoon picnic at Gulf Shores.

"France? . . . I read in the *Mobile Press Register* that the German army has occupied almost *all* of France! How's your son gonna be transferred to France if the Germans are in control?"

"I'm not interested in politics . . . so I don't follow the war. All I know is my boy says he's probably heading for France before the end of June this year," the surly woman started restacking the remnants into neat piles as the Camel dangled from her lips.

"Well, I wish him well . . . and thank you for your time but I'm not paying that much for two yards of organdy," Miss Alice had already started moving towards the front door to make her escape.

"Now don't you run off—I can give you a 25% discount and still make a nice profit," the woman grabbed the folded remnant and un-furled it across the oak table.

"No, thank you," Miss Alice paused at the front door where she reached to her hat's brim and pulled the lettuce-green veil down over her eyes. "I'll ask somebody else to find me some organdy."

"Hold it, Missy! I'll sell it to you for 50% off—now that's a nice price!"

"I wouldn't buy that organdy if you sold it for *99%* off! It's the principle of the thing—there's war going on all over the world—and all you care about is making money on the black market! You should be ashamed of yourself!"

"And just who you gonna ask to find organdy when I probably got the last piece in Mobile county?"

"*The good Lord*—that's who I'm gonna ask!" Miss Alice let the screen door slam behind her, slipped on her white gloves, and hurried across the intersection to Laurel Street.

She was in a quandary. She had used every scrap of white organdy for Mary Helen's prom dress so there wasn't even a one-yard remnant to squeeze a short-sleeved dress for Mickey's First Communion.

She phoned all her seamstress and tailor friends to see if she could find some white organdy. Nobody in town had any, but she did find two yards of silky white rayon right across the street where George Jumonville and his wife worked out of their house on Laurel Street, both sewing for the same society customers as did Miss Alice. It was while sitting in the Jumonville's brightly-lit sewing room having afternoon tea—which she did 2-3 times a week when one of them needed help with handwork to meet a deadline, a favor they repaid graciously whenever she was behind schedule—that Miss Alice mentioned she was looking for white organdy. George reached behind him and grabbed the remnant of shimmering white rayon. He held up the fabric and waved it over his head like a banner.

"I'll take it!" Miss Alice threw back her head and laughed heartily.

"You're not gonna find any cotton organdy till this war's over!" George sipped his tea.

"I know! . . . Alyce and I are short on money this month so I'll have to trade you something. I've got a half-yard of a nice black velvet you might find handy to trim a ball gown next Mardi Gras. . . . Not a *velveteen*, mind you, and not any of that crushed velvet stuff that we all find tacky—it's a fine classic velvet, midnight black so it'll go nicely with any color of taffeta!"

"You don't need to trade us anything," Lucille Jumonville smiled

145

as she looked up from a mound of pale green dotted-Swiss she was working on in her lap. "If it's for your grandchild, you can consider it a gift from the Jumonville family—every little girl needs a new dress for her First Communion!"

While Rappy was in the Pacific, Alyce wrote him every day. Actually, it was every *night*.

After she and her mother got all four children tucked away some-time between 7:00 and 8:00, Miss Alice returned to her sewing machine for another two hours labor, and Alyce sat at a small secre-tary in the dining room corner to report to Rappy the day's events. It was a promise she made to him in the middle of the craziness on the GM&O platform when he was kissing everyone good-bye. He hadn't demanded it—she volunteered.

At first she wondered if she would have enough news to fill two pages of stationary every night, but as the summer of 1944 pro-gressed—both Shirley and Tommy had July birthdays, and Mickey's birthday was ten days after her daddy's in August—Alyce realized that the children were growing so fast and learning so much that she was writing 5-6 pages every night. Some nights she could barely drag herself to the secretary in the corner and flick on the desk lamp, but once she started writing, she felt the words flow effortlessly, except for the nights when she fell asleep over the letter in mid-sentence.

She looked forward to Rappy's letters, even when they arrived in a bunch—3-4 letters written on different days but mailed on the same day by the censor officer after he had blacked out anything Rappy had written that should have been classified.

Dear Hickory,   June 14, 1944
                                                                  #133

You can't imagine my surprise when I received the gold wed-

ding band. All the young boys in my unit tease me that it's not really a wedding ring but a nose-ring to keep me in my place 10,000 miles from home, but I don't need a ring to remind me to be true to you. The ring arrived on June 6, just one day before our 10th wedding anniversary.

It's hard to believe that it's been a whole ten years since we were married. That was in the middle of the Depression when we could barely scrape together enough money to buy a gold wedding band for you, but not one for me. Each time I look at this ring, I'll think of you and of when we'll be together again after this war is over and I'm back home on Laurel Street.

You asked what we do here on this island. I'll try to explain as best I can, but don't be surprised if the censor blacks out most of this letter as I never have any idea of what's considered "classified" and what's not. Anyway, here goes:

We're a non-combat unit here on the island. Our job is to ▮ ▮▮▮▮▮ and ▮▮ planes (so I won't be seeing any combat unless they transfer me out of ▮). After these planes are ▮▮ ▮▮▮▮▮▮▮, they are sent back on missions to places like ▮▮▮▮▮▮, and ▮▮▮▮. If the same plane returns a second time, we refuel and repair it again. But if it comes back a third time, it's sent to ▮▮▮▮▮ where it's ▮▮▮▮▮▮▮ and ▮▮▮▮▮.

I just finished a 12 hour shift on the runway so this letter tonight has to be brief as I'm really tired. Sometimes I feel I'm too old to be here in this tropical heat and humidity and rain. But we're so tired at night that I sleep on my cot in these hot barracks like it was the Jung Hotel where we spent our honeymoon.

But I'm grateful for the opportunity to serve my country. And I'm grateful to you for holding down the home-front and being so understanding. Hickory, you're the best one!

Tell Shirley Anne I'm sorry that I will miss her birthday next month, but I hope I'll be home from this war for her fifth birthday. I'm delighted that little Tommy is trying to walk. Maybe he'll be running down the hallway before his first birthday on July 30th! I bet Grandma Hicks thinks he's so smart because he's named after her son and her husband. Tell her I send my best.

Kiss all the children for me. Tomorrow's letter will be longer—promise!

All my love,
Rappy

P.S. I received 6 of your letters today in one packet. Two of them had been censored—one heavily. Now, Hickory, I can't imagine what you were writing that they don't want us GI's to know about.

P.P.S Thanks for those bottles of Paregoric you sent. Headache medicines are hard to find on these islands. So if you want to send more Paregoric, I can always use it.

Dear Rappy,   July 11, 1944

Yes, Tommy is running through the house like a junkyard dog. You know, all babies don't walk at nine months. None of our other children were walking by themselves until their first birthday. Tommy won't turn one till the end of this month so in comparison to his older brother and sisters, he's even ahead of schedule.

You won't believe how much all four children have grown since you left in April, especially Tommy. Now, he'll never be a husky boy like Little Rappy because Tommy weighed only five pounds at birth, but he's strong for his size and is never sick, even when the older ones catch a cold.

Margie has been teasing me that Tommy's not your child because his hair has bleached out blond in the summer sun. By August I suspect his hair will be completely white. I don't know where he gets that blonde hair from, unless it's from the Hicks' side. Mama says Tommy's starting to look just like my father, his namesake, but she's prejudiced. Right now she thinks the child can do no wrong, but once he gets in the backyard and starts chasing your chickens, I suspect Mama'll change her mind.

Today I paid the mortgage. Romie went downtown to his accountant's office so he gave me a ride to the bank. That saved a postage stamp. Besides, I wanted to hang around the bank lobby to see if anyone knew of a job I might find for September that wouldn't take me away from the children all day. Everybody asked about you, especially Hank Sorrentino.

I kissed the children for you when I put them to bed to-night. Little Rappy asked if you had killed any Japs yet. He still can't accept the fact that you're not in combat. Shirley wants to send you a half-pack of her Wrigley's Spearmint gum. She refused to take 'no' for an answer so I'll put two sticks in an envelope, address it while she's watching, and then give it to the paper boy as a tip.

I feel my eyelids getting heavy so I'd better stop writing before my penmanship gets so bad you can't read it.

Mama sends her love, and I do too . . . as always.

I miss you so much that it hurts. I'm waiting for the day when we can take the children to the beach again, when I can lie at night in your arms again. I'm dying for a smacker, but tonight I'd settle just for your touch.

All my love,
Hickory

P.S. Be on the lookout for some more Paregoric.

As soon as she sealed the letter and put a postage stamp on the envelope, Alyce went to the kitchen where her mother was busy shelling pecans at the kitchen table, stacking the fresh meats into a pile at her elbow. Opposite her on the table was an empty 2-lb coffee can and a small dark brown empty 4-ounce bottle which had contained Paregoric that Alyce used to rub on Tommy's gums when he was teething.

While Miss Alice shelled pecans, Alyce poured Early Times bourbon into the small brown bottle and replaced the top. She placed the small bottle of bourbon into the empty coffee can. She scooped up handfuls of pecan meats and shoveled them into the coffee can until the small bottle of bourbon was buried under the pecans.

The next day she would pedal to the Post Office to mail Rappy the letter—and his weekly supply of pecans.

꒰꒱꒱꒦

The following Saturday afternoon Alyce left the children with her mother and pedaled to St. Mary's Church. Depositing her bicycle in the rack next to the side steps, she tied a cotton scarf under her chin to enter the Catholic Church with her head dutifully covered. It was time to make her weekly Confession.

"I don't think that's a sin, Alyce," Monsignor O'Donoghue didn't bother to lower his voice when he pronounced her name in the dark confessional.

"But, it's a lie, Monsignor," she whispered in hopes he would follow suit.

"But, my dear, you can't tell a soldier overseas any bad news about his children!"

"Do you mean that God understands?"

"Of course, He does! . . . Besides, you say that the little fellow *has* started walking by now, yes?

"Yes, Monsignor, but he's *barely* walking."

"So?"

"I wrote Rappy that Tommy was running through the house one full month before his birthday. I lied."

150

"God understands. . . . It's okay to lie to a soldier about his children. We do it all the time in Ireland."

"But what about leaving out the truth. Isn't that called a Sin of Omission?"

"Give me an example, my dear."

"Mickey fell off a swing at Hannon Park and broke her arm. It was a bad break so I didn't tell Rappy. I could have written that it was only a sprain, but that would have been a lie! So I just didn't write him anything. . . . I guess I'm guilty of a Lie of Omission, right?"

"Technically, yes, you're guilty of a Sin of Omission, *only* if you think a soldier far from home has a 'need-to-know.' . . . Do you think Rappy needs to know any bad news?"

"Well, he can't do anything about a broken arm halfway around the world—except worry himself to death—so I'd say he doesn't need to know!"

"Clever lass! . . . Now, Alyce, I'm giving you an official *dispensation* to lie all you need to when you write Rappy. Also, you may omit any bad news about broken bones or anything else. Just promise me you won't abuse this dispensation—and that you won't tell Miss Alice or a living soul!"

"I promise, Monsignor."

"Run along, dear, and kiss the children for me."

"But you haven't given me any penance for lying, Monsignor!"

"We don't give both penance *and* a dispensation, Alyce. It's an 'either-or' situation. You're free to lie to Rappy all you want!"

♪♪♪

In early August of 1944 Alyce received a phonecall from Sister Mary Consuela at the Convent of Mercy.

"I need a kindergarten teacher, Alyce."

"I don't know anybody qualified, Sister, but I think Margie knows a lot of girls who went to college."

"I want *you* to teach the Kindergarten, Alyce."

"Sister, I don't have a degree in Education!"

"Don't I *know* that, Alyce?"

"But I never even started college!"

"There's a war going on, Alyce! All I need is a teacher for a small class of five year-olds!"

"I wouldn't even know how to begin, Sister!"

"You begin with morning prayers and a hymn to the Our Blessed Mother . . . then you do anything that will keep them busy and hopefully learn something useful, like the "A-B-C's" . . . or how to hold a Crayon in their little fists. Next they take a mid-morning nap, wake up and drink some milk, if we manage to get ration coupons for milk that week. Then, you play some games to teach them to be coordinated, even if it's only tag or just running across the yard. Their mothers pick them up at noon . . . and you're free the rest of the day."

"How many will I have in the class?"

"I have six registered right now, but it could be as many as ten. Just imagine yourself home taking care of your own children, Alyce."

"Sister, I don't have *ten* children at home to take care of!"

"You don't *yet*, Alyce, you don't yet."

Alyce was ecstatic. It was the perfect job. Because the Kindergarten didn't take in until 9:00 in the morning, she had time to get Mickey and Rappy off to school with Molly Sullivan across the street who daily drove her two oldest to St. Mary's School. Then Alyce jumped on the second-hand Schwinn and pedaled the two miles down Dauphin Street till she arrived at Bayou where the Convent of Mercy was located. By car the trip was ten minutes, but she didn't mind the twenty minute bicycle ride because she saved so many gasoline coupons.

Throughout the school year of 1944-45, Alyce noticed how much stronger her legs were becoming. Although Mr. McDole next door cut her grass without even asking if she wanted him to, she discovered after a couple of months into the school year that she had so much energy from pedaling the bicycle that she wanted to cut the grass herself. She and Little Rappy, now seven, cut the grass themselves. On

Saturday mornings, instead of sleeping late, she found herself slipping into the McDole garage and grabbing the reel push-mower before her kind neighbor beat her to it.

The kindergarten job continued throughout the next school year, and even six months after the Pacific war ended. Because Rappy was stationed in the Fiji Islands with a non-combat unit, his company would be one of the last to leave the Pacific. The war in the Pacific ended officially in August, 1945 with atomic bombs on Hiroshima and Nagasaki, but Rappy's unit didn't leave for San Francisco until October. He didn't show up on Laurel Street until Christmas of 1945.

Meanwhile, thanks to her friend Sister Mary Consuela, Alyce had held a job for eighteen months during the depths of World War II and earned $10 a week.

♪♪♪♪

It was futile for Alyce to remain on the Cooke's front porch ringing the doorbell again and again. She should return to her backyard to finish planting the okra seeds in the Victory Garden. But the moment her mother came out the kitchen door with the brown mailer in hand, Alyce dropped her trowel, wiped her soiled hands on her slacks and shirt, and ran for the nearest house with a record-player.

She knew that her next-door-neighbor wouldn't be home on a Friday at 1:30 in the afternoon. Ever since completing that teacher training course last summer, Mrs. Cooke had been gainfully employed at Craighead School as a 4th grade teacher.

"*Still,*" Alyce muttered aloud, "she might have stayed home sick today. She's the only one in the neighborhood I know well enough to use her record-player!"

Alyce stopped ringing the doorbell and glanced at the record she clutched in her hand. The 78 rpm record was hidden inside a brown sleeve. Inside that sleeve was the surprise which Rappy had promised she'd receive before Mother's Day. She had heard on the radio that some New York record company was touring the Pacific islands giving soldiers a chance to record a song for their families. The company was sending the records to the families in the States. *Gratis.*

She was dying to hear Rappy's voice.

No telling which song he had recorded. He knew so many, and he was never shy about singing along with the radio. Having taken piano lessons as a child with Sister Cecilia at St. Mary's School, he still had the talent to pick out a melody to accompany himself on the piano. Every time he planted himself at Romie's piano at closing time at the New Spic, his brothers and sisters teased him that he couldn't carry a tune until after his third beer, but the truth is that he had a pretty good tenor voice.

"He probably recorded 'Alice-Blue Gown'," Alyce mused as she scooted around the side of the Cooke house looking for an open window. It was late April, hot enough for Mrs. Cooke to leave a window open so the house would be cool when she returned from her teaching job.

Pausing next to the massive bank of blue hydrangeas, Alyce notice that a window-screen on one of the dining room windows was slightly askew. She reached over the bushes and tested the screen's wood frame. It moved. The window screen wasn't latched. She gave a slight pull on the frame and discovered the latch was missing.

Holding the brown package in her mouth between clenched teeth, she struggled with the cumbersome window-screen until it crashed onto the ground behind the hydrangea bank. She squeezed through the bushes and slid her fingers under the window-frame. The window eased upward as if it were a stage-curtain rising before a performance.

Five minutes later she was sitting on the Cooke's sofa listening to her husband singing. The record's quality was poor. Rappy's voice was tinny but it was definitely Rappy's, strong and on-key. His attempt to sound cheery contrasted ironically with the melancholy lyrics he sang:

Each night I cry a little,
Since I went away, love.
Each night I die a little,
Since I went away, love.

Love to you,
I'm sending love to you
Home to you,
I'm coming home to you

After she placed the phonograph needle at the edge of the record to play the song again, Alyce pulled her legs under her and leaned back on the sofa. The tears were streaming down her cheeks. She wiped them with the sleeve of her shirt, caked with soil from where she had been working in the vegetable garden. She realized that her face was stained with dirt and tears but she didn't care. She ignored the tears as Rappy's voice launched into the song for the second time. Rather, she let them flow as she gulped to suppress sobs which were surfacing from her belly.

"Well, he's not bad," Mrs. Cooke stood in the front doorway holding a book satchel overflowing with student homework papers, "but he's certainly no Frank Sinatra!"

"He's *better* than Frank Sinatra!" Alyce managed to blurt before the sobs erupted.

She glanced towards the doorway to see if the older neighbor was angry with her for breaking into the house, but she saw only a blur through the watery flow of tears. She heard the music start up again, and then Rappy's voice:

Love to you,
I'm sending love to you
Home to you,
I'm coming home to you

Alyce looked up to see Mrs. Cooke ambling towards her. The tall neighbor with the wide padded hips slid onto the sofa and held Alyce in her long heavy arms. Alyce relaxed into the fleshy embrace of the older woman and permitted herself to be rocked to and fro as she listened to her husband singing his promise to return safely from the war.

Fawn River
South Mobile County, Alabama
January 21, 2012

AFTER LUNCH UPSTAIRS, my grand-daughter emerged from the elevator with my daughter on her arm. My daughter grabbed hold of the walker, crossed the wide living area, and again settled in her recliner as my grand-daughter returned upstairs in the elevator.

Before my daughter had a chance to doze off for an after-lunch siesta, I spoke up from the sofa where I'd been sitting.

"Your husband didn't *have* to ship out to the Fiji Islands, so why did he go?"

"He thought it was his duty to serve his country," she searched the end table for the remote control.

"Couldn't he have served *dutifully* here? Serving at Brookley Field or another base? . . . Still a soldier in the US Army?"

"He wanted to go overseas," she dropped the remote control on her lap, closed her eyes, and sank deeper in the recliner.

"And how did you feel about *that*?"

"You sound like *Dr. Phil*!" she chuckled.

"Well, what did you think about his decision to go overseas?"

"I didn't like it!"

"But you supported it?"

"He was my husband—the head of the house—and he was a *man*. I've always done what men tell me. It started with Bubber. I'd never have taken that Classical Course in high school if Bubber hadn't told me to do it."

"Women in your generation were taught that a man knows best, is that correct?"

"In my day few women went to college, even if they were smart. Everybody got married and had babies . . . and depended upon their husbands to make the decisions. Besides, I always trusted Rappy to know best."

"But he went off to war and left you with four children to take care of!"

"It wasn't that bad—Mama was there to help me."

"But soldiers over thirty-five didn't have to ship out, even if they'd finished their boot camp. So why did he go?"

"Why do you *think*? . . . For the *adventure*!"

"You mean he got married too young? . . . He felt he'd missed out on something, like traveling overseas?"

"He'd worked hard all his life—right out of high school—giving all his paycheck to his mother, and then the Depression came and hit us hard. He'd never have volunteered for the army, but when he was drafted he saw it as his duty."

"And despite the hardship of boot camp, when he got through it all, he wanted to follow it through overseas. . . . So it might've had something to do with camaraderie?"

"Maybe. . . . That, and the adventure."

"Did you believe his stories about stealing beer from the Officers' Mess Hall?"

"Half of 'em. Rappy could exaggerate a story, you know, especially after a couple of drinks," she chuckled again and briefly opened her eyes.

"Your son says his daddy volunteered for Kitchen Patrol in the Officers' Mess so he could steal beer. The draftees didn't have beer on the island."

"Tommy exaggerates as much as his daddy—that's where he gets it from."

"So your husband didn't steal the beer?"

"Look, I was at the kitchen sink when Rappy was telling Tommy that story. Tommy had just returned from a year teaching in Saudi Arabia, and the two were sharing adventure tales. Both of 'em were drinking bourbon so I didn't believe all those stories, especially Rappy's. . . . It's possible he stole a couple of beers from the Officers' Mess and drank 'em on the spot—no way to chill 'em on that island without ice—but I doubt if he stole the lumber from Supply to build a wooden ice-box—the plywood and 1x1 studs and the rope and all that! Rappy claimed he took his homemade icebox up in the mountains and lowered it into a cold stream to chill the beer."

"It makes a good story," I laughed.

"Tommy believed it! . . . He said, 'Daddy, if you'd been caught, they would've court-martialed you and put you in the brig for the rest of the war!' . . . But Rappy said, 'Hell, they needed every man they had! They wouldn't have done a damn thing to me!' . . . I hated it when Rappy cussed so much. It was the whisky—he didn't cuss near as much when he drank just beer."

"A non-combat tour in Fiji would've been a fantastic adventure for a young man with no responsibilities, some twenty-five year-old bachelor. . . . But your husband left you with four children!"

"And just how could I have stopped him from going?"

CHAPTER **9**

GERMANY SURRENDERED IN May of 1945. . . . Victory in Europe!

Alyce and the children celebrated *VE Day* by shooting off penny firecrackers all afternoon when Uncle Joe Midgette dropped by to supervise the children. That night the whole neighborhood around Laurel Street forgot about gasoline rationing, drove up to Government Street, and joined the caravan parading all over the city. Miss Alice sat up front holding Tommy on her lap. Alyce honked the horn incessantly and drove so fast that the running boards on the old Plymouth vibrated as she struggled to keep up with the cars ahead of her. Little Rappy, Mickey, and Shirley leaned out the windows shouting and waving tiny American flags.

As July of 1945 approached, the whole country had been filled with hope that the war in the Pacific would soon end with a Japanese surrender. Alyce felt sure that Rappy would be home safely by Labor Day. Every Monday for nine consecutive weeks that summer she pedaled her bicycle to St. Mary's Church at 4:00 p.m. for services at a Novena to Our Lady of the Miraculous Medal. Around her neck she wore a silver chain with the Miraculous Medal blessed by Bishop Toolen. She bought a second medal for Rappy in hopes the Blessed Mother would keep him safe on that tropical island for the few remaining months of the war that appeared to be heading for a climax.

In late May, the week that her kindergarten class at COM started the summer break—the same week that the Maryknoll missionary priest arrived at St. Mary's to begin the nine-week novena—Alyce wrapped a silver chain and Miraculous Medal in white tissue paper and laid it on top of the regular shipment of shelled pecans to Rappy. At the bottom of the coffee can, hidden under the pecans, was the usual paregoric bottle filled with Early Times.

Dear Rappy,   *May 31, 1945*

 I've been on the go all day so I hope I don't fall asleep in the middle of this letter.
 Margie's car has been in the shop all week so I had to pick up your mama and daddy tonight for Mary Helen's prom at the Convent of Mercy.
 Yesterday was the last day of school so the Sisters at St. Mary's had a lot of celebrations to start the summer vacation. Each class had its own little "show", some kind of play or music recital. Little Rappy's second grade put on a play about the animals which live in the Gulf. He was a starfish. His teacher wanted Mama to make three octopus costumes for Rappy and two of his classmates, but I explained to the Irish nun that we don't have many octopus in the Gulf of Mexico. She was happy with Mama's starfish costumes, but Rappy wanted to be a shark.
 Mickey's first grade sang Irish songs and Catholic hymns to the Blessed Virgin Mother because May is Mary's month. Thank God the kids didn't need costumes. Sister Mary Alice sent a note home asking for the girls to wear "party dresses", which saved Mama from having to make another animal costume, so Mickey wore her First Communion dress.
 Mama wanted to see Mickey and Rappy perform in the class plays, so we took Shirley and Tommy with us. I took Shirley into Mickey's classroom so she could see all the pretty party dresses. Mama took Tommy into the second-grade where he was thrilled with all the fish costumes. Mama said

the second-grade boys read their lines with lots of enthusiasm. I guess she meant the boys were loud, which must have thrilled Tommy because he's become quite boisterous himself.

After school Mama and I took the children to the Cotton Patch for ice cream. That was one trip in the car which I hadn't planned on this week so I'm glad this is the end of the month because I've run out of gas coupons. With Romie in the Caribbean islands serving with the Merchant Marine, I have no hero in Mobile to give me extra gas coupons at the end of the month. But, tomorrow is June 1 so I'll be first in line for coupons. With the children home from school for the next three months, I'll probably have gas coupons left over at the end of each month to trade for sugar and canned milk for Mama's hot tea. You know how much tea she drinks on a late night when she's sewing on school uniforms in the summer.

The children are doing great. Mickey and Rappy talk about you coming home in time for a Labor Day picnic on the Cedar Point wharf. Shirley turns five in July and is talking about going to kindergarten with me when classes start up again in September. I'm sure Sr. Mary Consuela won't object. But I can't very well let Shirley ride on the handlebars as I pedal two miles to the Convent, so I'll have to find more gas coupons to drive the car. With Romie gone, I'll have to find a new contact—somebody willing to trade gasoline for coffee.

Tommy's talking up a blue streak. He turns two at the end of July so he's right on schedule.

I miss you very much.

Here's a big smacker for you!

All my love,
Hickory

P.S. Be on the lookout for some Paregoric—and a surprise from the Blessed Mother.

163

Tommy was *not* talking up a blue streak.

He was barely talking at all. But Alyce felt no guilt about lying to Rappy. After all, Monsignor O'Donoghue had given her an official dispensation allowing her to lie to her husband about the children whenever Rappy couldn't do anything about bad news. And Tommy approaching his second birthday and still not speaking more than two words at a time was indeed bad news. In Fiji Rappy couldn't do a thing about it, so Alyce figured it was time to use her dispensation. And she knew better than to mention it to Monsignor next Saturday in the confessional.

But she needed to talk to a doctor about Tommy not talking yet.

"It's nothing to worry about," the pediatrician said as he tousled Tommy's white hair bleached from the summer sun.

"I want this child talking before Rappy gets home from the war. I want everything *right* when his daddy gets home," Alyce trusted Vaughn Adams, who had been the pediatrician for her children since 1937 when she first brought Rappy Jr. home from the Allen Memorial Hospital.

"Does Rappy have a discharge date?"

"Nobody gets discharged 'til the war's over, but everybody says it can't go on much longer—isn't that so?"

"That's the scuttlebutt, Alyce, but who knows? . . . At any rate, I wouldn't fret about this little guy here. He'll talk when he's ready."

"I think the problem is my mother! She gives him anything he wants so he doesn't have to talk. He just points. And his two older sisters are pretty bad about spoiling him, too!"

"Well, one day soon he's going to look up from the breakfast table and say, 'These grits are lumpy!' . . . And when you ask him why he hasn't spoken before now, he's going to say, 'Well, up 'til now, every-thing's been fine!'"

***

Romie was killed in August of 1945.

No one knew the exact date but probably it was before *VJ Day*

164

when the war in the Pacific officially ended and the Japanese surrendered. No one knew exactly how he died. All they knew was Romie was killed in Costa Rica where his ship had docked.

In 1944 Romie joined the Merchant Marine to avoid being drafted and sent overseas in the army. Being only thirty-two, he wouldn't have been eligible for the same waiver that was offered to Rappy who was over the cutoff age of 35. Romie was eager to make sacrifices for the war effort on the home-front, but he didn't want to risk losing his successful New Spic Supper Club if he were sent overseas for the duration of the war.

The Merchant Marine was the perfect solution. He shipped out to Latin America for two months at a time, and when he returned he had two months in Mobile to take care of his business until he shipped out again. While he was at sea, Romie left his supper club in the hands of his younger brother, Emile, who could be trusted to operate the business—and stop the kitchen help from stealing Romie blind.

When word reached the Perez family that one of their seven sons had been killed in the war, the family was devastated. It was especially difficult to accept that the one who had died was Romie, the golden boy.

Alyce and her children were visiting Margie and Bill Serda at their summer rental across the bay at Battles Wharf. Margie went next door to take a phonecall at the home of Pop Woods, her landlord, who had the only telephone within half a mile. When she came back to the bungalow, she stood at the screen door and wept openly.

"It was Papa calling from Mobile," she broke into sobs. "It's about Romie. He's been killed."

"But there's no combat where he is!" Bill Serda, Margie's husband, said in disbelief.

"My, Lord!" Alyce felt as if she had been slugged in the stomach. She couldn't imagine Romie dead, a man who was so vivacious and vital.

"We have to get back to Mobile!" Margie was hysterical. "Papa says he had to put Mama to bed! We've got to go!"

"What about Cleo?" Alyce's first thoughts were of Romie's wife.

"She's got sisters, doesn't she? We'll see her tonight, but first we've got to take care of Mama and Daddy!" Margie was grabbing damp bathing suits and towels off the backs of chairs as she rounded up her four children.

Alyce realized she wasn't crying for Romie. Not yet, anyway. Maybe she would break down tomorrow when she saw Cleo. Or maybe next month when they brought the body home in a coffin covered by an American flag. Surely she'd break when she heard "Taps" at the graveside.

Right now she had to take care of Margie who had gone to pieces over her brother's death. And when they got to Mobile Alyce would leave her children with her mother on Laurel Street so she could help at the Perez house where her mother-in-law would need someone to take care of the kitchen as the house filled up with mourners, both family and guests. Alyce welcomed the opportunity to take care of others so she wouldn't have to deal with her own feelings of loss and waste. Staying busy taking care of others meant she wouldn't have time to worry about Rappy getting killed on his way home from a war that had officially ended last week when the Japanese surrendered. Even in peace time airplanes crash over the Pacific Ocean, and ships sink at sea.

Early the next morning Alyce received a phone call from Romie's widow, Cleo.

"Will you come help me with all this paper work?" Cleo's voice sounded as if she was still in disbelief.

"Paper work? . . . Maybe you need a lawyer, Cleo?" Alyce hadn't been given the chance to express her condolences.

"Romie had a lawyer—and an accountant—so I got all the advice I need. The lawyer's gonna be here in an hour, but I've never met him. Besides, I don't trust lawyers. I want somebody like you here to help me figure out what I'm signing."

"Where're your sisters?" Alyce felt her anger rising that Cleo was alone.

"Both of 'em are in Pensacola waiting for their husbands to come in tonight on leave, but I just want someone from Romie's family here when the ship captain gets here."

"The ship captain? . . . What's he want?"

"He's gonna tell me how Romie died."

"They haven't told you yet?"

"They have to do it in person—and I want you here, Alyce."

"Well, I'm not 'family'—I just *married* into the Perez family, like you! But I'm glad to come over if you think I can help."

"You can help. . . . Neighbors have been arriving since dawn with food and layer cakes. And I expect a lot of people will be dropping by all day to pay their respects—you know how popular Romie was. Besides, I want you here to keep me company, you know."

In 1933 Cleo Constantine was a pretty twenty-one year-old brunette from the Greek-American community in downtown Mobile when she met Romie Perez who had turned twenty-one the same month. A year later she found herself married to the young man who was making a name for himself with his restaurant on Williams Street. Before the year was out, she gave birth to her first daughter. By the time Romie entered the Merchant Marine in 1944, Cleo had given him three daughters, the youngest born in 1942.

When Romie died at the age of 32, he left Cleo with three young girls—ages eleven, ten, and three.

Alyce had known Cleo when they were young girls. Both came from the south part of town, and both married into the lively Perez family, choosing the two brothers considered to have the most personality. After marrying, the two girls became friends. They understood the other's struggle to fit into a large family where she was expected to have fun at the party but still behave like a lady. She should not draw too much attention to herself. The spotlight should shine on the husband.

"I'll take care of the kitchen," Alyce whispered into Cleo's ear.

The young widow was seated at the table between Romie's lawyer and the captain of the ship on which Romie had sailed. Documents ready for Cleo's signature were spread all over the mahogany surface.

"If I don't like their explanation—or if I can't understand what I'm signing—I'll yell for you, so don't leave the kitchen, Alyce," Cleo whispered and squeezed Alyce's hand as she gazed up with eyes full of tears and gratitude.

In the kitchen Alyce got busy making room for all the food that had been arriving since daybreak. There were at least a dozen layer cakes which she lined up on the counter next to the sink. The rest of the food she arranged temporarily on the large kitchen table until Cleo and the men were finished in the dining room. Later Alyce would transfer the food to the dining room table so guests arriving to pay condolences wouldn't have to enter the kitchen to get something to eat. The roast turkey and the two baked hams appeared too big to fit into the refrigerator, even the large one that Romie's wealth had bought for the new house. But Alyce figured out how to remove a shelf from the refrigerator, rearrange some leftovers, and store the turkey and hams so they wouldn't spoil in the August heat until guests arrived towards noon.

She was glad that Romie's two sisters were busy taking care of their mother at the house Romie had bought for her. Alyce liked both Margie and Mary Helen but Margie, especially, had that confidence of taking charge in a crisis situation. Alyce would have liked to think that it was a Perez trait, but she had to admit that it was a characteristic that she herself possessed. She could only imagine how chaotic the kitchen would become if Margie and she were organizing the food at the same time.

As soon as she got the food stored and rearranged, Alyce made a pot of coffee for the two sailors sitting on the back steps. These two were not sailors with the U.S. Navy—rather they had arrived with the Merchant Marine captain who was sitting at the dining room table with Cleo. Alyce invited the two men to drink their coffee at the kitchen table, but they refused, content to sit on the back steps under the shade of a pecan tree as they sipped from their mugs.

Sitting at the kitchen table with her cup of hot tea, Alyce realized that the two sailors were talking about Romie. They were speculating on what the captain was telling Cleo about Romie's death in Costa Rica. Alyce strained her ears to listen.

The younger man spoke first:

"What ya think he's telling her?"

"That Pee-rez was running for a train and fell under it."

"Is that what happened?"

"Nobody knows what happened, now do they, Young-un?!"

"We shouldn't have sailed without him."

"The captain thought he went AWOL, so don't blame the captain."

"So, where's the body?"

"Nobody knows where the body is, Young-un

"But what'd the telegram from Costa Rica say?"

"They found a body on a railroad track—that's all it said."

"But they had a name didn't they?"

"Yeah. The name was Pee-rez, a common name in Costa Rica."

"But they found identification papers on the body, didn't they?"

"Merchant Marine ID, but it could've been in a wallet stolen from Pee-rez and found on the body of someone not really Pee-rez, you see?"

"Yeah, somebody could've stolen the wallet. Pee-rez always carried too much cash, him being the Purser and all. You know how he liked to flash around the cash!"

"Especially when he was drinking."

"You think it had anything to do with a woman?"

"*Could* have, Young-un! . . . Pee-rez was quite the ladies man—they couldn't keep their hands off him!"

"Yeah! . . . I remember that native girl I was with at that dockside bar in Honduras. I went to the john and when I came back, that sassy girl had crawled up in Pee-rez's lap!"

"All the telegram said was that they found a body on the railroad track with Merchant Marine ID saying he was Pee-rez."

"Did anybody see him fall while he was running after the train?"

"Didn't mention no witnesses—just a body lying on the track."

"You think those natives could've *thrown* him on the track after he was already dead?"

"Anything's possible, Young-un! . . . Pee-rez could've hit on a woman at a tavern, and her man and his buddies could've followed Pee-rez, slammed him upside the head, and thrown him on the track."

"For messin' with their women?"

"*Or,* . . . maybe they followed him to rob him."

"You mean he might've been flashing around money inside the bar?"

"Could've been."

"So, what's the captain telling the widow in there?"

"He's telling her something nice."

"Like, 'your husband was running after a train and fell under it' . . . something like that?"

"Or, like . . . 'your husband was jumping from one ship to another at the dock, fell between them, hit his head, and died instantly."

"This coffee ain't as good as what we drunk in Costa Rica."

ᒐᒐᒐ

That night Alyce sat down at the secretary in the dining room to write Rappy that his younger brother Romie had died. Before she started her letter, she picked up an envelope and re-read the letter she had received from Rappy that very afternoon.

Dear Hickory,   *July 30, 1945*
                                                                    # 544

Today's Tommy's second birthday. Nobody knows how much I want to be there with you all when the little fellow blows out the candles on his cake. I'd be proud to lead the family singing "Happy Birthday, dear Tommy!" And I'm delighted to hear that he's talking up a blue streak.

I can't write you any specific details because the censors would just black them out, but I think I can safely say that this war is coming to a climax. That's all I can say. But I doubt that I'll be home by Labor Day to take Mickey and Rappy to their first day of the new school year.

We haven't been as busy on the base these last few weeks, which should be significant, but that's all I can say in a letter. It's great that things have slowed down because July and August on this tropical island are the hottest months of the year.

With all this time on our hands, the brass are showing us more picture-shows. Yesterday I sat through three of them. They show movies that the young boys like—lots of pictures with Betty Grable and other pin-up stars, and lots of war movies with John Wayne and the tough guys. I'd give anything to see a movie with Al Jolson or Eddie Cantor up there singing on the screen. And I'd like to see some of those old comedies like Harold Lloyd or the Marx Brothers, but I think it's important to keep the younger boys entertained.

As soon as this war's over, I'll let you know my discharge date. I can't wait to get home to see you. I'm already planning to celebrate by taking you to the New Spic. I dream of sitting down with you and Romie and Cleo to one of those T-Bone steaks and a cold bottle of beer. Real cold, something we can't find on this island.

Kiss all the children for me. Tomorrow's letter will be longer—promise!

You're the only one I've ever loved . . . will ever love!

A big smacker for you!

All my love,
Rappy

With her mother sitting at her side for moral support, Alyce picked up her fountain pen to write the most difficult letter she ever had to write.

"Now, Alyce, you're not gonna tell him what those two sailors said, are you?"

"Oooh, Mama, I can't tell him any of those tales! Those sailors were just *guessing* what happened to Romie."

"So, what are you gonna tell Rappy?"

"I'm gonna tell him what the ship captain told Cleo!"

"And, *what* exactly is that?"

"That Romie didn't show up after liberty so the ship sailed without him . . . that after they sailed, the captain received a telegram from the Costa Rican police that Romie's body was found on a railroad track . . . that nobody knows exactly *how* he died."

"Just make sure, Alyce, that you tell him the *truth*."

"That's the truth."

"Then that's what you gotta write him."

"But Monsignor O'Donoghue said I didn't have to write Rappy the truth if he couldn't do anything about it."

"Well, Rappy can't do anything about Mickey's broken arm or about Tommy not talking much yet, but he surely deserves the truth about Romie."

"You're right, Mama. If he hears the truth from somebody else, he'll never trust me again . . . about anything!"

"So, what're you waiting for?"

"I can't do it," Alyce laid the pen on the desk.

"You're tired from spending all day at Cleo's house—all those folks coming through and bringing all that food. I can't imagine how many dishes you and Mary Helen had to wash all day long, just to feed those folks. You're exhausted, Alyce."

"Yes, M'am, I really am," Alyce rested her arms on the small desk and slumped forward.

"Well, let's go to bed. You don't need to be writing such a letter when you can't even see straight. You can write the letter tomorrow."

But Alyce never had to write the letter.

The next day when she returned to Cleo's house to man the kitchen again, she learned from Cleo that the Red Cross had sent telegrams to Romie's two brothers stationed overseas, Rappy and Charles. When Alyce realized that she didn't have to write the letter—that the Red Cross telegram would reach Rappy a week before her letter—she made a mental note to light a votive candle in thanks to the Infant of Prague. She reached up to her face to wipe away something in her eye and realized that she was crying silently.

She decided she wouldn't write Rappy until she had his letter in hand acknowledging that he had received the fateful telegram announcing Romie's death.

Dear Hickory,   *August 16, 1945*
                                                          # 560

Yesterday the Japanese surrendered.
And yesterday I received a telegram from the Red Cross saying that Romie is dead.

The International Red Cross regrets to inform you that your brother, Jerome Leopold Perez, was killed in a civilian accident in an unnamed Central American port. STOP The date of death and other details are still unknown at this time. STOP

That's all it said. I know you will send me details as soon as you learn them. I wish I could be there with the family. I know Cleo will need help with all the funeral details as soon as the body is shipped home. I really want to be there for Mama. I know she's going to take this really bad.
It's killing me that Romie is dead. He was more than a brother to me—he was my friend. People in Mobile are often critical of him because of his business practices during

173

Prohibition. But most people don't know how charitable he was. I know.

I kept his books at the Spic and Span and again at the New Spic. I know how much money he gave to the church and to other charities without ever taking credit. He asked me to make anonymous donations for him. And I did. His kitchen workers will tell you that they were instructed never to turn away any hungry soul who knocks on the back door of his restaurant.

When you get the details of Romie's death, please send them. Meanwhile, do whatever you can to help Mama. I know she's in a lot of pain and suffering.

I'm so sad.

All my love,
Rappy

꽃꽃꽃

Rappy didn't arrive home until December 23.

Although the war in the Pacific ended officially on August 15, his non-combat unit didn't make it to stateside until early December. The combat troops in the Pacific were transported home first. The non-combat forces, including Rappy's unit which had spent the war fueling and repairing B-29s on an island in Fiji, had to wait their turn. And when they finally were told in the autumn of 1945 that they were on their way home, they discovered they'd be transported not by air but by sea—on a troop carrier that took more than two weeks to cross the Pacific to San Francisco.

"It's long-distance, Rappy! Talk louder!" Alyce shouted over the telephone.

"I'm in Hattiesburg," Rappy shouted back.

"Where's that?"

"Mississippi, Hickory! . . . It's less than two hours from Mobile!"

"We're waiting for you, Rappy! Take a bus!"

"I'm not discharged yet!"

"What's the holdup?"

"They're trying to send me to a sanatorium!"

"Well, I always said you were crazy!"

"They have me confused with another Perez who's shell-shocked!"

"I'm coming to Hattiesburg!"

"No, Hickory! I'll have this straightened out in a few days."

"A few *days*? . . . It's already the 16th ! Will you be home for Christmas?"

"Hickory, I'll be home for Christmas if I have to *walk*!"

Exactly one week later on December 23, Alyce found herself in the front seat of Uncle Joe Midgette's car, sandwiched between her favorite uncle and her husband who was on the last leg of his journey home from war.

As the car left Hattiesburg and headed toward Mobile after sunset, she pulled her old wool overcoat more tightly around her shoulders and nestled her body deeper between the two men. She felt a delicious relief. She was in the hands of the two men she trusted most on the planet. She let her right hand fall limp into Rappy's as he clutched hers as if they were teenagers on their first date at the picture-show. She glanced at Rappy and found him staring out the window into the dark pine woods which sped by in a blur. When he gazed down at her, she saw in his face that he still couldn't believe that the war was over, that finally, after he and she had exchanged over 600 letters, he was speeding down a dark highway in the middle of the night towards the warmth of his home on Laurel Street. After ten years of marriage, Alyce realized she had learned to read her husband's thoughts.

He knows he's got to adjust to civilian life again. He never saw combat, but he's bound to have seen men on their way home with terrible injuries.

175

And surely he's aware of the war atrocities we've seen since Europe was liberated last spring. He's seen the same magazine photos we saw of US soldiers missing arms and legs, the same newsreels when US troops liberated those death camps in Poland and Germany. And all those dead US soldiers washed up on the beaches in the island battles in the Pacific.

Somehow, I've got to be a rock for him.

Lord, show me how.

But before any adjustment could begin, Rappy would have to learn that Romie's grave had not been located yet. Cleo was in the process of sending a private investigator to Costa Rica to find the grave. Somehow Alyce would have to find the opportunity and courage to tell Rappy what the most recent telegram from Costa Rica had reported:

A body with Romie's ID had been found on a railroad track the day his ship left port. The authorities wrapped it in a bedsheet and buried it without a coffin in a shallow grave. The Spanish family name, 'Perez', convinced the local police chief that Jerome Leopold Perez was a Costa Rican native whose body had not been claimed. The problem was to find the grave in the local Potter's Field.

As the car sped towards Mobile, Alyce glanced at Rappy's profile and decided she wouldn't say anything about Romie's grave until Rappy asked. She hoped to get through Christmas Day before she'd have to deal with the task.

Just two days, Lord! Please give me two days grace!

Rappy had been living under a military structure for two years whereby he was told what time to rise in the morning and what time to go to bed at night—and what to do each hour in between. He would rest at home for only two days, celebrate Christmas Day with his family, and then report back to the bank where his job was waiting for him. Without the Merchants National Bank supplementing

Rappy's salary for the past two years, Alyce didn't know how she could have managed.

But she *had* managed. She didn't know how to rate her performance. All she knew is that with her mother's help, she had done the best she could. She had proved her competence. Out of necessity she had become independent. But truthfully she was ready to hand the checkbook back to Rappy as soon as they walked in the front door on Laurel Street. And he could take over cutting the lawn as soon as the grass emerged from hibernation next March.

But, best of all, she would call Sister Mary Consuela immediately and resign her teaching job. She wouldn't return to teach kindergarten in January after the holidays. She had earned the luxury of getting her three oldest children off to school and then sitting down at the table with her mother to have their morning tea-and-toast in quiet as the sun peeked through the kitchen window before little Tommy stumbled out of bed.

The car sped towards Mobile through the winter darkness. Alyce closed her eyes and relaxed even more because she knew that Uncle Joe would get them to Laurel Street safely. She realized that Joe Midgette, a fine and honorable man—even though he was a non-Catholic and peppered his conversation with the salty language of a sailor from his years at sea—was as close to a father as she would ever find. Although he had five children of his own with her aunt, Olivia Fanane Midgette, he treated Alyce as if she were his own daughter—dashing off to Hattiesburg on a day's notice so Alyce could have two hours of privacy with Rappy in the car before he reunited with his children and the mob of relatives waiting for him on Laurel Street.

It occurred to Alyce as she felt the warmth of Uncle Joe's shoulder pressing against her own that she could stop searching for a father. She had one living just around the corner—three doors north of Laurel on Monterey Street. She knew that Joe Midgette would always be there to support her in the future through any crisis, to help her over any obstacle to happiness.

Watching the utility poles zoom past as the headlights reflected off them, Alyce realized that she had not only survived eighteen months keeping her family together while Rappy was at war, she had prevailed. Now a father would be a mere luxury in her life. The war experience had taught her that she didn't need a father.

Indeed, she had prevailed.

CHAPTER **10**

THREE DAYS AFTER her husband arrived home from war, Alyce found herself outside the Merchants National Bank with Rappy as he mustered courage to enter the building to resume his job. She pulled her overcoat lapels together to ward off the winter cold as she hurried behind Rappy who had taken off to circle the block again. She wanted to slip her arm into his to let him know she understood his anxiety, but his pace was too fast for her to keep up.

As she followed him around the corner of St. Joseph Street, she felt the chilled wind blasting up St. Francis Street from the waterfront. Her feet were killing her. Had she known she'd be scurrying around the block all morning, she would've worn flat shoes. Her calves, covered only by nylon stockings, were freezing. Her wool-tweed overcoat barely covered her knees.

She wanted to grab Rappy by the collar of his overcoat and drag him into the cozy warmth of the bank building, but she decided it was her duty to follow him around the block again until he walked off his nervousness. She was determined he would walk inside that bank today to resume his position in the Bookkeeping Department on the fifth floor.

Finally, after they circled the block nine times, Rappy made a dash through the revolving doors and entered the lobby. He paused next to a heating grate and blew on his hands to warm them as he gazed around the foyer with its plush red carpeting, marble walls, and polished brass fixtures as if he had never seen it before.

"So different," he scanned the elegant foyer from top to bottom.

"It's the same, Rappy. It hasn't changed in the two years you've been away," Alyce realized this wasn't the time to let her patience run out.

So different from *Fiji!*" he dragged his hand along a brass railing polished to a brilliant shine.

"Yeah, it's a lot different from the pictures you sent of the islands. Those people in the pictures looked destitute. The natives don't have any bank buildings like this, do they?" she was dying to reach the reception area to sit down and rest her feet.

"The people on my island have only one bank—it's in a thatched hut the size of our garage."

"Let's go in and see everybody! You *know* they're anxious to welcome you back!"

"It's so different, Hickory," he murmured as he slipped his hand under her elbow and guided her through the door into the main lobby.

"But *you're* not different, Rappy! You're still the same great fellow I married eleven years ago!"

He pushed open the glass door, took her by the hand, and led her into the lobby where four secretaries from the Bookkeeping Department stood holding a coconut sheet-cake big enough to serve fifty. Behind the four secretaries were grouped the entire thirty members of the Bookkeeping Department holding up a hand-lettered banner:

Welcome Home, Rappy!

That night Rappy returned from work in high spirits. Once inside the house he quickly discovered that little Tommy, unlike his older brother and sisters, was not running to greet him as he struggled out of his overcoat in the middle of the living room.

"He doesn't know who you are!" Miss Alice laughed as she swept Tommy into her arms.

Rappy kissed his three older children and gingerly approached his mother-in-law holding his youngest child.

"I'm your daddy, little fellow!" he knew better than to force himself on the child.

"Kiss your daddy, Tommy!" Miss Alice held the child closer to his father.

"No!" Alyce raised her voice from the kitchen doorway. "Don't force him! He was only seven months-old when you left for boot camp! All he knows about his daddy is that picture on my vanity!"

"Alyce, we've got to start somewhere!" Miss Alice protested, still holding the child close to his daddy for a kiss.

"Rappy, bring him a present from Woolworth's tomorrow. He likes trucks and jeeps—anything to do with the army."

The next day Rappy returned home with a small toy jeep from Woolworth's, a tiny thing that he could hide in his hand and let Tommy guess which fist held the surprise. The day after, it was a tiny army tank. After a week Tommy was waiting on the front steps each night to receive his toy. The third week the bribe was reduced to a penny candy hidden in Rappy's fist so that the child could guess which hand held the surprise.

After four weeks Rappy was able to enter his house without any bribe, and Tommy ran up to his daddy to receive his kiss just like his older brother and two sisters. Under his bed the two year-old had hidden a shoebox containing a dozen tiny army vehicles and a stash of penny candies.

By the time Mardi Gras season arrived, when Rappy returned at night from the bank, Tommy was pushing the older children aside to be the first to jump on his daddy and kiss him on the lips.

♪♪♪♪

True to her word, Alyce resigned her job teaching kindergarten. It was time to relish her mornings as a stay-at-home housewife. She was relieved from her wartime schedule when she rushed like mad to get the children off to school and then pedaled two miles down Dauphin Street to the Convent of Mercy. She still woke up early to turn on the gas stove in the central hall to warm the house before anyone else was up, but she luxuriated in the fact that on a cold January morning she didn't have to brave the chill on her bicycle.

After serving a hot breakfast to her husband and three older children, she kissed Rappy good-bye at the front door as he left in his buddy's car waiting at the curb which carried four MNB employees to work—a cost to Rappy of only $1.00 per week. This arrangement left the ten year-old Plymouth in the driveway all day so Alyce could pick up the children from school at three—and run errands for her mother or take one of the children to the doctor in an emergency. As soon as Rappy was out the door, Alyce waited with Mickey and Little Rappy at the front door for Molly Sullivan to carpool the children to school.

Miss Alice had breakfast waiting for Alyce in the kitchen where they warmed themselves next to the stove. The two women shared the *Mobile Press Register* as each silently planned her day while savoring steaming tea and hot buttered toast. Although the war had been officially over for five months, sugar was still rationed—and would continue to be so for two more years. But ration coupons were no longer needed to buy Carnation evaporated milk which Miss Alice used to dilute the strong English Breakfast tea she let simmer on the back burner all day while she worked at her sewing machine.

Before they could be disturbed by Tommy, who didn't emerge from Miss Alice's bedroom until nine, the two women took their time with the only hour they'd have alone for the rest of the day.

"Now, Alyce, what's all this about *The Servicemen's Readjustment Act of 1944?*" Miss Alice murmured as she read from the front page.

"Rappy says most folks call it the *GI Bill of Rights,*" Alyce dipped her toast into the hot tea.

"Now, I *have* heard about *that!* . . . George Jumonville says it's got something to do with war veterans getting government money to go to college," Miss Alice spooned some fig preserves onto a crust of toast.

"Uncle Joe says the main purpose is to help war veterans buy a house."

"You and Rappy already have a house. . . . But now, Thomas's gonna want to buy a house as soon as he gets married."

"Bubber hasn't even made it home from the Philippines, Mama!"

"In that last phonecall he said 'any week now!' He's stranded some place close to San Francisco. . . . Or is it San Diego?"

"And he doesn't need to buy a house until he finds a girl to marry."

"It's about *time* he got married!" Miss Alice chuckled.

"He's only thirty-five, Mama!"

"It says *here*," Miss Alice pointed to the front page of the paper, "that this GI Bill gives money to veterans to attend college. . . . Now, Thomas graduated from Spring Hill already, but what about Rappy? How in the world could *he* go to college? He certainly can't quit his job—not with four children to support!"

"He says the University of Alabama has a branch downtown that gives night classes."

"How can a married man hold a job all day long and go to college at night?"

"He wouldn't have time for more than two courses a semester, so it'd take eight years to earn his Bachelor's degree."

"Eight years? . . . I bet he wouldn't get home till nine every night! By that time the children would already be asleep!"

"Four nights a week—they don't hold classes on Friday nights—and I can't see Rappy Perez doing it for eight years."

"Well," Miss Alice folded the news section and slid it towards her daughter, "if Rappy's in line to be the next head of Bookkeeping, does he really need a college degree?"

"He says he doesn't need it to advance. He'd still get a raise every year without any degree, but he might need it if he wants to become an officer of the bank . . . sometime in the future."

"I'd leave the future in God's hands, Alyce. Right now, Rappy needs to be home at night to see his children grow up."

"He doesn't want to take those college courses at night—he's been out of high school for nineteen years—he's worried he'd fail!"

"He's plenty smart—he'd never fail. But, eight years of classes? By the time he finishes, Little Rappy'll be *sixteen* and Tommy'll be *ten*!"

"And the girls," Alyce said wistfully. "It's important for a girl to have her father around the house. I know how much I missed a father."

"Girls *and* boys!" Miss Alice ignored the mention of Alyce's father. "These children need their daddy at home, especially since he was away at war for two years and when he finally got back here, his youngest didn't know him from Adam's housecat!"

ﮔﮔﮔﮔ

Instead of college, Rappy made his mark with the *American Institute of Banking*.

When he returned to work after the war, Rappy was taken under Mr. McRae's wing. The bank president sponsored Rappy in the AIB, a national professional organization of bank employees that offered banking courses equivalent to those taught in university Business Administration departments. Only two years after the war, Rappy had advanced to teaching banking courses for the local chapter of the AIB. The classes were held twice a week in a seminar room above the downtown post office so that two nights a week Rappy didn't get home to Laurel Street until 8:30.

By 1948 he was President of the AIB's local chapter. His duties included representing the chapter at the national convention which in 1949 would be held in Portland, Oregon. Of course, the local AIB chapter was paying all expenses for Rappy to attend the week-long convention. To his delight Rappy discovered Mr. McRae offered an extra two week's leave so he could take the train to Portland instead of traveling by airplane. After flying from San Francisco to Honolulu in a troop carrier on his way to the Fiji Islands—and throwing up most of the flight—Rappy would have certainly insisted the chapter's Vice-President attend the convention in his place if it meant traveling by plane.

As soon as Rappy was elected AIB president in 1948, he and Alyce started saving spare change so she could attend the convention with him in June of 1949. For a full twelve months they dumped all their spare change into a cigar box hidden behind Rappy's socks in the middle drawer of their bureau.

Alyce was counting the weeks to the convention. A total of six men—and their wives—from local Mobile banks would be on that train, partying for two days and nights from Mobile to Portland, but as the date approached, she felt qualms about running off and leaving her mother with six children for three weeks, even if school would be out by the time she and Rappy left for the June convention.

In the four years since Rappy had returned from the war, he and Alyce had added two more children, both girls, to the expanding Perez family on Laurel Street. Only fifteen months after his return from Fiji, Alyce gave birth to their third daughter. Rappy insisted naming the baby girl after her mother. So their fifth child was christened 'Alyce Felicia Perez', and the birth certificate spelled the name 'Alyce'—not 'Alice' as the legal names of the infant's mother and grandmother were spelled.

Less than two years later the Perez family received a special valentine when Alyce gave birth to their sixth child on February 14, 1949. She named their fourth daughter 'Catherine Theresa Perez", the middle name in honor of Rappy's mother, Nellie, who had been christened 'Helen Theresa Callus'.

As the departure date for Portland neared, Alyce's qualms about leaving her Mother alone with six children under the age of twelve turned into Catholic guilt.

"Mama, I can't go off and leave you alone with all these children!" Alyce dunked her buttered toast into the hot tea and gazed at the May sunshine streaming through the windows. She hoped her mother wouldn't see the tears brimming in her eyes, tears of guilt at the thought of leaving her children with her mother for three weeks while Miss Alice started on school uniforms for September when the Catholic schools would re-open.

"Alyce, I can take care of the children for three weeks," Miss Alice didn't look up from the newspaper spread on the kitchen table. "You go with Rappy and enjoy yourself!"

"Cathy's only three months old!"

"Mickey can help me—she'll be out of school for the summer."

"Mickey's only ten, Mama!"

"She's turning eleven this summer—she can take care of Snook-ums and Tommy while I concentrate on the baby. This might be the only chance you ever get to travel and you've gotta take advantage of it—especially since you and Rappy spent a whole year saving all your change in that cigar box!

"Your problems will be Shirley and Little Rappy," Alyce turned to her mother and wiped the tears from her eyes.

"They won't be no trouble—they'll surprise you," Miss Alice mur-mured as she reached for a piece of toast, her eyes still scanning the front page.

"Rappy just turned twelve, and he's . . . well, he's all *boy*! And Shirley's only eight so she won't be as much help as Mickey, but if—"

"You're going on that convention, Alyce, and that's *that*!"

So it was decided that Alyce would accompany Rappy on the trip to Portland, Oregon with scheduled side trips to Sun Valley, Idaho as well as Lake Louise in Canada. She spent May getting her clothes ready for the trip. It was similar to putting together another honey-moon trousseau, but little in this travel trousseau would be new. Most items would be garments already hanging in her closet, outfits bor-rowed from friends and family, and a few garments fashioned on her mother's sewing machine.

Three weeks in chilly mountainous weather as far north as Canada, including the round-trip train ride, would require a wardrobe com-pletely different from her honeymoon trousseau for New Orleans that humid June fifteen years ago. She would need to borrow sweaters and woolen slacks. Miss Alice would have to make a cocktail dress with long-sleeves, something unheard of in coastal Mobile, Alabama.

To whip up a travel trousseau in only three weeks, Alyce called on her McHugh cousins who both wore a size 6. Euphemia lent a navy suit and Lucille provided a red-and-white cocktail dress and a hat to match with a jaunty red feather and veil. To fill in the gaps, Miss Alice tackled her sewing machine with the same gusto she used for a wedding with eight bridesmaids. The focal garment was a tailored travel suit of a lightweight British wool, pearl grey, worn with a variety of borrowed silk blouses, with or without the jacket.

One week before Alyce was to leave on the trip, Margie appeared at Laurel Street with her set of Samsonite luggage in fawn leather. The set consisted of the essential traincase, a hatbox, the Pullman suitcase, a three-suiter for Alyce, and a two-suiter for Rappy. When Margie arrived with the five pieces, Alyce had just left for St. Mary's School to pick up her three oldest children. Margie, always in a hurry to finish her errands, just dropped the luggage in the middle of the living room, chatted a few minutes with Miss Alice, and dashed out the front door.

Miss Alice decided to carry the five pieces to Alyce's bedroom to clear the living room before Alyce returned with the older children. Cradling the three month-old Cathy in one arm, Miss Alice struggled with the large Pullman case as she scurried through the central hall. In her daughter's bedroom, she tried to shift the infant into her other arm as she shoved the Pullman suitcase with her knee, but the 62 year-old grandmother stumbled, tripped over the suitcase and fell against the four-poster bed. Bracing herself to protect the baby as she fell, Miss Alice slid to the floor. Somehow she managed to land on her back with the infant safe on her stomach, but her left arm became twisted under her.

When Alyce came through the front door with the three older children, she was greeted by the new baby's cries coming from her bedroom. She noticed Tommy, now age five, standing in the hallway at the telephone table trying to dial a number.

"We have to call the police, Mama!" the little towhead shouted. "Grandma fell in the bedroom and broke her arm bone! She's stopped crying—but the new baby won't!"

Alyce found her mother sitting calmly on the side of the bed trying to quiet the infant who was unhurt. As Alyce moved closer to the bed, she saw that her mother's left arm hung helplessly at her side. The forearm had already started to swell. A faint purple bruise was becoming darker by the moment as it crept down her arm from wrist to elbow.

》》)

At Providence Hospital's emergency room, it took the ER staff only thirty minutes to set the bone in Miss Alice's forearm and wrap the arm in a cast from wrist to shoulder. Miss Alice was told by the ER staff that she should spend the night in a hospital room in case she had a reaction to the pain medication. Because of her age, they insisted on keeping an eye on her. The family doctor, Homer Dowling, knew Miss Alice well enough to surmise that she wouldn't get any rest on Laurel Street. Miss Alice wasn't one to take to her bed when six children needed to be fed supper.

Alyce was devastated. The sight of the thick cast on her mother's arm—blinding white and still damp from the plaster—sent a shiver of shame down her spine. Her mother had stood by her side all her life—especially during the war years when Alyce felt so vulnerable without Rappy home and in charge. After each birth Alyce was able to convalesce in the hospital for a full two weeks for two reasons: Rappy's group medical plan at the bank allowed her a traditional Victorian confinement in the Allen Memorial Hospital at the insurance company's expense but, more importantly, Alyce knew she could relax in her hospital room because her children were under the care and love of their Grandma Hicks.

Alyce watched helplessly from the doorway as her mother—aided by two nurses, a nun, and an orderly—struggled to climb into her hospital bed.

Well, there goes Portland!
I can't recall the last time I felt such guilt! . . . Why, I'm completely self-centered!

Selfish! . . . Rotten! . . . Mama's been so good to me, and all I can think of is a stupid train trip!

That night she lay in the dark and allowed herself the luxury of weeping into her pillow. Rappy pulled her close and let her cry on his pajama top as he held her.

"Now, Hickory, we can figure something out," he whispered, forgetting that his mother-in-law was not in her bed in the next room.

"It's hopeless, Rappy."

"Well, at least you're not blaming it on God's Will," he teased.

"Blaming *what*?" she became testy.

"The *broken arm*! What else?"

"But it *is* God's Will! . . . The broken arm is God's way of stopping me from getting on that train!"

"So, Hickory, is it God's Will that you don't go to Portland?"

"Evidently God doesn't want me to go."

"So, you've accepted it?"

"No! I have *not* accepted it! But I'm gonna *have* to accept it . . . tomorrow."

"And just how do you plan to do that?"

"I'll say a second rosary tomorrow night."

♪♪♪

But before she could say even one rosary, God changed His mind.

The next morning, before Alyce could get out the front door to bring her mother home from the hospital, Margie appeared in the living room with her mother, Nellie Perez.

"You're going on that trip, Alyce!" the older woman released Margie's arm as she slid onto the sofa.

"I can't go off and leave these children when Mama has a broken arm," Alyce felt her eyes filling up with tears.

"I'll help her," Nellie said as she folded her hands in her lap.

"Grandma, I can't let you do that—and how would you get down here? You don't drive!"

189

"I'll drive her down here every day," Margie stood at the mantle and folded her arms over her chest as if she were preparing for a fight.

"But you're not familiar with the house, Grandma, the kitchen, and the children's routine, and, you know" Alyce looked away, determined that the tears would not burst forth.

"I know I can't do a lot, but—," the older woman was interrupted by Margie.

"Of course Mama can't chase after the little ones, Alyce, but she can rock the baby when it cries and she can sit in front of a highchair to spoon vegetables into Snookums and sit on the front steps to make sure nobody runs into the street while your Mama is doing other things!" Margie had come prepared to accept only an affirmative answer.

"But Mama's got a broken arm—she can't even change a diaper!" Alyce realized she was almost wailing.

"She broke her *left* arm," Margie laughed, "and she's right-handed, isn't she? Together she and Mickey can change a diaper. Weren't you bragging last month that Mickey's changing diapers without even asking you?"

"I just don't know," Alyce glanced back and forth between the two women.

"Well," Margie started for the front door, "Mama's got high-blood pressure, you know, and a bad back but still there's a lot she *can* do. If nothing else, it'll be good for Miss Alice to have an adult around in the daytime just to talk with."

As Alyce stood in the doorway watching Margie escort her frail mother down the front walk, she wondered just how much help Nellie could really be to her own mother. Grandma Perez would turn sixty-eight in July. She needed a low-salt diet due to high blood pressure. And because of osteoporosis, the old lady had a severe humpback. She always turned down the volume to her hearing aid when she was around any large family gathering, especially if most of her twenty-eight grandchildren were cutting up.

I need to put on my thinking-cap!

My mother-in-law needs this opportunity to make herself useful. I've never called on her to baby-sit for a Mardi Gras ball or bank party because she couldn't handle all six children alone. And Papa'd be no help. Actually, he'd resent the children getting all of Nellie's attention.

But Nellie could serve as moral support to Mama. She'd feel useful during the day and go home at night to rest with Papa.

She wants to help.

I've got to realize that I'm not the only one who feels a need to help other folks. This time I have to step back and let somebody else do the helping.

A tough order.

Standing in the front door as she watched Margie's new Buick pull away, Alyce reached in her apron pocket and caressed her rosary beads. She decided to accept Grandma Perez's offer as a gift from God. Today it was easy to accept God's Will.

♪♪♪

What sealed the decision that Alyce would attend the convention was Rappy's suggestion to pay Josephine to come to the house every day for the entire three weeks.

Her name was Josephine Johnson. She had been working at Laurel Street for two years, since right after Snookums was born in 1947. Her main duty during six working hours was ironing white cotton school uniforms and table linens—a huge relief for Alyce—but Josephine also helped out in the kitchen, rocked the new infant so Alyce could tend to a jealous older child, and babysat when Alyce drove around the corner to Weinacker's grocery store or to pick up the older children from school. Having Josephine to baby-sit meant Miss Alice didn't have to leave her sewing machine, which gave Alyce the luxury of not having to rush back home to free up her mother from watching the children.

191

"I hate to say it, but I feel rich having somebody to iron three times a week," Alyce smiled at her mother-in-law who sat in the living room rocker as Alyce breastfed the three month-old Cathy.

"Alfred can *afford* somebody to iron for you," Nellie Perez never referred to her third son as 'Rappy'.

"Mama and I've been taking turns ironing the school uniforms, but if I'm gonna breast-feed this baby just like the other five, then I'm gonna need help cuz sometimes Mama can't take time away from her sewing to iron those uniforms, and neither one of us feels like ironing after nine o'clock when the children are finally in bed."

"Don't apologize, Alyce—you deserve it. Now, you don't iron Alfred's white dress shirts for him to go to the bank, do you?"

"No, m'am. That was the best advice you ever gave me—to send Rappy's shirts to the laundry instead of ironing them myself. It was the last thing you said just before I walked up the aisle to marry him, do you remember?"

"The same thing I told Margie and Mary Helen and all my sons' wives. If a man has a job where he needs a starched white shirt every-day, then he's got a salary large enough to afford a laundry bill!"

"Mr. Mack from the Imperial Laundry stops by Friday mornings to drop off six white shirts—starched, pressed, and wrapped around cardboard liners—and picks up six dirty ones. Rappy's never complained about the laundry bill. I just write Mr. Mack a check every week."

"School uniforms don't need to be pressed just so—that colored woman can do a fine job, and she's cheaper than the Imperial Laundry. Just don't forget to give her carfare every time she leaves the house," Nellie wagged her finger at Alyce.

"She's here for six hours so I give her two dollars and carfare—and usually I have some leftovers from the refrigerator to offer her cuz she's got three children she's raising for her sister who's feeble-minded, so she says."

"What'd you say her name is?"

"Josephine. . . . Those children call up here looking for 'Aunt Jo'.

And her friends call for 'Josie'. Now, her church members call for 'Mother Johnson' but her legal name is 'Jordan'. At least she told us it's 'Jordan'."

"You might ask Alfred if you need to do something about this Social Security thing with her."

"He's taking care of that now, which is how we found about the Jordan man. We think he was a common-law husband or something, but he's long gone. At this point Rappy can't figure out *what* her real name is!"

"Just so long she's good with the children."

♪♪♪

And she was indeed good with the children.

When Josephine first appeared on Laurel Street in the spring of 1947 she was already past fifty-five. She was a tiny thing, less than five feet tall and not even a hundred pounds of mere muscle and bone. Her small head was a sheen of tight curls which she kept coiffed with a dime-store hairdressing. She had a swayback problem which caused her fanny to stick out so her natural gait appeared sassy as she scurried down Laurel Street to catch her bus. Usually she carried two shopping bags of leftover food and hand-me-down clothes Alyce had given her for the three young children she was raising alone in Trinity Gardens in Africatown, a good thirty minutes north of Laurel Street on the edge of the city limits.

When Alyce told Josephine that she needed her to come to Laurel Street every day for the three weeks of the Portland convention, Josephine threw her hands up in the air and screamed "Thank you, Jesus! . . . I can use that money! Thank you, Jesus, thank you, Miz Pee-rez . . . and thank you again, *Jesus!*"

Because school was out for the summer there would be no uniforms for Josephine to iron. And any other ironing could be put on hold for three weeks.

"Now, Josephine , let's talk about your main job while I'm away," Alyce convinced the older woman it was perfectly all right for a maid

193

to sit on the sofa to discuss 'business' with the white lady.

"Yessum," Josephine sat in her white cotton uniform, her feet dangling over the sofa's cushion like a child's.

"The best help you can be to my mother is to take care of the two little ones, Snookums and the new baby. Snookums is pretty much potty-trained, but she might wet her pants during the day—so you'll have to keep her panties washed and dried on the clothesline cuz I don't have a big supply for her, and—."

"Yessum."

"And, of course, the new baby has to be changed several times a day. Mama can't help you with that cuz she's got a broken arm, so you'll have to make sure there's a steady supply of diapers—*and* rubber pants! You keep 'em washed in the laundry shed—now you do know how to use that wringer washing machine, don't you?"

"Yessum."

"And Mickey can help you hang 'em on the line if you get real busy."

"Yessum."

"Aside from those two little ones, you just ask Mama what you can do to help her when Snookums and Cathy are taking their nap."

"Yessum."

"Don't worry about the cooking as Mama can handle that—with Mickey's help—but you'll have to wash the dishes—especially the heavy pots Mama can't lift with one arm—before you leave at 6:00. I've told Mama y'all need to have an early supper so you can do the cleaning-up and get to your bus before it gets dark. But it's June and the sun doesn't set till eight or so."

"Yessum."

"And keep your eye on Mama so she doesn't fall again."

"Yessum."

♪♪♪

The next day, dressed in her new pearl-grey travel suit, Alyce met Rappy at the GM&O station for the trip to Portland. Before the train even pulled out, they made friends with the five other Mobile couples popping champagne in the club car. They toasted the 'All Aboard' party on the train that would pick up other banking couples in Montgomery, then Birmingham, and in cities all across the country on their way to Oregon.

As the Mobile delegation sat in the club car waiting to depart the GM&O station, Alyce found herself paired off with the wife of the First National Bank delegate.

"You don't look *old* enough to have six children!" the woman exclaimed.

"I'm thirty-six," Alyce sipped her bourbon-and-Coca-Cola.

"My God! I'd have put you at twenty-nine! How many more children you plan to have?"

"As many as the good Lord sends me!" Alyce chuckled as the train lurched forward.

"Well, just be careful having babies when you're over thirty-five—some doctors say it's risky!"

"I haven't had any trouble—I just pop 'em out!"

"I mean risky for the *baby*! . . . There can be birth defects."

"Well, that depends on the Will of God, doesn't it?"

"No sense in testing God, is it?"

Alyce dismissed the thought from her mind. The party in the club car felt like a Mardi Gras ball at Fort Whiting where she could have fun knowing her mother was home taking care of the children. She wouldn't entertain any idea that at her age she was risking birth defects. She'd leave that in God's hands.

But this vacation to Oregon and Canada—her first since that weekend trip to Fort Leonard Wood to visit Rappy during boot camp—would be the last she'd take for many years. The following summer of 1950 held a fate that would change her life dramatically.

CHAPTER 11

ALYCE STOOD ON the front porch of Laurel Street watching help-lessly as her mother's sewing machine was carried down the front steps. Sitting next to her in the porch rocker, Miss Alice cradled six month-old Cathy in her arms, tickling the baby's chin to get her to laugh. Alyce's brother, Bubber, stood in the driveway behind his tan Studebaker with the trunk open to receive the wooden cabinet. It was a handsome piece of cherry furniture containing the heavy sewing machine tucked inside, ready to pop up when the cabinet's lid was pulled open.

Alyce realized that her brother had chosen the wrong day to move their mother to his rented house across the street from Ladd Memorial Stadium. For one thing the August humidity was oppres-sive. But worse, she should have made sure the younger children, especially Tommy, had been taken to play at Hannon Park. The six year-old towhead stood on the bottom step holding out both arms, palms facing outward, the universal gesture to stop traffic. Everyone on the front lawn laughed, imagining he was ready to stop the sewing machine cabinet from falling, as if the kindergartener could prevent the machine from crashing down the steps if his daddy and older brother dropped the wooden cabinet.

Realizing the desperate child was actually trying to hold back his grandmother's departure, Alyce looked away. Tommy couldn't bear to see the sewing machine leave the house. He knew that following close behind the cabinet, his grandmother would descend the steps to move away—the loving woman who had nurtured him while his own mother was struggling to keep her family together during the war.

Alyce could tolerate any amount of pain herself but couldn't bear to see one of her children suffering, either emotional or physical pain. She turned from the scene, glanced into the McDole's front yard, and focused on the zinnias, vibrant in shades of orange and red. She gazed into the flower bed to hide the tears flowing down her cheeks. She recalled the bittersweet memories of her mother working at her side the past nine years, especially during the war years when Alyce counted on her mother's moral support as well as someone to run the house while she taught kindergarten and scurried around trading ration stamps.

She refused to give in to her emotions. Growing up on Bayou and Savannah she learned that working-class folks of Irish descent, especially good Catholic folks, didn't give into their feelings. She had seen her mother take a deep breath and just get on with the next task at hand.

"You just do what you have to do!"

Back in 1943 when Thomas Hicks, Jr. went off to fight in World War II, he promised his mother on the GM&O platform that he would return in one piece.

"And I'm gonna rent a whole house and have you move in with me, Mama!"

"Bubber," Alyce reassured her brother, "you're welcome to stay at our house when you get back from the war . . . as long as you want! You heard Rappy say that last night at your going-away party!"

Alyce felt her voice getting shrill over the clatter on the platform. Six months pregnant with her fourth child, she stood on one side of her mother while Aunt Olivia Midgette stood on the other, both women ready to support Aunt Alice if the need arose.

"Thomas," Miss Alice had no intention of showing frailty on a train platform in front of strangers, "don't you worry about me! You just concentrate on getting home from that war with all your limbs intact! . . . And your *mind*!"

"Just stay close to the Lord!" Aunt Olivia reached out and touched the woolen sleeve of his army uniform.

"But Rappy and Alyce need the room!" the slight Thomas shifted his duffel bag to his other shoulder and glanced away to avoid appearing panicked. "By the time I get back they'll have this fourth baby to find a bed for."

"Little Rappy's moving into your bed *tonight*, Bubber! And we can put the crib in his room cuz I just know this baby's gonna be a boy!" Alyce didn't need to fake her cheerfulness.

"Just look how high she's carrying this baby!" Olivia searched for conversation to distract the soldier from the terrifying uncertainty of going off to war.

"Absolutely! This baby's gonna be a *boy*—and he's going in your room with Little Rappy!" Miss Alice realized her son's fretfulness was about getting killed in the Philippines, not finding space for a crib safely stored in the attic.

♪♪♪

And the baby was indeed a boy. Three months after Thomas Hicks shipped out for the Philippines, Alyce's fourth child was born. She named the boy after her brother, "Thomas". Two and one-half years later the baby's namesake returned from the war in one piece, both body and mind. He resumed his white-collar job in the Purchasing Department of the International Paper mill and immediately started dating Emma Gallagher who had written to him faithfully while he was at war.

Upon return to Mobile in 1946 at the age of thirty-four, Thomas Hicks found himself on Laurel Street sleeping in his old bed in the smallest bedroom with Rappy, Jr. But Uncle Tom's stay on Laurel Street lasted only four months. In May he and Emma Gallagher were married and they moved into the garage apartment behind Mrs. Cooke's house on Laurel Street.

Next door, the two year-old Tommy Perez slept in a child's bed in the corner of Miss Alice's room where she kept an eye on him. During the war while Alyce taught kindergarten and took care of the older three children, she counted on her mother to act as primary caretaker for Tommy who was only six months old when his daddy went off to boot camp.

Miss Alice and her fourth grandchild bonded quickly. It was the grandmother who fed him, changed his diaper, and bathed him while his mother taught kindergarten. And when the child reached the age of two—the war still raging in the Pacific—he found a favorite spot on the floor next to his Grandma's sewing machine where he gathered her discarded wooden spools and constructed army barracks or turned them into army jeeps which rolled across the hardwood oak floor.

"It's not just that he's named after my son—*and* my dead husband," Miss Alice confided to her childhood friends from downtown who took the bus out to Laurel Street for afternoon tea once a week, "it's that he's starting to *look* like my husband! I know it's much too early to tell what this child's gonna look like when he's all *grown up*, but he does have the nose . . . and the mouth . . . and the *hairline*! My stars, the resemblance is so striking that naturally—although I know a grandmother shouldn't admit it—I tend to favor *this* one!"

And now, six years after Tommy's birth Miss Alice sat on the front porch wondering how she would get down the steps and past the child into the Studebaker. Bouncing the six-month old Cathy on her lap, Miss Alice struggled to make conversation with her daughter. She tried to distract herself from her conflicted feelings as she played patty-cake with the baby on her lap.

"You *know* I wouldn't move in with Thomas if Emma didn't need me more than you," Miss Alice didn't glance at her daughter standing next to her.

"I know, Mama," Alyce continued gazing in the direction of the brilliant zinnias.

"I don't see how Emma can handle this new baby—he's not even a month old yet—what with Little Tom going through his Terrible-

Twos and running all over the house breaking everything he can get a hold of!"

"It's more than the Terrible-Twos, Mama."

"You don't believe that stuff about Tom being Mongolian, now do you, Alyce?"

"*Mongoloid.* . . . That's what Bubber called it."

"Well, just cuz Thomas graduated from Spring Hill College doesn't mean he knows anything about medicine. He shouldn't make a diagnosis just because the child looks funny."

"Sooner or later they're gonna have to take him to that specialist in Birmingham," Alyce looked down at her mother in the rocker to gauge her reaction.

"Well, let's wait till Emma recuperates from her delivery with this new baby before you say anything to her about Little Tom!"

"I'm not about to say anything to Emma! It's none of my business! But Bubber *knows* what he's gotta do!"

"He told me one of the doctors said it was dangerous for a woman to have her first baby if she's over thirty-five. . . . I've never heard of such a thing!"

"And to think how easy it's been for me to have babies!" Alyce was almost whispering.

"There's nothing to do, Alyce, but trust in the Lord."

"I wouldn't know how to raise a baby who wasn't . . . *healthy,*" Alyce said wistfully, as if she were talking to herself.

"You'd just take care of him, Alyce, just like he was any normal child!"

"Well at least Emma's new one seems normal. . . . 'Patrick', after her brother?"

"She's already calling him 'Pat'!"

"Well, your leaving's for the best, Mama. Right now Emma needs you more than I do because her own mother's dead, and her only sister, Marguerite, can't be any help. . . . Poor thing."

"I just hope we get along in the kitchen! A daughter-in-law ain't the same as your own *daughter.*"

201

"Y'all are gonna do just great, Mama."

"Now what're we gonna do about little Tommy out there?" Miss Alice pointed to the six year-old standing at the foot of the steps with tears running down his cheeks.

"He'll do great!" Alyce realized she had raised her voice to convince herself.

"Now that I'm leaving, there'll be room in that bedroom for Little Rappy to move in with Tommy."

"Everything'll be great, Mama," Alyce turned her attention again to the zinnias.

"It'll only take ten minutes to walk here from Thomas's house—I can walk over here any afternoon while Emma and the children are napping if you need me for something."

"I know, Mama."

"And any night you and Rappy need to go to a bank party or something, you know I can get Thomas to drive me over here to baby-sit!" Miss Alice's voice rose as she handed the baby to Alyce.

"I know, Mama."

"It's not like I'm moving to Mississippi!" her voice elevated to a high level of anxiety.

"No, M'am, it's not."

Miss Alice grabbed her train-case from the floor next to her rocker. Quickly she scurried down the front steps to deal with Tommy whose upper lip was trembling in an effort not to cry in front of his daddy and older brother.

♪♪♪♪

Alyce was certain she conceived her seventh child on the night of October 12, 1949, Columbus Day. The local council of the Knights of Columbus staged a big spaghetti supper and dance to celebrate the birthday of their celebrated Italian explorer.

Knowing her children were safe at home with Josephine, Alyce arrived at the KOC hall to have fun. This was her first night out since she and Rappy returned from Oregon three months earlier. As soon as

202

the spaghetti supper was over, the hall was cleared of the long folding tables and the area was turned into a dance floor with a band on the stage.

Alyce danced the first number with Rappy, but after that she lost him as she danced the rest of the night with Rappy's buddies from the *IFT* crowd. She was glad that the KOC had allowed non-Catholics to buy tickets to the benefit. That assured she'd dance with guys she saw only once a year at Mardi Gras balls. One of her favorite dancing partners was Rappy's bank colleague, George Sandoz, a one-time beau from her youth who at every dance looked her up when the band started 'their' song from their courting days, "I'm Dancing with the Prettiest Girl on the Floor."

Towards the end of the evening Alyce found herself sitting at a table sipping her second bourbon-and-Coca-Cola and laughing with Peg Sorrentino at a joke about an Italian butcher on his wedding night. Rappy was on the floor dancing with a clerk from the bank's Bookkeeping Department, some Semmes girl half his age who had drunk too much Chianti and insisted on dancing with her boss.

Out of nowhere Father Eddie Kerns appeared at the table with a bottle of Carling's Canadian Ale and took a chair opposite Alyce. He greeted Peg briefly, hardly glancing at her, so it was obvious that he wanted to talk to Alyce alone.

"There's Hank signaling me to meet him on the dance floor," the savvy Peg had already risen and was sidling from the table.

The Irish-American priest who had married Alyce and Rappy fifteen years ago was a personal friend of Rappy's parents. Julius and Nellie lived behind the New Spic Supper Club in a house Romie bought for them before he joined the Merchant Marine, a house within walking distance of Little Flower Church where Kerns now served as Pastor.

Kerns' relationship with the Hicks family was even tighter. Until Miss Alice and her brothers sold the family house to pay back taxes which Grandma Fanane had neglected to deal with during her lifetime, Kerns was a regular guest for Sunday dinner at Bayou and Savannah.

Sitting next to the fiftyish priest at the KOC party, Alyce braced herself for what she knew was coming. The laconic Irishman stared at the white linen tablecloth as he prepared his spiel to Alyce.

"Alyce, we need your help . . . in convincing Rappy to join the Knights of Columbus," Kerns widened his lazy smile as if his Irish charm would influence Alyce.

She felt her spine stiffen. She had been brought up to respect all priests. They're God's representatives on earth. This priest was a genuine friend of her family, and Kerns had been like a father to Bubber when he was a child. But she refused to let herself be used as a pawn in the plot to get Rappy to abandon his principles.

She took a sip of the bourbon-and-Coca-Cola while she stared into the priest's smiling face. Rarely did she indulge in a second drink on a night out. This was one night when she wished she hadn't, even if it came after a generous serving of spaghetti and meat sauce. The last thing she wanted was to sass Father Kerns.

"You said 'we', Father. Who're you talking about?" she refused to return his smile.

"The nominating committee. Every year they put up Rappy's name for membership, and every year he refuses their offer. This year they've asked me to approach him."

"So, why *don't* you? . . . Father?" she added the 'Father' so as not to sound disrespectful.

"Do what, Alyce?"

"*Approach* him! . . . Why don't *you* approach him, Father Kerns? Isn't that what the committee suggested . . . Father?"

"He'll listen to you, Alyce. Everybody knows how crazy he is about you."

"I respect Rappy for not joining the Knights of Columbus."

"Romie's been dead four years, Alyce."

"That doesn't matter to Rappy, Father."

"Mother of God, Alyce, Rappy plays shortstop on the KOC softball team!"

"He plays ball with his *friends*, but he's not gonna join an organization that blackballed his brother!"

"If Romie were alive today, I'm sure they'd let him join."

"Too late, Father. The Church pressured the KOC to deny Romie membership during Prohibition cuz he was selling bootleg beer. And *you*, Father, . . . went along with the Church."

"You can respect Rappy's principles, Alyce, and still talk to him for me. Can't you just *talk* with him?"

"It's not just Rappy, Father. It's me! I don't *want* him to join the KOC . . . not after the way you all shunned Romie! He was the only one in town who'd sell you priests bootleg whisky! Besides, Father, I'm proud of Rappy for not joining. I hope he never joins. But you should feel free to 'approach' him about it."

"It won't do any good, will it?"

"I hope not, Father. I certainly hope not."

Alyce rose quickly from her chair and hurried to meet Rappy on the floor for the last dance. As she passed behind the priest still slumped in his chair, she resisted the urge to give his bony shoulder a patronizing pat. She really shouldn't have had that second drink.

Alyce and Rappy didn't get home from the KOC dance until 1:30. Of course, the six children were asleep in their beds. Josephine was asleep on the sofa. Although a bit tipsy from too much beer, Rappy remembered to take off his shoes and tiptoe through the house to their bedroom.

Alyce stood at the end of the sofa and gazed at Josephine covered by a patchwork quilt made by Grandma Fanane in the late '20s for Alyce's hope chest. Luckily it was too late to awaken Josie and drive her out to Trinity Gardens. That meant Alyce would have to be up at six to get Josie home early to work in her vegetable garden on Sunday, her only day off from cleaning white folks' houses and caring for their children.

"Lucky I've never needed a lot of sleep," Alyce murmured to herself as she slipped out of her pumps and padded through the house.

In the bedroom she found Rappy sitting on the edge of the bed in only his boxer shorts, grinning like a school boy privy to a naughty secret.

"He talked to you, didn't he?" Rappy's grin evolved into a smug smile.

"Shh! . . . You'll wake up the children!" Alyce whispered as she placed her shoes on top of her cedar chest and quickly stepped out of her skirt.

"Father Kerns talked to you about me joining the KOC, didn't he?" he cocked his head, pleased with himself.

"How did you know?" she stood facing the window and reached behind her neck to unfasten the buttons which trailed down the back of her navy rayon blouse.

He sprang from the bed and pressed close behind her, the two of them standing in the light of the October harvest moon peeking through the Venetian blinds. He removed her hands from behind her neck and unbuttoned the blouse, quickly from top to bottom.

"I *knew* Father talked with you because he didn't even *try* to talk with me!" Rappy whispered, his mouth close to her ear as he slid the blouse down her arms.

"So, what does *that* mean?" she gave a hushed throaty laugh in the half-darkness.

"It means you convinced him it would be pointless to talk with me about joining the KOC!"

"I don't want you to join," she turned slowly to face him.

"Because they wouldn't let Romie in?" he slid the blouse down her arms and let it fall to the floor, leaving her standing in the moon-light in only her lace-trimmed nylon slip.

"Because you've taken a stand. And I respect you for that," she cocked her head.

"Ah, you *respect* me!" his hands started at her elbows—he slowly worked his way to her shoulders as he massaged her upper arms.

"Now don't get the bighead!" she slid her arms around his neck.

She leaned into him as he kissed her on the lips. She pulled him toward her more closely. She rolled her head to the side as his lips slid down her neck. Over his shoulder she imagined a silhouette in the doorway. She blinked her eyes twice until she could determine which child had stumbled into their bedroom. It was six year-old Tommy in his red flannel pajamas rubbing his eyes and staring at his Mama and Daddy in the moonlight.

"What do you need, Tommy?" Alyce remained in her husband's arms as she whispered over his shoulder.

"I need to go to the bathroom and I can't find Grandma! *Rappy's* in her bed! What'd Rappy do with Grandma?!" the child gazed at his parents in bewilderment.

"Grandma's living with Uncle Tom and Emma now. Did you forget?" Alyce whispered.

"I need Grandma! I need to *tee-tee!*" his voice bordered on quiet hysteria.

Quickly Alyce broke free and swept the child through the hall and into the bathroom. Five minutes later she returned to the bedroom expecting to find Rappy asleep under the covers. But he was still at the window, gazing through the blinds at the moon. She came up behind him, slid her arms around his bare chest, and laid her cheek on his back.

"I respect you, Rappy. I really do."

Their seventh child was conceived that night, and was born on July 11, 1950. Rappy wanted another boy, and he was determined to name him after Romie.

♪♪♪

"Bless me, Father, for I have sinned. It's been two weeks since my last Confession."

"Ah, Alyce, always lovely to hear from you! . . . You and Rappy are the Salt-of-the-Earth! Bringing Christ all these lovely lambs for his flock!" As usual, Monsignor O'Donoghue spoke so loudly that everyone in the back of the Church knew which penitent had entered his confessional.

"Something happened, Monsignor, that I might have to confess. I don't know if it's a sin or not—you'll have to decide that—but I don't like the way I handled it. I'm guilty of some bad thoughts."

"Well, Alyce, the good Lord doesn't expect us to control what thoughts come into our minds, but He also doesn't allow us to *entertain* bad thoughts, like planning to murder someone."

"I didn't actually *entertain* the thought—I tried to get rid of it—but I blamed something on somebody and it wasn't her fault."

"You're too mysterious, Alyce! Start from the beginning."

"Well, Mickey came home from school last week with a terrible itch."

"There's always some child at St. Mary's with lice. What grade is Mickey in?"

"Sixth, Monsignor, but it wasn't lice. I checked her head."

"So, where was the itch?"

"She had a rash all over her body, mostly her arms and legs—and some on her stomach."

"Sounds like bedbugs."

"That's what I thought, Monsignor. I thought she had sat next to some classmate who'd brought bedbugs from home, but the Sister said no other parent had called with a problem. That's when I checked everybody else in the house and all the mattresses."

"You need to boil the sheets.—that's what my mother does in Ireland."

"I boiled the sheets on Mickey and Shirley's bed—they sleep in a double—and then put Mickey in a rollaway bed in the living room until we found out what it was."

"What was it? . . . Impetigo?"

"I'm getting to that, Monsignor. Before I found out what caused it, I blamed Josephine. That's my sin, I think."

"Now, who's Josephine?"

"The colored woman who works for me. She slept on the sofa all night when Rappy and I went to the KOC dance last month, and I blamed her for leaving bedbugs on the sofa."

"Maybe she did! . . . Where's the sin, my dear?"

"Before I found out it wasn't bedbugs—or *any* bug—I blamed it on Josephine because she's a colored person."

208

"A lot of colored people don't have adequate plumbing to bathe regularly. Just like most *white* people in my country! The Irish don't bathe everyday like you do here in this great country, Alyce."

"But Josephine is cleaner than a lot of white people! And I *knew* that! She smells of lye soap when she walks in the door so I know she bathes before she leaves home—or maybe the night before—and she wears a starched white uniform to work! Clean and spotless!"

"So, your sin is that you blamed your colored woman for leaving bedbugs on the sofa?"

"I blamed her because she's colored."

"Maybe you blamed her because she's the only person outside the family who slept overnight—whether she's colored or not—assuming that Mickey didn't pick up the bugs at school?"

"The skin doctor said it was the shingles, Monsignor."

"Ah, the *shingles*! . . . One of our holy Sisters came down with that two years ago. Very painful! It's caused by stress, they say."

"The shingles can be *set off* by stress. But I think Mickey's itch was only hives. She's too young to have shingles."

"Hives?"

"Hives *or* shingles. . . . Either one can be set off by stress, but shingles don't itch—they hurt! That's what Dr. Dowling said, and I trust him more than the skin doctor. So, you see, it had nothing to do with Josephine."

"Where's the sin, Alyce?"

"I blamed her for the itch."

"Did you confront her?"

"No, Monsignor, by the time she came back to work, I had taken Mickey to the skin doctor and found out it was shingles . . . or hives."

"You weren't entertaining bad thoughts, Alyce, you were merely trying to find the cause of the itch in case all your other children had been exposed to the bedbugs, . . . if indeed it *had* been bedbugs."

"I boiled Mickey's sheets right away but I didn't want to have to boil every sheet in the house before I found out what was causing the itch!"

"So, Mickey's in the sixth grade, eh? You should consider finding the cause of stress, don't you think, Alyce?"

"She might be putting *herself* under stress, Monsignor. She makes straight A's and plays basketball, sings in the choir, and all that. And she helps me at home a lot—I couldn't get supper ready on time if she and Shirley didn't help in the kitchen."

"A twelve year-old girl like Mickey may be feeling the advent of womanhood, if you know what I mean, Alyce."

"But, Monsignor, she's awfully young to be going through that just yet."

"Well, a young girl's body at that age can have stirrings that cause her concern because she has no idea what's going on inside of her, eh?"

"Maybe, Monsignor."

"Tell her to stay close to the Blessed Virgin and all will be fine!"

"We just made another novena to Our Lady of the Miraculous Medal, Monsignor."

"Now, before I give you absolution, Alyce, tell me why Rappy won't join the Knights of Columbus!"

♩♩♩♩

By February of 1950, shortly after her 37th birthday, Alyce felt certain she was pregnant again. Because her periods had been irregular all her life, she often went two months without a menstrual cycle. After skipping four consecutive periods this time, she felt safe in telling Rappy that she was expecting their seventh child. A week later she made an appointment with Dr. Dowling who merely confirmed what she already knew—she was four months along.

"Well you know I want to name him after Romie," Rappy was standing in the kitchen doorway finishing a second cup of coffee before catching his ride to work.

"It might not be a boy," Alyce was individually wrapping four ham sandwiches with waxed paper and sliding them into brown paper bags for the children's lunches.

"But if it *is*, we name him Romie, okay with you, Hickory?"

"Let's name him 'Jerome', not 'Romie',"

"Of course! His birth certificate will say 'Jerome Leopold' but we'll call him 'Romie'."

"*You* can call him 'Romie'—I'm gonna call him 'Jerry'."

"Jerry?"

"I don't like the name 'Romie',"

"You were *crazy* about Romie!"

"I was crazy about your *brother*! But I never liked his nickname."

"Hickory! . . . You never said anything about this before *now*!" Rappy grabbed his overcoat as he heard his co-worker at the curb blowing the horn.

"It sounds like a *gypsy* name . . . 'Romie' does," Alyce reached down to pick up Cathy hanging onto her knees to avoid Rappy's stare.

"Well, we'll just wait and see," he turned in a huff and headed for the front door.

"You can wait and see," she murmured to his back, "but any *boy*-baby's gonna be *called* 'Jerry'."

♪♪♪♪

That afternoon when Josephine finished ironing the boys' white shirts, she appeared in the kitchen where Alyce was getting an early start on supper. Alyce stood at the counter chopping onions while she held the one year-old Cathy balanced on her hip. Shirley sat on one side of the kitchen table struggling through her fourth-grade Arithmetic homework while Snookums sat on the other side eating a bowl of Rice Krispies.

Tommy was across the street playing doctor-and-nurse with his first grade classmate, Mimi Sullivan. Both Rappy and Mickey were at basketball practice after school. He would ride home on his bicycle—she'd walk with three friends who lived in the neighborhood. Safety in numbers—no need to worry about the four girls walking the ten blocks from St. Mary's, as long as they were in their homes before five o'clock.

"I guess you're ready to get your carfare and leave," Alyce placed Cathy in the highchair and washed the onion juice from her hands.

"No'm, I ain't ready to leave just yet," Josephine said, glancing around the small kitchen in search of some utensil.

"What're you looking for?"

"I need them little black frying pans—the *iron* ones!"

"Josephine, are you planning to make cornbread right now?" Alyce knew what was coming next.

"Mr. Pee-rez be home for supper tonight? He ain't got the banking school tonight—not on Monday, do he?" Josephine gazed at her employer with wide hopeful eyes.

"He's coming home for supper, but you don't have to make him cornbread."

"One of 'em' gonna be for *me*! . . . And you don't never make him *yellow* pan-bread—the kind he likes!"

"I can't make any cornbread very well—mine's always too dry. And I don't see how you cook it on top of the stove—I bake it in the oven but it still comes out dry."

"Well, I guess I could show you, but—," Josephine was reluctant to share her bargaining chip.

"I never have time to bake bread, Josephine, you know that! Now, I was hoping to get the supper underway right now."

"I'm gonna help you! . . . I got a mess of turnip greens in my bag back there—you know how Mr. Pee-rez likes my turnip greens and yellow cornbread—so what was you planning to fix?"

"Pork chops."

"Mmm, pork do real good with the greens and cornbread. Let's get started," she headed for the cupboard to pull out the corn meal.

"Oh, Josephine!" Alyce rolled her eyes in surrender and searched the lower cabinet for the two little cast-iron skillets which she'd inherited from Grandma Fanane.

Alyce abandoned the stove to Josephine. With Cathy on her lap she sat at the kitchen table to help Shirley with long division. She knew better than to argue once Josephine made up her mind to make cornbread for Rappy. Any day that Josephine arrived at Laurel Street with a mess of greens and set out to make "pan-bread" for Mr. Pee-rez, Alyce was powerless to dissuade her. It had become a ritual about 4-6 times a year, usually when Josephine's quarterly Blue Cross bill arrived for her health insurance.

The greens and yellow cornbread were collateral for the loan. Usually Josephine wanted to borrow $5.00, a sizeable sum for a domestic maid in 1950 when her wage for a full day's work was only $2.00 plus carfare.

Josephine knew that she could soften up Rappy with the cornbread and hit him for a loan. It always worked. The minute he came in the front door and smelled the cornbread on top of the stove, his resistance collapsed. And the cornbread was inevitably accompanied by a dish of fresh turnip greens from Josephine's garden. The greens were boldly seasoned with bacon drippings and a ham-hock.

"Thank you, Mr. Pee-rez, for the loan! I pay you back next month after the other white folks pay my wages. You *knows* I gonna pay you back!" the tiny woman promised as she struggled out the back door under all her shopping bags and bundles, hurrying to catch the last bus to Trinity Gardens.

But she never paid back the loans.

"You know she's taking you for a ride," Alyce felt it her duty to remind Rappy.

"Well, *you* don't have time to make cornbread!" he was mildly defensive as he sopped the last of the greens' liquor with the last crust of cornbread.

"We'll never see *that* five dollars again," she stopped clearing the dishes and sat at the dining table next to her husband.

"Or any of the other ones," he leaned back, gave a smile of gourmet contentment, and patted his stomach, recently expanding at the age of forty-two into a middle-aged spread.

"*Or*, any in the future! . . . So what're you gonna do?"

213

"Well, Hickory, I'll just put $5.00 less in the collection basket at church this month."

"I guess you're right, Rappy. . . . Charity is charity. And Josie deserves it as much as anyone."

♪♪♪♪

That February of 1950 was the third year Rappy rode the Mardi Gras float as a member the *Infant Mystics* crewe. The year before he rode in the parade, but he had to attend the ball alone. Olivia and Joe Midgette took the four older children downtown to see their daddy on the float, but Alyce, eight months pregnant with Cathy, stayed home with Snookums while she nursed swollen ankles and varicose veins.

But this year Alyce was preparing early by having her mother create a new ball gown for the Grand March. When Rappy emerged from the stage tableau and descended the steps with the other nineteen members from Float #5, she planned to be sitting in the middle of the dance floor in her folding chair with all of the other Call-outs. This year Rappy wouldn't be standing behind an empty chair.

Three years after induction, both Alyce and Rappy still marveled that he had been tapped to join one of Mobile's more elite Mardi Gras associations. The *Infant Mystics* was the second oldest crewe that still paraded. There were a couple of older Mardi Gras societies that hosted a ball, invitation only, but they no longer built floats and paraded. Only the *Order of Myths* was older than Rappy's society, and they were older by one year only. The *OOM's* were founded in 1867 and staged their first parade in 1868, the same year that the IM's were founded and paraded through downtown Mobile.

"I'm still amazed that Rappy got in the *IM's*. We're not *Old* Mobile society," Alyce was helping her mother glue silver sequins onto the floor-length skirt of a red tulle strapless ball gown. The two women sat on the living room floor with the full-skirt spread between them like a giant red camellia as they spaced the single sequins six inches

214

apart. At a given signal from Miss Alice, they lifted the skirt on opposite sides and turned it twelve inches clockwise until, two hours later, the entire skirt was splattered with silver sequins. The two women had created a meteor explosion of tiny silver stars showering across the vermillion tulle.

"Frankly, I was surprised that Thomas got in," Miss Alice spoke through a mouth full of straight pins clenched in her teeth, a habit of any good seamstress.

"But Bubber still has his Spring Hill College contacts—he had lots of Old Mobile boys in his classes—and then there's his boss at International Paper."

"Rappy's lucky that Mr. McRae's taken such a shine to him," Miss Alice murmured.

"Rappy says it's because so many *IM* members were killed in the war—or came back so depressed from combat-fatigue that they don't want to do Mardi Gras anymore."

"That many?"

"He says they needed to replenish the ranks. Mr. McRae called a bunch of department managers into his office—Rappy included—and told them to go to the next *IM* meeting, even gave them directions to the secret location of the den, and told 'em they'd been voted in. They were already *members*!"

"I noticed a lot of the new *IM* members are Catholics, like Crane, Sorrentino, Mattei."

"Yes, M'am," Alyce continued working on the skirt. "Rappy says if there hadn't been a war the *IM's* surely wouldn't have let in *that* many Catholics, not at one time anyway."

"You know, Alyce, when I worked for Mr. DeCelle he told me how the *Infant Mystics* was founded to begin with. It seems that the first members were *sons* of the *Order of Myths* members. Those Old Mobile daddies in the *OOMs* didn't want their grown sons in the same organization for fear the boys would tell their mamas what really goes on after those meetings at the secret den."

"So that's why it's called *Infant* Mystics?"

"Apparently so! . . . The first *IM* members were the sons of the *OOMs*. But I'm sure they did the same stuff after their secret meetings as their daddies did."

"Rappy's already told me about the crap game," Alyce continued working on the skirt.

"*Crap?* . . . That's a cuss word, isn't it?"

"*Dice* game, Mama! . . . After the meeting they hang around and drink and shoot dice. Rappy sets a limit for himself. He never loses more than $5.00, and not even that much if Josephine fixed yellow cornbread that afternoon and took his last five dollar bill."

"Let's see how this looks *on* you!" Miss Alice struggled to her feet, dragging the red net gown after her.

"I'm gonna have to wear that Merry Widow," Alyce took the dress from her mother and laid it on the sofa as she searched the room for the corset.

"I hope that Merry Widow don't squeeze the baby too much!"

"Mama, I'm only four months along."

"You're already showing a bit."

"Only cuz my stomach muscles are stretched from being pregnant six times already!"

"You're gonna need that Merry Widow to hold up your bosoms. Nursing those six babies made your bosoms sag, you know."

"You don't need to remind me, Mama!"

"Well, that Merry Widow'll hold 'em up and point 'em out real nice. I made the bodice nice 'n roomy cuz I know you're gonna fill it out."

Alyce located the Merry Widow corset in an overstuffed chair. She sank into the chair and held up the corset, stretching it back and forth to test its elasticity. Miss Alice got down on her hands and knees to search for any straight pins that may have become embedded in the living room carpet.

"We can't have any of these children running barefoot in here and sticking a straight pin through the big toe!" Miss Alice slowly ran her palms over the rug in large sweeping circles.

"Is it too good to be true, Mama?" Alyce spoke softly as she continued to play with the corset.

"What's true, Alyce?" she spoke absent-mindedly as her gaze swept back and forth across the rug.

"My *life*! . . . Next month we pay off the mortgage on this house—it's been nine years since we moved in here in March of '41, and somehow Rappy managed to pay it off in less than the ten year contract."

"Rappy's good with money—he just don't have a lot *of* it."

"But they still haven't made him a bank officer yet—and he's been with 'em for twenty-one years," Alyce played with the label on the corset.

"Well, I still say he did right by not going to college at night. He gets a raise every year, don't he?"

"Yes M'am, but the younger boys with college degrees are just climbing up the ladder and stepping right over Rappy."

"You might count your blessings, Alyce."

"And they are *many*, Mama! . . . When we were downtown on Bayou and Savannah, did you ever think that Bubber and Rappy'd belong to the *Infant Mystics*?"

"I'll tell you what *I* never thought! . . . I never thought I'd end up with all these grandchildren—your six, seven come summer, and two of Thomas's."

"We've got a lot to be thankful for, Mama."

"Indeed you do! . . . All your children are healthy and . . . *normal*."

"You're thinking of Little Tom Hicks, aren't you?"

"Just stay close to the Lord, Alyce, and He'll take care of you."

"I pray every night to the Blessed Mother to make this one healthy too."

"This should be your lucky year, Alyce. Pope Pius XII's gone and declared it a *Holy Year*"

"What's that mean?"

"I have no idea. But the pope says 1950 is a *Holy Year*!

Fawn River
South Mobile County, Alabama
January 21, 2012

"YOUR HUSBAND NEVER joined the Knights of Columbus, did he?" I stood at the window gazing towards the marsh.

"What're you looking at?" she opened her eyes and shifted herself in the recliner.

"I'm waiting for your blue heron to return."

"Ever since that BP oil spill, he doesn't keep a regular schedule."

"Did the oil come this far up into the river?"

"No," she closed her eyes, "we're quite a few miles from Dauphin Island—from the coast—and the river current pushes water into the bay and eventually into the Gulf, but ever since the oil leak, the birds have been confused."

"Disoriented, I'd imagine."

"These marshes up here in the river were spared the oil pollution, but probably the birds don't trust *any* marsh, not after all they've been through."

"You didn't answer me," I said. "Did your husband ever join the Knights of Columbus?"

"They stopped asking him."

"Would you consider yourself a devout Catholic?

"I never knew what that means," she chuckled.

"Everybody says you have such a strong faith in God."

"I've done a lot of charity work for the Church, if that's what you mean."

"That's not what I was getting at."

"Sometimes I think Rappy had a stronger faith than me—he had the responsibility of feeding us all."

"You were president of the Ladies of Charity, weren't you?"

"Everybody had to take a turn at that. It was no big deal."

"So what about this Knight of St. Gregory honor?"

"Rappy deserved it. He took care of money for St. Mary's for years—as well as accounts for other parishes. The bishops had him raising funds for all kind of causes, and then there were all those spaghetti suppers."

"It was your spaghetti sauce recipe, right?"

"Anybody can make a decent spaghetti sauce if the ground beef isn't too fatty."

"You got the volunteer help together and organized all the ladies, no?"

"But Rappy telephoned all the wholesalers to beg for free food—ground beef, pasta, bread, salad fixings—he had a tough job."

"So you two worked as a team."

"You could say that," she opened her eyes wide as if she had just witnessed a revelation.

"They don't have an honor for a *Lady* of St. Gregory?"

"The Church doesn't think much of women, not even the Sisters."

"What about all the changes in the Church after Vatican II?"

"What about 'em?"

"Did you agree with them?"

"It was great not having to wear a hat in church anymore."

"Is that all?"

"I didn't like the way they chopped up that beautiful high altar in

220

St. Mary's. Somebody'll have to answer to God for that!"

"What about eating meat on Friday?"

"You know," she laughed as she closed her eyes again, "right after they said we could eat meat on Friday, Rappy cornered every priest we came across—even in the middle of a nice restaurant—and asked him if Julius was burning in hell right now. Julius was an older brother who was known to eat hot dogs on Friday when he owned the Tiny Diny . . . And you know, not one priest would dare to make a judgment. Rappy'd keep needling the priests to give a 'yes-or-no' answer, but they never did. He could be devilish, Rappy could."

"So, would you say that your faith got you through the bad times?"

"Is that heron back yet? . . . The blue one?"

CHAPTER **12**

Why am I still groggy from the anesthesia? It's never taken me this long to come around!

Who was that sitting by the bed just staring at me while I tried to wake up? Rappy? Where'd he go?

And who stuck his head inside the door a minute ago? That man wearing a funny collar. . . . A priest?

Where's Dr. Dowling? He always drops by when I wake up.

Where's the baby? . . . Why won't that charge-nurse bring me the baby? Where's the baby?

ALYCE'S SEVENTH CHILD was born on July 11, 1950 at four in the afternoon.

Although he was full-term, he weighed only 4 pounds, 10 ounces.

He was baptized ten minutes later in the delivery room. Alyce, still in that twilight half-sleep from ether given in the last stage of labor, had been swiftly carted away to her room as soon as Dr. Dowling realized the baby was in distress. When he held the infant by his feet, he noticed immediately that the baby's legs were limp. Unlike a normal newborn, this one wasn't squirming. His arms were flailing a bit and he was crying feebly, but he wasn't squalling like a healthy newborn.

The hall outside the Delivery Room filled with nurses as soon as word spread that a newborn in Delivery was 'in trouble'. Some nurses rushed to offer assistance while others gathered in curiosity as they sipped Coca-Colas and nibbled on cheese crackers from the vending machine.

Dowling calmly instructed a nurse to fetch the chaplain. This baby might not live even an hour. The Allen Memorial Hospital was operated by the Catholic Diocese. Any newborn in distress was baptized immediately, regardless of the mother's religious affiliation.

"You don't need a priest, Doctor," his attending nurse said as she put drops in the infant's eyes. "I'm a Catholic. I can baptize a baby in an emergency."

"You might *have* to! . . . But let's give the chaplain five minutes. Besides, we might need him to console the parents if the little fellow dies. . . . Tell one of those nurses to find the father and bring him in here!"

A third nurse was sent to find the staff pediatrician. Dr. Dowling had seen this deformity before but he'd forgotten the medical terminology. Yet he didn't need the correct vocabulary to make his own diagnosis as a General Practitioner:

> *Apparent paralysis of the legs, maybe more. Affixed to the base of the spine is an exterior growth the size of a small egg.*
> *The head appears larger than normal. Possible hydrocephalus.*

Within two minutes the nurse returned with Rappy who stood next to the bassinet at the doctor's elbow. Rappy stared at his newest son, this tiny listless child with his legs frozen as his torso squirmed in discomfort.

Seconds later the pediatrician arrived. After giving the newborn a quick examination, he made his pronouncement:

Spina bifida.

He sent a nurse to Providence Hospital next door to find a neurologist. A specialist was needed to confirm the hasty diagnosis, and then to explain the dismal prognosis to the parents.

The chaplain arrived empty-handed. He grabbed a stainless-steel cup from the sink and filled it with tap water. The attending nurse reached to lift the baby's head but the pediatrician grabbed her hand.

"Let me do it," the doctor carefully rolled the infant on his side to examine the *bifida* at the base of the spine.

"Have you chosen a name?" the priest asked impatiently as he held the metal cup with water dripping down the side.

"It's a boy," Dr. Dowling placed his hand on Rappy's shoulder.

"Why are we baptizing him? Is he going to die?" Rappy gazed in bewilderment at the physician who had delivered five of his six older children.

"We have to play it hour-by-hour," the pediatrician supported the infant's head with one hand and examined the limp legs with his other.

"If he's about to die, I can't name him 'Romie'," Rappy gazed at the baby rolled on his side.

"A name is not essential to baptize him, Mr. Perez," the priest held the cup of water over the baby's head, "but if he dies in the next few minutes, it'll be more personal for your wife if he has a name!"

"My brother Louis," Rappy mumbled. "Name him 'Louis', after my oldest brother."

The priest launched into an impromptu ritual to administer the sacrament of Baptism:

"Louis, I baptize you in the name of the Father, and of—" the priest let the water dribble down the back of the infant's head covered in fine black hair and still damp from the birth canal.

"A second name!" Rappy blurted.

"And of the Son, and of the Holy Ghost," the priest ignored Rappy's outburst.

"Alyce would want two names!"

"You can add a second name when you fill out the birth certificate, . . . and when your parish church types up the baptismal certificate. For right now, we welcome our newest member into the Communion of the Faithful. . . . And his name is 'Louis'."

"Is he going to die?" Rappy repeated the question to the pediatrician.

"I told you, Mr. Perez, 'we play it *hour-by-hour*'!" he was towel-drying the newborn's hair from the baptismal water.

"He's baptized into the Church now, Mr. Perez," the young chaplain joined his hands in prayer at his chest. "If he dies now, he'll go straight to heaven."

"I just can't name him 'Romie,'" Rappy was gazing at the newborn as the pediatrician pushed gently on the tiny chest in an effort to help him breathe more easily.

"Now, we need prayer," the priest closed his eyes and began to murmur.

"Now, we need a neurologist," the impatient pediatrician glanced at Dr. Dowling. "What's taking him so long?"

♪♪♪

Alyce was prepared for the worst. She knew there was something wrong with the baby when the nurses hadn't brought him to her. She estimated it had been more than two hours since she woke up in her room. When she asked why they hadn't brought her the baby, they avoided eye contact and offered feeble excuses.

"Some country-woman just had triplets, and we're understaffed on this 3-11 shift, and some nurses are on supper break! We'll bring him as soon as I can free up a pair of hands! . . . Why don't you just lie there and rest? You just had a baby!"

Alyce reluctantly took the sleeping pill they gave her at 8:00 p.m. and dozed off. When she awoke, it was 7:00 the next morning. The sun was streaming through her window—she was ready to nurse her baby.

At 9:00 a.m. the door opened and three men entered to tell her what she'd already figured out.

Monsignor O'Donoghue pulled up the straight-backed chair and sat close to the bed. At age sixty the tall Irish priest was still able to sit erect in the chair with his knees close together. Rappy and Dr.

Dowling stood at the foot of the bed. Rappy cranked the bed into a higher position so she could see everyone at once.

"God has sent you an angel, Alyce!" the monsignor beamed as he placed his large hands on his knees and leaned forward in the metal chair.

"An angel? . . . Does that mean it's dead?" Alyce glanced at Dr. Dowling for a frank answer.

"He's alive, Alyce," the doctor smiled and touched the covers at the foot of the bed. "But we have him on oxygen."

"Oxygen! . . . What's *that* for? . . . And did you say '*he*'? . . . It's a boy?" she propped herself up on her elbow.

"To help him breathe, Alyce. He's weak and struggling to breathe, but that's probably exhaustion from just being born," Dowling stared at the floor.

"Did something happen during the delivery? . . . While I was under the ether?"

"It was routine—like all your deliveries—but it's called 'labor' not just for the mother! It's work for the baby too, you know!" he gave his wide compassionate smile.

"You have an angel, Alyce!" the kind monsignor leaned forward again and touched her on the forearm.

"Why's he an angel?" she glanced at all three men, one at a time.

"He's crippled, Alyce," Rappy said. "Paralyzed."

"*Paralyzed?*"

"Only from the waist down, Alyce," the doctor continued to smile.

"So he's crippled! Lots of children are born crippled. Why's he on oxygen? Why does it take three of you to come in here just to tell me my baby's crippled? What's going *on*?" she heard her voice becoming louder. She was determined not to become hysterical, but she needed answers.

"He has a serious problem with his spine. The base of his spine is open and the nerves don't extend into the legs. The nerves are in a ball—a growth—at the base of the spine. And fluid has backed up the spinal column into his head. Probably there's some pressure on the brain. I've brought in a neurologist to examine him—a specialist on the brain and spinal column. He's with your baby now."

"We baptized him, Alyce," Rappy said quietly, "just in case . . . in case something happens."

"So there's a chance he could die any minute?" she asked matter-of-factly.

"The baby-doctor said we'll have to play it 'hour-by-hour'," Rappy fidgeted.

"We'll know more as soon as I return to the nursery and talk to the neurologist," Dowling turned for the door.

"He could already be dead by the time you get back, right?"

"He'll go straight to heaven, Alyce," the monsignor sat back in the chair and sighed in smug conviction. "He's been baptized into Holy Mother the Church. If the good Lord has already taken him, then he's joined the Communion of the Saints! . . . You have an *angel*, Alyce!"

"But if he's not dead yet, Monsignor, how can he be an angel?" she glared at the priest.

"He has a physical affliction, Alyce! God gives afflictions only to those who can bear them. You have an innocent baby who's done no ill to anyone, who hasn't yet committed any sin against God. The holy waters of Baptism have removed all trace of Original Sin which we inherit from Adam. As an innocent soul, with God's infinite grace, your baby-boy will bear his affliction joyfully. Whether he lives or dies, Alyce, he's a true angel!"

"I don't want an angel, Monsignor. I want a healthy baby."

"We're going to do whatever we can, Alyce," Dr. Dowling said as he slipped out the door. "And try to get some sleep—you were in labor most of yesterday."

The monsignor followed the doctor out of the room, leaving Rappy alone with his wife.

"If he lives, I want to call him 'Jerry'," Alyce adjusted her cotton bed-jacket as she slid farther under the bedcovers.

"You don't have to worry about that," Rappy eased himself onto the metal chair.

"I imagine you baptized him 'Jerome', but I don't want to call him 'Romie'—you already *know* that—and you ought to do this for me. I don't ask for much, Rappy, but I'm asking for *this*," she let her head sink more deeply into the pillow.

"I couldn't name him 'Romie'—I mean "Jerome"—I just couldn't do it," he turned away, knowing his face would betray his shame. His vanity prohibited him from assigning his favorite brother's name to this crippled child who probably wouldn't live.

"Oh," she was speechless.

"He's named 'Louis'."

"*Louis*?"

"He's having a hard time in New Orleans right now. Maybe this will help him somehow if he finds out we named a baby after him."

"You've got to stop sending him money," she muttered as she squirmed to get comfortable in the bed.

"I thought he really needed surgery when he wrote me," he said weakly.

"You know he's drinking again. That story about needing surgery was just a lie to get money out of you for booze."

"Well, maybe God'll help both of them—Louis *and* this new baby—cuz both of them need God's help."

"You've got to stop trusting Louis," her voice had become hollow, as if she were talking to herself.

"I think they'll be able to cure this baby someday, Alyce, if he lives long enough. Surely science will figure out how to fix this little fellow so he can walk. Or surely God will send a miracle. Jesus made the lame walk in the Bible, didn't He? You believe in miracles, don't you, Hickory? . . . I know you and your mama are big on God's Will, but can't we accept this as God's Will and pray for a miracle at the same time?"

She couldn't answer. She was staring at the sun rays streaming through the Venetian blinds.

An hour later Alyce finally saw the baby. The door opened and the nurse swept into the room with the newborn cradled in her arms. Despite the July heat outside and the lack of air-conditioning in the old hospital building, the infant was swaddled in several layers of white flannel receiving blankets. Only the very top of his head—covered in glossy black hair—was visible.

"Your pediatrician's in the nursery," the nurse waited patiently until Alyce shifted herself into a sitting position against the headboard.

"Dr. Adams is here?" she was unbuttoning her bed-jacket to get to her nightgown.

"We've already started him on formula," the nurse continued to wait.

"But I'm gonna nurse him!" Alyce was unbuttoning the front of her nightgown so she could breastfeed the infant.

"Dr. Adams said you're not," the nurse's voice was curt.

"I nursed all my children!"

"I told you, Mrs. Perez, we've already started him on formula—doctor's orders! This infant has too many complications. Dr. Adams says you're *not* nursing him, but you can hold him for ten minutes," the nurse gently lowered the baby into Alyce's arms.

Alyce cradled the baby as the nurse stood close to the bed.

"Can you leave so I can be alone with him?" Alyce gazed at the infant asleep in her arms.

"No, M'am, I can't leave. If he gets into trouble, I'll have to hurry him to the nursery and put him back on oxygen."

"Can I take these blankets off? . . . So I can see his legs?"

"There's nothing to see—they look like any baby's legs only he can't move them."

"I want to see the growth on his back."

"It's not his back—it's on the base of his spine—but Dr. Adams won't let me take off the bandage. He said to keep it dressed to protect against infection—at least until the neurologist shows me how to change the bandage. Now, *he* might say the bandage isn't necessary, but until he gets here, we're keeping it dressed . . . and *I'm* keeping him wrapped up in these blankets."

"Where *is* this neurologist?"

"He's still making his rounds at the Mobile Infirmary. When he gets here, I'll wake you up so you can talk to him."

"I'm not going to sleep."

"What's the name of that neurologist Dr. Adams called in?"

"Dr. Patton."

♪♪♪

That night Miss Alice helped Alyce into her dressing gown and slowly the two women walked to the nursery. They stood in the hall with their noses pressed against the glass picture window.

"He looks like all your babies, Alyce!" Miss Alice chirped.

"Yes, but I think he's the prettiest. . . . Isn't that ironic?" Alyce talked softly, still weak from the delivery the day before.

"Why? Because he's crippled?"

"His skin is so white—it's translucent," Alyce was almost whispering.

"My, he does have a beautiful face!" Miss Alice laughed, determined that her daughter wouldn't slip into melancholy.

"His head doesn't look too big to me."

"Well, maybe it won't swell! . . . We'll just trust in the Lord, Alyce!"

"Dr. Patton said it should start soon . . . the swelling."

"He looks normal, Alyce, except that he's not moving his legs."

"And except for that oxygen tank standing next to his bassinet."

"Well, I don't think this baby's gonna die."

"Why do you say that?"

"For one thing, he's got too many people praying for him! I tell you, Alyce, the phone's been ringing off the hook at Laurel Street. It seems everybody in Mobile—not just Catholics—I mean, *everybody's* praying for him, . . . and for *you!*"

231

"I wonder what I did to cause this, Mama," Alyce's voice became shaky.

"What *you* did? . . . You didn't do anything, Alyce! Babies are born crippled all the time! This was just God's Will!"

"I've been thinking it might've been caused by something I did during the pregnancy, you know? Maybe towards the end I shouldn't have been reaching down to lift up Cathy so much. Sometimes I'd pick her up and find myself off balance. You know, with your belly so big and swaying all over the place, it's easy to get off balance. Sometimes I'd even fall down. Well, not all the way to the floor—I'd catch myself on one knee."

"Fiddlesticks, Alyce!"

"Seems like toward the end I was falling down a lot—getting off balance and falling down while doing housework."

"That don't hurt a baby! A pregnant woman has too much padding. All that water floating around in there *protects* the baby. You're talking crazy!"

"I recall Rappy's mama saying I shouldn't have bounced Cathy on my stomach like I did, but I thought Grandma Perez was just being overly cautious."

"She *was*! . . . Nellie's an alarmist! That's where Margie gets it from!"

"I wonder if I'm being punished for something," Alyce's voice echoed Catholic guilt.

"My stars! Punished for *what*?"

"I don't know, Mama, maybe something I did when I was young."

"God don't work that way, Alyce!"

"But I was a good girl. I mean, nothing happened before we got married. Rappy was the first man I ever . . . I ever—*you* know!"

"You're a good wife, Alyce, and a fine mother! You're not being punished for a single thing!"

"Then what is it, Mama?"

"It's the will of the Lord."

One week later when three Sisters of Mercy made an unannounced visit at the hospital, Alyce was fully dressed to go home. Sitting on the edge of the bed, she was waiting patiently to be discharged by Dr. Dowling when the three nuns breezed in without knocking. With only one metal chair to offer the three, she escorted them down the hall to host them on the overstuffed furniture in the Labor & Delivery waiting room.

The lazy ceiling-fan didn't do much to cool the spacious room. It merely dissipated the heavy mid-summer heat through the dank room. Alyce sat in one of the overstuffed chairs while the three Sisters squeezed onto one sofa, leaving the opposite sofa empty. It was a peculiarly odd feeling for Alyce. Usually when she received the obligatory visit from the Sisters of Mercy to meet a Perez newborn, she was at home sitting on her own living room sofa in her favorite dressing gown and cradling the infant in her arms.

"Will we be able to see the precious little angel?" Sister Mary Dorothy cooed in her Irish brogue.

"Of course, Sister! He's with the neurologist right now, but you can see him on the way out," Alyce relaxed into the easy chair and prepared herself for the unwelcome flood of flattery the nuns delivered after a new baby was added to the Perez family.

"Ah, you're the *Salt-of-the Earth*, Alyce!" the prim Sister Mary of Mercy spoke through pursed lips. "You and Rappy are just the Salt-of-the Earth!"

"Bringing all these new lambs to the flock!" Sister Mary Dorothy fluttered her hands as if she were shooing sheep.

"Our Lord, the Good Shepherd, is mighty pleased with you and Rappy!" Sister Mercy held up her right hand as if she were going to bestow a hand-blessing on Alyce.

The third nun sat at the end of the sofa in silence. Alyce had never met her before and concluded that since no one bothered to introduce her, she wasn't a force to reckon with. Each time someone spoke, she nodded her head vigorously in agreement and beamed until her fat, fleshy face—squeezed into a mound of pie-dough inside the white starched wimple—turned apple-red with childlike glee.

"We're all praying for the little angel, Alyce!" Sister Mary of Mercy continued.

"Praying you can take him home soon!" Sister Dorothy gushed. "Home to all his older brothers and sisters just waiting to receive him into their arms! . . . So when's the little darling going home?"

"We don't know, Sister," Alyce shifted in her chair. She realized these naïve nuns had no idea what awaited her newborn at home. "We didn't know he'd live this long—he's only one week old and still needs oxygen most of the day. The neurologist says we have to play it a week at a time."

"So, maybe he'll be home in the bosom of his family *next* week?"

"I doubt it, Sister. You see, it's not just that he's paralyzed—he's got these neurological problems that—"

"New-row *what?*"

"Problems with *nerves* that don't extend into his legs, and problems with the fluid in his spine that backs up into his head, so that—"

"Ahh, the good Lord can take of that!" Sister Dorothy's brogue had become musical.

"Our entire Mercy community is praying for him, Alyce. Not just the sisters in Mobile but in Pensacola, Birmingham, and even our Mother House in Baltimore!"

"We appreciate the prayers, Sister. Billy needs them."

"*Billy?* . . . Monsignor O'Donoghue said his name was *Louis!* We've been praying for a little angel named *Louis* Perez!"

"That's the baby's first name, . . . 'Louis William Perez'. Rappy and I know lots of fellows named 'William' among friends and family— Bill Serda, Billy O'Connor—so we added 'William.'"

"But shouldn't you call him *Louis?* . . . Wasn't he *baptized* as 'Louis'?!" Sister Mercy's face showed concern, as if a sacrosanct Church law had been broken.

"The staff in the nursery have fallen in love with him. They started calling him 'Billy-Boy', so I went along. They're with him more than I am. And now that I'm going home today, he'll be with them all the time. Besides, I've always liked the name 'Billy', you know."

"But we've been praying all along for *Louis*!"

"Ahh, woman!" Sister Dorothy snickered. "The good Lord surely knows which little angel we're praying for, don't you imagine? . . . No matter which name we use, the Lord will send the miracle, right Alyce?"

"A miracle, Sister? . . . Dr. Patton says he'll never walk. Right now we need a miracle just to keep him alive."

"And there *you* are, Alyce, talking so calmly about keeping the little angel alive when another mother would be crying her heart out. You're such a brave woman, Alyce, and you have so much faith in God's Will. You're an inspiration to all Catholic women!"

I don't feel brave. And I certainly don't feel an inspiration to anybody. I wanna hide under the covers and cry. If I could just sob like a child, I might feel better.

But I've got six children and a husband waiting at home. And with Mama now living with Bubber and Emma, she won't be in the house to help out. If ever there was a time to accept God's Will, this is it.

I'm gonna have to remind myself every hour of the day of Mama's advice:

'You just do what you have to do!'

♪♪♪

Three months later in mid-October Alyce and Rappy sat in the neurologist's office waiting for his latest report.

Billy was still in the hospital.

"When can we bring him home?" Rappy asked cheerily.

"You might never bring him home, Mr. Perez," Dr. Patton used a curt tone to deny Rappy any false hope. "This child is still not out of the woods. You don't understand the severity of the situation."

Alyce liked Dr. Patton. She wasn't intimidated by his apparent brilliance. Better yet, he was able to explain Billy's condition in layman's terms so Alyce could understand at least the basics of her child's complex deformity. And more so, the neurologist encouraged Rappy and her to ask questions. She asked a few. Rappy, on the other hand, was full of questions, all of them leading to the possibility of a cure.

"Don't you have some kind of operation to fix our little boy, Dr. Patton?" Rappy refused to be pessimistic.

"There's no cure.

"But you said he's improving."

"He *is* improving, but he still needs oxygen several times a day. If he makes it through the winter, he might have a chance. But there's the danger of catching an infection in the hospital. A mere virus, like the common cold, could be fatal."

"Rappy, I don't want to bring him home until he's stronger," Alyce spoke up. "It's fall already, and with six children at our house, you know *one* of 'em's gonna bring home a cold from school before Christmas."

"If I see any appreciable change either way—either a marked improvement or a turn for the worse—then I'll call you at home. Otherwise, you all come back for another report in mid-November," the kind doctor had risen from behind his desk to urge them towards the door.

"Rappy," Alyce reached for her purse as she rose from the easy chair, "tell him about the Knights of Columbus offer."

"They've offered to send Billy to a special hospital in Texas," Rappy stopped in the middle of the office. "They plan to raise the money to cover all costs . . . for as long as he needs to stay there."

"*Which* hospital?" the doctor's face showed concern.

"I don't know—some hospital which specializes in treating kids like Billy."

"*Where* in Texas? . . . Which city?"

"They didn't say."

"Find out and let me know."

"We want to know, doctor," Alyce stood next to the chair, "what *you* think of the idea—what you think of sending him to that hospital out there."

"You mean to institutionalize him? . . . If he were my child, I wouldn't do it."

"But what if they can cure him?" Rappy was persistent with the 'cure'.

"Mr. Perez, there *is* no cure for *spina bifida*, and there never will be. Medical science cannot restore nerves where God didn't put them in the first place. The nerves to Billy's legs are rolled up in a ball at the base of his spine. In some cases we remove the growth which stops the fluid from building up in the head, but—"

"When're you gonna do that?" Rappy interjected.

"*But*," the neurologist had become impatient with Rappy's insistence, "although it's too early to tell for sure, it appears that Billy's case is too complicated to remove the *bifida*—that is, the mass—without causing irreparable damage to the brain."

"So you'd never remove it?" Alyce asked.

"Too early to tell. But if you take him to a hospital specializing in rehabilitation, they'll go ahead and remove it without considering the consequences. Their primary concern—I'm assuming from my past experience with these kind of 'miracle-workers'—is to get the child into leg braces and crutches as soon as possible so they can claim a success."

"Well," Rappy said, "maybe a miracle-worker is what we need! . . . . . No offense to you, doctor!"

"None taken, Mr. Perez, but someone would have to go to Texas *with* the child. You can't leave him out there alone with strangers for two or three years."

"Three years?" Alyce was horrified.

"But he's with strangers here at *this* hospital," Rappy said.

"I visit him every day, Rappy!" Alyce had become aggravated.

"If you leave him out there alone," the doctor interrupted, "the emotional stress alone could kill him."

"You visit him everyday, Alyce," Rappy ignored the doctor's warning, "but you say he doesn't know who you *are*!"

"He doesn't know I'm his *mother*, but he does recognize me! He smiles when he sees me . . . *sometimes*! He relaxes in my arms! He's comfortable with me!"

"Mr. Perez, if your wife stays with Billy in Texas, who'll take care of your six children at home?"

"Rappy, Mama *cannot* move back into our house!"

Rappy didn't answer. He slowly approached the door and stared at the brass doorknob. Without turning to face Alyce and the doctor, he then spoke softly.

"We need a miracle. You doctors have to find a cure."

"There *is* no cure, Mr. Perez. You should listen to your wife."

Suddenly Rappy rallied. He spun around and grinned at Alyce.

"Did you hear that, Hickory? The doctor says I should listen to *you*! . . . Man, Doctor Patton, I listen to her all the time. Because when I don't, she reminds me I *ought to*!"

"Besides, Mr. Perez, I doubt your local Knights of Columbus chapter could even afford the cost of daily care for three years at a hospital like that—much less the cost of rehabilitation therapy."

♪♪♪

Alyce didn't visit Billy in the hospital *every* day.

It was her intention to do so, but the logistics were daunting. During the week the four oldest children were at St. Mary's School until three o'clock. The problem was what to do with Snookums at age three and Cathy at age twenty months, both too young for kindergarten. Pre-schools and day-care centers didn't exist in 1950's Mobile.

On days that Mickey and Shirley didn't have basketball practice—or Field Day training in the spring—Alyce charged the two older girls to watch their baby sisters after school so she could dash to the hospital for a 3:30 visit. Back home at 5:00 she dove into preparing supper for a family of eight.

"Stop worrying, Alyce!" Miss Alice reassured her daughter. "It's

238

not like you're putting Mickey and Shirley in charge of two *infants*! Mickey's real responsible at twelve. And although Shirley's a daydreamer, she's a big help when she puts her mind to it. Certainly, they can make sure their little sisters don't burn the house down while you're gone for an hour! . . . And on afternoons when they have basketball practice, you can always drop off those two little girls at Bubber's. Emma and I can watch 'em while you visit Billy."

But Alyce couldn't drop off the two little girls at Bubber's house. Emma had her hands full with her own toddler, Pat, who was six months younger than Cathy. In addition she was learning how to cope with Little Tom Hicks who, at age three, had been diagnosed with Down Syndrome. Emma was overwhelmed with Little Tom's uncontrollable behavior which resulted in most of her wedding china being destroyed piece by piece.

Because Miss Alice spent most of the day helping to corral Little Tom, she struggled to find time to sew. In addition to her steady school uniform clients, her dressmaking business was thriving in the postwar boom when Mobile's middle-class matron could afford a private seamstress rather than settle for a ready-made dress off the rack.

Alyce's other option was Josephine. When Josie arrived to help out—two or three times a week after Billy was born, if Rappy could afford it—Alyce dashed to the hospital for a half-hour visit before noon. But there were days when Josie wasn't scheduled to work for Alyce, and Mickey and Shirley didn't get home from basketball practice until five o'clock. On those days Alyce had to forego her visit to Billy in the Allen Memorial Hospital.

If she missed a visit during the week, she made it up on Saturday. With Rappy home all day to care for the children, she could leave the house at 9:00, early enough to catch the round of basketball games at St. Mary's gym to see Little Rappy, Mickey, and Shirley play in their respective games of Seniors, Juniors, and Tinymites against teams from other parish schools. With Rappy at home taking care of the three smaller children, she made sure her Saturday visit with Billy was two hours long. She tried to schedule it around noon—the three older children could find their way home on bicycles after their games—so she could feed Billy his lunch.

"What time will you be back?" Rappy stood at the kitchen door, itching to get in the back yard to take care of his chicken coops.

"It depends," Alyce searched for the car keys. "I think Mickey plays at 3:00, unusual cuz the Seniors usually play in the morning, and I'm gonna try to get some Christmas shopping in."

"I thought you'd finished all your Christmas shopping."

"I'm never finished—not when I've got to do the whole thing on $50.00."

"I might find some more money if I can defer this month's hospital bill until January."

"Don't do that, Rappy! The last thing we want is to get behind in the hospital bill. Are you sure the bank insurance policy won't cover *some* of Billy's expenses? Can't they cover at least the oxygen?"

"Thornton's looking into it. They've never had a precedent for our situation with Billy."

"It's ugly outside. Don't keep these children out in that damp all day. Cathy's already got a runny nose. And keep your eye on the girls that they don't wander down the driveway and out into the street!"

"Go on, Hickory! . . . Go do your errands."

"There're some eggs in the icebox you can scramble for lunch. Or there's always peanut butter and jelly—I might not get back till five or six."

"Get out of here, Hickory!"

When Alyce arrived at the nursery, she found Billy in Miss Angstrom's lap. From the day Billy was born, the middle-aged spinster had fallen hard for this beautiful infant with so many needs. All the nurses in the Nursery had become smitten with the baby during the past five months, but it was Miss Angstrom who had taken charge of his care during her day-shift.

"Is he sitting up?" Alyce became excited when she saw her child in the nurse's lap.

"It's more like he's leaning back against my stomach," the nurse chuckled, "but it's a start, right?"

"Indeed, it is! Tell me what to do so I can hold him like that and feed him!"

"You have to be careful of the *bifida* on his back. Place your palm on his back right above it so you can measure how far it sticks out without actually touching it. And don't be nervous—all the gauze and padding and the surgical mask protects it."

Alyce took Billy onto her lap and gazed down at him. Sitting up—although supported by both her hands so he wouldn't topple over—the child was far more vulnerable than the typical five month-old learning to sit. But she had confidence he would be sitting alone, propping his weight on his arms, in a few more months.

"His skin reminds me of a Dresden doll, Mrs. Perez," the nurse gazed dreamily at the child.

"It does. I told my mama he's the prettiest of all my babies. Just look at those long dark eyelashes."

"Like a chorus girl!"

"What color do you think his eyes are?" Alyce leaned over to look closely.

"If I didn't know better, I'd say *jet-black*, the same color as the pupil! . . . . But probably the iris is a brown shade so dark that it just appears black."

"The same as Cathy's eyes," Alyce smiled. "His look so much darker in contrast to his skin. He's so white—we're gonna have to get him outside in the sun as soon as the weather gets warm in the spring."

Alyce sank back in the rocker and relaxed. She had two hours for Billy . . . and for herself. She needed to be home by six to fix supper. Before that, she had to make it back to the gym for Mickey's 3:00 game. And some time before six tonight, she needed to dash downtown because Hammel's Annex had a Christmas sale, today only.

But meanwhile, she indulged herself in feeling maternal. She slowly rocked her child as he gurgled like an ordinary baby.

241

If I ever get him home, I'll make sure he receives as much attention as I can find in my daily routine. I won't spoil him just because he's afflicted. But I'll have to make allowances for his handicaps.

Somehow I'll find a balanced approach. I have no idea how to do it, but I'll learn.

I'll trust the Lord to show me.

For the next hour or so, she could forget about basketball games, Christmas shopping, and her other duties on Laurel Street. She could relax and take care of her youngest child who needed his mother.

)))

At St. Mary's gym, Alyce sat between Eunice Usher and Sister Mary Grace as Mickey took the court to captain the Senior team, girls who weighed over 105 pounds. Although Mickey weighed only ninety she was allowed to play for both the Juniors and the Seniors.

Sister Mary Grace and Alyce were the same age, both born in January. They had been friends for eight years, ever since Sister Grace taught Little Rappy in the first grade. Since then, she had taught Mickey and Shirley, and just last year she taught Tommy. Alyce felt closer to the vivacious nun than any of the other nuns on the faculty. Possibly, it was because Sister Grace was from Apalachicola, Florida, only two hours east of Mobile. She was one of the few nuns on the faculty who wasn't born in Ireland, who hadn't arrived from the old country armed with a hickory stick and prepared to use it on unruly students, especially 'bad boys'.

Before Mickey lined up at center court for the tip-off, she made the Sign-of-the-Cross and glanced at her mother on the sidelines.

"Look!" Sister Mary Grace grabbed Alyce's arm. "Mary always looks this way before each game to see if you're here!"

"That's because she never knows if I'm gonna make it or not."

242

"You can always bring the little ones! We have two student baby-sitters in the kindergarten classroom to take care of the little ones during the games!"

"Frankly, Sister, if I can find a free baby-sitter, I like to get away from home once and a while to have some time to myself—and I do like to watch my children play sports!"

"I have to dash to the convent to check on Sister Mary Gregonius who's bedridden. I'll be back by halftime to see how many points Mary's scored," the slender nun bolted from her metal folding chair and headed for the exit.

"Look at that *pot licker* for Cathedral, Alyce!" Eunice Usher leaned over and whispered in Alyce's ear.

"Which one?" Alyce laughed.

"That tall one with the hips! She jiggles when she runs down the court! She must weigh 150 pounds!" Eunice sneered.

"But so far, she's high scorer!"

"Cuz she's so damn tall! . . . Can't you just see her licking the pot after it's been drained of all the collard greens and ham-hock?"

"Definitely a pot-licker, Eunice," Alyce chuckled in conspiracy.

"Probably comes from the Home."

"St. Barbara's Home? . . . Oh, yeah! All the girls from the Home attend Cathedral, don't they?"

"It's hard to tell who's an orphan and who's not," Eunice mumbled. "Our girls are gonna have to trick her into fouling out! We've got to get Miss Pot-licker off the court!"

♪♪♪

"Bless me, Father, for I have sinned. It's been six weeks since my last haircut—I mean my last *confession*!"

"Your last haircut, Alyce?"

"I'm just thinking of all the things I need to do while Rappy's keeping the children today. Emma, my brother's wife, is really good at cutting short hair like mine—I can't see paying a beauty parlor when I can save that dollar for Santa Claus shopping," she realized she was

243

talking a mile-a-minute, a sure sign her mind was racing with all the things she needed to get done by 6:00 p.m.

"Ah, Alyce! The good Lord wants us to receive the sacrament of Confession more often than every six weeks," Monsignor O'Donoghue admonished her gently.

"I realize, Monsignor, but it's a week before Christmas and I'm a bit overwhelmed. You see, Little Rappy's serving Midnight Mass, Mickey and Shirley are singing in the choir. And by Wednesday I've gotta find presents for each of the children to give to their classmates—I wish the sisters would stop that silly tradition of drawing names for a gift cuz I never know which child I have to buy for! . . . And I'm not half-finished with my shopping!"

"Sometimes the Lord provides the best bargains for the last days of shopping, no? . . . Tell me, dear, have you brought the little angel home from the hospital? Little Louis?"

"We call him 'Billy', Monsignor—and, no, he's still at the Allen Memorial. The doctors don't know when we can bring him home."

"Ahh, we're all praying for him, Alyce! You know that God has sent you an angel! A true angel!"

"Yes, Monsignor."

"Tell me your sins, my dear."

"I committed a sin of uncharity. . . . Is there such a word? . . . I was unkind to a child."

"What did you say to him, my dear?"

It was a girl, and I didn't say anything *to* her. . . . I gossiped about her."

"Gossip is uncharitable—we all know that."

"And to make it worse, she's an orphan, I think, from St. Barbara's Home."

"Why were you gossiping about an orphan from St. Barbara's, my dear Alyce?"

"It was at a school basketball game, Monsignor. She plays for Cathedral. She's a great player, but she's tall and fat. Another mother and I were making fun of her from the sidelines because Cathedral was winning."

"Were you *shouting* at her from the sidelines?"

"*No,* Monsignor! We were whispering and laughing about how fat she is and speculating on what she eats to get so fat. . . . And then I realized that most of the Cathedral players live at St. Barbara's, so she might be an orphan."

"Well, Alyce, it's no worse to gossip about an orphan than to gossip about your next-door neighbor's child. But, still, it's a sin against charity."

"I realize, Monsignor, and I'm very sorry. I feel . . . ashamed."

"For your penance, Alyce, say a rosary for that poor orphan girl."

"I already have, Monsignor."

"Well, . . . say another one. . . . *Te absolvo en—*"

CHAPTER 13

CHRISTMAS WAS FUN.

Alyce and her mother managed to continue Grandma Fanane's tradition of baking three fruitcakes before December 10. In the two weeks leading up to Christmas the cakes had to be properly aged with a daily dousing of bourbon. Shirley, age ten, jumped at the chance to take charge of the chore. She had to soak the fruitcakes everyday by removing the cheese-cloth from each moist cake, soaking the cake with Early Times, then rewrapping it and replacing it in its tin.

Alyce felt the child would develop self-esteem if she could meet the responsibility of aging the fruitcakes. And Shirley met it. Everyday after school, she dropped her book-bag on the sofa, washed her hands, and made a beeline for the kitchen pantry where the fruitcakes were stored. She never missed a day. And after Christmas dinner she proudly brought the largest cake to the table and served the first slice to Grandma Hicks who showered her second oldest grand-daughter with effusive praise.

Alyce empathized with Shirley who had to follow behind her older sister, Mickey, two years older and teacher's pet for every nun who taught her. Following Mickey through school was no different for young Shirley, petite like her mother, than Alyce following Bubber through St. Joseph's some thirty years earlier. Consequently, Alyce was vigilant for opportunities to give Shirley responsibilities to build

247

self-esteem. Hence, the fruitcakes were a grand success.

Three days before Christmas Josephine was wandering around the kitchen threatening to cook yellow pan-bread. Miss Alice was busy making oyster dressing for the Christmas turkey, so Alyce took advantage of two free baby-sitters to visit Billy.

"Mama, after I leave the hospital I'm dashing downtown to finish my Christmas shopping—and a couple of errands—so I might run late. Can you start supper if I'm not back by six?"

"Take all the time you need, Alyce. I'll call Thomas to pick me up on his way home from work."

'Downtown' meant more than Christmas shopping. Alyce would be in the neighborhood of the Cathedral, right across the street from St. Barbara's Home which housed most of Cathedral girls' basketball team who had edged out Mickey's team. Alyce needed to make amends to the girl she and Eunice Usher had called "Pot-licker." The mere sound of the derisive nickname rolling around in her head caused shame all over again. Atonement would require more than another rosary.

That morning she made phone calls to Florinda O'Hara and Willie Mae Andrews, two ladies in St. Mary's parish who did a lot of charity work, to find out who was president of the St. Barbara's Home Ladies Auxiliary. It was time for Alyce to expand her charity work. Ever since Little Rappy had started first grade, she had made time to be a Room-Mother, almost every year, even during the middle of the war when she and her mother were struggling with the gasoline ration.

After the war she joined the Altar Society which decorated the altar with flowers and washed and ironed the linen cloths for the altar, as well as the white surplices for the altar boys and priests. Since Alyce didn't have an automatic washer in the late 1940s, she volunteered to take charge of candle inventory. It was an easy task. Once a week she ordered new candles from the liturgical supply house in Chicago. Because the candles were consecrated annually on Candlemas Day, Alyce had to make sure that no used candles, often burned down to a stub, were thrown out with the trash. She turned them over to Father Nolan, the Altar Society's moderator, and assumed he disposed of them properly.

Now, Alyce needed to join the St. Barbara's Home Ladies Auxiliary. Not just *needing* to join, she wanted to. On the phone the Auxiliary president explained that most children at the Home were not orphans—they were from 'broken' homes. According to the president, that could mean neither of the divorced parents was able to provide for the children, or neither wanted the children. At times the parents were still together but were too poor to provide for the children, or both were in the throes of alcoholism. Or worse, one was afflicted with a mental illness.

Whatever the reason for a child having to live at the Home, it caused Alyce to pause and count her many blessings. Neither she nor Rappy suffered from any mental illness. And neither had an alcohol problem. Rappy occasionally partied too much at a Mardi Gras ball, but that was typical in Mobile. So far, they were able to pay the monthly hospital bill for Billy's care. If he stayed longer in the hospital, she was confident the Lord would show them how to meet the costs.

The most important thing was that their family was intact. Her children had a mother and father who loved them and were willing to sacrifice for them. Her children were secure on Laurel Street. They weren't living at St. Barbara's Home in a downtown neighborhood that was losing its luster every year, a 100 year-old brick building that needed a new staircase.

After dashing into Woolworth's at four to buy some last minute stocking-stuffers, Alyce found herself in the St. Barbara's kitchen arranging homemade Christmas cookies on silver serving trays for the children in the dining hall. Standing between Willie Mae Andrews and Florinda O'Hara, she worked quickly to get into the dining hall and find the girl she had called 'Pot-licker.'

"Now, Florinda and Willie Mae," Alyce continued to work while she talked, "both of you have as many children as I do, so tell me how you manage to do so much charity work!"

"Well," Willie Mae spoke slowly and distinctly as she concentrated on the chocolate brownies she was arranging, "I have only two left at St. Mary's and none at home, so it's getting easier for me every year."

"All of mine are either at St. Mary's are still at home just like you, Alyce, and here I am pregnant again," the rotund Florinda laughed loudly and popped a Danish wedding cookie into her mouth. "I'm a terrible housekeeper, which makes it easier for me to take off. I tell the older ones to watch the little ones, I step over all the clutter on the floor, and I just walk out the front door."

"Well, I have Josephine who comes two or three times a week. And I have Mama close by—the other side of Government next to Ladd Stadium—so I manage to find *some* free time, but I'd like to do more," Alyce arranged the iced Santa cookies on a doily-lined silver tray.

"Isn't Little Rappy in the eighth grade with my daughter, Pat? He'll be getting his driver's license in a couple of years—that'll help you with errands and such—and your two older girls are big enough now to baby-sit after school, and—" Florinda popped another cookie into her mouth.

"When they don't have some kind of sports practice or Girl Scout meeting," Alyce interrupted.

"That's not *every* day! . . . You can work it out, but the important thing is to free up your mornings to do your charity work so you'll be there when the children get home from school."

Five minutes later Alyce slowly circulated the dining hall with a tray loaded with iced Santa cookies as she served the children scattered around the room. She kept her eye out for the tall brunette who played center on Cathedral's Senior team.

The first thing that impressed Alyce was that the children were so well behaved. The little ones were seated at low tables where they nibbled cookies and drank Coca-Colas, giggling and talking quietly. The little girls were dressed in hand-me-down party dresses with matching hair ribbons, their long gleaming tresses freshly shampooed and brushed, probably by older sisters also living at the Home. The little boys sported white dress shirts and homemade red bowties, obviously the handiwork of the six nuns who wandered separately around the room to assure that the children behaved themselves.

The older children—girls attending Bishop Toolen High whose teenage brothers lived at Catholic Boys Home—were standing in clusters, giggling among themselves as they sipped their Coca-Colas. Alyce continued passing out cookies, smiling at each teen and urging her to "take more than one—take a handful!"

Then she spotted her. The big brunette stood with two other girls next to the hall door. She wore a holly-green taffeta party dress with a four inch-wide belt covered in the same fabric—a full skirt much shorter than the 1950 look—obviously a hand-me-down from an Auxiliary matron, but it fit the 13 year-old well. With her long raven hair pulled back with green plastic barettes on each side of her head, the child looked sweet.

"Won't you have a Christmas cookie?" Alyce approached the girl and her friends.

"Yes M'am," the girl smiled shyly.

"I saw you play against St. Mary's. You're really great!" Alyce gazed up at the girl who was a full head taller than she.

"Thanks," she blushed as she nibbled on the iced cookie.

"My daughter played against you, but you beat us."

"Oh?" her eyes lit up momentarily. "Who *is* she—your daughter?"

"Mickey Perez. She plays for both the seniors and the juniors. She's only in the seventh grade, you see. But aren't you in the eighth?" Alyce realized she was rambling nervously.

"Mickey?! . . . Oh she's a great player!" the girl said sincerely. "She's usually high scorer for St. Mary's cuz she's so small that no-body can guard her, especially big girls like me! And we have a lot of big girls on Cathedral!" she giggled.

"You have a great team, Cathedral, and you're the best. And I bet you're always the high scorer for your team, right?"

"Not *always*," she blushed again.

Driving home at 6:30 Alyce revised her weekly schedule in her mind so she could volunteer two hours a week at St. Barbara's. It would have to be a day when Josephine was ironing. Miss Alice's sewing schedule was too erratic to ask her to baby-sit once a week on a specific day at the same time. Somehow Alyce would squeeze her grocery budget to find $1.00 a month for dues to join St. Barbara's Home Ladies Auxiliary.

♪♪♪

Billy was six months-old, still living at the Allen Memorial in the nursery, when the hospital's accounting department became aggressive in collecting the $200 per month on the burgeoning bill.

"Mickey said the hospital called today," Alyce sat at the dining table where she and Rappy were eating supper alone. Because some nights he moonlighted by keeping books for small businesses and didn't get home till eight, she often fed the children earlier and waited to eat supper with her husband.

"They called yesterday, too!" Shirley spoke up from the other end of the table where she was copying a map from her 5th grade Geography textbook.

"You didn't tell me that, Shirley!" Alyce was further miffed that the hospital's phone-calls were becoming a daily harassment.

"They said I'm late?" Rappy spooned black-eyed peas into his mouth as he gave a lop-sided smile. "I *know* I'm late!"

"They left a message with Mickey," Alyce picked at the food on her plate.

"Nothing wrong with that," Rappy said.

"Rappy, the nun didn't just say 'Tell your mama and daddy to call the business office'. She *said* 'Tell your parents their bill is six weeks overdue and subject to penalty.' . . . *That* was the message she left with a twelve year-old child!" Alyce struggled to keep her voice down.

"But, Mama," Shirley looked up from her map, "yesterday she didn't leave *that* message with *me*. The Sister just said 'Tell your mama

252

to call us at the Allen Memorial'. That's all she said."

"Shirley, take your homework into the living room. You can draw that map better if you spread out on the floor."

"You sound aggravated," Rappy tried to repress his own anger.

"*Aggravated*?! . . . These nuns belong to an order called the Daughters of *Charity*!"

"We can't expect charity from them, Hickory," he muttered. "It's a hospital owned by the diocese, all right, but still they have to cover operating costs."

"This is no time to sound like a banker, Rappy! . . . They shouldn't leave a message like that with a *child*!"

"I'll drop by the hospital after work tomorrow."

"Wednesday? . . . Isn't that the night you keep books for that hardware store?"

"I can be late.

♪♪♪

Word spread throughout the Perez extended family that Rappy and Alyce were struggling to put food on the table. They never asked for help, but someone had sent out the alarm. Alyce suspected it was Margie, Rappy's sister, married to Bill Serda who had opened the first independent supermarket in wealthy Spring Hill. Almost every Tuesday morning Margie appeared in Alyce's kitchen with two large bags of groceries. Margie pulled up to the back of her husband's supermarket where Bill's manager had already filled twenty bags with groceries. The manager and Margie loaded the back of her car with groceries for Catholic Charities to deliver to needy families.

"I feel bad, Margie, taking these groceries away from people who need them more than Rappy and me," Alyce peeked into the top of the bag hoping for two pounds of ground chuck, an item she could stretch into three meals.

"It's not *my* idea," Margie fibbed. "You know how crazy Bill is about you! He told me to go through the Catholic Charities bags and pick out the best stuff for Laurel Street!"

253

"I couldn't have gotten through the war without Bill Serda," Alyce felt her eyes misting up.

Alyce suspected it was Margie who had called Rappy's Aunt Pauline, the *grand dame* of the Perez clan.

'Aunt Pauline' was Leopoldina Perez Gonzalez, Rappy's aunt, the widow of Sebastian Gonzalez. In the 1890s, when Rappy's daddy was boarded at Spring Hill College to attend their elementary school, his oldest sister was boarded at a private school after her father brought his nine children from Mexico's Yucatan peninsula to learn English in Mobile. Because the girls at Leopoldina's school had trouble pronouncing her name, they rechristened her 'Pauline'.

After high school Pauline married Sebastian Gonzalez, a young entrepreneur, who had immigrated with his family to Mobile directly from Spain. By starting out slowly in a fish stall, he gradually made his fortune on the Alabama Gulf Coast with a small fishing fleet. By the time he reached his mid-thirties, Uncle Sebastian had turned his family's Star Fish and Oyster Company into a thriving enterprise with fleets that trawled through the Gulf into the Caribbean. After Sebastian died in the mid-1920s, Aunt Pauline continued to help out her huge family in any way she could.

In February, 1951 when Aunt Pauline appeared at Laurel Street with her daughter, Emilie Dekle serving as chauffeur, Alyce didn't ask questions. She welcomed the older lady because she realized it wasn't just Pauline's *charity* she was accepting. It was known throughout the extended family that Rappy was one of Pauline's favorite nephews. And, aside from being his wife, Alyce was treasured in her own right by Aunt Pauline.

"It's just stuff I grabbed out of my pantry," the old lady fussed as she poked into the two paper bags Emilie had deposited on Alyce's kitchen table.

"Mama," the stately and poised Emilie tried to urge her mother out of the kitchen, "Alyce can go through the bags when she gets time."

"Some lard, you see, and flour and rice and . . . oh! These potatoes are a week old but I'm sure they're still good! They'll do fine in a beef stew! Emilie, did you put that stew meat in here? I told you to take it out of the icebox so we wouldn't forget it! I always buy too much, Alyce, and then it spoils in the icebox, so you're doing me a favor by taking this stew meat off my hands! Besides, I need the space in the icebox!" Aunt Pauline was taking the items out of the bags, one by one, and holding them up for Alyce to inspect.

"You know how much I appreciate it, Aunt Pauline . . . and Rappy does too—I mean, 'Alfred'!"

"We all go through bad times sooner or later, Alyce!" she patted Alyce's hand. "You just need to concentrate on getting that baby home so he can be here . . . with you and Alfred—and the children!"

After Emilie finally steered her mother out the front door, Alyce stood in the kitchen doorway gazing at the grocery items strewn all over the table.

Should I be too proud to accept charity from Rappy's aunt?

I never knew Uncle Sebastian, but Grandma Fanane always said how much money the Star Fish and Oyster Company makes. And everybody knows how Aunt Pauline helps anybody in the family who needs it.

Well, now Rappy and I need it! . . . We're not starving, thanks to family like Margie and Bill, but compared to other employees at Rappy's bank, we're definitely poor. To meet that Allen Memorial monthly bill we're going through our savings like Sherman through Georgia!

Can I swallow my pride and accept this charity? Do I have any pride left?

The priority is to pay the hospital on time every month until Dr. Patton says it's safe to bring Billy home . . . . . or until he dies. Nothing else matters but Billy. That $200 payment might be a huge chunk from Rappy's salary, but it comes off the top each month.

I'm learning how to plan really inexpensive meals. Nobody in this house will ever go hungry! They'll get a hot meal every night, even if supper means grits and weenies!

）））

During that winter of 1951 Miss Alice established a Sunday routine so Rappy and Alyce could go to the hospital together to visit Billy. After attending Mass on Sunday morning with her son, Thomas, while Emma stayed home with the two children, Miss Alice walked over to Laurel Street to help Alyce with the big Sunday dinner served at 1:00 p.m. After the dishes were washed and everything was put away, Miss Alice kept the older children while Alyce and Rappy were at the Allen Memorial.

When they returned around 4:00, Alyce and her mother spent the late afternoon getting the St. Mary's uniforms ready for the four school children to wear the next week. On Monday Josephine arrived to iron the white shirts and blouses—white cotton shirtwaists for the girls in the fall and the spring—but the clothes had to be starched and ready for Josephine when she arrived at Laurel Street.

"You need a new pot to boil this starch," Miss Alice glared at the gallon-sized Dutch oven on the stove-top. The large pot was filled to the brim with Staley's starch bubbling like white lava.

"We need a lot of things, Mama," Alyce murmured as she ironed a shirt for Little Rappy to wear the next morning before Josephine arrived.

"One of these handles is missing a screw! If you're not careful picking up this pot, this handle can twist in your hand! All this boiling starch'll scald your feet! You'll never walk again!"

"I'll get Rappy to fix it next Saturday."

"Promise yourself you won't use it again till it's fixed! . . . *A Phillips screwdriver and one small screw!* That's all it needs. I'm sure you can find that in his tool box—you don't need to bother Rappy!"

Alyce didn't respond. She ironed the damp, stiff shirt in silence, pleased to watch the wrinkles disappear as she pressed hard with the iron.

"Did you know they have a new iron that spits out steam?" she said finally. "You don't need to dampen the shirt before you iron it."

"Well, you need a lot of other things before you go buying something fancy like that."

"Before we do anything, Mama, we have to pay that hospital bill every month . . . *on time!*"

"Now, tell me again why the bank won't pay anything on this hospital bill?" Miss Alice was ladling the hot starch into a metal pitcher rather than pouring from the pot with the cracked handle.

"It's not the bank, Mama—it's the insurance company that issued the medical policy. They say Billy couldn't be insured before he was born, that all his problems were caused by his birth—which is true—at which time he wasn't listed on the family policy."

"Now, if Shirley Anne got real sick—say meningitis cuz that's what the doctors are afraid might kill Billy if that thing on his back gets infected—and Shirley ends up in the hospital, would the bank insurance cover her expenses?" Miss Alice stopped ladling and gazed at Alyce.

"Every penny! The policy gives full coverage for me and the other children, just the same as for Rappy, the employee!"

"Well, the thing to do is bring Billy home tomorrow! . . . Then the next day stick him back in the hospital and file a claim that what he's got is some new-fangled disease! Won't that do the trick?"

"Mama!" Alyce laughed heartily. "That's a devilish idea! And it just might work, but we can't bring Billy home until Dr. Patton officially discharges him."

"And when does he think that'll be?"

"He can't say. But we have our monthly visit with him Friday. I'll get Rappy to press him for a time frame."

"Now, tell me again when Rappy's gonna buy you that automatic washing machine?" Miss Alice shouted from the bathroom where she was pouring the hot starch over a mound of white shirts and blouses in the bathtub.

"As soon as we save enough money to buy it!"

"Thomas and Emma bought their machine on the installment plan."

"*You* try to convince Rappy Perez to buy something on credit! Obviously, I haven't had any success!"

"How're you gonna save money for an automatic washing machine at the same time you're saving to send Little Rappy to Spring Hill College?"

"College is four years down the road, Mama. And the way we're living from month-to-month, four years is an eternity!"

"You just might have to break down and borrow money from the bank for some of these necessities—even if only for the automatic washing machine."

"I *have* to get an automatic washing machine before Billy comes home. Nurse Angstrom says all his bed linens have to be changed every day—and the surgical masks that cover that growth on his back—not to mention the diapers. He goes through twelve diapers a day cuz a wet diaper can cause the growth to become infected—which would probably kill him in a matter of days, even with these modern antibiotics. . . . So, the automatic washing machine is at the top of our list."

"Just don't get a Bendix like Emma bought. It's got a door on the front where you throw the dirty clothes inside. Little Tom and Pat crawl in there every time I forget to close the door."

"Sears and Roebuck sells Kenmore—with the door on the *top*."

"That's more sensible."

♪♪♪

When Billy celebrated his first birthday, July 11, 1951, he was still living in the nursery of the Allen Memorial Hospital. He had not yet seen his home on Laurel Street.

Nurse Angstrom took it upon herself to stage a birthday party in the large grassy courtyard behind the hospital. The party was attended by most of the doting staff from the nursery—the nuns, nurses, orderlies, and volunteer auxiliary—who all brought small gifts for the honoree.

258

None of Alyce's children had seen their youngest brother. According to hospital rules, only children over twelve were allowed to visit on the nursery floor. Little Rappy and Mickey were over twelve, but Dr. Patton had told Alyce—and had left strict orders with the nursery staff—that Billy could have no visitors under eighteen. The neurologist was trying to assure that his vulnerable little patient would not be exposed to any childhood diseases, especially mumps, measles, whooping cough, and chicken pox.

At three o'clock in the afternoon Alyce arrived in the courtyard with her six children and her mother. Nurse Angstrom had pushed a gurney covered with a baby-blue crepe paper tablecloth under a spreading oak tree to host the party out of the hot July sun. The gurney was filled with candies, party favors for the brothers and sisters, and a huge birthday cake. And every guest received a helium-filled balloon.

"His head's so big!" Snookums exclaimed when she got her first glimpse of her little brother.

"Hush!" said Shirley, who was holding hands with her little sister as they approached the tree, yanked the child close to her side. "Grandma said not to mention his head!"

"Leave her be, Shirley Anne! She's only four!" Miss Alice slid into a lawn chair as she balanced the two year-old Cathy on her lap.

As the party got under way and the older children moved in shyly to make a fuss over their little brother sitting on Nurse Angstrom's lap, Alyce stepped back to observe.

Out here in the open air, he looks so different! . . . His head does look awfully big! It must have been slowly swelling this whole past year. I guess I didn't notice cuz I see him every day—well, almost every day. But still, it doesn't look that huge to me! I wonder what Mama thinks. She sees him only once a week.

Oh, God! He looks so delicate with the sunlight shining on him through the trees. So pale! How can we ever take him home? . . . It's been a whole year! We can't leave him in this hospital indefinitely, not with me being pregnant again!

259

She hadn't made an appointment with Dr. Dowling yet, but she knew she was 2-3 months along. This new baby would arrive in February or March. She hadn't told Rappy yet. She'd tell him tomorrow, a full two weeks before he started his vacation. She wouldn't wait to tell him in August when he was home the whole month on vacation. She didn't want him trudging around the house for a week after she broke the news, him worrying about where he was going to find the money for another hospital bill. She'd tell him tomorrow morning on the way to work, just before he got out of the car so he would have to rally to get through his day in the Bookkeeping Department.

He'd have two weeks at work to worry—and to talk with Mr. McRae if he had to line up financing for the next baby's delivery. Having a baby at the Allen Memorial Hospital was cheap if you were a Catholic. The Labor and Delivery cost only $25.00. For the first seven babies, it had been no problem for Rappy to save the $25.00. After all, he had advance notice that a baby was on the way. By the time Alyce told him she was pregnant, he had at least seven months to save $25.00.

But this time would be different. It would be impossible to pay Billy's bill of $200 a month, meet the routine household expenses, save money for Rappy's college and the new washing machine . . . *and* still save $25.00 plus semi-private room expenses. Alyce realized she'd have to make another nine-week novena to Our Lady of the Miraculous Medal. A miracle was needed.

 ♪♪♪

Three months later, against the advice of the neurologist, Rappy and Alyce prepared to bring Billy home to Laurel Street.

The child had been living in the Allen Memorial nursery for fifteen months.

"My best advice," the neurologist played with the paperweight on his desk, "is to leave him where he is."

"We can't afford it any longer," Rappy said flatly.

"I'm having another baby in February," Alyce glanced at her hands and realized how threadbare her white gloves had become.

"I can see that," the doctor smiled.

"Tell me, doctor," Rappy cocked his head, "is he gonna get any better living at that hospital?"

"Probably not."

"We need to save up for Alyce's next hospital stay in February," Rappy volunteered.

"Besides," Alyce ventured, "when the new baby arrives, I just won't be able to go back and forth to the Allen everyday to visit Billy. It's time to bring him home."

"I sympathize with your reasons," Dr. Patton leaned forward, "but as Billy's physician, I have to advise against bringing him home."

"What's the danger?" Alyce asked matter-of-factly.

"He could have a convulsion."

"What's that?" Rappy glanced at the doctor, then at Alyce.

"Like a *fit*, Rappy," she continued gazing at the doctor. "What else?"

"He could go into respiratory arrest and stop breathing . . . and die."

"We'll get one of those oxygen tanks," Rappy glanced again at Alyce.

"I wouldn't!" Dr. Patton held up his hand like he was trying to stop traffic. "One of your children might tinker with it and cause it to explode. The whole house would go up in flames. Besides, the cost would be exorbitant."

"Thank you for everything you're doing for the little guy, Doctor," Rappy rose and stood beside his chair, "but we've decided to bring him home."

"I understand. And although I have to advise against it as his physician, I want to commend y'all for not putting him in an institution. Most parents would."

"I could never do that," Alyce slowly rose from her chair.

"Over the past year I've become quite attached to little Billy—I know he'll receive the love and care he needs in your home."

"Anything you need to tell us, Doctor?" Alyce hesitated before crossing to the door.

"Make sure he's not exposed to any childhood diseases, especially measles, chicken pox, whooping cough, and mumps. He could die from any of those."

"You've got to be kidding!" Rappy laughed sarcastically.

"You *know* we've got six other children, Doctor," Alyce glared at Rappy. "I'll do my best, but I can't promise he won't be exposed to germs!"

♪♪♪♪

On a bright October morning in 1951 Billy arrived at Laurel Street at nine o'clock. He cried for ten hours straight. Unrelentingly. The child was inconsolable. Obviously he missed Charge-Nurse Angstrom who had been his primary caretaker for the first fifteen months of his life.

Alyce was at a loss. Miss Alice sat in Grandma Fanane's bedroom rocker gently rocking the child for hours on end while he cried. Rappy took Tommy and Little Rappy outside to rake leaves. Josephine had arrived at eight to look after Cathy and Snookums while their mother and grandmother tried to establish a routine to accommodate Billy as he adjusted to his strange new environment.

"Mama," Alyce stood in the bedroom door watching her mother slowly rocking the child, "I've got all kind of things to show you about taking care of him—especially how to keep the bandages sterile on that growth—but we can do that later when he goes to sleep."

"That'll be a while if he keeps this up," the older woman rocked patiently.

"And you need to know what to do if he has a convulsion."

"My stars, Alyce! . . . Don't even think about such as that!"

"Dr. Patton said we have to be ready for any kind of emergency—he taught me everything we need to know!"

Five minutes later Alyce had crowded Josephine, Mickey, and Shirley into the bathroom as she demonstrated the most important lesson she had learned from Doctor Patton.

"One of you might be baby-sitting Billy when I'm not home and

262

nobody else is around. You need to know what to do if he gets sick," Alyce leaned over the bathtub and placed the rubber plug in the drain.

"Oooh, Mama!" Shirley gasped. "I don't want to baby-sit him alone—I'm only eleven!"

"You won't be alone with him, Shirley. Not right away, that is. But once Mickey gets older and starts dating, you might *have to* baby-sit alone—when you're fourteen or fifteen—so you need to know this. Now, pay attention!" Alyce turned the cold water tap until the flow was steady and moderately forceful.

"Miz Pee-rez," Josephine shyly hid her hands under her white apron, "you needs to think twice 'fore you put that crippled baby in dis big tub!"

"That's right, Josephine! The doctor says to give him a sponge bath while he's lying in bed, before we even get him up. But if he has a convulsion, you—"

"She means 'a fit', Josephine," Mickey turned toward the maid and enunciated slowly.

"Yessum," Josephine nodded her head slowly and rhythmically. "I knows about them *fits*! . . . Last summer we had two junkyard dogs in my neighborhood what got the fits! Rosie's man had to shoot 'em . . . dead!"

"You're right, Josephine," Alyce turned off the water, "we don't put him in water unless he's having a fit."

"What does a fit *look* like?" Shirley asked.

"The doctors says he'll be trembling, so you—"

"That means 'shaking'," Mickey turned to Shirley and Josephine.

"Right!" Alyce continued. Shaking a lot and maybe drooling at the mouth."

"I've read where the eyes roll to the back of the head," Mickey said matter-of-factly.

"Maybe that too," Alyce continued. "Now when you lower him into the water, he has to be in a sitting position."

"But you said he can't sit up alone!" Shirley was wide-eyed.

"Right! . . . So you have to support his back."

"Yessum," Josephine had been nodding her head during the entire instruction.

"But the most important thing, . . . the *most* important thing is not to let that growth on his back get wet."

"How do I do that?" Shirley's voice was fearful.

"Look in the tub! . . . See how much water I put in? Barely three inches. And it's cold water. The doctor said as cold as you can get it. But only three or four inches—not deep enough to get that growth wet. That's the most important thing: *Don't get the growth wet!*"

"And then what?" Mickey stared into the tub visualizing her brother sitting at the bottom.

"You have to hold him up with one hand, and with the other hand splash cold water all over him, especially his chest to shock the lungs into breathing regularly, and the shoulders, and the face—well, *just all over him!*" Alyce's voice had taken on such a sense of urgency that she realized she might be frightening Josephine and Shirley.

"Well," Shirley eased towards the door, "I'm not gonna baby-sit him alone until I'm sixteen and have my driver's license! I'm not gonna be blamed for getting that thing wet!"

CHAPTER **14**

ON THE FIRST Friday of December Alyce stood alone in the backyard gazing at the stars. At 5:30 in the morning the air was freezing.

It's still dark. Thank God I don't need much sleep.

In her new routine since Billy had arrived home only six weeks ago, she crept out of bed at 5:15 to begin her day before anyone in the house was awake. Her first task was to take down Billy's dry diapers and bedsheets that had been hanging on the clothesline all night long.

Before going to bed each night, she dumped a load of the family's dirty clothes into the new Kenmore washing machine crammed into a corner of the breakfast room. She set the dial for 'Normal' cycle, turned on the machine, and slipped into bed next to a snoring husband. With rosary in hand she drifted off to sleep, smiling in bliss to the gentle purring of the automatic washer.

When she rose before dawn—each morning, including Sunday—she pulled the damp laundry from the washer, divided the wet clothes between two metal pails and slipped into Rappy's khaki wool army jacket. Outside she worked her way down the clothesline in the light of a single naked bulb Rappy had installed on the corner of the eaves on the Cooke's side.

But today, unlike most mornings, she wasn't able to speed down the line shoving the wooden clothespins deep into the pockets of the GI jacket as she snatched the dry diapers one-by-one from the metal wire.

These diapers are stiff as a board after hanging in the freezing air all night! Now, I'm certain I wouldn't be able to tolerate this cold if I wasn't so pregnant!

And to think Grandma Fanane always teased me that I'm so cold-natured! If she could only see me now!

The next step was to hang the damp clothes from the two metal pails so they could dry when the sun finally appeared over the pecan trees in the Cooke's backyard. She flounced each garment with one hand as she dug into the pocket with her other hand to grab two clothespins.

On this particular morning—seven months pregnant with a baby Rappy hoped would be Jerome Leopold Perez, II—she paused in the dark backyard before hurrying to the warmth of the kitchen. Her arms clutched the stack of clean sheets and diapers, the stiff icy garments crunching audibly against her swollen belly. She craned her neck and gazed into the northern sky where the stars shone brightly with no hint of a sunrise in the east.

She tried to spot the constellations Bubber had pointed out when they were children on Bayou and Savannah, back on a summer eve when they lay on their backs in the soft grass, smoking homemade cigarettes made from crushed pecan leaves wrapped in toilet paper which burned much too rapidly to give any effect—back when they had their whole lives ahead of them. But now the only constellation she recognized was the Big Dipper, the easiest to find.

She glanced toward the back fence at the row of raised chicken coops Rappy had built from used plywood and chicken-wire Mr. Cooke no longer needed. The chickens were quiet, all huddled into corners of the coops, too cold to cackle. She noticed the film of ice on the water in the drinking troughs.

266

Just like the previous December she wondered how she and Rappy could afford to stage a Christmas holiday to meet their children's expectations, especially the older ones hoping for trendy new clothes for the unending social functions demanded by St. Mary's students. And now Little Rappy was a freshman at McGill and, ironically, a pledge with the Delta Sigma fraternity which Alyce had fought for the Battle House ballroom when she presided over the ADK sorority so many years ago. Little Rappy managed to pay his fraternity dues with the wages and tips he made bagging groceries at Serda's supermarket, but there was the winter formal assessment, the tuxedo rental, and other expenses his parents would help the teenager finance.

Standing in the backyard under the naked light-bulb, she gazed at her ankles swollen with fluid from another pregnancy, her left ankle hidden under a mass of varicose veins knotted into a glob the size of a golf ball. Those veins would be removed in February at the same time she delivered her eighth child, a simple surgery covered by the bank's medical insurance policy.

It was time to climb the back steps, enter the kitchen and start Rappy's coffee. She loved the smell of coffee brewing in the morning, but she couldn't stomach it, even when she wasn't pregnant. She'd have hot tea and toast, as usual, after Rappy and the older children had left and the two little girls were up and seated at the table.

Then she would start the task of getting Billy bathed in his bed, the *bifida* on his back dressed in sterile bandages. After coating it with Vaseline to protect it from bacteria, she would cover it in a surgical mask which tied around his belly. She would gently lift him, slowly, so the fluid in his spine wouldn't rush to his head and launch a debilitating headache—and finally place him in a high chair, turning him at an angle so the growth wasn't pressed against the chair's wooden back.

Before she made the beds she'd put another load of dirty clothes in the washer. Since nobody in the house owned more than three pairs of underpants, it was necessary to wash often during the week. She discovered it wise to wash at least one load everyday so she

267

didn't get behind and discover someone needed clean underwear at the last minute, especially if they'd had an accident.

When Mickey and Shirley got home from school everyday, they hurried to the backyard and took down the dry clothes their mother had hung that morning. Then the two girls would hang another load of wet clothes Alyce had washed while they were in school.

At night she put Billy's second set of sheets and diapers in the washer and started the routine all over again. She was grateful for the automatic washer, but last weekend she saw her first electric clothes-dryer. Of course, it was at Margie's house. Margie was the first in the family to get any new appliance or gadget. This dryer was an amazing invention. Ever since Billy arrived home from the hospital, Margie volunteered to dry the Perez laundry on rainy days when Alyce couldn't get outside to hang the clothes. Margie even came by Laurel Street to pick up the wet laundry, take it home and dry it in her new dryer, then return it to Alyce later that night.

Alyce wouldn't dream of suggesting to Rappy that she 'needed' a clothes-dryer—not right now when they were still paying off the huge balance at the Allen Memorial—but at least once a week she experienced a dream when she saw a Kenmore clothes dryer enthroned next to her new washing machine.

But on this particular Friday morning in early December, she would wake up the older children fifteen minutes earlier. After feeding them breakfast, she would usher them out the door so they'd be on time for First Friday Mass of the Sacred Heart. She embraced the Twelve Promises that Our Lord made when he appeared to St. Margaret Mary Alacoque, that for those who honored nine consecutive First Fridays, He would 'comfort them in all their afflictions'. Alyce was especially reassured by the last promise in the list of twelve, that of final penitence—that the penitent 'would not die without receiving the sacraments, that she would not die in God's disgrace'.

There was no way she could throw Snookums and Cathy in the back of the car and make it to 8:15 Mass this morning, not without someone to stay with Billy, and not with her ankles swollen and her varicose veins acting up. But she believed that her older children could attend Holy Communion on nine First Fridays as her proxy so that the Sacred Heart would establish peace in her house, as He promised.

Before she left the backyard to enter the kitchen and begin another task-filled day, she took one final look at the starlit sky. For another thirty seconds she relished the quiet of being alone with no one to care for at the moment . . . no one to *do* for.

Lord, we need a deep-freeze and one of those new automatic clothes dryers. But Rappy's talking about buying a boat sometime down the road—says he can trawl for shrimp and crabs and flounder that live on the bottom of the bay and save us a fortune in groceries, especially Friday dinners. But I'm gonna fight him on this boat thing. And the older children are dying for one of those television sets.

Of course, the deep-freeze WOULD save money so you probably should send it first. However, maybe you can find a way to send the clothes dryer at the same time—or even before the deep-freeze, maybe? Most of our financial problems would be solved if You'd just convince Rappy it's okay to buy appliances on the installment plan. I mean, sooner or later the bank's gonna make him an officer even though he doesn't have that college degree, and then we'll have more money each month to pay the installments.

But we need a clothes dryer. Not just me, but my two older girls shouldn't have to take down the dry clothes in the dark after basketball practice! They need more time to do their homework and just talk on the phone—they're getting to that age. We REALLY need a clothes dryer!

Are you listening, Lord? . . . I'm not just talking to hear myself talk! . . . This is a prayer!

In the central hall she adjusted the flame in the huge gas stove which heated the entire house. Standing before that stove the four older children jockeyed for position to stand closest to the fire while waiting to use the bathroom one at a time before they dashed back to their bedrooms to change into their school uniforms. She made a mental note to add a second bathroom to her prayer list.

Rappy was kneeling at the side of the bed in his pajamas, his arms resting on the mattress as he mumbled his morning prayers. His eyes were closed, not tightly but as if he were sleeping. His features at age forty-three now showed signs of middle-age. Alyce saw in his face a certainty that the Lord would answer his prayers about Billy. Rappy had confided that he still held hope God would cure Billy, but he feared that their financial situation wouldn't improve for many years. He admitted that he had to dig deeply to trust in God's Will. She reminded him that if he had hope, then trust would follow. All he had to do was pray. And he did pray, both morning and night.

Meanwhile, she prayed that the Lord would send Rappy what he needed to trust more and worry less. Gazing at Rappy on his knees in prayer as he prepared to face a whole day at the bank and then two more hours keeping books for some small restaurant owner, she realized that if Grandma Fanane were alive, Alyce would be hard-pressed to find words to explain to her skeptical grandmother how much she loved Rappy. But more than that, how much she admired him. . . . Respected him.

♪♪♪

The following Friday morning Alyce left Billy and the two little girls with Josephine and drove her mother downtown to finish their Christmas shopping. After scouring for a matching sweater and skirt for Mickey on Lerner's clearance rack, they hurried over to Hammel's Bargain Annex to find a sport-shirt for Little Rappy.

"My stars, Alyce!" Miss Alice held up a short-sleeve boys' sport-shirt in a sunset-orange Hawaiian pattern, "I can't believe high school boys are wearing this in the winter time!"

"Those must be left over from the summer, Mama. As sure as I buy that shirt, they'll be out of style come springtime, don't ya' know?"

"Well, I could make a shirt just like this—it don't have no placket

270

down the front like a dress shirt so it'd be simple—if I had the *time!*" she refolded the shirt and gently replaced it on the clearance table.

"I had hoped that this would be the last Christmas when I had to do it all on just $100."

"It *will* be, Alyce. Now that Billy's home from the Allen, you don't have that monthly hospital bill anymore—so that's a $200 you have each month!"

"Not so, Mama! . . . We have an outstanding balance at the Allen that'll take two years to pay off at this rate of $200 a month. And that's a big chunk out of Rappy's salary. I'm afraid that nothing's changed with Billy home—financially, that is."

"So that means y'all have to postpone buying that deep-freeze . . . as well as the automatic clothes dryer, I suppose?"

"Rappy Perez doesn't believe in buying anything on credit if he can save up the money," Alyce said wistfully.

"Does that have something to do with that dinette suite his daddy dumped on y'all when you ended up postponing your wedding?"

"I imagine so," Alyce said nonchalantly. "The last purchase we made on the installment plan was all our furniture at Adam Glass, *and* Papa's dining room suit. . . . Somehow Rappy managed to save enough for my automatic washing machine. . . . And can you believe that Sears and Roebuck gave us a trade-in on that old wringer washer I've had for seventeen years?"

"Well, buying a deep-freeze might be good sense!"

"I just hope we can save a lot of money with a freezer, enough to buy the clothes dryer later on down the road!"

"Go to the farmers' market and buy vegetables by the bushel. Sit those children down on the back steps shelling black-eyed-peas and butter beans to freeze—that's what I'd do!"

"And freeze chickens! All those fryers in the backyard will turn three months at the same time. We can't kill fifty chickens and eat 'em all on the same weekend, so—"

"Last Sunday I fried three chickens while you were bathing Billy and getting him all bandaged and everything. *Three* chickens! . . . It's

271

Little Rappy who's starting to eat like a field hand! And Tommy! I ain't never seen an eight year-old eat like that child! He's as thin as a rail so I don't know where he puts it!"

"He *runs* it off—never sits still—talks a mile-a-minute and never shuts up! But, as long as we've got those coops in the backyard, I don't begrudge anybody all the chicken they can eat. Baby chicks are cheap, Mama."

"It's the feed that costs so much. Thank God that Joe Midgette works for Lamey's and gets an employee's discount."

Outside on the sidewalk the two women walked briskly down Royal Street to the parking lot. At the corner of Dauphin they stopped for the light to turn green. Although still chilly, the weather had warmed a bit and both women were wearing light topcoats over their wool dresses. Overhead the noon sun was brilliant.

"It's hard to believe that it's all gone, Mama," Alyce gazed wistfully into the window of Three Sisters at an expensive tweed overcoat with lapels trimmed in a rich chocolate velvet.

"*What's* all gone?"

"All our savings, everything we've saved since we got married."

"Yeah, I suspect it would be gone with what you've been through with Billy."

"*Seventeen* years of savings gone in *seventeen* months."

♪♪♪♪

Alyce and Rappy managed to put on a fine Christmas with a budget of $100. The two oldest children—Rappy and Mickey—received store-bought clothes they both needed to attend sock hops at McGill where Rappy was a freshman. Mickey, in the eighth grade at St. Mary's, attended boy-girl parties in her classmates' homes where teenagers learned to dance with each other under the supervision of parents as chaperones. Grandma Fanane would have approved.

For the middle children—Shirley, 11 and Tommy 8—Alyce found inexpensive puzzles and games that thrilled them both. For the two little girls—Snookums, 4 and Cathy 2—there were all kinds of toys on sale at the last minute at Kress and W.T. Grant. For all the children she stuffed their stockings hanging on the fireplace mantle with apples, oranges, satsumas, lots of hard candies and Hershey kisses. Each child dug deep, eager to discover what tiny surprise toy might be found in the toe of the red flannel stocking. The stocking had been embroidered with the child's name by Grandma Hicks before she moved out three years earlier.

For each other, Rappy and Alyce exchanged gifts with a special meaning. He gave her a box of six Hershey bars—without almonds—as he had done every year since returning from World War II. Her gift to him usually was something he direly needed. When money was tight, she gave him six pairs of black dress socks to wear to the bank. In years when she had $5.00 left in her Christmas budget, she gave him a dozen Tampa Nugget cigars from Albright and Wood.

Alyce made sure Josephine arrived at 7:00 in the morning so she could be at the tail end of the line, right behind Little Rappy, when the children gathered in the central hall behind the closed doors. For Alyce it was a joy to hold the hand of the youngest child as she led the line into the living room. She reveled in the gleeful delight as each child, especially the younger ones, saw what Santa had left for them under the fir tree.

At the back of the line, Little Rappy, now even more devilish at fourteen, teased Josephine that Santa hadn't left her anything because she had been naughty. Josie hooped and shouted in playful fun, "Miz Pee-rez! Rappy's goin' at me agin! You make him stop! He be bad!"

Under the tree was a gift for Josephine, a beige cardigan sweater Alyce found on Lerner's clearance table on Christmas Eve minutes before the store closed. Holding the sweater high for all to see, Josephine literally screamed in delight. When she opened her present from Shirley, a ten-cent bar of scented soap from Kress, Josie took a deep whiff of the heavy perfume, pressed it to her tiny bosom and shouted over and over again, "Thank you, Jesus! . . . Thank you, Jesus! . . . Thank you, Jesus! . . . Thank you, Jesus! . . . Thank you, Jesus! . . . Thank you, Jesus!"

What was lacking in expensive gifts was made up in the festive food, drinks, and Christmas traditions prepared weeks in advance by Alyce, her mother, and Rappy as well. The three labored lovingly to assure the house was decorated with fragrant southern-pine boughs on the mantles and loads of colored lights lining the window frames outside. A live Douglas fir dominated the living room window, a tree so tall that the halo of Sweet-Angie-the-Christmas-Tree-Angel scraped the low ceiling. Since there was little extra money available, the trio compensated by spending a lot of time and energy to create a memorable holiday season.

Of course, there were the three traditional fruitcakes and dozens of homemade iced Santa cookies for the younger children. Rappy made sure he had two bottles of bourbon on hand for visiting guests and for the traditional eggnog. The turkey dinner was sumptuous and plentiful with both chocolate and lemon meringue pies for those who didn't like their fruitcake soaked in bourbon. Alyce worked diligently to provide the luxuries of a festive holiday so that her children would grow up learning that the joy of Christmas lay not in 'presents' but in brothers and sisters, cousins, aunts and uncles, friends who dropped by Laurel Street with their large families, special holiday foods—and in the place of honor in the center of the mantle, the manger scene.

♪♪♪♪

On an early January morning—moments after she had risen from her tea-and-toast at the kitchen table—Alyce heard the doorbell ring.

Who in the world could that be at 8:30 in the morning?! . . . I've got to get Billy up, strip his bed and start a load of wash with all his bedsheets and diapers and get it on the line so it'll be dry when Mickey and Shirley get home!

And the radio said this rain might turn into sleet before the day is out!

Lord, can't you please find a way to send me a clothes dryer before Rappy goes out and buys that deep-freeze?

274

Peeking out the front window as she waddled to the door, Alyce recognized Peggy Walsh standing on the front porch with a large paper bag, probably full of groceries from Aunt Pauline. Peggy was the youngest of Aunt Pauline's six children. Married to Jack Walsh who worked with his family's successful Walsh Stevedoring, Peggy reveled in her domestic life raising her seven children, even though she had earned a Bachelor's degree from a college in Quebec and was fluent in French and Spanish.

Before meeting Peggy, Alyce feared she'd be intimidated by Rappy's educated cousin who had traveled to Europe before settling down to marry, but when she finally did meet Peggy, Alyce found her delightful and unaffected. Just chatting with her about raising teenagers, one would never know that Peggy was so well-educated.

"Alyce! . . . You look like you're ready to have that baby right here in the doorway!"

"I *feel* like it, Peggy! Come in and get out of that cold!"

"Mama wanted to come with me, but I'm not about to bring her out in this weather. She just can't admit how old she's getting!"

Alyce led Rappy's cousin to the kitchen where they passed through the hallway strewn with three makeshift clotheslines draped with clothes drying over the large gas stove.

"Excuse the laundry," Alyce gestured to the clotheslines stretched from wall to wall.

"My goodness, Alyce! Every time I drop by here you've got somebody's pajamas drying over the stove," Peggy laughed.

"That's because everybody owns only one pair of pajamas! . . . But today I have a whole wash-load drying over the stove. I left it outside on the line all night and it's all stiff as a board from that freeze."

"Jack just bought me an electric clothes-dryer, Alyce! As soon as you and Rappy get back on your feet," Peggy glanced awkwardly at Alyce's belly, monstrously big at eight months pregnant, "you're gonna *have* to get one! . . . Your whole life will change!"

"I can't wait, Peggy!" she laughed heartily.

"Mickey's in the eighth grade this year, right? Is she going to the Convent next year like you did?"

"I hope so! . . . You know the Sisters of Mercy give a full scholarship to the St. Mary's girl who's tops in her class."

"The girl with the best report card?"

"It used to be the best report card, but with two eighth grades they figured one teacher might grade easier than the other one, so now they give some kind of academic test."

"Probably a standardized exam," Peggy mused, "but from what they tell me, Mickey'll come out first—don't worry!"

"Well, she's gonna have to beat Helen Andrews who's real good at taking tests."

"I'll get Mama to say a rosary for Mickey . . . to *Our Lady of Guadalupe*. You'd be surprised how quickly Mama's prayers are answered!"

"No, I wouldn't!" Alyce gazed at the bag of groceries still in Peggy's arms and thanked God for Rappy's generous and loving family.

♪♪♪

The second Jerome Perez was born on February 8, 1952.

At seven pounds he was a healthy baby with enough stamina to carry the name of Rappy's favorite brother who six and a half years earlier had been found dead on a Costa Rican train track.

The previous July when Alyce first confirmed she was pregnant for the eighth time, she realized that the baby, if born a boy, would definitely be called "Romie." Not that she was giving in to Rappy, but it was no longer in his control—or hers—because Rappy's sister-in-law had thrown a wrench into the name debate.

In the middle of World War II, Rappy's youngest brother, Joe, got married in 1943 while still in the Navy. He married Mary Johnson, a Catholic girl who had attended high school at the Visitation Convent with the French nuns. When Mary delivered her third child in the summer of 1951, Alyce had just discovered she was pregnant with her eighth child, the one Rappy hoped would be a boy to name 'Jerome', so he

276

could call him 'Romie', although he knew Alyce was opting for the nickname of 'Jerry'.

Mary Perez announced to the extended Perez family that she was naming her second boy after the Patron Saint of Mothers, the popular St. Gerard. Before she brought the baby home from Providence hospital, she was already calling him 'Jerry'.

"She *knew* I was planning to call this baby 'Jerry' if it's a boy," Alyce tried not to show how bitter she felt.

"She probably didn't even know you were pregnant when she decided on that name! . . . Now, which saint is it?" Rappy struggled to sympathize with his wife.

"*Gerard*! . . . I've told you twelve times already! *Everybody's* naming their baby boy 'Gerard' these days! It's a fad!"

"Hickory, if this baby's a boy—and we won't know for another seven or eight months—you can still call him 'Jerry', can't you?"

"How *can* we?! . . . The two boys'll be only one year apart in high school! Grammar school won't be any problem—Mary and Joe send their children to Little Flower! But they'll be at McGill at the same time! You can't have two Perez boys named 'Jerry' at McGill *at the same time*! Think of the confusion!"

"Well, then we'll just have to call our boy 'Romie', won't we?"

"You'd like that just fine, wouldn't you!?"

"Aw, Hickory, the baby might be a girl."

"Not with all the prayers you've been saying morning and night on your knees at the side of our bed!"

"I'm praying God'll send a cure for Billy!"

"*And* you're praying for a baby boy come February that you can call '*Romie*'!"

"So, you think my prayers have been answered?" he teased.

"Not if I can help it!" she turned on her heel and headed for the washing machine behind the kitchen.

Jerome Frederick Perez came home from Providence Hospital not as 'Jerry', but as 'Romie'. And ironically, fifteen years later when the two cousins were at McGill high school, the grades for Gerard Perez were mistakenly entered into record for Jerome Perez, and *vice-versa*, on more than one occasion.

The day after Romie arrived, Alyce was taken to the operating room for varicose vein surgery. Dr. Dowling had first tried to convince her to have the veins removed when she was pregnant with Billy, but Alyce postponed the surgery.

"You should've had this procedure done when Billy was born," the genial Dowling said as he examined Alyce's legs in January, just a month before Romie was born.

"Well, I'll have it done this time," she winced as he poked around her swollen ankles.

"You can wait until the spring—there's no real hurry."

"We better do it this time. Once I leave that hospital you'll never get me back in there—not with two babies home in diapers and still no clothes dryer."

"You've got seven places I need to cut out."

"*You*? . . . I thought you were a General Practitioner!"

"I am. . . . But I deliver your babies, don't I? So I can cut out these varicose veins just as well. It's not complicated like brain surgery."

"Sure, go ahead! I trust you more than some expensive surgeon I don't even know. Just make sure you've got me knocked out good!"

"Like I said, you've got seven places I'm gonna cut out—the worst being the left ankle and that bad place behind the right knee."

"Just do what you have to do, and make sure you order a full two weeks recuperation *in the hospital*. That's what the bank policy covers—fourteen days—and I want every one of 'em."

〽〽〽〽

Just look at my stomach all sticking out as if I'm five months pregnant!

With each baby it gets worse. Dr. Dowling says the abdomen muscles are all stretched from so many pregnancies. I hope he was joking when he said I need to do sit-ups. Even so, when would I find time? . . . I can just see myself on the floor

278

*trying to do sit-ups while balancing a new baby on my stom-
ach and a three year-old toddler vying for attention and Billy
lying in his bed waiting for me to bathe him, change him, and
get him up! . . . Maybe I should gain twenty pounds on my
hips and fanny so my stomach wouldn't stick out so much.*

*And my hair! . . . Just look at it! Barely thirty-nine years old
and I'm more grey than brunette! And it's not a pretty grey—
it's yellowish! If I dyed it like all the other bank wives do,
Rappy would throw a fit! Easy for him to be so cavalier about
it all—he doesn't have a grey hair in his head!*

*All right! If the Lord wants 'grey hair', then it's grey hair.
Maybe when it ALL turns grey I won't mind it so much. And
maybe if I stand up real straight I can hold in my stomach and
not look five months pregnant when I'm not!*

*No self-pity, Alyce! Think of all the folks who're much
worse off than you and Rappy! Those poor orphans growing
up at St. Barbara's home! Think of that sweet girl you called
'Pot-licker' who needs to lose weight. And I bet she could
use a new party dress this spring like Mickey—not a hand-
me-down, but a dress made just for her. Does that girl have
a grandmother who can sew for her? Does she even HAVE a
grandmother?*

*Time to get out of yourself and do for others. It's springtime
and the city's bursting with azaleas, wisteria, dogwood, and
bridal wreath and everything! Do some charity work a few days
a week so you can return home with a better perspective.*

You need to get out of the house more!

Mickey didn't win the scholarship to the Convent of Mercy high
school. Helen Andrews did.

That meant next September Rappy would be paying tuition at
three different schools—McGill Institute for Little Rappy, Convent of
Mercy for Mickey, and St. Mary's for Shirley, Tommy, and kindergarten for Snookums.

Tuition was just half the problem. The Brothers of the Sacred Heart at McGill were not so bad about assigning class projects that cost more money, but they were guilty of changing the textbooks every two or three years—especially the science books—which meant Little Rappy's books couldn't be saved for Tommy's use six years down the road.

The Sisters of Mercy at both St. Mary's and the Convent were forever sending home notes to the parents asking for money for all kinds of class projects, not to mention the endless contributions to the African missions. One enterprising nun even concocted a scheme to 'ransom pagan babies from China.' Tommy collected Coke bottles and returned them to Weinacker's to earn ten cents a week for twenty weeks so he could name a pagan baby after himself, trusting that a Maryknoll missionary in China would baptize the baby with Tommy named godfather. The baby was placed, supposedly, in a Roman Catholic orphanage and raised as a Catholic, not a pagan.

And then there were the benefit events to raise money for the school's PTA. Because Rappy worked for a bank, the nuns, priests, and brothers at all three schools expected him to keep the books and provide strategies to raise funds for reducing the school debt and financing new building projects. .

"A what?" Alyce stared at Rappy as they finished a spaghetti and meatball dinner alone after he came in late from moonlighting at the Tiny Diny where he kept books on Tuesdays for his brother, Julius.

"A benefit dinner, Hickory. Monsignor O'Donoghue wants me to organize a benefit dinner to raise funds to pay off the school debt."

"They just moved into that new building three years ago! It takes years to pay off a debt that big! You need to tell him that!" she speared the last meatball and cut it in half.

"He knows it, but he doesn't want to pay it off out of the Sunday collection. He's thinking of an annual benefit, some kind of special dinner for 1,000 people or more who pay $1.00 a plate."

"You don't know how to cook a dinner for 1,000 people, Rappy! You wouldn't know how much ingredients to buy, proportions and all that! Every time you cook crab gumbo it comes out different! Sometimes it's good—sometimes your roux has so much flour that I can't taste the seafood!"

"*You* could do it," he gave a sidelong glance, expecting her to hit the roof.

"Me? . . . I've never cooked for that many people," she calmly dismissed the idea.

"You cook for ten people every night, Hickory! Just multiply the ingredients by a hundred and you're all set to go!"

"You're talking crazy, Rappy!"

"I'll help you with the Math to determine proportions and all that!"

He stared at his empty plate for a full minute, knowing better than to press further.

Finally she spoke.

"What does Monsignor want you to cook?"

"Anything that'll make a big profit. We need to find something where all the ingredients can be donated," he turned abruptly in his chair and leaned toward her.

"You'll never get *everything* donated," she gazed into the mirror over the sideboard as she considered possible menus.

"He can get fish donated from Star Fish and Oyster—my Gonzales cousins donate seafood all the time, *everywhere*. What about a fish fry?"

"You'll have to get the cooking oil donated. You're gonna use a lot of oil to fry that many fish. And what will you serve with the fish? Hushpuppies? French fries? Cole slaw?"

"What about grits?"

"Grits?!" she laughed and cocked her head flirtatiously. "Rappy, few folks in St. Mary's parish would think fried mullet and grits is a fancy meal—not enough to pay a whole dollar a plate!"

"It doesn't have to be fancy—just tasty!"

"Besides, I wouldn't be able to find enough Room Mothers willing to stand over a hot frying pan to fry that many fish. Think of something else."

He glanced at the half of a meatball remaining on her plate.

"What about *that?*" he pointed at the meatball.

"Spaghetti and meatballs? . . . Maybe. . . . But it takes too long to press that many meatballs together. What about spaghetti and *chili?*" she was becoming more enthused by the minute.

"You mean like Dew Drop chili—a bowl of Mexican chili, or the kind they put on the hot dog?"

"Just leave out the chili powder and add more tomatoes. You've got the recipe, don't you? From your Uncle George Widney?"

"You mean from when I worked for him in high school? When he opened that first Dew Drop at Government and Ann? . . . . I think I lost that recipe when I changed our safety-deposit box at the bank."

"I make a pretty good spaghetti sauce—if I don't have to cut back on lean ground beef. That's the secret . . . *lean!*"

"I'll get Haas-Davis or somebody to donate the best beef," he urged her on.

"Now, the school cafeteria has all the canned tomato sauce we need. They get it free from the federal government—in those big gallon cans. Mr. Gordon Smith will surely donate the French bread—he likes you—and we've got butter from that federal government program. And you *know* Numa Kearns will donate all the lettuce and carrots and produce for a salad, as well as onion and garlic for the meat sauce."

"So what's left?"

"Spaghetti. You'll have to find somebody to donate the spaghetti. *Then* you'll have a spaghetti dinner benefit."

"So you'll do it?" he held his breath.

"Only if you make sure I've got help at home the week you host the benefit. . . . The *whole* week! Mama'll be here to baby-sit at night, but I want Josephine here during the day—*every* day that week!"

And that's the moment when Alyce and Rappy brought forth their legendary "Spaghetti Suppers" that were staged in the Mobile diocese for twenty years, even after their last child was graduated from McGill high school in 1976. After the rousing success of the first Spaghetti

282

Supper, the couple was besieged by PTA presidents from Catholic parishes all over Mobile to advise them on how to stage a profitable benefit.

Usually 'advising' meant that Rappy and Alyce spent four weeks planning the event and then put on white aprons to direct the supper in the cafeteria kitchen of the neighboring school. At one point in the 1960s they were called upon by St. Rose of Lima's parish on Mon Luis Island to stage a fish fry. Alyce warned Rappy against wandering from their spaghetti expertise, but he convinced her to go along because the Creole parishioners at St. Rose on the coast were fantastic fry-cooks. The fish fry was not only profitable—it was a triumph for the parish.

"Did you say that *Mobile Press Register* photographer takes our picture *tomorrow*? In the cafeteria at St. Mary's? . . . Ten o'clock?" Rappy muttered as he slipped on his pajama top.

"They don't want me—they want *you*!" Alyce sat in the bedroom rocker giving Romie a bottle.

"It's Josephine's day to iron tomorrow, isn't it? . . . There's no reason why you can't come."

"I've got a lot to do tomorrow, Rappy! I don't need to be in the picture."

"You're the one who came up with the recipe—the whole idea to serve spaghetti!"

"Yeah, but you're the one who's president of the PTA, who keeps books for Monsignor. And what does Mr. McRae say about you taking off to have your picture taken in the middle of the morning?"

"He thinks it's great. He wants all his employees to do some kind of community service. He encourages it cuz it looks good for the bank."

"Tell him it'll look even better if the photograph caption reads, 'From left to right, Rappy Perez, president of the PTA and Assistant Vice-President of Merchants National Bank', . . . wouldn't you think?"

"If they ever make me an officer, Hickory, they'll start with 'Assistant *Cashier*'."

"They passed you over again in January this year, but Aunt Pauline says she's doubling her efforts with Our Lady of Guadalupe."

"Then maybe next year'll be my year."

"You'll need a white chef's hat for that photo tomorrow."

"Where am I gonna find *that*?"

"I've already called Sr. Mary Rosario and told her to find you one . . . or else she should have her art teacher make one out of crepe paper and white cardboard."

"What'd she say?"

"When I told her the chef's hat in the newspaper picture would double her ticket sales, she jumped on the idea. That Sister can smell money behind a steel door!"

Fawn River
South Mobile County, Alabama
January 21, 2012

"You never did explain why you did so much charity work," I stood at the window keeping my eye out for the blue heron.

"You mean the spaghetti supper benefits? . . . That was Rappy's idea," she pushed her walker across the tile floor on her way back from the bathroom.

"It was *your* recipe."

"Don't start that again! I *told* you! . . . Monsignor O'Donoghue asked Rappy to stage a benefit to reduce the debt on that new school building. Rappy thought it'd be a one-time event, but it just grew into an annual thing. Before we knew it, parishes all over the diocese were calling on us to teach them how to do it."

"Why didn't you just give 'em your spiral notebook and let 'em take it from there?"

"I'd never part with that yellow spiral notebook! It has wedding plans in it and a lot more!" she glared at me as if I had asked her to give away the family Bible.

"But you didn't have to go back to the same parish every year, did you?"

"Not usually, but sometimes we had to if they forgot to keep careful records! Most parishes gathered a volunteer team that ran with the ball the first year. I made 'em get their own spiral notebook and take notes. They needed an inventory of ingredients, all the way down to parmesan cheese."

"Forget the spaghetti suppers! I wanna know about your own charity work. Why'd you do so much?" I crossed to the sofa and sat down.

"It wasn't all that much," she settled herself into her recliner and closed her eyes.

"The Altar Society, the Ladies Sodality, the—"

"It started with the Altar Society right after the war, I think, but it might've been with the Sodality . . . I can't remember."

"What made you volunteer for all these charities?"

"The Altar Society and the Sodality were *church* organizations—not charities!"

"But you volunteered for the Ladies of Charity and St. Barbara's Home, and probably a bunch of other groups you don't brag about, like the March of Dimes."

"I wanted to get out of the house."

"I think you realized there were a lot of folks much worse off than yourself . . . worse off than you, Bubber, and your mama when ya'll were so poor on Bayou and Savannah, even before that Great Depression."

"And to get away from all my children on Laurel Street. On days when Josephine came in the back door, I was already halfway out the front door!"'

"You must've felt a moral obligation to help folks less fortunate than you and Rappy."

"I needed free time! . . . Caretakers need free time. That's why I urge Mickey and Pal to go out to eat alone and leave me here. If I fall and break my neck while they're gone, then I'm just dead!"

"It was your mother, wasn't it? She was your example. Ya'll were poor—her refusing to touch that $2,000 I left her in life insurance—but

286

she helped neighbors worse off than the Hicks and Fanane families. It was in your blood to help others, even when you and your husband were so poor in the early 1950s."

"Mama shouldn't have given Pike Garrett that money."

CHAPTER **15**

THE FREEZER ARRIVED on the second Saturday in October, 1952.

Alyce wasn't notified the appliance was on its way until Sears and Roebuck called the day before to ask what time they could deliver on Saturday.

"*What* freezer?" she shouted into the phone.

"It's an 18 cubic-foot Kenmore, *upright* with a door that opens like a refrigerator," the shipping manager sounded as if he were reading from an invoice.

"I didn't order a deep-freeze!" she had just finished dressing and bandaging Billy's *bifida* and was about to lift him off her bed when the phone rang. "Maybe my husband did! Lemme call him at the bank and I'll get back to you! What's your number?"

"It's a gift—an anonymous gift, Mrs. Perez. What time tomorrow can we deliver it?"

"A *gift*?! . . . Who's giving us a deep-freeze?"

"*Anonymous*! . . . I can't say! . . . And we call it a 'freezer'. Nobody calls it a deep-freeze anymore."

Are you sure it's not really a clothes-dryer you're supposed to deliver?"

Rappy and Alyce never found out who gifted the freezer. Rappy assumed it was Timmy Dimatteo, a teller at the bank who was his teammate on the YMCA basketball and baseball teams in the 20s and

30s when both were new at the bank. Timmy was a bachelor in his early fifties who lived with his mother within walking distance of the bank. With no family to support, he saved most of his salary and often helped out his colleagues in need.

Alyce speculated it was the girls from the Bookkeeping Department where Rappy was manager. He supervised forty employees, mostly young single women with cash to spare, who adored him because he treated them so well. Because of his sense of fair play—and without even realizing it—Rappy had become an advocate for every female employee in the bank, not just his Bookkeeping girls. Before World War II all the tellers in the cages were men. When Rappy returned from the war, he discovered that women had been hired to work as tellers to replace the men fighting in Europe and the Pacific.

"Mr. McRae," Rappy stood before the bank president only two weeks after returning to work in 1946, "are those nine girls gonna keep their jobs as tellers—or will they be sent back to the file room?"

"We lost too many men in the war, Rappy. We need those girls as tellers. They've been at it for two years and are doing fine."

"Then, don't you think we ought to pay them the same salary as the male tellers, sir?"

"Well, Rappy, I never thought about it."

"They're doing the same job."

"Then they'll be making more than your girls in Bookkeeping."

"But my girls don't have to stand up all day in high heels and smile at customers."

"Do you want me to bring it up before the Board of Directors?"

"I'll leave that to *you*, sir, but giving them equal pay would entice a real smart girl to apply here instead of at the First National . . . or the American."

Alyce figured that the girls in Bookkeeping passed the hat for their boss as they did twice a year for Christmas and Rappy's birthday and bought the freezer. Probably they overheard him at work talking on the phone to the Amana salesman as well as the folks at Sears and Roebuck.

If only he'd been asking for quotes on a dryer instead of that silly deep-freeze—I mean, 'freezer'. . . . But I see an upside to this. Whatever money he's already saved in that separate account for the freezer can be earmarked for my clothes-dryer!

So I'm gonna act real thrilled about the freezer and encourage him to continue scraping money off the top of his salary for that special savings account. If they make him an officer next January, I'll have that dryer.

When the Sears and Roebuck truck arrived the next morning, Saturday, Rappy was puttering in the backyard, keeping one eye on Billy who was sitting in his high chair in the middle of the St. Augustine lawn. The child, now over two years old and stringing together a few sentences, sat watching Snookums and Cathy jump into piles of fallen leaves.

Rappy was the first to spot the delivery truck backing into the driveway. Shirtless and in work shorts, he sprinted down the driveway with a garden hoe in one hand shouting like a kid on Royal Street as a Mardi Gras parade approaches from far down the street:

"Alyce! It's here! Get *out* here, Alyce! It's here!"

"All *right*, Rappy!" she calmly walked to the front door from the kitchen. "Stop yelling! The neighbors'll think we've never had furniture delivered in our whole lives!"

It was a white mountain of an appliance. There was no place for it in the small kitchen so it ended up in the dining room. Rappy and his oldest son quickly slid the china cabinet out of the way as two delivery men guided the huge freezer—teetering on a trolley—through the living room and into a dining room corner.

"It looks like something that fell out of the North Pole," Alyce murmured from the kitchen doorway.

"A glacier," Little Rappy chuckled at his mother's irritation.

"Think of all the money we'll save!" Rappy stood next to Alyce, still shirtless, sweating in excitement.

"I *know* you're heading out to the farmers' market this afternoon, so let me give you a list of vegetables the children like! Don't you come back here with six bushels of stuff they won't eat!"

"Just cook it and put it in front of 'em, Hickory! Tell 'em they *have* to eat it!"

"But why not give 'em vegetables they *like*? . . . Besides, *I* might not like what you buy and bring back here to freeze! I'm not like *you*! I don't like *all* vegetables!"

ﻭﻭﻭ

At the end of the month Rappy bought another 100 baby chicks at a Post Office auction. Although the notice in the newspaper announced 'bidding open to the public', he was the only bidder. It was a Sunday afternoon, so nobody else showed up on the steps of the main Post Office down the street from the Merchants National Bank. When the postal clerk emerged through the front door at four o'clock sharp, he didn't find the usual crowd of anxious farmers waiting to bid on the baby chicks unclaimed by the addressee. Running into Rappy Perez's family in Sunday dress and Catholic school uniforms at the foot of the steps, he almost dropped the carton containing the peeping chicks.

The Perez family had just come from the Christ the King parade and benediction in Bienville Square, celebrated annually (pre-Vatican II Council) on the last Sunday in October.

Rappy, having marched with St. Mary's chapter of the Holy Name Society, stood on the bottom step in his navy blue suit, white shirt, and necktie. Alyce stood behind him dressed in her pearl-grey travel suit—tailored by Miss Alice in 1949 for the Oregon bank trip—with white gloves and a veiled charcoal felt hat. Shirley and Tommy were dressed in St. Mary's School uniforms—freshly laundered and ironed—as was required to march in the parade to honor Jesus as 'Christ the King'. Rappy Jr., a sophomore at McGill, was dressed in a suit and tie like his father. Mickey, a freshman at Convent of Mercy, sported her band uniform.

After the benediction by Bishop Toolen was concluded—and the

292

crowd of participants swarming all over the azalea bushes in Bienville Square had dispersed—the Perez children made their way to the front door of the bank building, as they did every year after the parade, to meet their parents. But this year, instead of hurrying directly to the parking lot, the family strolled to the Post Office to bid on the baby chicks.

Rappy bought the chicks with an opening bid of $1.00. No other bidder showed up.

Walking to the car Rappy carried the heavy carton and smiled contentedly like a farmer who had just purchased a prized steer.

"Now, Hickory, when these little fellows become frying size in three months, we can butcher them all at once and freeze 'em! Three fryers per meal means we've got enough chickens in this box for thirty Sundays!"

"Assuming they're all alive in there!" she smiled back, delighted to see her husband so optimistic.

On the way home in the car, Rappy Jr. refused to allow the flat carton of chicks to rest on his lap. He shoved it over to Tommy who peeked into the box and found that six of the chicks were dead from suffocation.

"Good," Little Rappy muttered. "That's six less I'll have to kill."

As the oldest son at fifteen, it was Rappy, Jr. who, every Saturday afternoon after coming home from his half-day bagging groceries for Bill Serda, hastily grabbed three hapless chickens from the larger coop against the backyard fence for Sunday dinner the next day. Alyce assumed she and her husband were the only faithful in St. Mary's parish who—thanks to an antiquated ordinance allowing livestock within the city limits—raised chickens and turkeys in the middle of the city. Every Saturday Little Rappy beheaded three fryers with an old Boy Scout hatchet and threw them into the center of the backyard where they flopped around headless, spraying the St. Augustine grass with swaths of black syrupy blood. Then he had the nauseating job of dipping the three birds into a washtub of steaming water to loosen the feathers before plucking them naked. As a result of the weekly slaughter, at the dinner table the teenager avoided the pieces of legs, thighs, and backs which reminded him he was eating a bird. He ate only the breast which had no hint of bones and joints.

If Josephine by chance was working on Laurel Street on Saturday, Alyce would ask her to kill the chickens for Sunday dinner. Rather than use the Boy Scout hatchet, Josephine would wring the chicken's neck—not with her hands but by a method she claimed was passed down by her grandmother, a plantation slave raised in Conecuh County.

The first time Josephine stepped into the backyard to slaughter the three chickens, Alyce hurried to the back bedroom to observe through the window. It was the first and last time Alyce witnessed the ritual.

Josephine stood under the double clothesline and pulled the two metal wires together with one hand. She lapped one wire over the over. She slipped the neck of the chicken between the taut wires. Then she jumped back as she let go of the two wires. They sprang back to their original positions. The head of the chicken snapped off as the body rocketed across the yard like a white feathered missile. Upon landing, the headless chicken spewed an arc of blood from its neck as it ran in circles.

"So that's what they mean by 'running around like a chicken with its head cut off,' huh?"

Alyce quickly pulled down the window shade and hurried back to the kitchen.

In addition to providing meals for the new freezer, the chicken project was a source of summer clothes for the girls in the family. The first time Uncle Joe Midgette delivered the chicken feed to Laurel Street, Alyce discovered that the 50-lbs sacks were made of brightly colored fabrics.

Look at those sacks! Cotton fabrics! Flowered patterns! All different colors! . . . Mama can make shorts and halter tops for the girls this summer! Matching outfits!

Cute little play-clothes good enough to wear around to Hannon Park! We'll add a little white rick-rack to trim the halter and they'll be snazzy! All I have to do is make sure Rappy doesn't throw away the sacks when they're empty!

To make sure the feed sacks weren't burned in the trash, Alyce convinced her husband to find two 50-gallon metal drums with lids to store the feed—one for chicken feed, the other for turkey feed. When Uncle Joe Midgette delivered the feed, usually on a Friday afternoon, Alyce stood in the garage and supervised the emptying of the sacks into the drums. She made sure Little Rappy used a sharp kitchen knife to cut the top of the cloth sack—she wanted the empty sack handed to her in one piece with no rips down the side.

Outside the kitchen door she turned the sacks inside out and shook them vigorously to get rid of the feed dust. Then she ran them through the washing machine . . . twice. When Miss Alice came over for Sunday dinner, she took the squares of fabric home where she slit open the sides, laid them out on her bedroom floor, and designed shorts and halters for her four grand-daughters—no sewing pattern needed.

♪♪♪♪

It was the day after her fortieth birthday, January 21, 1953 when Alyce concluded she was pregnant for the ninth time. By her own reckoning she had probably conceived in late October which meant the new baby would arrive in July. Romie wouldn't turn one until February and here she was—already pregnant again.

Forty! . . . Three months pregnant! And look at this streak of yellow running from my widow's peak. It's so ugly against my black hair. I want to dye my hair. I admit it. I can stand the grey, but this ugly yellow has to go.

I tried to laugh when Mickey and Rappy gave me their birthday present last night with that newspaper column pasted on the gift wrapping. . . . BEAUTY AFTER FORTY. . . . I don't really need to be reminded how old I am. . . . As if I have time to read that newspaper column to learn beauty tips! Or to use them! Or to afford that moisturizing night cream, whatever she advised in that silly newspaper column!

And why do so many of my babies come in the summer?! . . . Mickey, Shirley, Tommy, Billy—four of them! And now this one!

Lord, help me get through next summer! I can put Billy in his bed at noon for his nap, but Romie'll be only 18 months and tearing all over the house. So, you know he won't be ready for a nap when I am. And nobody'll be able to nap in July in this house with only a window fan and a bunch of small oscillating fans.

I'm not asking for one of those new air-conditioners . . . yet. Margie's got three of them sticking out of her windows. But let's think about them down the road, okay?

Now about the clothes dryer! . . . Are you listening, Lord? . . . I'm not just talking to hear myself talk! . . . This is a prayer!

At age fourteen Mickey had become aware that Alyce had a life other than being mother to eight children.

As a freshman at Convent of Mercy high school, Mickey pledged ADK sorority, the social organization which Alyce had founded in 1931 which now inducted girls in their first year of high school. Going through the old scrap books in the ADK archives, Mickey discovered that her mother had been a *very* popular girl before marriage. There were many snapshots of Alyce taken by her friends where they mugged before the camera at a slumber party. Mickey found lots of newspaper clippings of ADK social activities, including the first Winter Formal where "Miss Alyce Hicks, radiant in a white gown of *peau de soie*, led the ball as president. She chose as her escort Mr. Alfred Leonard 'Rappy' Perez, employee with Merchants National Bank."

When Alyce approached Mickey in the 8th Grade and offered

a basic explanation of the birds and the bees, it was shortly before Alyce delivered baby #8. When Romie arrived a month later, it was the first time that Mickey—at the age of thirteen—was able to fully comprehend how a woman became pregnant, what labor and delivery really entailed. And a year later, watching her mother standing at the stove three months pregnant with baby #9, Mickey realized that her parents evidently enjoyed an active sex life. Probably more active than the fourteen year-old could imagine.

Now she and her mother were sorority sisters. Mickey wanted her mother to enjoy life again as she had back in the 1930s as a popular girl in the ADKs. There was little Mickey could do to help, except offer to baby-sit so that her mother and daddy could go out more often to forget the many responsibilities at home, especially taking care of Billy. Mickey decided she could share with her mother her daily life at the Convent of Mercy, Alyce's alma mater, from where her mother had so many memories of carefree days.

"Now, Mickey," Alyce pointed to six serving bowls on the kitchen table, "I agree with your Home Ec teacher that each dinner plate needs some 'color and texture', but Sister Andrea probably doesn't realize that I don't serve the plates in the *kitchen*—I carry serving bowls to the dining room so everybody can serve themselves."

"Sister says that's called 'family style', Mama," Mickey was rummaging around in the silverware drawer.

"We're talking about eleven hungry people at that table, assuming your daddy's not keeping books on a given night, and few people in this house like the same vegetables!"

"Yessum," Mickey placed a large tablespoon in each empty bowl, "but Sr. Mary Andrea says we just need to make sure each meal has a *few* different colors and at least two or three different textures."

"Well, she'd love this meal! . . . We've got *white* mashed potatoes, *orange* carrots, and *red* weenies! . . . The weenies are kind of firm, the mashed potatoes are gooey, and the carrots are . . . well, overcooked. I ought to get an 'A' for 'color and texture' on this meal, don't ya' think?"

"It's colorful all right," Mickey laughed. "But Sister says something green always perks up the dinner plate."

"A green vegetable?"

"Yessum! . . . Like spinach."

"I don't like spinach, Mickey," Alyce declared solemnly.

"Neither do I," Mickey furrowed her brow and then giggled.

"The only greens I serve are *turnip* greens. Your daddy and I love 'em, and so do Rappy and Tommy, especially when Josephine cooks 'em with yellow cornbread. Most of the time I just serve vegetables everybody'll eat, like black-eyed peas, field peas, crowder peas, pork-and-beans, and—"

"None of them are green!"

"There's always *green beans*! . . . Everybody likes green beans!

꒰꒰꒰

The next night Alyce noticed Mickey was unusually quiet at the dinner table, not offering any anecdotes about what went on at the high school that day.

"What happened at school today?" Alyce deposited the stack of dirty plates on the kitchen counter next to the sink where Mickey was washing and Shirley was drying the dinner dishes.

"Nothing," Mickey concentrated on the mound of silverware in the sudsy water.

"You can tell me," Alyce glanced at Shirley drying the glasses. "Shirley won't repeat it—or should she leave the room?"

"She can stay," Mickey didn't look up from the sink. "It wasn't such a big deal."

"So, why're you so quiet all night?"

"Sr. Andrea said something in Home Ec that embarrassed me," she mumbled, afraid that her complaint might seem self-centered.

"What'd she say?" Alyce felt her stomach tighten.

"She was teaching us about laundry stains and used *us* as an example," Mickey glanced at her mother.

"*Us?*" Shirley exclaimed. "You and the girls in your Home Ec class?"

298

"Us!" Mickey snapped at her younger sister. "This *family*!"

"She *did*? . . . What'd she say? . . . About *us*?" Alyce felt an age-old conflict rising in her breast. On the one hand she respected nuns as a band of religious women serving Christ, but she resented those individual Sisters who took liberties at a child's expense—whose behavior was so cavalier.

"She was talking about how to remove an ink-stain from a white shirt and she said, 'Now, if one of the little Perez children is playing with a bottle of ink and spills it all over his sister's white uniform blouse, how can we remove the ink-stain?' . . . Or something like that."

"Did you say anything? . . . I imagine you kept quiet," Alyce held her breath.

"Somebody needs to tell *that* sister to mind her own beeswax!" Shirley had stopped drying dishes and stood spellbound.

"I *said*," Mickey began slowly, "I said, 'The little Perez children aren't allowed to play with ink, Sister.'"

"And then?" Alyce urged her on.

"Then Sister said 'Well, let's just imagine that somehow one of them *got a hold* of the ink and spilled it all over your white blouse.' . . . Or something like that."

"That's why God invented Clorox! You don't need Home Ec to know how to bleach white cotton," Alyce didn't try to hide the fact that she was miffed.

"I said, 'Sister, in our house Mama keeps the ink on top of the china closet next to the checkbook. It's so high up that even *I* have to climb on a chair to reach it.' . . . Or something like that."

"That's okay," Alyce downplayed her approval, trying her best not to show that she was tickled her child had stood up to the nun, something Alyce could never have done as a freshman in 1927.

"Do you think she'll report me to Sr. Mary Alda for sassing her?" Mickey looked up from the sudsy water at her mother. "Are you mad at me?"

"No, she's not gonna report you, and I'm not mad. That wasn't sass—it was the truth—unless your *tone* was sassy."

"I tried to sound respectful, but I didn't like being singled out. I mean, there're other girls in Home Ec with little brothers and sisters, so why did she pick on me?"

"She thought she was being cute. Besides, she knows *me*. I would *not* worry about it," Alyce refrained from saying 'I'm proud of you!' for fear of encouraging her daughter to rebel against the nun's authority in the classroom.

Later that night as she lay in bed with her rosary in hand next to her sleeping husband, Alyce reflected on her decision as a high school senior in resisting Sister Consuela's pressure to enter the convent and become a nun.

If I had become a Sister of Mercy, I might be at the Convent right now teaching Home Ec, or Sewing, or Typing and Shorthand. Surely they'd never let me teach Latin or Math!

And Sr. Mary Alda would be my principal, my supervisor! Lord, I haven't seen her in over five years—except at those annual COM reunions. I spoz I ought to call her, but I just don't have time. Now, if Sr. Andrea wants to make something of that business today in Home Ec class, Sr. Alda might be phoning to tattle on Mickey.

If she does, I'll just deal with it. Besides, I don't like any Sister implying that I let my children play with permanent ink! . . . even if she IS a friend from high school.

I never thought of becoming a nun. Frankly I just couldn't see the benefits. Of course, the Sisters don't have to worry about money, that's for sure. They take a vow of poverty— which just means they have no personal savings account at the bank—but all their needs are taken care of, so you could hardly describe that as POVERTY! I bet they eat steak twice a week! The Mother House in Baltimore pays all their medical expenses, which sounds great to me!

But a nun doesn't have a man sitting across from her at supper to share the daily problems of just living. At night she has no one lying next to her whose mere presence gives comfort and peace, even if he's snoring. She's alone.

I can't imagine life without Rappy. We're struggling, of course, but I'm as crazy about him as much as I ever was— and he knows it. And I know how much he loves me.

A nun will never know how that feels.

♪♪♪

On June 1, 1953, Miss Alice walked through her daughter's front door at two o'clock on a blistering afternoon and found Alyce, seven months pregnant, lying on the dining room floor next to the window fan whirring its three huge blades at top speed. In a loose-fitting maternity skirt and sleeveless 'hatching-jacket', Alyce lay on her back with her eyes closed, resembling a swollen sea creature washed up on the beach. The sixteen month-old Romie was asleep at her side, both lying on an old cotton quilt that Grandma Fanane had crafted as a teenager.

"Mama? . . . Is that you?" Alyce opened her eyes as she heard someone walking across the hardwood floors, but she made no attempt to even wave her hand in greeting.

"Don't get up, Alyce!" Miss Alice knelt down next to the baseboard and placed her palm on the forehead of the sleeping Romie.

"It's the coolest place in the house—here on the floor—you get a nice draft blowing over you from this window fan," Alyce said lazily.

"This child's hot as blazes but I don't think he has a fever," Miss Alice quickly rose from her knees with an agility belying her age.

"Mama, go check on Billy for me, please. Make sure that oscillating fan goes back-and-forth. I want it to blow *over* him—not *on* him—and lemme know if he's sleeping."

"Where's Cathy and Snookums?" Miss Alice dropped her purse on the dining room table.

"Shirley's supposed to have them napping in my bed. You might check on them too."

The next day Bill Serda dropped by at noon and found Alyce lying

301

in the same place under the window fan. By five o'clock that afternoon two of his stock boys had arrived at Laurel Street in a pickup carrying two industrial fans that stood on six foot-high stems with wide bases.

"You sure you don't need these fans, Bill?" Alyce asked over the phone later that night as she sat on the floor in the central hall.

"When's the last time you shopped in my store, Hicks?" his voice over the phone was somewhat flirtatious, but raspy from years of cigar-smoking.

"March, I guess. Since I've gotten so big with this baby I don't fit behind the steering wheel real well. It's too uncomfortable to drive all the way out to Spring Hill!"

"I just put in central air-conditioning! The whole store! We're the first supermarket in Spring Hill to be fully air-conditioned! . . . So, you see, Hicks, I don't need those old fans anymore. You're welcome to 'em! Put one of 'em in your bedroom so you don't have to take a nap on the floor to keep cool!"

"Bill, those are some *big* fans!" she chuckled.

"Have you turned 'em on yet? . . . They sound like those new jet airplanes rearing up to take off. Helluva noise, but they do put out a lot of wind!"

"Well, I thank you cuz I can really use 'em."

"The pull-chain on one of 'em is broken off. Just stick the plug in the wall—it runs on just one speed . . . 'High'. You can adjust the other one to run on three speeds. They'll be great for the day, but at night the roar'll keep you awake."

꒰꒱꒰꒱

Rappy's mother, Nellie, suffered a severe stroke on June 15, just one month before Alyce delivered her ninth child. When Alyce got word on the phone, she called the bank and left a message with Rappy's secretary. She turned the house over to Mickey and dashed to Providence Hospital.

If Rappy's mother dies, he won't be able to accept it. He still gets down on his knees twice a day to pray for a cure for Billy—he thinks the child'll walk some day—so how can we expect him to accept the inevitable about his mother's death? It's not the first stroke—she's been on blood pressure medicine for years! It's not like she ignores her diet. I mean, when she and Papa came for Sunday dinner last year, I knew she couldn't eat fried chicken so I had Little Rappy kill another chicken to broil after Mama skinned it good.

If she's unconscious, she could lie there for weeks, not responding to anything! Maybe that'll give Rappy time—not to mention Margie and the others, especially Mary Helen up there in Pittsburgh—give them time to adjust to the fact that their rock is leaving them.

If Margie needs someone to relieve her at Grandma's bedside, I'll surely volunteer. Now I know they'll all say I can be excused from taking my shift cuz I'm about to have this baby any day, but that's the point! I'd rather sit in that air-conditioned hospital room keeping an eye on Grandma Perez than lie on my dining room floor trying to find relief from this god-awful heat!

Lord, you know Rappy'll never be ready to lose his mama.

I can think of only one prayer at a time like this: 'Help us, O Lord, to accept Your will, whatever it may be.'

Two weeks later Miss Alice returned to stay with Billy for the Fourth of July holiday when the whole family left to spend the weekend at Margie and Bill's rented home on the eastern shore in Battles Wharf. Rappy's mother had been in and out of a coma for two weeks. All his brothers and sisters had agreed that they should go about their lives. "That's what Mama would want." They had accepted that their mother would never recover, that her death was imminent. At least it appeared that they had accepted it.

Alyce was looking forward to sleeping on the expansive screened porch, furnished with eight sets of bunk beds, where the luscious bay breeze would blow in from the west all night long.

They arrived on the afternoon of July 3 and spent a fun-filled evening with Margie and her family of seven children, Bill and Rappy drinking beer at the end of the wharf supervising the older children shooting off firecrackers over the moonlit water. Alyce and Margie sat on the screened porch with the smaller children and drank iced–tea after the little ones were put to bed. For Alyce, at eight months pregnant, it was bliss to escape the stifling humidity and heat of midtown Mobile.

But on the next day, the Fourth of July, word came at noon that Rappy's mother had died.

Margie and Rappy immediately grabbed car keys and dashed for the back door. Alyce and Bill Serda had the task of calming them down, reminding them that between the two families, there were fourteen children to take care—half of them diving off the end of the wharf at that very moment.

Within fifteen minutes it was decided that the four adults would drive to Mobile and leave the children in care of their older brothers and sisters. Bill, Jr. at 18, and Rappy, Jr. at 16 were both licensed to drive, so the children would have no problem getting to Mass the next morning, then back to Mobile safely. Mickey would turn 15 next month while her twin cousins and classmates, Joan and Joy, had turned 15 the previous January—all three girls responsible and capable to care for their younger siblings. The refrigerator held a cooked turkey, ham, roast tenderloin and potato salad, four pounds of bacon, two gallons of orange juice, and six dozen eggs. Bill Serda never invited guests to the beach without stocking his larder to the brim from his supermarket. The three COM cousins could use what they had learned in Home Ec to feed the two families for twenty-four hours until they could get everybody packed up to drive the 25 miles back to Mobile.

On the ride back to Mobile alone with Rappy, Alyce avoided conversation for fear he would burst into tears.

This one's a toughie, Lord! Rappy thought his mother hung the moon—and so did I. She imagined her 'Alfred' could do no wrong, probably cuz he kept that family afloat during the Depression by handing his mama his paycheck every two weeks when Papa was having 'hard times'

I don't see how Rappy's gonna make it through this funeral. And me being eight months pregnant, I need to rally some energy to help him.

'Help us, O Lord, to accept Your will.'

In Roche's Mortuary the wake took on an air of Irish festivity. With most of Nellie's twenty-eight grandchildren running up and down the air-conditioned hall and ducking out onto the verandah to chew gum and drink Coca-Colas, Papa., the grieving husband, sat stoically on a brocade settee receiving mourners. He ignored his grown children milling through the guests receiving happy condolences on what a fine woman their mother was, how she surely deserved her reward.

When it came time to seal the coffin, only the two youngest siblings—Joe and Mary Helen—broke down and wept. Their older brothers and sisters rallied with smiles and hugs to remind them that "Mama's better off now".

Rappy made it through the ceremony at the Catholic Cemetery just fine, Alyce observed, until it was all over. At the graveside he comforted his baby sister Mary Helen who, together with her older sister, Margie, was exhausted from the two week hospital vigil, by gently massaging her shoulders as the priest sprinkled dirt on the coffin. But as he walked back to their car after the graveside rites had finished, Rappy collapsed onto the hood of the car. Miss Alice sprung to Rappy's side before anyone else. She urged him to "let it all out, Rappy! Your mama's gone, so it's okay to just let it all out."

In an instant Alyce was at his side, her hand on his shoulder as his whole body shook with grief while he wailed 'I could've done more for her! Oh, Mama! Mama! Mama! Mama!' Because he was inconsolable, Alyce realized he couldn't drive, so she took the car keys out of his hand and threw them to Little Rappy who had already opened the driver's door. As they drove to Papa Perez's house on Johnston Avenue, Rappy wept uncontrollably for three miles as Mickey, Shirley, and Tommy squirmed in the back seat. Then his sobs subsided little by little. By the time they arrived at his parents' house, he was in control of his emotions enough to walk into Papa's house with a smile on his face.

The scene inside the house was even more festive than the funeral home. Rappy's brothers from out-of-town hadn't seen each other in several years and turned the occasion into a party. Rappy's two oldest brothers—Louis and Julius—were both divorced, both drank too much, and both moved from city to city in hopes of settling down. Charles was an Army career officer who had flown in from his base in Hawaii.

Alyce stood in the doorway to the kitchen where the clan had gathered to celebrate their mother's life. Bill Serda grabbed a dining room chair and made her sit down. She was settling into the chair when she saw that her father-in-law had emerged from the bedroom where he had been sedated. At the far end of the kitchen he appeared in the doorway leading from the hall. He was wearing a sleeveless undershirt and white full broadcloth underpants which had three snaps down the front across his broad belly. With one hand he reached to support himself on the doorjamb, staggering with grief. His face showed a scowl of disapproval.

"How can you boys drink whisky like that when we just buried your mother?" he was on the verge of tears.

"Now, Papa," Louis, standing closest to his father—and also the drunkest—tried to put his arm around him, "You know how much we all loved Mama! This is just the only way we can tolerate our loss!"

"You're disrespecting your mother! And you're disrespecting my wife," the old man refused to be patronized. As his knees buckled, he threw off Louis's hand and fell against the kitchen sink.

Four men rushed to his side—two sons as well as two son-in-laws. They caught him as he slid to the floor, guided him out of the kitchen and back to the bedroom where they settled him into his bed.

How pathetic Papa looks! But I'm glad he didn't let Louis humor him. I wish we hadn't named Billy after Louis. At least we don't call him 'Louis' . . . or 'Louie' . . . . . or 'Lou'! Unless you read Billy's birth certificate you'd never know his real name is 'Louis William Perez'.

Papa's gonna have a hard time without Grandma. She was the glue holding this family together. When Romie died, Grandma rallied to support everyone. When Louis went through all his women trouble and several divorces, Grandma was there. And when Julius got in trouble at the bank almost twenty years ago, Grandma stood by him through all his legal problems. And now just look at Louis and Julius getting drunk in their mama's kitchen two hours after we just buried her.

I wonder if Julius knows that he's probably the reason why Rappy hasn't been made an officer at the bank yet. Mr. McRae said he didn't think Rappy was in cahoots with Julius when it happened, but Rappy was questioned for three days by the Board of Trustees. . . and those federal bank examiners who came all the way from Washington as well! They never accused Rappy of helping Julius, but through all these years the Board's never trusted Rappy enough to make him an officer. That's what Mr. McRae tells Rappy every year when he's passed over. It's as if Rappy's been on probation for seventeen years. But Mr. McRae has control of salaries cuz he's the president. He makes sure Rappy gets a small raise every year. So he must not believe Rappy guilty of "aiding and abetting" his brother, or whatever they call it.

I hope Rappy doesn't invite Julius to Laurel Street for a home-cooked meal. If he's staying with Margie and Bill, it's best for all concerned if he just eats with them and gets on a train for Atlanta as soon as he can. At nine months pregnant, I'm not sure I can be civil to Julius, much less make him feel welcome in our home.

307

James Dowling Perez was born on July 23, 1953, less than three weeks after Rappy's mother was buried. Weighing 5 pounds, 5 ounces, he was small but apparently healthy. At two weeks he developed an allergy to cow's milk, manifested by a pink rash on both cheeks. The problem was solved easily by switching to a powdered milk from the pharmacy, but it was an added expense to the monthly budget—which meant Alyce would have to rob from her grocery money to buy the powdered milk. The bigger problem was where to put the new baby's crib.

With only three bedrooms for nine children and their parents, the bungalow on Laurel Street was desperately overcrowded. Little Rappy at age sixteen was squeezed into a small bedroom with Tommy and Romie. Over the summer Mickey had just turned fifteen and Shirley thirteen, both needing privacy from their two little sisters in a double bed next to a second double bed in the larger bedroom.

In the parents' bedroom Rappy fashioned his version of 'crib bunk-beds'. At age three Billy was sleeping in a larger crib—almost a youth-sized bed—with high sides that folded down so he could be lifted. On top of that crib Rappy perched a smaller one with three foot legs on casters. He merely placed the small crib on top of Billy's bed and tied the crib's legs on to the bottom bed with heavy twine. There was enough space for Rappy or Alyce to lean in and lift Billy from the bottom 'bunk' without bumping their heads.

"We're gonna have to mortgage the house," Rappy said wistfully as he lay under a small oscillating fan in only his undershorts.

How do you do that?" Alyce held the infant Jimbo in her arms as she fed him his midnight bottle.

"We just borrow against the house. The house is collateral. We make monthly payments on the interest until we can start paying back the principal."

"Rappy, that's like buying the house all over again!"

"That's right, Hickory," his voice was steady as he stared at the ceiling with his hands clasped behind his head on the pillow.

"We just paid off that mortgage two years ago," she murmured. "So how long would this mortgage be?"

"Ten years. . . . Same period."

"Is this the only answer?"

"Look on the positive side, Hickory! . . . We'll borrow enough money to add a room on the back of the house—a big room for two sets of bunk beds!"

"I want a walk-in closet with sliding doors."

"You want something real modern, huh?"

"And build that room big enough for the freezer. I'd like to get it out of the dining room so we can fit more chairs around the table," she placed the empty baby-bottle on the night-table.

"Rappy can have his own room if we close in the screened porch out front."

"*Close in* the front porch?"

"Yeah. . . . Replace the screen with some kind of windows so it's a room. We'll have to put a space heater out there cuz there's no insulation, but he'll be fine."

"I want *jalousies*," she lifted the infant to burp him.

"What's that?"

"Those wide blinds made out of frosted glass the Cooke's have on their porch."

"Yeah, they'll keep it cool in the summer."

"All right, Rappy, that'll give us a total of five bedrooms. Now what can we do about Billy's hospital bill."

"Keep paying it."

"Two hundred dollars a month?"

"We'll take out a large enough mortgage to cut the balance in half. Let's hope I'm made an officer in January."

"Will we have enough money to add a second bathroom?" she ignored the mention of a possible promotion at the bank.

"Not after we do all that construction and cut the hospital bill in half. We can wait on the second bathroom."

"What about my clothes dryer?"

"That'll have to wait too, Hickory. Right now we have two priorities—*one*, add more rooms, and *two*, pay off the hospital. We'll just have to count on Mickey and Shirley to hang the laundry on the line."

Since Jimbo's birth in late July, Mickey and Shirley had been hanging out diapers in the backyard at least twice a day. Alyce needed clean diapers for the new infant and for Romie, who still wore diapers at the age of eighteen months. And Billy, paralyzed from the waist down, wore diapers all his life. With three children in diapers Mickey and Shirley were given responsibility of washing and drying diapers until school started again in September.

Those girls fill two clothes lines with diapers twice a day! And that's' just DIAPERS! But once school starts again next month, we'll go back to our normal routine where they just bring in one load of dry clothes after they get home from school.

So in September I'll be on my own with regular laundry to do plus all the diapers for three babies!

Now about the clothes dryer! . . . Are you listening, Lord? . . . I'm not just talking to hear myself talk! . . . This is a prayer!

CHAPTER 16

SPINAL TAP.

The mere words sent a bolt of terror through Alyce's entire body. She abhorred the trips to Dr. Patton's office for Billy's spinal tap. All through the years she had learned how to 'get on top' of her own pain so that she never dreaded labor and delivery of her babies. Nor did she panic on the occasions when she sliced her finger deep while chopping onions for a crab gumbo.

Yet nothing upset her more than one of her own children in pain. If it was unavoidable, such as the eight year-old having a tooth filled, the child could endure the fear because it wouldn't last long. Since the child had to get used to having cavities filled, Alyce never remained in the treatment room holding the child's hand while Dr. Doody drilled. Instead, she buried herself in a *Redbook* short-story in the waiting room.

Watching one of her children having his scalp sewn up after a fall from his bike was a bit different. If the child screamed in fear because he wasn't able to see what Dr. Adams was doing with that sharp needle at the top of his head, Alyce reasoned that the trauma was a one-time event for that child, unlikely to be repeated. In that case she sat next to the terrified child—she massaged his shoulders to help him relax.

But the excess fluid in Billy's spine had to be drained once a year.

Sometimes twice. Dr. Patton scheduled the procedure for once a year. But if Alyce noticed Billy grabbing the side of his swollen head, she suspected the fluid was building up on his brain and called Patton.

"Billy, does your head hurt?

"Yessum," the child murmured and gazed at his mother through eyes opened to mere slits.

"Where does it hurt, Billy?

"It hurts here!" he pointed to his temple with a tiny index finger. "Everywhere. It hurts bad, Mama."

Alyce dreaded the procedure. Billy suffered excruciating pain as the long needle pierced his spine through the tender *bifida* at waist level. If only the doctor could enter the spine below the waist—Billy was paralyzed from the waist down—then the child wouldn't feel a thing. But the needle had to enter the spine through the *bifida*.

Whenever the spine was tapped, Rappy took the afternoon off from work. Alyce drove while Rappy sat in the passenger seat with Billy balanced on his lap. When they arrived in Dr. Patton's office for the first spinal tap, Rappy settled himself atop the treatment table with Billy on his lap.

"Is this all right Doctor?" Rappy turned the child so his back was exposed to the doctor.

"He can't move so it doesn't matter. But he may be more comfortable lying on his side."

"He'll feel more secure if I hold him," Rappy declared confidently.

As soon as the needle entered the *bifida*, Billy let out a piercing scream. Rappy's forehead broke out with beads of sweat. His eyes glazed over.

Alyce dashed for the table. Dr. Patton withdrew the needle and grabbed the child as Rappy slid to the floor in a faint. Alyce took Billy from the doctor and laid him on his side on the table. She held Billy's hand and stroked his face while he screamed as the doctor finished the procedure. The nurse tried to rouse Rappy from the floor with spirits of ammonia.

At the next spinal tap, Dr. Patton insisted Rappy sit in a chair next to the open door so he could benefit from an air draft from the hall. Rappy could hear the child screaming but he didn't view the procedure. Still, he fainted and silently slumped off his chair onto the floor. Patton instructed the nurse to let him lie there and wake up on his own.

After that second visit, Rappy wasn't allowed into Patton's treatment room. He sat on the front porch glider—out of earshot from Billy's screams—thumbing through old issues of National Geographic in hopes of finding photos of the Fiji Islands where he had served in World War II.

"Now, how old is he?" Dr. Patton held up the beaker of spinal fluid to check the color.

"Three last July, so he's three and a half now," Alyce sat in a chair holding Billy tightly to her chest to comfort him as he sobbed and trembled in her arms, his oversized head wobbling on his thin neck.

"That case of measles last fall should've been fatal," the doctor murmured as he handed the beaker to his nurse and leaned against the treatment table.

"It doesn't seem to have affected him, Doctor. He still can sit alone and balance himself by holding onto his knees, you know like one of those oriental monks."

"Amazing. . . . It's only January so winter's not over yet. Try to keep him from catching a bad cold until spring gets here."

"Doctor, I can't keep him away from his brothers and sisters."

"I know, but if he gets another serious childhood disease, it might be fatal."

"Which childhood diseases do you consider *serious?*"

"Mumps . . . chicken pox . . . whooping cough . . . meningitis."

"Is meningitis a *childhood* disease?"

"Not really, but that's the one I worry about the most. He was born with an open spine so bacteria can enter his spine easily. Meningitis attacks the spinal column and brain."

"I keep the *bifida* as sterile as possible."

"I'm sure you do, Mrs. Perez."

"Could he survive meningitis?

"Possibly . . . but he'd be so weak, he'd probably waste away in a matter of months."

"Then we have to pray he's never exposed to meningitis."

"All right, Mr. Billy, what do you say about all this, little fellow?"

"I wanna go home," the child murmured and buried his head in his mother's bosom.

In the car Alyce gripped the steering wheel before she turned the ignition key. She girded herself for what she feared would be a confrontation with her husband.

"Come on, Alyce, start the car."

"Not until we agree on something, Rappy."

"Start the car and get the heater going! Billy's cold!"

"So am I, but you've got to stop the weekend outings in the car with Billy."

"Hickory! . . . What're you talking about? Billy loves to ride in the car—he needs to get out of the house!"

"He doesn't feel *secure* in the car, Rappy. He wants to be in his chair . . . or in his bed!"

"We can't keep him cooped up in that house for the rest of his life! . . . In that damn high chair!"

"Stop cussing," she said calmly. "And for all we know, all that fluid in his spine may be affected by the motion of the car moving, like people who get carsick. That could make those headaches much worse!"

"He loves to ride in the car! Don't you, Billy?!"

"I wanna go home," the child's tiny fingers clutched the sleeve of his father's navy suit jacket. His pale white hand quivered like a wounded baby dove.

Lord, don't let this child suffer.

If you're gonna take him, don't let it be a long drawn-out disease. Rappy couldn't endure anything that agonizing. As

314

for me, if it's your Will, I'll have to endure it, won't I? . . . But,
frankly, I'd rather not.

Don't let him fade away slowly.
When the time comes, take him quickly, . . . please.

ﮗﮗﮗ

By the time Jimbo was six months old, Alyce was dependent on Paregoric.

Not for herself. She couldn't conceive of taking drugs to ease emotional pain, but she relied on the prescription opiate to knock out her babies when teething. It was the only way she could get any sleep during the teething phase.

Ever since Cathy cut her first tooth at the age of eight months in October of 1949, Alyce enjoyed an open Paregoric prescription at Nixon Drugs on Old Shell Road across from the Dew Drop Inn. Her pediatrician, Vaughn Adams, had offered her the prescription with unlimited refills.

"*Now* you won't have to call me if she starts teething on a weekend," the doctor picked up his fountain pen and scribbled on a pad.

"They usually start teething in the middle of the night," Alyce chuckled. "They wake up screaming."

"If I'm remembering correctly, Alyce, I've been prescribing this for a couple of years?"

"Lord, Dr. Adams, I've rubbed Paregoric on all my babies' gums— starting with Little Rappy!"

"Then you know the correct dose and how to administer it?"

"We couldn't find it during the war when Tommy started teething, so Mama just rubbed bourbon on his gums."

"Did it work?"

"Killed the pain for a couple of hours, but he didn't sleep through the night like they do with Paregoric."

"As long as you realize it's an opiate—so you have to be sparing."

"You can't get much of that liquid on the tip of your pinky finger."

In January of 1954 Jimbo, six months-old, cut his first tooth on a late Saturday afternoon. It was then that Alyce was grateful for the unlimited Paregoric refills at Nixon Drugs. Standing on the front steps cradling the screaming baby as the winter twilight rapidly turned to night, she waited for the Nixon delivery boy to arrive on his bicycle with the tiny treasure in his pocket. At her side stood Shirley, with Romie balanced on her hip, who tried to quiet the 23 month-old toddler traumatized from the incessant crying from his infant brother.

Tending three babies around the clock required most of Alyce's energy and resourcefulness. Even though Billy was three, Alyce considered him a baby because he required constant care. He had to be put to bed and lifted from it twice a day. He had to be bathed while still in bed, and his *bifida* had to be dressed and bandaged daily. At age three he ate mainly Gerber's strained baby food twice a day with oatmeal or a scrambled egg for breakfast.

Romie, about to turn two in February, was slow to potty train, but Alyce figured she'd have him out of diapers in another six weeks. Then she'd have only Billy and Jimbo, the six month-old, left in diapers.

She wasn't that concerned with finding energy and time to keep the house going. Sure, she was exhausted when she finally climbed into bed at night, usually between midnight and one after ironing a uniform shirt or sewing on a button for somebody—but once her head hit the pillow, she fell asleep immediately. She found it hard to sympathize with folks who complained of insomnia. On the rare occasion when she tossed and turned because one of her children had suffered a crisis at school that day, she asked the Blessed Mother to help her drift off to sleep. Of course, as any mother of nine children would do, she slept with one ear cocked for a crying toddler or the tiny voice of someone standing at the side of her bed because he got lost on the way to the bathroom.

As for finding time to do all the things that needed to be done every day, she did what she could *when* she could. Unlike Rappy who composed a written list every morning, she kept her list in her head. But her *modus operandi* was to do the task that was staring her in the face at the moment. And with ten people in the house to take care of, including Rappy, there was always a priority that rose to the top of her list and cried out for attention.

No, her major concern was neither finding energy nor getting more sleep. It was saving money on meals. Rice-and-gravy was a staple she could serve every night. If she had no fish, chicken, or meat, she still could brown flour in oil and make a gravy. A dab of bacon grease melted with the rice would give it a pork flavor. Served with pork-and-beans as a protein dish, the meal contained enough nutrition until the next night when she hoped to have some ground beef for a shepherd's pie or a meat loaf. She would love to serve a tasty meal each night to please the whims of each child, but even excluding the three babies, she had six older children with varied tastes. She refused to be a short-order cook. If someone didn't like the meal on any given night, the next night he might find his favorite main dish, if he were lucky.

"I'm sorry, buddy, but if you don't like this leftover stew you can find peanut butter and jelly in the kitchen. That'll fill you up tonight. Maybe tomorrow I'll have something you like."

No one dared to leave the dining room table to make a peanut butter sandwich.

♪♪♪

After twenty-five years of service to the Merchants National Bank, Rappy finally was made an officer in January of 1954. The phone call came on a Friday afternoon at one o'clock when Alyce was putting Billy to bed for his nap. Knowing that today was the annual meeting when the bank named new officers, she drifted through the morning on automatic pilot, often reaching up to clasp the Miraculous Medal dangling from the sterling-silver chain around her neck as she murmured the prayer, "Help us to accept your Will, Lord, but Rappy really deserves it this time, . . . and you know it!"

"Guess where I've been all morning, Hickory!" Rappy's voice over the phone was smug and flirtatious.

317

"Why didn't you call me *sooner*? . . . I've been going crazy *wondering*! . . . Did you get to eat lunch in the board room? What'd ya'll have?" she felt her eyes misting with genuine joy.

"I *couldn't* call you beforehand! They grabbed me from my desk and marched me into the board room!"

"Who was there?"

"The Board of Trustees! . . . Most of 'em, anyway."

"Were any bank officers there?"

"Every one of 'em! . . . Everybody was there for induction of new officers."

"So who do you think went to bat for you?"

"Mr. Michael, of course, Mr. Cleverdon, Mr. Conover, and Mr. Smith."

"Mr. *Gordon* Smith? . . . Smith's *Bakery*? . . . I'm not surprised he stood up for you. Last month at the Ladd's Christmas party, he was standing right behind me in the buffet line. He leaned over and told me what a great man you are, and what an important contribution you make to the bank. I just smiled and said, 'Yes, sir, I *know* he's a great man.' . . . I'm glad I didn't say something smart like 'If you think he's so great, Mr. Smith, then make him an officer!' . . . Huh?"

"They're always looking at the wives, Hickory."

"I know it! That's why I hate those bank parties cuz most of the officers' wives went to those fancy girls' colleges in South Carolina and Virginia!"

"But I bet none of them took four years of classical Latin!"

"For whatever good *that* did me!"

"Well, you must've passed muster with the board, Hickory, cuz here we are! . . . We finally made it."

"And it's a Friday. Bad day to celebrate when you're Catholic. If I had time, I'd run down to Star Fish and Oyster to get some fresh snappers for tonight, but we'll celebrate with tuna casserole."

"See if Mickey or Shirley can babysit tomorrow night. I'm taking you to Korbett's to really celebrate. Fried chicken and chocolate ice cream!"

"I might even have a Brandy Alexander for dessert!"

As an Assistant Cashier, Rappy's raise in salary was somewhat higher than in previous years, but not enough to seriously reduce debt. Yet as an officer he was able to participate in the stock purchase plan. For every share of bank stock he purchased, the bank matched it. It would be five years before he could begin purchasing any shares, but he and Alyce looked forward to investing for their retirement once they paid off the Allen Memorial Hospital and reduced the new mortgage considerably.

Meanwhile, Alyce continued to drop dimes, nickels, and pennies into the mayonnaise jar hidden behind the washing machine where she was saving for her clothes dryer. Any coin larger than a nickel was left at the bottom of her purse for emergency grocery errands when she sent Tommy on his bike to Weinacker's to pick up a loaf of bread or quart of milk between weekly shopping trips to Serda's in Spring Hill.

> *Every time we manage to make a dent in our debt, I get pregnant. So there's another hospital bill—not to mention another mouth to feed. Down the line that means more tuition fees at either McGill or Convent of Mercy.*
>
> *The secret to reducing the finances is to stop getting pregnant. But my periods are so irregular that I can't trust that Rhythm Method. And the Church forbids any artificial means of birth control. I'd be mortified to ask Dr. Dowling about birth control anyway! I just couldn't imagine him taking out all those devices and lining them up on his treatment table for me to examine.*
>
> *So, I guess the only thing to do is to have less intercourse. I'm just gonna have to find something to do late at night until I know Rappy's sound asleep. I can always iron school uniforms until one—that'll keep me awake and on my feet. That should prevent another pregnancy. I doubt the Church considers ironing uniforms as 'artificial' birth control.*

The next night Alyce darned every sock in the house that had a hole in it. She cleaned out the refrigerator. Then she ironed uniforms until 1:30 a.m. After she turned off the gas stove in the central hall, she proceeded to circle the front of the house turning off lamps and overhead lights. She picked up toys from the living room floor and gathered school jackets tossed on dining room chairs. On the bathroom floor she found a towel soaked with water. She wrung it out and hung it on the rack over the tub.

By the time she changed into her nightgown and slipped into bed, she was shivering from the January cold. Her feet were like ice. She snuggled up to Rappy who was sound asleep. She pressed her feet against his. He flinched from the touch of her cold feet but in his sleep he didn't push her away. Without opening his eyes, he slipped his arm around her shoulder and drew her close as she let out an audible sigh.

Mercy, he's warm!

I can't think about birth control tonight! It's too cold! And he's so warm!

I'll think about it tomorrow.

Maybe tomorrow night this bedroom won't be so cold when I finally get to bed.

♪♪♪♪

A week before Valentine's Day Alyce returned home from a Room Mother's meeting for Snookum's class and found Shirley at the dining room table making valentine cards to exchange with her eighth grade classmates.

"It's almost dark outside, Shirley. Did you bring in the diapers?" Alyce dropped her purse in the captain's chair.

"No m'am, but I haven't forgotten!" the thirteen year-old murmured as she traced a heart onto a sheet of blood-red construction paper.

"Has Mickey brought in her line? Alyce struggled out of her overcoat.

320

"I think so," she continued tracing without glancing at her mother.

"We're leaving for the Mardi Gras parade in less than an hour, and if you don't bring in those diapers, you're not going. You can stay home with Mickey and babysit Billy!"

"Yessum," she reached for the scissors to cut out the heart.

"You know, Shirley, you're gonna need to marry a rich man so you can have a maid everyday."

"I'm gonna marry Howard Keel!" she put down the scissors and grinned at her mother.

"He doesn't have to be *that* rich—just rich enough to afford you a clothes-dryer! . . . Now, put down that valentine stuff and bring in those diapers!"

"I don't see why your husband doesn't buy *you* a clothes-dryer!" the child sashayed past her mother as she headed for the kitchen door.

"Don't be disrespectful of your daddy, young lady! You're not too old for a spanking! You speak ugly about your daddy again, and you'll have to *wear* one of those diapers for a *week* after I get through paddlin' your fanny!"

I had no idea John Quigley's child was in that first grade with Snookums. Since he and Alfreda live in Spring Hill, I just assumed they send their two boys to St. Ignatius—it's much closer than St. Mary's. When Alfreda walked into that meeting today, I almost dropped my teeth. I don't know if she didn't recognize me or if she just doesn't remember me—we only met that one time at the OOM's dance. She's tall—and those high-heels make her two inches taller—and those broad shoulders! Those china-blue eyes, and so blonde. She's the complete opposite of me! And to think I was his first choice!

What would it be like to be John's wife now that he's president of Mobile Coal and Ice? . . . For one thing I'd have a clothes-dryer by now. And probably a maid every day. Maybe

321

even a cook. But John and Alfreda have only two children,
which means that one of the parents isn't all that fertile—
probably John. So, if I'd married him I wouldn't have to worry
about birth control.

Am I spoz to imagine my life would be that much better
if I didn't have all these children? . . . All I know is if I want
Rappy Perez, I have to take his fertility in the bargain. And he's
a fertile son-of-a-gun!

The next night, Wednesday, Alyce and Rappy attended the *Fifty Funny Fellows* ball at Fort Whiting. Thursday night it was the *Stripers* ball, after they had taken the children downtown to catch throws from the floats and then rush back home so the parents could change into their formal dress—a full length gown for Alyce, white tie-and-tails for Rappy.

For a couple attending a Mardi Gras ball, 'getting dressed' was as time-consuming for the gentleman as for the lady. First, he had to slip into the white tuxedo shirt, a detached collar, and a white bowtie. On top of the shirt he wore a white starched vest which buttoned down the front. The shirt and vest had no buttons, but rather a second row of buttonholes down the front. The gentleman pushed a silver stud through one button-hole and then through its matching buttonhole. After that, he had to thread cufflinks through the French cuffs. He maneuvered himself into trousers held up with suspenders that buttoned inside the waistband. Next he wrestled with the white bowtie and, finally, he donned the coat with split-tails.

For Alyce she only had to select one of three ballgowns, slap on some rouge and lipstick, and douse her earlobes with Lanvin.

Friday night was the same routine for the *Crewe of Columbus* parade and ball—one they didn't want to miss because both Bill Serda and Rappy's youngest brother, Joe, were members. Saturday night was the *Mystic of Times*, both parade and ball. Sunday was a day off to recuperate for Monday when Rappy rode the float of his own mystic society.

At noon on Monday Rappy left work early to have lunch at home. The annual tradition was for Alyce to prepare him a fatty beefsteak to coat the stomach lining for an evening of drinking that began when the maskers gathered at the club den to costume themselves to ride the floats. By the time the parade was over at 8:30, each masker was high enough with Mardi Gras spirits to carry him into the ballroom to meet his lady for the Grand March.

For Alyce and Rappy that last week of Mardi Gras season proved grueling. But both loved it, Alyce as much as Rappy. It gave her a chance to catch up with old friends at the ball and to dance with men whom she'd dated when she was a carefree teenager living at Bayou and Savannah. Rappy didn't mind. He enjoyed watching her whirl around the dance-floor, radiant at forty-one, energy to spare after caring for nine children all week. He wished he could afford to buy Alyce new evening gowns every year, but with her mother's creative expertise, she made it through each season with only the three gowns. The next year Miss Alice recycled the gowns—adding a layered skirt on one gown, a huge bow at the waist on another one, and even dyeing a gown a new color.

Alyce didn't go to the balls to model her gowns—she went to dance. And after the ball ended at one in the morning, she and Rappy hurried home to get four hours sleep. At dawn they rose in the February chill when he rushed off to work and she scurried to get the children off to school. That final week of the Mardi Gras season was a roller coaster, but both of them looked forward to it every year—well into their seventies.

♪♪♪

When Miss Alice left Laurel Street in 1949 and moved in with her son, Alyce vowed she would never take advantage of her mother as a free babysitter. But all that changed when Billy came home from the hospital two years later. Besides, Miss Alice adored Billy so much that she relished the chance to babysit, even after Bubber bought a house in west Mobile and someone on Laurel Street, usually Mickey or Little

Rappy, had to drive fifteen minutes to pick up their Grandma Hicks.

In August of 1954, a month after Billy had turned four, Rappy devised a way for the family to spend the first two weeks of his vacation 'down the bay' in a rented cottage. The rent was nominal because the cottage belonged to Aunt Olivia and Joe Midgette on Hollingers Island where they had retired in the early 1950s. Joe and Olivia offered Rappy and Alyce the small cottage behind the larger bungalow. And the Perez family was welcome to share the long wharf projecting 150 feet into the shallow bay with Lee Lee and Uncle Joe. Everyone sat under the pavilion and enjoyed the bay breeze.

Two days before departing Laurel Street Rappy stood next to the garage admiring his twelve-foot speedboat resting on two wooden horses. Perched on the back of the small boat was a 12 horsepower Buccaneer outboard motor. Both the motor and the boat were third-hand. As Alyce stared at the boat—white paint peeling from the bow and forest-green paint peeling from shallow keel—she saw it as some large decaying beast. She had been told a rich parishioner had given Rappy the boat when the guy bought a new one, but she looked at the old boat as some decrepit monster set on consuming gasoline, oil, and unexpected expenses.

"That saltwater air'll be great for Billy!" Rappy exclaimed.

"Billy's staying here, Rappy," Alyce declared flatly.

"He'll love it on the water, Alyce!" he persisted.

"He'll hate it. Besides, he can't tolerate the ride in the car. He gets headaches just riding ten minutes to the doctor's office. That ride to Hollinger's Island is *forty-five* minutes!"

"We can't afford Josephine day and night for two weeks, Alyce."

"Mama's staying with Billy."

"You said you'd never ask your mama to babysit overnight unless it's an emergency."

"I *didn't* ask—she offered."

"What about her uniform orders. It's August."

"She can use my sewing machine—it's a White, just like hers."

"Then everything's settled?"

"Except for that boat and motor," she cocked her head towards the rig.

"I told you I didn't pay anything for it!" he sounded like a little boy who had brought home a stray puppy.

"Yeah, it just *followed* you home, huh? . . . Rappy, you promised you wouldn't get a boat till I got my clothes-dryer!" she was determined not to sound whiny.

"I didn't buy it, Hickory! . . . It's free!"

"The gasoline for that motor isn't free!"

"Gasoline's cheap!"

"Twenty-one cents a gallon is not cheap, Rappy! . . . I can buy a quart of milk with twenty-one cents! Besides, you'll have to buy motor oil, and paddles, and life preservers and—"

"We don't need life preservers," he muttered as he coiled the long rope leading from the bow.

"You're not taking the children in this little thing without life preservers and at least one paddle!"

"It's gonna save a lot of money, Hickory. All we need to buy is a trawling net so I can catch shrimp and crabs and flounder and sheephead and anything that lives on the bottom of the bay! . . . We've got two empty shelves in that freezer just waiting for all that free seafood!"

"Well," she softened a bit, "you ought to ask your Gonzalez cousins if they have any old nets at Star Fish and Oyster they don't need anymore."

"So you agree that the boat's gonna help us save money?"

"Little Rappy's next door in the Cooke's workshop this very minute trying to make a pair of wooden water skis. Water-skiing just eats up gasoline!

"This motor's not big enough to pull him up—it's only got twelve horses."

But it *was* big enough to pull Little Rappy on water skis. It took a while for him to get up on the skis, but as long as the seventeen year-old didn't fight the outboard motor, he managed to get up. If he remembered to lie back, relax, and give the small motor time to rev up slowly and reach its twelve horse maximum, the little rig slowly eased the teenager onto the water's surface so he could glide across the glassy bay on his homemade wooden skis with shoe-fittings made from inner-tubes.

For the younger children, the small motor was plenty big enough.

Mickey, Shirley and Tommy took turns on the new water-skis after Little Rappy taught them the basics. Nobody had a problem getting up. The little Buccaneer motor popped them out of the water without straining. Rappy drove the little boat while Little Rappy stood in chest-deep water teaching Tommy and his sisters how to lie back, relax, and "just let the boat pull you out of the water. Just don't fight it. Twelve horses are a lot stronger than *you!*"

Alyce sat at the end of the wharf with Aunt Olivia and Uncle Joe under the pavilion. With Jimbo in a playpen and Romie on her lap, she kept her eye on Snookums and Cathy at the foot of the wharf where the water was only up to their waists. When Mickey and Shirley weren't skiing, they dragged the two little sisters through the water in their small inner-tubes.

Alyce gazed eastward towards the middle of Mobile Bay. It was six o'clock on an August afternoon when the water reflected a luscious salmon sheen of the setting sun. She marveled at how glassy the bay had become, still and flat, perfect for skiing. Little Rappy on the water skis appeared a silhouette in the rays of the sunset as he skimmed effortlessly across the horizon.

I wanna do that! . . . I wanna water-ski!

Rappy's afraid I'll get hurt, so he says. So what if I get hurt a little bit? It'll be a lot of fun! If he's afraid I'll get hurt, why isn't he afraid that one of the children'll get hurt? I mean, one of them could run smack into a buoy . . . or fall off and sprain their back . . . or break an arm.

But if I fell off and sprained MY back, who would run the house? Who's gonna cook and clean and do the laundry and

*get the children to school while I lie in bed with a bad back?
I bet that's what he's thinking.*

*Or maybe he's remembering that convention trip to
Portland when we stopped off in Sun Valley to ice-skate. He
was pitiful! He was down on his fanny most of the time! I
didn't have any trouble. I took off and skated right across to
the other side. Of course, I wasn't going real fast, but I wasn't
on my fanny the whole afternoon.*

*Hmm. . . . If I learn to water-ski, then he'll have to try
it. And with all that extra weight he's put on in the past five
years, I don't imagine that little motor could pull him up. And
he doesn't want to look bad if I got up and he didn't. I can
understand that, but still . . . I wanna ski!*

I'm so mad I could cuss!

After two weeks on Hollinger's Island, Rappy and Alyce brought
the children home to Laurel Street on August 14, just one day before
the feast of the Assumption of the Blessed Virgin Mary, a holyday
of Obligation in the Catholic Church. For Alyce, that meant almost
everybody in the house had to attend Mass the next day, just as if it
were a Sunday.

Luckily Rappy was home from work for another two weeks—he
took the whole month of August for his vacation—so he'd be able to
get the older children to Mass in the morning. Little Rappy had his
driver's license now, so he was good to chauffeur for one Mass. And
if Alyce and Rappy went to separate Masses, they could cover three
Masses to make sure everyone older than six fulfilled their Holyday
of Obligation, which included Snookums who had just made her First
Communion last May.

As soon as she walked in the front door upon returning from
Hollingers Island, Alyce headed straight for the washing machine.
She filled it with the first load of shorts, Tee-shirts, and halter-tops grit-
ty with beach sand. At midnight she finished the third load of laundry
after Mickey and Shirley had hung the first two in the dark. Miss Alice

worked in the kitchen cleaning fresh seafood Rappy had caught that day in a shrimp net borrowed from a bank buddy. She labored at the sink where a large ice chest at her feet contained nine nice flounders and twenty pounds of shrimp. In the back yard under the outside light bulb Rappy cleaned four dozen blue crabs he'd brought home in a burlap croaker sack. After the cleaning, washing, and packaging, the prized seafood would be stashed in the massive 18 cubic foot freezer now standing upright in the new room added to the back of the house.

Before going to bed Alyce took care of minor first aid the children hadn't noticed until they got home to Laurel Street. Several needed their sunburned backs sponged with vinegar, and a couple needed calamine lotion for mosquito bites. And Billy needed to be put to bed.

"Billy's been listless since yesterday, Alyce, and *irritable*!" Miss Alice said as she headed for the car where Little Rappy was waiting to drive her to Bubber's house."

"You didn't feed him anything other than baby food, did you?"

"My stars, no! . . . I asked him if his head was hurting, but he said 'no,' so I don't imagine it's time for one of those spine taps. . . . I think he just missed you too much!"

"Yessum. He doesn't have a good concept of time, so telling him 'Mama'll be back in two weeks' is just the same as two years."

"But I'd keep an eye on him, Alyce."

And she did. For the next two days she kept a close eye on Billy.

Thursday night he appeared worse. He complained of a headache, but that wasn't all that unusual. She gave him a low dose of Paregoric at nine but he awoke at midnight, whimpering. He kept rubbing his neck with his little hand.

"Does your neck hurt you, Billy?" Alyce leaned into the lower bunk-crib and whispered so she wouldn't awaken Rappy.

"Yessum," the child whispered in return.

When she put her hand on his forehead to test for a fever, he whimpered more loudly. She gave him a larger dose of Paregoric and sat with him, holding his tiny hand until he dozed off at one.

She climbed in bed with her rosary and said a full five decades of Glorious Mysteries before dozing off herself. At five o'clock, she was wide awake.

It was a Friday. If Dr. Adams would agree to a house-call, it had to be today. He might be out of town on the weekend, or relaxing with his family at his Point Clear summer home.

"I don't know, Alyce," the pediatrician rested his hand on Billy's forehead while he took the child's temperature with a rectal thermometer.

She sat on her bed holding the child's hand and reassuring him that the doctor wasn't there to give him a spinal tap. Rappy stood in the bedroom doorway with a glass of lemonade as if his presence could minimize the dread of Dr. Adams' diagnosis.

"I can't tell if he has a fever," Alyce said, "since he doesn't hold a thermometer under his tongue very well, but his forehead feels cool to me."

"The stiff neck and the headache scare me. You know what we're worried about, don't you, Alyce?"

"Don't even say the word, Dr. Adams!"

"Today's Friday. . . . Take him to that neurologist this afternoon— before the weekend. This could turn into an emergency."

Spinal Meningitis

The neurologist confirmed the worst. In the car on the way to Dr. Patton's office, Rappy chattered to Billy on his lap that everything was just fine as the child held his head with both hands and quietly sobbed with pain. Alyce drove silently as she prayed:

> *I'll try to accept anything you send, Lord. . . . But why do you want this child to suffer?*
>
> *Forget about me. Forget about Rappy. I can get him through this. But why let Billy suffer?*
>
> *Help us to accept your Will.*

To confirm his diagnosis of meningitis, Dr. Patton had to do a spinal tap. For the second time in the past six months he inserted the long needle through the *bifida* and extracted a sample of cerebrospinal fluid, the fluid that envelops the brain and spinal cord.

"Go directly to Providence Hospital," the doctor said as he sent his nurse for Rappy who was waiting on the front porch.

"Don't you have to wait for the laboratory to examine the fluid?" Alyce continued to stroke Billy's cheek.

"The lab's closed on the weekend. We can't wait till Monday. I'll start treatment tonight with antibiotics. I'm going ahead with meningitis treatment, if that's all right with you."

"Of course! . . . We can't wait till Monday."

"I'm sure it's meningitis, Mrs. Perez."

"I hate to sound stupid, Doctor, but what exactly *is* meningitis?"

"It's an inflammation of the protective membranes covering the brain and spinal cord. The inflammation's caused by infection with viruses, bacteria, or other microorganisms."

"*Bacteria?*" Alyce hung her head. "Maybe I didn't keep that *bifida* sterile enough?"

"Don't blame yourself! . . . Yes, bacteria could easily have entered through the *bifida*, but he could've just as easily breathed in a virus floating through the house. His immune system is terribly compromised since he never goes outside except to visit a doctor's office."

"You said not to expose him to germs."

"Exactly. . . . So he isn't building up immunities like your two younger boys. We just can't take the risk. It's not unusual that he's contracted this disease. After all, Mrs. Perez, his spinal cord membrane is protected by a thin layer of skin, only two millimeters thick, covering the *bifida*. . . . Even normal people get meningitis! With his birth defect of an open spine, he was primed for this disease!"

"What about the other children?"

"It can be contagious—or infectious—*if* it's viral."

"Our house is the gathering place for all the neighborhood kids! On a given summer afternoon there might be fifteen children in and out of our living room. And everybody makes a fuss over Billy! . . . My God! Have I infected the whole neighborhood with *meningitis?*"

"If it's a virus, healthy kids won't get infected. I suspect Billy's body's been weakened by inactivity. He has no resistance. He picked up a virus . . . or bacteria entered through the *bifida*. Either way, you could never have prevented it."

"Doctor, meningitis can be fatal, can't it?" Alyce didn't bother to whisper the question because she was certain Billy didn't know the meaning of "fatal".

"Alyce!" Rappy spoke up from the doorway. "Don't think like that!"

"Of course it can be fatal. But I'm starting treatment in an hour if you get out of here and take this child to the hospital."

♪♪♪♪

After one week in Providence Hospital, Billy was back home before Labor Day.

But he would never be the same again. The intensive treatment of antibiotics and antiviral drugs knocked out the meningitis, but he arrived home debilitated. Alyce had to tie him in his high chair so he wouldn't slide out under the tray.

Apparently he had been weakened from the disease's toll on his body. Also it appeared that the drugs had weakened his immune system because he had little resistance to any virus that floated through the house on Laurel Street. And he caught every childhood disease that one of the older children brought home from school.

By the age of eight he had suffered bouts of mumps, chickenpox, whooping cough, influenza, and a multitude of common colds. He survived them all, but each one weakened him as he grew older in a life that consisted of being lifted and carried twice a day from bed to chair.

Billy's new chair was a godsend. While Billy was in the hospital with meningitis, Monsignor O'Donoghue announced Billy's name from the pulpit as the newest member on the list of Prayers for the Sick and Afflicted. He went one step further and described Billy as "an angel right here in our midst in St. Mary's Parish". A couple in

331

their late thirties decided they wanted their six children to meet an angel so they called Alyce and asked if they could visit Billy when he arrived home.

Four weeks after Billy's homecoming, the Drumm family paid a visit—the father, mother and six children all under the age of ten. The mother gushed over Billy while the older children hung back. The three little ones pointed at his large head. The father circled Billy in the high chair with great intent. He asked Rappy why it was necessary to tie the child into the chair with a folded diaper around his waist.

Alyce felt she had made a mistake by showing off Billy as if he were part of a sideshow at the Greater Gulf State Fair. But later that night Mr. Drumm called and asked if he could make a new chair for Billy. His hobby was carpentry and he had his own workshop in his garage where he crafted custom-made furniture for neighbors and parish members in need. He claimed he had a novel idea for a new chair for Billy that would give him freedom and comfort.

The new chair was innovative. The seat was as high as a kitchen counter. The wide tray in front of Billy was the same dimensions as a bridge table. It lifted out so Billy could sit on a six-inch high cushion of foam rubber. When the tray was replaced, it fitted under his armpits so that he was snug against the backrest with this expansive tray in front for him to hold his toys.

When Monsignor O'Donoghue arrived at the house for his monthly visit, Alyce let him know how much his Prayer List had changed Billy's life.

"You know, Monsignor, if you hadn't described Billy as an angel, that Drumm man wouldn't have come to visit. And Billy wouldn't have this great new chair."

"Oh, Alyce, it is indeed a fine chair!"

"Look! . . . It has casters on the legs so I can roll Billy up to the dining table, into the living room, just any place! So much better for me than having to lift that high chair if he wants to be in another room with the other children."

"The good Lord provides, doesn't he, Rappy?"

"Indeed, he does," Rappy smiled.

"I brought you this marvelous book from Ireland, Rappy. . . . You and Alyce must read this and see how a crippled child can be a blessing in your life."

"What's the name of it, Monsignor?" Rappy was wary.

"It's by a crippled man in Ireland. His name is Christy Brown. He's become a nationally famous painter! An artist! And he paints only with his left foot!"

"Interesting," Rappy took the book and examined the cover.

"*My Left Foot*! . . . He has some kind of palsy and can control only his left foot! And here our little Billy can move both his arms and both his hands!"

"Well, Monsignor," Alyce glanced at the book's cover over Rappy's shoulder, "since the meningitis episode Billy's having a hard time holding a crayon in his hands."

"We'll read it, Monsignor," Rappy clutched the book to his chest.

"Of course," Alyce tried to sound respectful. "We might learn something that will help Billy."

My left foot! . . . Hmmph! . . . I bet this Christy Brown didn't have a disease attacking HIS brain! How do we know Billy's mind wasn't affected by that meningitis?

I don't want him to paint pictures. And I don't want him to be an angel. I just want him to have a half-decent life with no headaches, no pain, and no more spinal taps.

And I don't want him to wither away before my very eyes.

CHAPTER **17**

"HICKORY! . . . It's the end of the month and we've got $20.00 left over!"

At the end of November, 1954, Rappy and Alyce were surprised to have a cash surplus after paying the monthly bills and setting aside cash for groceries and routine expenses. There was a tiny light at the end of the tunnel.

Only three monthly payments remained on Billy's bill at the Allen Memorial Hospital.

Rappy, Jr. was earning spending money from a couple of after-school jobs. Most Saturdays he made over $5.00 in tips carrying grocery bags to the cars of rich Spring Hill housewives at Uncle Bill Serda's supermarket. As a McGill senior he managed to pay all his school expenses, minus the tuition.

Mickey learned to make earbobs to sell to family, friends and neighbors. Her handsome profits bought high-heel shoes, hats and handbags. Grandma Hicks was always eager to sew frocks and ball-gowns for ADK activities, but Mickey knew her parents couldn't afford matching accessories for several new dresses each season.

After finishing her homework at the foot of the double bed she shared with Shirley, Mickey sat at the end of the dining room table—often while her daddy sat at the other end keeping books for some small entrepreneur—and sewed tiny colored glass beads onto pique buttons the size of quarters, then glued a clip to the back of the button with glue to make model airplanes. Because she participated in so many extra-curricula activities, the junior at Convent of Mercy didn't have time to hold a steady part-time job after school. There was basketball or cheerleading practice, a Sodality of the Blessed Virgin Mary meeting, or band practice.

Shirley, a freshman at age fourteen, had figured out a few schemes of her own to earn spending money. The previous summer, immediately after Eighth Grade graduation, she spread the word through the neighborhood that she was ready to babysit. The three Baumhauer children across the street and the five Drake children at the corner of Hannon and Laurel became her regular charges. That summer she earned $20.00 by watering Mr. Fulcher's prized roses—just two doors away—when the Murphy High biology teacher took his wife to Mexico for two weeks.

Too young to hold a steady job after school, Shirley concentrated on selling raffle tickets for various school benefits to earn the privilege of riding the COM float in the annual Floral Parade the following Mardi Gras.

Both these girls are popular! . . . I'm not complaining— because I was popular enough at the Convent—but now that I'm older, I wonder if being popular is all that important. I encourage them to participate in as many school activities as they can manage, and I'd never restrict them, not as long as they help around the house as much as they do.

Mickey's my right hand. She's always in the kitchen doing what needs to be done without being told. She walks in after school, puts down her books and dives in to help me get supper on the table, or fold diapers, or put away clean laundry in everybody's dresser drawer—without having to be asked.

On the other hand, Shirley needs to be told what to do. She's as good as gold, willing to help when asked, but I do have to ask her. When Mickey comes in the front door after school, she picks up toy trucks and clothes from the living-room floor as she moves through the house and makes her way to her bedroom. Shirley walks in the front door and just steps over all the stuff on the floor . . . or kicks it aside. I honestly think she doesn't SEE it. It's the difference in personalities, I guess.

But Shirley makes a real contribution when she takes the little ones outside in the fresh air, or around to Hannon Park to play on the swings and see-saw. Once the little ones are out of the house, I can get a lot done. That's when Shirley's a big help to me!

)))¸

Alyce began pilfering clothes from the Ladies of Charity to clothe her nine children in November of 1954. Upon joining the diocesan organization, she volunteered to chair the ongoing clothing drive for St. Mary's parish. Each parish chapter of the Ladies of Charity named a member to collect donated clothing and deliver it downtown to the office of Catholic Social Services so it could be distributed to the poor.

"Well, *we're* poor," Alyce muttered as she approached the mound of clothing tumbling out of paper bags piled in the dining room corner where the freezer once stood. "I really don't think the good Lord expects me to get Bishop Toolen's permission to rummage through these bags and see what I can find for my own family before taking these clothes to Sister Roberta. I mean, after all, St. Mary's *is* a rich parish and some of this stuff came from Raphael's and Metzger's, and some of it's barely been worn. . . . My Lord! This pair of trousers still has the price tag on it! Maybe they'll fit Little Rappy. He's gonna need some new pants for all those graduation parties next spring!"

She threw the pants on the dining room table and dug through the rest of the bags.

"The way I look at it, the Lord sent me all these clothes. He expects me to take what I need before giving them to Catholic Social Services. I mean, it isn't like I'm gonna sell this stuff to make a profit—we're gonna use it!"

In addition to the Ladies of Charity donations, she relied on hand-me-down clothes from family and friends.

I don't know what I'd do without Elsa Schultz. And I'm thrilled she likes to shop so much. Every time she goes shopping with her Spring Hill friends—which is at least once a week—she buys something for her daughter. And that little Marilyn has quirky taste in clothes. Half these clothes Elsa gives me have never been worn—some with the tags still on them. I'm not gonna have to buy anything for Snookums and Cathy until they enter high school and insist on picking out their own clothes.

As long as Mama is able to sew, Tommy's wardrobe is taken care of. She has no trouble altering Little Rappy's hand-me-downs to fit Tommy. I don't know how she does it! I mean, when Rappy was eleven, he was a husky boy. But Tommy's just skin-and-bones. Any of Rappy's clothes I've saved have to be drastically cut down to fit Tommy. But Mama can reshape a suit so it looks like it just came off the rack from Stoll's! I still have that suit she cut down for Tommy to wear to Romie's funeral right after the war. And that suit actually belonged to Tommy's DADDY . . . but Mama cut it down so it'd fit Tommy perfectly for the funeral . . . and he was only three at the time!

Hand-me-downs from family and friends turned up spasmodically at Laurel Street. But the donations to the Ladies of Charity clothing drive arrived regularly. At least once a week some parishioner knocked on the front door with two or more large bags of nice clothes for the poor.

In addition to collecting clothing for the charity drive, Alyce was responsible for another task for the Ladies of Charity. Once a week she went grocery shopping for the Carmelite nuns. Living in a cloistered monastery on Holcombe Avenue these Carmelites emerged from be-

338

hind the walls only for an emergency. The Ladies of Charity agreed to provide a volunteer to shop for the nuns. For Alyce, who did her own major shopping at Serda's once a week, piling eight extra bags of groceries in the back of the station wagon behind her own eight bags was no problem. She delivered the sisters' groceries at the monastery on her way home from Serda's. And the chore was easier in the summer when Tommy was out of school and went along to help her.

"This bag's so heavy, Mama! What's in it?" the eleven year-old struggled with the last of the eight bags as he lined them up on the cool tiles of the monastery's dark foyer.

"Groceries!" Alyce approached a curtained area which looked like a confessional.

"These sisters have *air-condition*, Mama! . . . I thought you said they practice obedience, chastity, and *poverty* at this place! Poor people don't have air-condition! *We* surely don't have air-condition!"

"Shh! . . . Keep your voice down and just do what I tell you!" she pulled a rope next to the curtain. There was no sound, but she knew that a bell had rung across the courtyard in the Sisters' living quarters.

"Will we get to see the Sisters?" Tommy whispered.

"No. . . . And there's only one I ever talk to. She's able to see me, but I can't see her."

Alyce swept aside the curtain to reveal a large wooden barrel that had been cut in half vertically and was positioned at waist level.

"Now, Tommy, put a bag in the bottom of that barrel."

After he placed the bag, Alyce gave the barrel a push. The bag of groceries disappeared as the barrel slowly spun around, leaving her and Tommy staring at the back of the barrel.

A chirpy voice erupted from the other side.

"Oooh, potatoes!" the nun's voice was pleasant.

"Yes, sister," Alyce chuckled. "There're always potatoes on the list."

"We really should cut back on potatoes. You know, we don't get much exercise in here, except working a bit in the vegetable garden."

"I'll lend you some of my children to take care of. You'll get so much exercise chasing after them that you can eat all the potatoes you want!"

The nun laughed heartily as the large wooden barrel spun around revealing it empty where the grocery bag had been removed.

"Now, Tommy," Alyce whispered, "Put another bag in the barrel."

"This one's got potatoes too, I think," the child struggled with the heavy bag.

Methodically, Alyce and her son placed all eight bags in the barrel one-at-a-time. Tommy spun the barrel to deliver the bag to the unseen nun on the other side of the wall. When the barrel returned empty—as if by magic—Tommy's face broke into a grin each time.

"It's like the old man behind the curtain in *The Wizard of Oz!*"

After the last bag was removed, the barrel spun around with a white piece of paper resting on the bottom.

"The grocery list for next week," Alyce murmured as she reached for the paper.

"You mean we get to do this every week?" Tommy exclaimed.

"Guess what's on the top of the list?" Alyce smiled as she guided Tommy towards the door.

"Potatoes?"

♪♪♪

Three weeks before Christmas of 1954 Alyce burned her left hand severely in a kitchen accident. The culprit was the gallon-sized Dutch oven she used every Sunday to boil starch for the school uniforms. As her mother had predicted three years earlier, the handle on the big pot finally came off in Alyce's hand as she tried to lift the pot of hot starch from the kitchen stove.

When she felt the handle separate from the pot, she dropped the pot and jumped back. Too late. She watched the river of bubbling white liquid flow over her left hand as it cascaded in slow motion onto the linoleum floor. Instinctively she grabbed a dishtowel and wiped the thick starch from her hand. She held up her hand to the afternoon sunlight coming through the window to examine it. The entire top of her hand was scalded. It wasn't bleeding but it was bright crimson, yet very dry. Why wasn't it wet from the starch?

She stared at the dishtowel soaked with hot starch and realized that when she had wiped the liquid starch from her hand, she pulled off the top layer of skin. She held onto the counter as she slowly stepped through the slick of starch spreading across the floor and made it to a corner. She lowered herself into a chair and held her left wrist tightly. She gripped it—allowing the hand to dangle like a piece of raw meat on display.

Why doesn't this hurt more? It barely tingles. When will it start to throb? How'm I gonna get through Christmas with only one hand? And what if I need skin grafts?

Oh, God, who's gonna dress Billy's bifida if I can't use my hand?

Suddenly the hand was ablaze. It throbbed. She squeezed her wrist even tighter and closed her eyes. She steeled herself against the excruciating pain.

"Mama, are you okay?"

She opened her eyes to find Shirley staring at the puddle of hot starch still spreading on the center of the floor.

"Go get your Daddy," Alyce managed to say as she gasped for breath, determined not to scream.

The fourteen year-old Shirley stood frozen, gaping at her mother's hand dangling in mid-air.

"Hurry, Shirley!"

As soon as the child bolted out the front door, Alyce let out a muffled scream.

Within seconds Rappy dashed in from the front yard. He was running so fast he couldn't stop before he slid through the puddle of slick starch and fell on his side. Pulling himself up on the kitchen counter, he looked first at the wet starch dripping down his right side from shoulder to pants-cuff. Then he saw Alyce's raw hand. He grabbed the counter to keep from fainting.

"It's Sunday!" he shouted. "Providence emergency room!"

By this time Alyce was struggling to her feet as Shirley threw dish towels and aprons on the floor to soak up the wet starch so no one else would slip and fall. Rappy struggled to guide Alyce out the front door and into the car.

Getting through the holidays one-handed was difficult for Alyce. Her mother arrived everyday to tend to Billy, dressing his *bifida* and changing the bandages. Josephine dropped by whenever she could leave early from another domestic job. Margie picked up wet laundry three times a week to dry in her clothes dryer.

Mickey and Shirley did Christmas shopping for their mother after school. Since their high school was located downtown, the girls could easily walk to the big stores to finish Alyce's Santa Claus list after school.

The worst part of the ordeal was changing the dressing on the burned hand. Because the top layer of skin had been removed, the bandage had to be changed daily to prevent infection. Bubber's wife, Emma, was a trained nurse who knew how to change the dressing with minimal pain for Alyce. But when Emma wasn't able to drive over on some nights, Rappy had to change the bandage.

Rappy couldn't bear pain—not his own, not anyone's. Because he wouldn't trust Mickey to change the bandage, after supper he sat Alyce down and braced himself for the procedure.

"Wait a minute, Rappy!" Alyce sat at the dining room table next to the window, as far as she could from the central hall which led to the bedrooms.

"You're not ready?"

"Roll Billy's chair into the living room so he can't hear us. Then close the French doors. Red Skelton's on the T-V, and Billy's crazy about him. Turn the volume up loud so he won't hear me if I let out a yell."

Two minutes later Rappy hovered over Alyce sitting in the captain's chair at the head of the dining room table.

"Go ahead, Rappy! . . . Yank it quick. It won't hurt as much!" Alyce's eyes were filled with tears as he tried to ease the gauze off slowly.

She screamed.

The younger children escaped to their bedrooms and closed the doors to avoid hearing their mother's painful wails. Little Rappy dashed out the front door and sat in the car behind the steering wheel until the procedure had ended.

Once the old gauze was removed, Rappy had to spread an anti-bacterial ointment over the top of the hand before he bandaged it with sterile gauze.

"What's all that yellow junk?" Tommy stood next to his mother, frightened every time she moaned, but curious as to the procedure.

"It's some ointment that prevents infection," Alyce was grateful to answer the child's question which distracted her from the pain.

"Mama, if you rub Paregoric on your hand, it might put the pain to sleep," the eleven year-old glanced at his mother for reassurance.

Rappy glared at the child but Alyce managed a weak chuckle.

♪♪♪

Alyce visited Dr. Dowling weekly for him to monitor the healing process. On her final visit in late January, he declared the danger of infection had passed. He suggested a routine obstetrics exam which confirmed her suspicions. She was pregnant with her tenth child.

It was the day before her birthday, January 21, 1955.

How can this BE?

I tried to take care—darning socks till midnight, ironing uniforms, and watching Steve Allen till all hours and all those late shows I don't even like!

Two months ago? . . . That would've been November. So, what happened in late November that would've caused me to get pregnant? . . . Oh, my God! That bank party at the Cleverdon's. I had a second highball. When all those wives

343

started reminiscing about their college days—all that chit-chat about Sweetbriar, Hollins, and Randolph Macon where they learned to pour tea—I got nervous, as usual. But, I know I should never have a second drink! Every time I do, I get pregnant!

The Catholic Church has to DO something! At this rate Rappy and I will end up having seventeen children!

When does this change-of-life start? . . . I'm ready!

The next day Alyce celebrated her 42nd birthday with anxiety. Before she told Rappy about the pregnancy, she let the older children host a birthday party after supper. Mickey made a devil's food cake with chocolate icing from a Betty Crocker box mix—her mother's favorite—and Shirley made chocolate brownies, a double batch so there'd be plenty left over to add to the brown-bag school lunches the next morning.

After the girls cleared away the dessert dishes and teacups, Little Rappy decided—after three brownies—that he wanted a second piece of birthday cake.

"Take this piece to your daddy in the living room. He's in there watching something with Billy," she passed Little Rappy a dessert plate, favoring her left hand which was still a bit sore six weeks after the burn accident.

"I'll have this one," the seventeen year-old declared without budging from his chair. "Tommy, take Daddy a piece of cake."

Alyce stopped slicing the cake. She stared at her oldest son.

"I *said* . . . 'Take that piece of cake to your Daddy'. . . . *Then*, you'll get your second piece!"

"But I'm your firstborn!" the teenager tried to disarm her with charm.

Alyce pointed the long knife at him. She declared solemnly:

"I was a *wife* long before I became a mother! . . . Your father comes first!"

"You sound serious, Mama," the boy, somewhat chastened but

344

still flirtatious, rose from his chair and moved towards the living room with the slice of cake.

"Damn right, I'm serious," she muttered as she returned to cutting the cake.

"Mama!" he stopped in his tracks. "I've never heard you cuss!"

"You've never heard me this *serious*! . . . Listen here, young man, don't you even think you're gonna talk your daddy into buying a bigger boat until I get my clothes-dryer. And I don't want to hear any foolishness about you needing an Evinrude 25 so you and your buddies can ski double behind a bigger boat."

"Daddy wants a bigger boat to pull a longer shrimp net . . . so ya'll can store more seafood in the freezer," the teen held the dessert dish in one hand and gestured gallantly with the other.

"And people in hell want ice water! . . . It's time, young man, that you thought of other folks in this house beside yourself. As long as you paid for all your hobbies—and there's been a hundred of 'em—you figured you could bring whatever you wanted into this house. It started when you were ten and you brought home that stray puppy!"

"Mama, he *followed* me home," the teen shrugged.

"In a cardboard box? . . . I've put up with hamsters, white rats and, white mice. Those mice multiplied almost overnight till we had fifty of 'em running all over the house and ending up in everybody's dresser drawers! We had parakeets dirtying the valance over the new living room picture-window! I've put up with dead lizards in test tubes filled with rubbing alcohol and live snakes three-feet long for Biology experiments. I let you bring home baby squirrels you and Ralston Renema robbed from some poor mother's nest—dead ducks from your hunting trips you threw on the kitchen table where you cleaned 'em, . . . and that stupid tropical fish tank!"

"Daddy bought most of the fish!"

"After *you* got him interested in the darn thing! . . . And who was up at three in the morning mopping the floor when the aquarium busted a wall and flooded the entire front of the house with twenty gallons of water?"

"Daddy and I helped!"

"But *you* weren't eight months pregnant!"

"I never said we're looking at a bigger boat," he grinned.

"I wouldn't be surprised if your daddy's got a secret savings account for that boat with the Evinrude 25!"

"So this is about the clothes-dryer?"

"Next time you pass Dauphin and Broad, take a look in the Delaney's showroom window and you'll see my clothes-dryer—the second machine on the right. I pass it every morning when I drive your daddy to work. You're not getting a bigger boat until I get the clothes-dryer."

"He'll probably buy a Kenmore cuz Sears and Roebuck give such a good warranty."

"Now take that cake to your daddy and come back and get this one for yourself."

♪♪♪♪

Seven months later, August 20, 1955, Alyce delivered her tenth child, David Clarke Perez. When she arrived home from the hospital with the infant, the new clothes-dryer was sitting next to the washing machine. Little Rappy had supervised the installation by the delivery crew and learned how to operate it so he could teach his mother. It was a Kenmore from Sears.

No longer did Mickey and Shirley have to bring in dry diapers from the backyard after school everyday. For them, the clothes dryer arrived in the nick of time. Mickey, now a high-school senior, was serving as treasurer for the ADK sorority, Drum Major for the school band, and Prefect of the Sodality of the Blessed Virgin Mary. Shirley, now a sophomore, was busy with varied after-school activities, especially selling raffle tickets to ride the COM float in the Floral Parade.

Thanks to the new clothes-dryer, as well as the older automatic washing machine, the diaper detail now consisted of a single manual task—folding. It was the responsibility of anyone sitting in front of the television with idle hands. By the time school reopened in September,

Tommy and Snookums were drafted for the diaper detail and trained to fold diapers for their three litte brothers who wore them.

"These big rectangular ones with the Curity label are for both Billy and Jimbo. These square ones are for the new baby," Alyce dropped two stacks of clean diapers at her feet as she squatted in the middle of the living room floor.

"These square ones are a lot thicker than the others," Snookums observed from where she knelt between her mother and her older brother.

"I think she's too little to do this, Mama," Tommy whispered.

"She's eight! . . . And she's smart! She can fold a diaper as good as you, I bet!"

"I hope so," Tommy was chastened.

"Now pay attention! . . . For Billy, you take this big rectangular one and fold it twice—once from the left, once from the right—so that it's three layers thick."

"Easy," Tommy said.

"For Jimbo, you use the same rectangular diaper," Alyce proceeded.

"The one called 'Curity', right?" Snookums asked.

"Right! . . . I told you she was smart, Tommy! . . . Now, for Jimbo you fold the Curity once in half, then again in half, so you end up with—"

"Four layers!" Snookums declared triumphantly.

"But that means Jimbo has four layers and he's almost potty-trained, but Billy has only three layers!" Tommy exclaimed.

"But Billy wears two diapers at a time—so he's actually wearing *six* layers!"

"And what about the new baby?" Tommy asked.

"You fold the square once. That's all!"

"And we put them in three separate stacks?" Snookums was already practicing with a Curity spread out on the floor.

"Then leave the stacks in the middle of my bed. I'll put them away before I go to sleep."

The next day Tommy sat folding diapers on the floor in the wide doorway between the living room and the dining room where the double French doors were opened. From that location he could feel the air-conditioning from the new unit in the dining room window and still be able to view the T-V screen where he watched the Mickey Mouse Club.

When Rappy passed by with Billy thrown over his shoulder as he headed for the front door, Tommy glanced up but continued folding and stacking without asking where his daddy was taking Billy in the car. But when his mother appeared dressed to 'go downtown', Tommy took note.

"Who gave us the air-conditioner, Mama?" he observed Alyce stop in the dining room to use the sideboard mirror to put on her lipstick.

"Ask your daddy," she blotted the lipstick with a single square of toilet tissue.

"Why can't *you* tell me?" he stared at the T-V as he continued to fold the diaper.

"Because I don't know," she laughed as she headed for the front door.

"Was it Mr. Anonymous? Like the freezer?"

"*Anonymous*? . . . Where'd you learn that fancy word? . . . Now, Shirley should be home from babysitting at the Drakes in an hour so she'll watch Romie and Jimbo. The baby's in his crib and will sleep till we get back. Josephine's in the back room ironing—she won't finish, I imagine, till Shirley gets back. Just make sure none of the little ones sneak out the front door."

"Is the doctor gonna stick a needle in Billy's back again?"

"I don't think so. He's just doing a yearly checkup."

"Mama, is Billy ever gonna get better?"

"You shouldn't worry about Billy, Tommy . . . Finish those diapers and do your homework or you won't be able to watch Davy Crockett tonight!"

"You know, Mama, instead of 'David Clarke Perez,' we should've named the new baby 'David *Crockett* Perez'!"

With Billy balanced on her lap, Alyce sat on a stool in Dr. Patton's office. The doctor squatted down so he'd be on eye level with the child.

"Billy," the kind physician smiled, "does your head hurt?"

"No, sir," the child's large head seemed like a watermelon wobbling on his thin neck.

Patton handed the child a wooden tongue depressor.

"Here Billy, you hold onto this," the doctor observed the child's hands as he reached for the depressor.

"Look, Billy! It's a really big popsicle stick!" Alyce laughed.

"How old are you now, Billy?" the doctor continued to watch the child's hand loosely wrapped around the depressor.

"Five."

"He turned five in July," Alyce said.

"Well, Mrs. Perez, because he hasn't complained of headaches since the meningitis last year, we don't need to do a spinal tap this visit."

"Do you think the headaches are gone for good?" Alyce didn't want to seem too hopeful.

"Possibly. . . . The meningitis could have affected the flow of fluid from the brain to the spine. . . . But the headaches might reappear. You never can tell. But I don't want to invade the *bifida* with a needle and risk the chance of infection again. He couldn't survive another case of meningitis."

"What are you looking at, Doctor?" Alyce glanced down at Billy's hand.

"His grasp is weak. He's not able to clutch that depressor."

"He can still feed himself with a spoon, but he's messier than before."

"We have to expect some residual weakness from the meningitis."

"But, Doctor, it's been over a year!"

"What about his learning skills? I don't suppose you plan to send him to school?"

"With that growth on his back, he can't sit in a wheelchair, and even if he could, his arms aren't strong enough to wheel the chair around by himself."

"There's a huge risk of infection from childhood diseases, especially now that he's had meningitis."

"I could teach him to read and write myself—and some basic arithmetic—but I have three more boys at home all day—all three younger than Billy!"

"Have you accepted that he's probably mentally retarded, Mrs. Perez?"

Alyce noticed her gut tightening. She felt her defenses rising.

"What makes you say that?"

"He may have been retarded at birth. But even if he was born with normal intelligence, typical *consequences* of meningitis are mental retardation and learning disorders."

"Billy remembers every visitor who comes through our front door," Alyce realized she was desperate to contradict the neurologist.

"Can he read?"

"He's only five, Doctor Patton."

"Has he shown any interest in reading?"

"No," she answered curtly. "He loves children books with illustrations the older children read to him, but he shows no interest in learning to read *himself*. . . . and I don't have time to read to him."

"Did any of the older children try to read before they started school?"

"All of them," she sighed, "but Billy remembers what time his favorite shows come on television—like Red Skelton and especially when Ed Sullivan has Elvis Presley scheduled. And if your wife walked in our front door tonight and didn't return for a full year, Billy'd greet her next year with, 'Hello, Mrs. Patton!' . . . just like that!"

"Well, maybe he's an *idiot savant* . . . of sorts."

"What's that?"

"A person who is mentally retarded but is gifted in a certain area, like playing the violin. Usually the gift involves memory—such as mathematics or music or, in Billy's case, possessing a gift for remembering names and faces."

350

"And record labels. . . . Billy has a small 45 rpm record player on his tray where he plays records. Of course, the older children have to help him stack the records on the spindle and lift the arm to place the needle on the edge of the record. Even though he can't read the labels, he knows what's on the flip side of all his records, especially Elvis's."

"Billy, you ain't nothin' but a Hound Dog!" the doctor imitated Elvis as he removed the tongue depressor from Billy's hand.

The child's face broke into a wide grin. He laughed uproariously, his frail upper body—the size of a three year-old's—convulsing with delight against his mother's bosom.

"If I were you, Mrs. Perez, I'd abandon any idea of Readin', Writin', and Rithmetic' and just enjoy him during the time he has left."

"I just want him to memorize the Baltimore Catechism by age seven so he can make his First Communion like a normal child."

ﻝﻝﻝ

Two weeks before Easter of 1956 Alyce started saying a second nightly rosary to spur the Blessed Virgin Mary to intercede with her Son. Alyce needed money for the children's Easter clothes. Mickey, Shirley, and Little Rappy were able to buy their Easter outfits with earnings from their part-time jobs. The problem was to buy a new shirt for Tommy and fabric to make Easter dresses for Cathy and Snookums.

Of course, Miss Alice could take time off from the June wedding she was sewing to create two dresses for the younger girls—and even a shirt without a placket for Tommy—but the problem was fabric. The empty chicken-feed sacks were fine for summer shorts and halter-tops, but Easter frocks required a far better quality of cotton.

The Blessed Mother sent Aunt Pauline. Early Friday morning before Palm Sunday, she arrived with Emilie Dekle, her oldest daughter. Two years earlier when Rappy became a bank officer, Aunt Pauline stopped sending groceries to Laurel Street. Instead, she arrived herself every other month with some practical gift for 'Alfred's' family which

351

promoted health, nutrition, or general well-being. This time it was an economy-size tube of Colgate toothpaste.

As usual, the old lady made a fuss over Billy. After each visit she indulged Billy with a ritualistic good-bye: He held his hand palm up, she rolled up two one-dollar bills and shoved them into his hand as he made a tiny fist. She turned to Alyce and instructed her to "buy some orange juice for our little Billy—and something nice, like a chocolate bar."

But on this Easter visit the two rolled-up bills turned out to be two *ten-dollar* bills. "Now, Alyce, you can buy the dear child an Easter basket bigger than all his brothers' and sisters'!"

Alyce laughed and promised she would do so, but she was eyeing the ten-dollar bills with the same contrivance as Scarlett O'Hara sizing up Miss Ellen's portieres to fashion the legendary green velvet gown to save Tara Plantation from the taxman.

Alyce didn't need to buy Billy an Easter basket. She had ten large baskets stored in the attic so she didn't need to buy new ones every year. She even saved the grass for the baskets. Besides, Billy didn't like chocolate or any sweets that much. At the age of 5½, his diet still consisted primarily of Gerber's strained baby food. She'd make sure his basket had lots of small toys he could play with on his tray, but she had plans for those two ten-dollar bills the Blessed Mother had delivered via Aunt Pauline.

On Monday when Josephine came to iron, Alyce dashed downtown to Zoghby's to buy four yards of cotton fabric—a print of red cherry bunches repeated in pattern on a pale blue background—for the two Easter dresses with full gathered skirts with a lace trim around the neck and on the puffed short-sleeves. She had $3.99 left over to buy a long-sleeved pink shirt for Tommy to coordinate with his black pants, the latest trend for seventh graders who were hosting record parties to learn the dirty-bop.

But by Holy Saturday Alyce could no longer ignore her conscience. She welcomed the Church's dictum to confess her sins annually during the six week Easter season.

"Bless me, Father, for I have sinned. It's been four weeks since my last Confession."

"Ah, Alyce, always lovely to hear from you!"

"I've got some serious sins to confess, Monsignor, like Pride and Despair and Thievery."

"Thievery? . . . Not *you*, Alyce!"

"Not stealing, actually, but it might be just as bad. Rappy's aunt gave Billy $20.00 for Easter and I spent it on clothes for a brother and two sisters."

"And a nice Easter outfit for the little angel as well?"

"Billy doesn't go anywhere, Monsignor."

"Well, surely you'll bring him to holy Mass tomorrow for Easter Sunday!"

"He doesn't ride well in a car, Monsignor."

"Ah, I see. . . . But he has all the clothes he needs, I assume."

"Yes, Monsignor, but Aunt Pauline said to spend the twenty dollars on sweets and chocolate for Billy but he really doesn't digest chocolate all that well and it really frightens him when he vomits, so you can see that—"

"I'm sure you take excellent care of him, my dear, and I'm sure he'll receive all the festive luxuries he needs to celebrate the holy feast of Easter! . . . Now, you mentioned the sin of Pride?"

"And Anger as well, Monsignor. Spring Hill College called us out there and explained that Little Rappy had failed some courses his first semester and would probably fail some more this semester. It made me mad cuz the priest implied Rappy can't learn college material."

"Ah, the arrogance of the Jesuits! . . . If there's a sin of Pride here, Alyce, it's probably on *their* account and not yours."

"It did hurt my pride, Monsignor. I felt the priest was telling me I had a stupid son, and I just hated hearing that."

"But Little Rappy was one of our brightest altar boys here at St. Mary's. I found him remarkably industrious . . . resourceful!"

"The problem was high school . . . at McGill. His daddy told him to take the Commercial Course—typing, accounting, bookkeeping—

instead of an Academic Course. We never dreamed we'd find college money for any of our children. Besides, the Commercial Course taught the skills he'd need if he went to work at a bank—like his daddy— which is probably one of the reasons Rappy advised him to take that course in the first place, and—"

"So what's the lad to do?"

"Get a job or join the army, I guess, Monsignor."

"Or stay out one year and go back."

"Back to *Spring Hill College?*"

"Once he's finished sowing his wild oats, he can try it again, my dear!"

"Really? . . . I thought once you left, you could never return to college . . . *anywhere!*"

"And this sin of Despair, my dear?"

"It's about Billy, Monsignor."

"And how is the little angel?"

"He's *okay,* Monsignor, but he's still weak from that meningitis last year. The doctor says he may never get his full strength back."

"Then we'll pray for a miracle, won't we Alyce?"

"*Rappy's* praying for a miracle, Monsignor."

"And you, my dear?"

"The neurologist says that medical science can't restore nerves where God didn't put them in the first place. The nerves to Billy's legs are rolled up in a ball at the base of his spine."

"It sounds like a case for St. Jude, the Patron of Hopeless Cases."

"This time, Monsignor, I prefer to accept God's Will."

"Ah, we mustn't give up hope, Alyce!"

"Is it a *sin* to give up hope, Monsignor?"

"It's a sin to give up *faith*! . . . Faith in God the All-Powerful"

"If by faith you mean 'belief', Monsignor, I do believe in God but I don't have any hope that Billy will ever walk."

"Maybe not walk, Alyce, but he can gain back his strength and paint beautiful pictures. He may write a book like Christy Brown and entitle it, *My Left Hand!*"

"That *would* be a miracle, Monsignor, considering he's right-handed. And we'd need a genuine miracle for him to gain enough manual dexterity to guide one of those fine paint brushes with his little hand."

"You have a strong faith, Alyce. Now you must pray for hope!"

"I'll try, Monsignor, but I'm not promising anything."

After receiving Absolution, Alyce emerged from the confessional and knelt in the dark corner in front of the Infant of Prague's statue.

Monsignor always gives me the same penance—one Our Father, one Hail Mary, one Glory-Be-to-the-Father.

If I confessed to suffocating the Fuller Brush man in my clothes-dryer, Monsignor would still give me the same penance.

He says to pray for hope. Rappy's got enough hope for both of us. He prays every night and every morning that Billy will regain his strength and live to be seventy—that he will one day even walk!

I'm keeping my prayer simple, Lord:

'Give us the strength to accept Your Will—whatever it may be! . . . And, don't let Billy just wither away before our eyes . . . please!'

CHAPTER **18**

WHEN SEPTEMBER ARRIVED, no one mentioned that six year-old Billy was old enough to enter the first grade. Nor was it suggested he could wait to start school the following September, a year behind schedule. The possibility of Billy ever attending school was never brought up.

Since Billy's last visit to Dr. Patton, his health had not deteriorated noticeably, in spite of weathering chicken pox along with all his siblings under twelve. But neither had his health improved.

What *had* improved was the financial situation on Laurel Street. No longer enrolled at Spring Hill College, Rappy Jr was working fulltime as an accountant with Ryan Stevedoring. Mickey, having graduated from high school the previous June, worked fulltime as private secretary to the Chief Medical Officer of the Mobile County Health Department.

According to a financial arrangement initiated by Papa Perez when Rappy lived at home as a bachelor while working at the bank, the grown child contributes 12½ % of his paycheck to his parents in exchange for room and board. Because Alyce continued to mingle Mickey and Rappy's dirty clothes with the rest of the family laundry—and she made sure that as breadwinners they were served meat, chicken, or seafood entrees at each dinner—the 12½ % was a bargain.

Now that Rappy Jr. and Mickey were high school graduates, Rappy had to pay COM tuition for only Shirley. Next year Tommy would start McGill with the higher tuition, but for one academic year Rappy would have a slight respite from tuition fees at private high schools.

Alyce was delighted to have her oldest daughter home at night with no homework to do. Mickey helped her mother prepare supper while she related her day at work and kept Alyce updated on her steady beau away at Troy State University. But something was amiss with Alyce. When she saw Mickey coming through the front door after a long day's work in a Mobile county bureaucracy—instead of returning home from a day on the Spring Hill College campus—Alyce felt a pang of guilt.

Rappy and I should've figured out a way for Mickey to attend college. We could've planned better! I mean, Mickey graduates from high school second in her class and she doesn't get to go to college! It's not fair! We manage to send Little Rappy to Spring Hill and he has to leave after two semesters!

Just because Mickey's a girl—even though her high school grades were light-years above Rappy's—she's not allowed college because her daddy expects her to get married, have babies, and depend upon a husband to support her! And to think she would've been Valedictorian at COM if she'd taken math and sciences instead of Typing, Shorthand, and Sewing! Instead, Helen Andrews becomes Valedictorian because her "all A" average counts more than Mickey's. But Salutatorian's still a big honor.

Now, one thing I don't think twice about is sharing Mickey's new wardrobe. She's taken this 'working-girl' thing to heart! Every season she makes the rounds of Burks, Butler's, and Baker's to pick up 3-4 pairs of stylish high-heels. At $2.99 a pair—and cheaper when on sale—why shouldn't she indulge her passion for shoes? And should I feel ashamed that she and

358

I have the same shoe-size, same dress-size, same hat-size?

The hand-me-downs from the Ladies of Charity clothes are always welcomed, of course, but I do so enjoy borrowing one of Mickey's cocktail dresses for a bank party, or her tailored suit for the NCCW annual luncheon. I do take care not to snag a run in her hose so she'll always have a pair for work the next morning.

At eighteen she's of legal age to attend Mardi Gras balls. I hope she has at least one ball-gown that's not too youthful for me to borrow!

ꜱꜱꜱꜱ

The 1957 *Infant Mystics* ball was the first occasion when Rappy did not call out his wife in the Grand March. Instead, he escorted his oldest daughter and started a tradition of calling out each daughter and grand-daughter when she turned eighteen. In effect this rite-of-passage marked the Perez girl entering womanhood. When a son took a wife, Rappy welcomed the new daughter-in-law into the Perez family by calling her out at the *IM* ball the year after she married his son.

While Mickey was being sewn into her new ball-gown by Miss Alice on Laurel Street, Alyce was downtown making sure the younger children got to see their daddy on Float #5 as the *IM's* parade of twelve floats and marching bands passed the corner of St. Michael and St. Francis. In fact, the family watched the parade twice: First, in front of the Merchants National Bank building right after the parade got underway at 6:30. As soon as Float #5 passed, Alyce herded everyone back into the station wagon and shot out Congress Street to park the car and have the children positioned on Broad Street for the chance to catch throws from their daddy a second time.

As Rappy's float approached the corner of Broad and Dauphin—just as when it had neared the bank building earlier in the route—Rappy stopped throwing to the crowds in the street below. Instead, he held arms full of serpentine rolls, moon-pies, and Cracker Jack pressed to

359

his chest as he scanned the darkness and the crowds for Alyce and the children in the throng below. He felt a tug on his pants leg. He looked down and saw Tommy running alongside the float. The teen dodged the spewing sulfur from the flares mounted alongside the float's base as he pointed ahead to where the family was waiting a half-block away.

"*Not yet! . . . Not yet!*" the thirteen year-old held up his palm to halt his daddy from unleashing the cornucopia of goodies before the float arrived at the corner. Tommy shouted to his daddy, "*Dauphin Street! . . . Dauphin Street!*" but he couldn't be heard over the din of '*Mister! Mister! . . . Throw me something, Mister!*"

"No use yelling 'Daddy' at him!" Alyce had instructed the children. "Every man on that float's a *daddy*! . . . Shout '*Rappy*'! . . . Real loud!"

And they did. When the float was fifteen feet away—when they saw Tommy running along side pointing at them—they shouted themselves hoarse until they saw through the eyeholes of their daddy's full-faced mask that he recognized them. His eyes locked onto them with a desperate attempt to shower love and affection.

As soon as he saw his family on the front row of the crowd, Rappy leaned right to tap Bubber on his shoulder, then left to punch Billy O'Connor. Within seconds both men shouted the alarm around the float with the single code word, '*Alyce*'!—pointing at her in the crowd so the *IFT* guys could shower her with a tribute of Mardi Gras sweets and trinkets, like college boys serenading a fraternity brother's sweetheart.

Holding Jimbo high in her arms like a beacon on a dark sea— while the other children scrambled on the asphalt for throws—Alyce watched her husband connect with his children in a way he wouldn't again for a whole year. It was vital that he unload the treasure at their feet at the exact moment his float passed by. It was a fleeting chance that came only once a year, rarely twice in the same parade.

Alyce felt her eyes misting slightly as she shouted and laughed in the February damp chill. In Rappy's eyes, vibrant behind the face mask, she saw memories of the war years on Fiji. Again she was reading the daily letters of his loneliness on the island and his yearning to be home with his family. But Rappy had never been very demonstrative with his affections. And as their financial situation worsened with each new birth, he became less so.

But he loved his children—and they knew it. And if he needed to show his affection by precisely aiming a load of Mardi Gras throws at their feet once a year, then Alyce would do her part to help him, even if she had to chase the parade all over town—cutting through alleys with a toddler in arms and five others running behind—to provide him with two chances to make it happen.

After all that, she still had to speed home to change into her ball-gown, drive to the Fort Whiting Armory where the ball was held, and have Mickey seated in her folding chair amidst the long line of other call-outs on the edge of the dance floor before the curtain went up on the tableau at 9:00.

♪♪♪

In the liturgical calendar of the Roman Catholic Church, the month of May is dedicated to the Blessed Virgin Mary. For the Sisters of Mercy at St. Mary's School—where Mary was both namesake and revered patroness—the month of May meant prayerful devotion to the Mother of God.

To Alyce it meant making crowns for the Blessed Mother's statues, not only for each of her children at St. Mary's but for her high school girls at Convent of Mercy as well. The year Mickey was a senior at COM, Alyce had to make five crowns during that May of 1956: two for her girls at COM and three for her children at St. Mary's. By the time her last child finished the eighth grade at St. Mary's in 1972, she had become so expert at tying tiny florets on a crown only 4" in diameter that she even considered a part-time job with Demeranville Florist fashioning corsages for fraternity boys during Winter Formal season.

In each classroom in St. Mary's school a three-foot statue of the Blessed Mother presided on a pedestal from the corner—all year long.

But it was during Mary's month that the statue was adorned daily with a garland of fresh flowers fashioned onto a wire crown. Each child in the class was responsible for bringing the crown on his specified day. But it was his mother who decorated the crown the night before—if her child had remembered to bring home the crown of wilted flowers that had been placed on the Virgin's head earlier that morning.

After the children were seated in their desks and lunch tokens were dispersed to those without a brown-bag lunch, the nun directed the crown-bearer to the back of the classroom. Because the school building had no air-conditioning, the child's mother had sprinkled the crown with water droplets and wrapped it in waxed paper to save the florets from the Gulf Coast's high temperatures, almost as brutal in May as eight weeks later at the height of summer.

The rest of the class rose dutifully and stood by their desks as the nun led them in singing the processional hymn dedicated to the Blessed Mother:

Bring flowers of the fairest, bring flowers of the rarest
From garden and woodland and hillside and vale!
Our full hearts are swelling, our glad voices telling
The praise of the loveliest Rose of the vale!

O Mary, we crown thee with blossoms today,
Queen of the angels, queen of the May!
O Mary, we crown thee with blossoms today,
Queen of the angels, queen of the May!

When Alyce first sat down at the dining room table to start on the crown for her second-grader Cathy, it was already 9:00 p.m. She had just checked on David in his crib to make sure he wasn't caught up in his blanket. She had tucked Romie and Jimbo in one set of bunk-beds in the new room at the back of the house. In a few minutes she would get up to make sure Cathy and Snookums were headed for bed. She would try to catch Tommy shining a flashlight under the bedcovers reading a Hardy Boys

362

mystery. After she put Billy to bed, it would be ten before she could focus on the crown without interruption and have it finished by midnight.

She positioned herself at the table next to Billy's chair so they both had a clear view of the television in the living room corner. On the table she spread out a triple thickness of newspaper on which she had placed two pie-pans filled with water. In the pans she had floated tiny bunches of blue hydrangea blossoms snipped at dusk from Mrs. Cooke's bushes. Next to the pans she had lined up the materials she needed to fashion the crown: a roll of white florist tape to cover the wire after she had stripped off the dead flowers; a spool of green thread for tying the blossoms; Rappy's garden shears for snipping the florets; and a baby-blue satin bow to hide the stems where the final two bunches would dovetail at the back of the crown.

Cathy'll get brownie points for this blue ribbon, not to mention the blue flowers. I suspect this Sister favors the Blessed Mother's special color over any pink, or white, or yellow flowers. The sisters at St. Mary's really do consider the Blessed Mother their own, but then so do the sisters at the Convent of Mercy.

Rappy has some Shasta daisies along the driveway that are just budding. Now, those little yellow and white buds would make a pretty crown, and so would those pink sweetheart roses he's got climbing up the clothesline post. But these blue hydrangeas are always a safe bet with any of the Sisters of Mercy. They just go crazy over Blessed-Mother-blue!

"I think *Medic*'s coming on, Billy. Try to stay awake and watch it. It's about doctors," she examined the crown before she started pulling off the wilted flowers from today's crowning in Sr. Mary Leonardo's second grade.

"I don't like doctors," Billy muttered. He was propping up his large head with one hand, his elbow resting on the expansive tray as he slowly paged through a Little Golden storybook about a pokey puppy, stopping momentarily to look at the illustrations.

"Does your head hurt?" she focused on the crown, pretending she wasn't worried about the possibility of another spinal tap.

"No'm. . . . But it feels heavy," he exchanged hands to prop his head.

"Let me watch the show while I'm working on this crown," she wrapped white floral tape around the crown, now stripped of the wilted flowers.

"I wanna go to bed," he murmured as he stopped to gaze at an illustration.

"You never go to bed before ten—sometimes eleven. Let's try to stay awake for another hour. This is my favorite show," she chatted nonchalantly, hoping to disguise any hint of concern.

The child continued to listlessly turn the pages.

"Are there any shows on tonight with music?" she took a delicate bunch of hydrangea florets from the pan, shook the water off, and began tying them on the front of the crown.

"I don't know," he dropped the book.

"Then just look at your picture books till I finish this crown."

"Why can't I read, Mama?" his eyes opened wider as he stared at his mother. He held up his head with both hands.

"God has other plans for you, Billy. You're special!" she glanced at him briefly, then returned to the crown.

"I wanna go to bed," his eyelids were starting to droop over his darkest-brown irises.

"You want me to put down this crown and read to you for a few minutes?"

"I wanna go to bed."

Maybe he's coming down with a little cold, or a stomach virus, or . . . something!

He didn't slide at all after that chickenpox last year.

He seems to be on a plateau.

But some nights he does tire out earlier than usual.

"What do you think about us having another baby, Billy?" Alyce reached for a bunch of hydrangeas.

"David's a baby. He sleeps in the baby crib. He wears a diaper."

"But we're gonna have another baby in October."

"What's October, Mama?"

"When Halloween comes, Billy, when they put on scary masks."

"Cathy's a witch—an ugly witch."

"When that happens, we'll have another little brother or sister."

"A boy like me?"

"A girl would be nice this time."

♪♪♪♪

In early September when she was eight months pregnant, Alyce stood in the kitchen at the ironing board pressing a white cotton uniform for Snookums. After eleven pregnancies in twenty years, her stomach muscles had stretched so much that she had to lean forward to reach the ironing board. Her swollen belly pressed against the board's edge like an over-inflated basketball.

Tommy stood at the kitchen counter squeezing lemons for a pitcher of homemade lemonade. Next to his elbow rested an unopened five-pound bag of Domino's granulated sugar.

"Now, Tommy, don't you use half that bag to sweeten the lemonade!" Alyce huffed as she sprayed the shirt with water mist.

"Nobody likes it tart, Mama, except Daddy."

"I'm not saying to make it tart! Get a saucepan out, heat a cup of water—not boiling, mind you, just too hot to put your finger in it—and add two heaping tablespoons of sugar. If you dissolve the sugar in hot water, you need only half as much to sweeten lemonade, or iced-tea for that matter!"

"You could teach Chemistry at McGill, Mama!"

"When you know your way around a kitchen you learn a lot about chemistry. I'm not bragging, but you can't get laundry clean if you don't know about chlorine and a bunch of other chemicals."

Mickey, sitting at the dining room table with her back to the open kitchen door, was typing a term paper for her beau at Troy State University on a typewriter borrowed for a week from Euphemia McHugh, Alyce's cousin around the corner in Monterey Place. She had positioned herself next to Billy's chair where he was able to catch the cool air from the only A/C window unit in the house while he watched television through the French doorway.

"Lord!" Alyce's audible whisper sounded more like a moan. "Why do you keep sending me all these *babies*?!"

Mickey stopped typing and turned in her chair.

"Are you all right, Mama?"

"Yeah, I'm *all right*! I just wanna know when these babies are gonna stop! I'm forty-four years old!"

"Mister Mueller says a Catholic can now get a dispensation to use birth control," Tommy spooned sugar into the saucepan.

"*Birth control*! . . . They're teaching birth control at McGill?! . . . And who's this Mr. Mueller?" she lowered her voice to keep Mickey from hearing at the dining table.

"He teaches freshman Religion to the two higher tracks."

"What's a layperson doing teaching Religion?!" Alyce rested the iron on its heel, put her hands on her hips, and turned all her attention on Tommy.

"He's a 'Jebbie', Mama. Studying to be a Jesuit, but not ordained yet, so we have to call him 'Mister' instead of 'Father'."

"I knew the Jesuits teach at *Spring Hill*. When did they start teaching *high school*?"

"He's doing his practice-teaching. Six Jebbies teach at McGill this semester—they're students from Spring Hill College. I've got Mr. Mueller for Religion and Mr. Rodriguez for Latin, just until January. Then they go back to Spring Hill for their last semester to graduate."

"They shouldn't be talking about *birth control* to fourteen year-old boys!" she pushed the swinging door shut to close off the dining room where Mickey was typing.

"Somebody asked him a question about birth control thinking it would embarrass him, he being celibate and all—you know, that marital stuff—but he didn't flinch. He just went ahead and answered it."

"What'd he say?" Alyce fingered the hem of her maternity jacket and stared at the iron.

"He said that artificial birth control is a mortal sin because the purpose of marriage is procreation, but you can get a dispensation."

"A dispensation? . . . From who? Who gives this dispensation?"

"He said a bishop . . . and only for extraordinary reasons, such as, if a pregnancy would constitute mortal danger to the mother."

"Oh, the bishop," she rolled her eyes and picked up the iron to finish the uniform.

"He said the Jesuits disagree with that teaching. The Jesuits think any priest can give the dispensation during Confession. It's best if the woman gets the dispensation from her Confessor, he said, if she has a certain priest she goes to all the time."

"Monsignor," Alyce muttered as she turned the uniform on the ironing board. "Not likely he'd give it. . . . And how come you know so much about all this marital stuff?"

"Daddy told me a little bit when I turned thirteen."

"He didn't tell *me* he had talked to you."

"You told him that I was confused cuz Sister Virginia said it's a sin to kiss a girl before marriage, and I asked you how would a boy know if he really loved a girl enough to marry her if he didn't first kiss her, and you told me to 'ask your daddy' . . . so I did."

And what'd he tell you?"

"He said that marriage was sacred and that I should respect women. Then he said 'if you have any more questions, just lemme know' . . . but he hurried out the room before I could ask anything."

"You should talk to a priest. Not Monsignor, or any of the priests at St. Mary's. You might talk to this Jebbie Mister from Spring Hill. Everybody says the Jesuits are brilliant."

On October 9, 1957 Alyce delivered her eleventh baby which she named Richard Gerard, in honor of St. Gerard, the Patron of Mothers among Catholic saints. The name, 'Richard', wasn't in honor of anyone. It edged out 'Stephen' when the children voted after Shirley campaigned hard for 'Richard'. Billy wanted to name the new baby 'Elvis Presley Perez'.

Here I sit in Grandma Fanane's rocker burping this new baby waiting for the nuns to arrive for their obligatory visit. There'll be two of 'em, at least, because a nun can't go out alone. Probably they'll be a trio of 'em. And they're gonna tell me that I'm the Salt-of-the-Earth! And Rappy too!

Today this baby's twenty-one days old. His oldest brother turned twenty last May and has just started back at Spring Hill College. To think my first two years of marriage I prayed daily to get pregnant. Since then I've been pregnant 99 months of the past twenty years. We don't need any more children!

Now, if you're thinking about another baby, Lord . . . . . Are you listening? . . . I'm not just talking to hear myself talk! . . . This is a prayer!

Alyce didn't rise from the rocker as Miss Alice greeted the three nuns and escorted them to the living room sofa. It was the same trio that visited the hospital seven years ago when Alyce was checking out two weeks after Billy was born—the same nuns who, after the hospital visit, visited Laurel Street immediately after the births of Romie, Jimbo, and David. And the three sisters looked the same as seven years ago. None of the three had aged, but the silent one with the jowls who smiled incessantly had added a third chin inside her wimple.

"You're the *Salt-of-the-Earth*, Alyce!" Sister Mary of Mercy led the litany of praise.

"And Rappy too!" Sister Mary Dorothy echoed.

Alyce continued rocking as she massaged the baby's shoulders while he slept on her lap. She smiled cordially but decided she didn't have the energy to be coy and deny that she and Rappy were the most devout Catholics in St. Mary's parish simply because they had added the most lambs to the Good Shepherd's flock.

"The Lord sent me eleven children. And I took 'em!"

The three nuns stared at Alyce. Even the ever-loquacious Sr. Dorothy was speechless.

Finally, it was the silent fat nun, the one who had never spoken a word on four previous visits to welcome a Perez newborn, who broke the awkward silence with a chirpy quip:

"Well, Mrs. Perez, if you and your husband have one more baby, they can make a movie about your beautiful family—*Cheaper by the Dozen* . . . Part *Two!*"

"I'd just as soon keep the number down to eleven and pass up the discount!"

ᒐᒐᒐᒐ

A year later Alyce decided it was time for Billy to make his First Holy Communion. After all, he had turned eight, a year older than what the Church considered 'the age of reason'.

Is Billy capable of reasoning like a normal child? Memorizing the flip side of Elvis Presley records is one thing, but does he know right from wrong?

Can he understand what sin is? Can he learn to 'examine his conscience' to make his First Confession before the First Communion?

What kind of sins could he confess anyway? He's never even sassed me. How could he possibly understand what it means to 'entertain bad thoughts'? . . . To 'wish harm' on someone?

Around the same time that Father Oliver Adams encouraged Alyce to start Billy on the *Baltimore Catechism*, she was introduced to Sister Catherine Peter at a function for St. Barbara's Home. Alyce took to the Trinitarian nun immediately and found it refreshing to meet a sister whose ministry was not in the classroom but in social work. Somehow Sister Catherine Peter had heard that Alyce nursed an afflicted child at home who didn't attend school. The vivacious nun offered to visit Laurel Street once a week to prepare Billy for his First Communion. Nothing was said about a First Confession.

When Sister Catherine Peter arrived, she brought along as her companion and helper Sister Philomena, a twenty-ish Irish American from Boston with a head full of flaming red curls who, like the older nun, doted on Billy and made him feel even more special. He looked forward to the class and even suffered having his hair wetted down and combed before each visit from the two nuns, giggling the whole time in anticipation of seeing his new friends.

Between visits from the Sisters, Shirley instructed Billy on the *Baltimore Catechism*, beginning on page one. Having graduated from high school the previous May, she was free in the evening when she returned home from her secretarial job. After the supper dishes were washed and dried, she took off her apron, placed the catechism book on Billy's tray, and tried to drill him on the basics of Catholicism.

"Let's try it again, Billy! . . . Who made you?" Shirley was a stern taskmaster.

"I don't *knooow*!" he pressed his temple with his left hand.

"*God* made you! . . . Now, repeat after me! . . . '*God* made me!'"

"*God* made you!"

"Not *me*, Billy! . . . *You*! . . . Now, say 'God made *me*!'"

"That's what I said, Shirley! . . . *God* made you!" he made a small fist and feebly hit the tray in exasperation.

"Shirley!" Alyce called from the kitchen doorway where she was drying a large gumbo pot with a faded dishtowel. "Take a break! We don't want to give him a headache."

A year later, after Shirley had tried to drill the *Baltimore Catechism* 2-3 times a week—and despite faithful weekly visits from the devoted Trinitarian nuns—little progress had been made in indoctrinating Billy in the teachings of the Roman Catholic faith. Each week the two nuns arrived eager and delighted in Billy's baby-like joy in greeting them, but the child was unable to remember a basic answer such as, "God made me to know, love, and serve Him in this world and to be happy with Him in the next"—much less understand the sophisticated concept that the wafer of bread he would swallow was actually the flesh of his Lord, Jesus Christ.

Finally Father Adams came to the rescue and put a halt to the Catechism drills.

"We've got to stop this, Alyce."

"He's never gonna learn it, Father."

"It really doesn't matter. . . . I'll talk to Bishop Toolen and get a dispensation."

"What about his First Confession? He'll never learn how to examine his conscience."

"He has no sins to confess, Alyce. He's as innocent as the day he was born."

"I don't think he can swallow the host *whole*. If he chews it, is that a sin?"

"I'll give him a small piece of the wafer—less than half—and he's free to chew it."

"Can you get a dispensation for him to chew it?"

"Don't worry Alyce! I'll get a general dispensation to cover all the bases."

"Thank you, Father. This means a lot to us."

"Well, young man," the young priest looked across the expansive tray at Billy holding his head with both hands. "What do you say to all this?"

"Take it *away*, Father!" he pushed the green paperback copy of the *Baltimore Catechism* across the tray until it fell over the edge and into the priest's lap.

♪♪♪♪

Between the time Richard was born in October 1957 and Mickey was married in January 1959—a total of fifteen months—there were 13 people living in the small house on Laurel Street. Sometimes Alyce felt she was directing traffic from her station in the kitchen as she scurried every morning to get the family out the front door: Three people headed downtown to work before 7:30; at that same time Rappy Jr was picked up by a buddy to drive in the opposite direction to Spring Hill.

Tommy had to get to McGill by 8:15; three younger children were delivered by carpool to St. Mary's at 8:45; Jimbo was driven to Kindergarten at 9 and picked up at noon to return home; and in between Alyce tended to the three children still at home.

The fact that Billy usually stayed up late watching T-V till ten and slept late was a blessing for Alyce. She was grateful he wasn't awake in bed each morning waiting for her to change his diaper, bathe him, and change the dressing on his back before she could lift him into his special chair. Every winter he managed to survive his annual cold with no apparent side effects. He even made it through a mild case of the mumps. When he first came down with the mumps after Romie brought them home from school, Alyce became alarmed about long-term effects on all the boys in the house:

> *Except Billy. . . . He's the only one I don't have to worry about the mumps 'dropping'. I've never seen that happen, but Dr. Adams says a young boy with the mumps needs to lie flat on his back so the swelling doesn't end up in his scrotum — which, I guess, is why they call it 'dropping' — and make the boy sterile so he can't ever father a child.*
>
> *Since Billy's paralyzed below the waist, he can't feel anything in that private region. He's never gonna get married — much less father a child — so that's one less thing I have to worry about. And to think Dr. Patton told me seven years ago to make sure Billy never comes down with any childhood diseases.*
>
> *The one I have to keep my eye on is Tommy. He's fifteen,*

and he's really going through puberty fast. He was slow to get there, but this is the year he seems to be racing through it. If he comes down with the mumps, I'll get Rappy to tie him to his bed for two weeks just to make sure those things don't 'drop'.

On August 24, 1957—two months before Richard was born—Mickey became engaged on her nineteenth birthday. Because her fiancée was studying at Troy State University, they planned a long engagement: He would continue studying until graduation in December, until he found a job while Mickey continued at her new job with the Social Security Administration. Because Rappy and Alyce couldn't afford a large society wedding, Mickey saved most of her salary to stage a wedding worthy of any seen at St. Mary's Church. She even budgeted a bridal consultant.

Alyce helped as much as she could. She rallied her in-laws—especially Margie, Mary, and Emma—to make finger sandwiches of chicken salad to save on reception costs. However, Mickey didn't want to cut corners on certain items, such as, floral arrangements for both the church altar and the mantelpieces at the reception hall, as well as champagne.

It was Julius who agreed to bootleg the champagne to Mobile from Schwegmann's superstore in New Orleans where it was half the price of the 'state stores' in Mobile due to a high Alabama liquor tax. Julius avoided paying the tax by smuggling twelve cases of champagne into Alabama under an army blanket in the back of the Perez family station-wagon.

Alyce took mental notes when Mickey returned from an appointment with the bridal consultant, Flossie Barrington. Eventually Alyce pulled out her spiral notebook with her notes on planning spaghetti suppers. She designated the back half of the notebook as a planner for future weddings. One day Shirley, Cathy, and Snookums would probably marry. No use to hire a bridal consultant again if Alyce could do all the planning herself. The next time she wouldn't have a six month-old baby to care for when Shirley married in a couple of years. And if Shirley agreed to let her mother plan the wedding, Alyce wouldn't have to deal with a bossy consultant like Flossie Barrington.

Meanwhile, she avoided the overbearing Mrs. Barrington and offered her advice directly to Mickey:

"Don't skimp on a photographer. Get a good one! Your daddy and I didn't have a photographer so there's no picture of my wedding dress. And this dress Mama's making for you is an original! You need a photo of the *dress*, if nothing else."

The big surprise of the wedding reception was that Mr. McRae and his wife showed up. With so many bank employees inviting him to their children's weddings, the bank president declined most invitations—except from the senior vice-presidents.

After the wedding party had been photographed in the parlor of the reception hall, Flossie Barrington arranged everyone in a receiving line. Alyce stole a glance out the window and was startled to see the McRae's standing on the verandah in the January chill, waiting first in line to greet the bride and groom.

"You *know* why he was at the head of the line!" Mary Perez whispered into Alyce's ear when she leaned forward to kiss her cheek as she breezed through the receiving line.

"I'm surprised he's here at all! You know Rappy's only an Assistant Cashier!"

"Everybody knows he's crazy about Rappy! . . . But when the McRae's arrived on the steps, the whole crowd—and I mean *everybody*—parted like the Red Sea!"

"Well, that was nice!"

"Being *nice* had nothing to do with it! . . . Everybody in this line owes money to the Merchants National Bank!"

ﮞﮞﮞ

Papa Perez died in May of 1959 at the age of eighty-one. After undergoing surgery for a routine removal of the prostate gland, he never awakened from the anesthesia. For twelve hours he lay in the

374

hospital bed as his children and daughters-in-law kept vigil—Alyce included.

It was during Alyce's shift, late at night, when her father-in-law slipped away. Because the doctor allowed only two people at a time in Papa's hospital room, Alyce was alone with one of Rappy's younger brothers during her shift. She was chatting at the foot of the bed with Emile when they noticed a different rhythm to Papa's breathing. Emile slowly walked to the head of the bed, leaned his ear to his father's mouth and stared at Alyce.

"He's stopped breathing, Alyce."

"Call the nurse, Emile."

"Yeah."

Seeing that Emile, staring at his father's face, had become immobile, Alyce reached for the buzzer. Then she stepped into the hall to alert Margie and the others that Papa had stopped breathing. Within seconds two nurses were taking vital signs of the Perez patriarch who had apparently died. There was no CPR; no tubes stuck up his nose or down his throat; not even an oxygen mask. It appeared that the two nurses never even considered heroic measures. The octogenarian was allowed to pass peacefully.

The irony of it all! . . . That I'm the one in the room when he dies.

And what a relief. . . . Now I can give up any hope that I would be a favored daughter-in-law, much less that he and I could even become close. What a silly dream!

Finally, I can surrender the fantasy that he'd ever be the father I never had.

Two months later Bill Serda died.

For years Alyce was aware that Bill suffered from some rare blood disorder that could lead to a stroke. Although his lab tests over the past two years had been a cause for vigilance, his death was a shock.

Within two months Margie lost her father and her husband. Three of her children were grown, two living outside of Mobile. Aside from Joy at Spring Hill College, Margie had four younger children in school. Her immediate concern, after grieving for her husband, dead in his mid-fifties, was to support her children attending Catholic schools, the oldest a sophomore at the Convent of Mercy.

When Alyce discovered Rappy had been named Executor of Bill Serda's estate, she was not surprised. After all, Rappy was the brother-in-law who helped Bill obtain commercial loans through the years as he expanded from his small store on the midtown corner of Dauphin and Lafayette to a modern supermarket in the heart of prosperous Spring Hill.

"We're not gonna sell Serda's supermarket," Rappy reported when he returned from the attorney's office where the will was read.

"I thought Margie was gonna sell it to Greer," Alyce sat down at the dining table to keep Rappy company as he ate a late supper alone.

"It's thriving right now, doing more business than Greer. That's why Greer wants to buy it—to kill the competition."

"So, who's gonna manage it?"

"Margie'll be there until three. We'll keep Bill's same staff: Mr. Lawson as manager; Mr. Sardis as butcher; Freddy Britten as produce manager."

"I know Margie's been taking business courses for the past two years—ever since Bill's blood tests took a turn for the worse—but *managing* a supermarket with thirty employees?"

"And I'll go out there at night to look over the receipts and . . . just keep my eye on things."

"At night? . . . *Every* night?"

"After supper, Hickory."

"*Every* night?"

"Bill's estate pays me an Executor's fee as long as we keep the store. I can give up keeping books for all those small business owners I've been doing for so many years!"

"*Every* night?"

At first, it'll have to be every night. After that, we'll just have to see."

"Have to see," she repeated.

"Margie's youngest is only nine. If we sell the store now and invest the proceeds to earn income, by the time Michael's ready for college in ten years the economy might be bad and Margie's investment income could dry up. By keeping the store she has a steady stream of income to raise those four younger children, . . . as long as we can keep the store thriving."

"I'm willing to try it, Rappy, as long as you don't forget you have *eight* children still at home who need your attention. And two of 'em haven't even started school yet."

Margie needs Rappy to run the store. I'm aware of that.

And I want Rappy at home most nights to help me with the nine children still living here. Now that Shirley finished high school last year, she can take care of herself even if she's still living here.

Bill and Margie were so good to us when we were struggling right after Billy was born. Margie picked up the laundry to dry in her clothes-dryer anytime it was raining or too cold for me to hang diapers outside. She even drove over here herself—leaving her little ones with Joan or Joy—to deliver the dry clothes.

And I'd never have gotten through the war years without Bill Serda slipping me coupons when I ran out of sugar rations, or meat, or butter. Right after Billy was born he sent a bag of groceries down here every week with Margie on her way to Catholic Social Services.

This might not irk me so much if I didn't think Rappy relishes the idea of another challenge—this time in an area definitely outside of his expertise. Rappy doesn't know a thing about running a big grocery store, but that's not gonna stop him. Everything to him's a challenge.

I can't begrudge Margie a thing. I just hope this doesn't go on forever.

377

Are you listening, Lord? . . . I'm not just talking to hear my-self talk! . . . This is a prayer!

⟫⟫⟫⟫

A year later Serda's supermarket was holding its own. Revenue had not increased—as it had done annually when Bill was alive and in charge—but neither had it fallen.

Every Saturday Margie stopped by Laurel Street after closing the store at 6:00 to drop off groceries. Alyce realized Margie felt bad about needing Rappy to oversee her supermarket on a daily basis. After putting in a full day at the bank, Rappy drove to the store after supper to make sure his sister's enterprise was on track. He pored over the books to make sure the managers and checkout girls didn't steal her blind.

It had been seven years since Margie delivered groceries to Laurel Street once a week. After Rappy was made a bank officer, Alyce told Bill to stop sending them so that Rappy could recoup his pride after those lean years since Billy's birth.

But now Margie dropped off a few groceries at least once a week.

Are these groceries a guilt offering?

I shouldn't be so cynical!

But I expect Margie does feel guilty that Rappy's gone from home every night. Maybe Margie needs to show her gratitude to me, personally, for not complaining about Rappy's absence. Well, I complain to Rappy now and then, but never in front of Margie—and I'm sure he'd never mention my complaints to his sister, no matter how close they are. Both he and I agree that marital squabbles shouldn't be aired like dirty laundry.

If I were in Margie's place—a widow with four children to put through high school and college—I'd probably expect Bubber to help me, even if it did take time away from Emma and his two boys.

I guess I should relax and welcome the groceries, espe-

cially the chocolate. I wonder if Margie puts it in the bag just for me?

And Alyce did appreciate the groceries, especially the rare treat Alyce found in the bag only 3-4 times a year, such as the twelve pound tenderloin Mr. Sardis had cut for Mrs. Hereford Hooper which she later cancelled. It was routine for the notorious lady to phone in orders for special meat cuts to serve during her weekend houseparties at the family's Point Clear summer home. But if the weather turned foul causing the socialite to postpone her houseparty—and the Alabama Gulf Coast has the highest rainfall in the country—she would cancel the order in her own sweet time, always after Sardis had cut and packaged the expensive roast.

A twelve-pound roast could sit in Serda's display case for five days with the risk of going rancid before anyone would buy it—and even then it would sell only if the butcher cut it into fourths. Margie reasoned that Alyce could serve the huge roast for Sunday dinner and still have enough leftovers for brown-bag school lunches all the way through Thursday, until Alyce made tuna-salad sandwiches for Friday, still the weekday when Catholics were required to abstain from meat under the pain of mortal sin.

♪♪♪

In the spring of 1959 before Bill Serda died, Tommy, looking forward to turning sixteen in July, searched all over Mobile for a fulltime summer job. On the last day of school in May, Uncle Bill offered the teen a bag-boy position in Serda's supermarket. In Tommy's first week he learned to bag groceries in the large brown paper sacks without putting the tomatoes on the bottom, to balance a bag in each arm without the paper splitting, and to carry the bags to the station wagons of the Spring Hill ladies in hopes of receiving a tip—usually a dime for each bag.

Because the bag-boys had to work all day Saturday, the busiest day at Serda's store, each bag-boy received an afternoon off during

379

the week. It was on Tommy's half-day-off that Uncle Bill collapsed on the stairs leading to his office above the storeroom. Alyce was relieved that Tommy had been spared the sight of Bill lying on the cement floor at the foot of the wooden stairs, surrounded by six-foot high stacks of cardboard cartons containing Carnation Evaporated Milk on one side and Pet Milk on the other.

On Tommy's next afternoon off, Alyce picked him up at 1:00 in front of the store so she could drop him off at Mayo's barber shop to have his flat-top trimmed.

"What this family needs is another car!" the teen quipped as he slid onto the front seat next to his mother.

"Your daddy'll buy a bigger boat before he gets a second car," Alyce muttered. "Tell you what: You drop me off at home and you can have the car the rest of the afternoon, as long as you pick up Romie from altar-boy practice at four."

"He's too young to be an altar boy! He'll never memorize the Latin!"

"They're starting them early these days. . . . The sisters say Romie's real pious. Maybe he'll be the 'religious' I've always wanted."

"The 'religious'?"

"A priest! . . . Or a nun or a brother! Mrs. Andrews has three 'religious' in her family—a priest, a nun, a brother of the Sacred Heart—and she's got only *six* children! You'd think with eleven children I'd get at least *one* 'religious'!"

"But, Mama, *you* didn't become a nun."

"I didn't have the vocation."

"Obviously none of us do either. Besides, why would you want one of your children to choose a life *you* rejected?"

"I might need a priest in the family to pray me into heaven," she laughed heartily.

"Don't give up. There're four more boys coming along after me. And maybe Snookums or Cathy'll 'go off' to the convent."

"All I can do is pray."

"Just don't pray for *me* to 'go off'. And you just might consult with the younger kids as well before you add them to your rosary list!"

When Tommy arrived home at four after picking up Romie, he marched straight into the kitchen, grabbed his mother by the elbow and, without a word, guided her out the back door where they stood at the foot of the kitchen steps.

"Mama! Why didn't you tell me how Uncle Romie died?!"

"I did! . . . They found his body on a train track. They think he was running for a train and fell under the wheels."

"Then how come he had a bullet in the back of his head?!"

"I never heard that!" Alyce was incredulous.

"The *barber* told me. . . . When he asked me which of the Perez boys my father was, he said he didn't know Rappy but that he was in Romie's graduating class. Then he said, 'Terrible that he had to die like that in Honduras'."

"He died in *Costa Rica*."

"Mr. Mayo said 'Honduras'. . . . Anyway, I said, 'Yeah, must be brutal to die under the wheels of a train—unless you're drunk, and then you wouldn't feel a thing'."

"What'd he say then?" Alyce held her breath in anticipation.

"Uncle Romie got in a poker game with a bunch of Honduran sailors in some dockside warehouse. He was drinking a lot, according to Mr. Mayo, and winning a lot. But instead of letting the guys win back some of their losses—which is etiquette in a poker game—Uncle Romie got cocky, swept up his earnings, and headed back to his ship. Evidently a few of the sailors followed him down an alley, shot him, got all the money back, and threw the body on the railroad track."

"Mr. Mayo doesn't know what he's talking about! . . . Besides, that's just *one* version!"

"Maybe so, Mama. But probably Daddy knows the whole story. I'll ask him," Tommy started up the back steps.

"No, you won't!" she grabbed him by the shirtsleeve and held tight.

"Uncle Romie's dead! . . . What does it matter, Mama?"

"Although Romie was four years younger than your daddy, Rappy worshipped him! It would kill him to hear a story like that, even if it's true—and we can't be sure it is!"

"You *know* Daddy's heard *something* during these past fifteen years about how Uncle Romie really died!"

"All your Daddy knows is what that ship captain told Cleo. And I was right there at her house listening to every word. Your daddy knows only what *I* told him the day after Christmas when he got back from the war. . . . And it's gonna stay like that, you hear me?"

"Yessum," the teen said meekly as his eyes remain fixed on her hand still clutching his sleeve.

"You promise me you'll *forget* what that Mayo man told you! And if you can't forget it, you take that story to your grave! Cuz if you tell *one* soul in this town, it will surely get back to your daddy . . . and he would never be able to deal with it . . . true *or* false!"

"I promise," Tommy said as he wriggled free from her grasp.

)))(

When it was time for Billy's annual visit to the neurologist in October, Alyce found herself in a quandary. She had read in the newspaper six months earlier that the genial Dr. Patton had died. His partner had taken over all of Patton's patients, but Alyce worried that Billy wouldn't trust a new doctor—especially if he had to administer the painful spinal tap. Because Billy hadn't experienced any excruciating headaches in over a year, she assumed the spinal tap wasn't necessary this year. Still, she wanted Billy to have his annual checkup with a neurologist instead of his pediatrician.

"He can't see Billy this month?" Alyce had slumped to the hall floor to calm herself.

"He's booked throughout October. He's taking care of all of Dr. Patton's patients as well as his own," the nurse on the phone was cordial.

"How long do we have to wait?"

"Is it an emergency?"

"Not exactly," Alyce was hesitant to share specific information

382

with the nurse on the phone, although the woman had assisted Patton over the past ten years whenever Billy visited the office.

"Does Billy need a spinal tap?"

"I don't think so."

"Mrs. Perez, I'm asking if he's having those excruciating headaches."

"No bad headaches, but it's time for his annual checkup."

"We can see Billy on the first Friday in November. . . . Shall I schedule it?"

"Yes, go ahead and make the appointment."

"If it's an emergency, Mrs. Perez, I can—"

"That's all right. I'll get our pediatrician to come out and look at Billy."

Dr. Vaughn Adams arrived the next evening after completing his office hours, and he didn't like what he saw.

"Alyce, the bedsores are getting worse but, of course, you know that."

"I rub on that ointment you gave me but it just seems to make the skin tenderer."

The doctor held Billy's legs apart to examine the ulcers on his inner thighs, one on each leg the size of a quarter.

"This one, Alyce, looks like it's about to break down."

"You mean pop open?"

"The problem is Billy won't feel the pain when it does so."

"What causes bedsores? I wash his sheets every day!"

"This condition has nothing to do with cleanliness. It's caused by pressure hindering the circulation. Only a thin cushion of fat lies between his skin and the thighbone, and it's wearing away. We call them 'bedsores' because patients get them from lying in one position for weeks at a time. . . . Even rotating the patient hourly can't prevent bedsores over a long period of time."

"Well, Billy sits in that chair all day—not able to move his legs— so I guess it's the same as if he were sick in bed all the time."

On the front steps Dr. Adams paused and leaned close to Alyce to give her more bad news. In the dark he spoke quietly so no one in the house could hear:

"His chest sounds bad, Alyce."

"It was that whooping cough last month—it spread through the little ones like Sherman through Georgia! I just couldn't keep Billy from catching it!"

"The whooping cough was surely rough on him, of course, but I've noticed a steady decline over the past two years."

"Should I keep the appointment with that neurologist?"

"Only if Billy gets headaches again and he needs a spinal tap."

"Is he dying?" her voice was flat.

"He's slipping away, Alyce."

"What's the problem?! . . . You said 'chest'! Is he coming down with pneumonia? Does he have some kind of disease?"

"His lungs are giving out, probably all his organs, but I imagine he'll die of respiratory arrest."

"How long?"

"I can't say. Maybe as long as a year."

"Is there anything we can *do*?"

"Let's just keep him comfortable."

After Dr. Adams drove off, Alyce remained outside. She gazed upward at the night sky, overcast and not a star in sight. Columbus Day and the weather was still muggy with a hint of summer. Rather than enter the house to hear somebody's Spelling words or iron a uniform shirt, she sat on the top step and clasped her arms around her shins. She yearned to just sit there until Rappy returned from Serda's at nine so they could discuss if they should confide to the younger children how sick Billy was. But people inside were waiting for her . . . depending on her.

Well, they could wait a few minutes more. She bowed her head over her knees and took a deep breath to keep from sobbing in the dark. Letting the hot tears stream down her cheeks and onto her skirt, she allowed herself a rare moment of self-indulgence. She wept quietly with her head buried in her skirt. The wool fabric wet from her tears pressed against her nose and smelled like something acrid.

Fawn River
South Mobile County, Alabama
January 21, 2012

"WHERE'VE YOU BEEN?" she lay in the recliner with her eyes wide open.

"You were dozing again so I stepped outside to look for the blue heron," I took my usual place at the end of the sofa opposite her chair.

"His schedule's off. Something's wrong."

"That was a busy year for you and your husband—and, especially, his sister,"

"Which year?

"The year your father-in-law died. . . . Was it 1960?"

"May of 1959. . . . If you give me a minute I can come up with the exact date."

"And then Bill Serda . . . the year you saw your son taking a steady decline."

"That was the hardest thing I've ever been through . . . watching Billy going down."

"Why were you so relieved when your father-in-law died?"

"I never said I was relieved," she snapped.

"*Somebody* said you were relieved!" I stood my ground.

"I told Tommy not to put that in the book," she reached for the remote control.

"Did you ever forgive your sister-in-law?"

"Mary? . . . She had the right to call her baby 'Jerry' if she wanted. He was born first."

"The other one—the one with the grocery store."

"Margie! . . . Now, what did I have to forgive Margie for?"

"Taking your husband away at night for so many years to run her store."

"That wasn't *her* fault! . . . He claimed it was his duty as her brother, but the truth is, simply, he loved a challenge.

"So you didn't blame Margie?"

"And I didn't blame Betty Drake when Rappy helped her on weekends run those four filling stations after Ross died. . . . Cancer at thirty-eight! Left Betty with five children under the age of ten! . . . Again, Rappy was the Executor for Ross's will, so he got a fee, but he didn't mind spending every Saturday driving from filling station to filling station to see if he could keep 'em going. . . . But like Serda's store, he finally sold 'em and invested the money for Betty."

"And during all that time your son was withering away?"

"Don't use that word . . . 'wither', I don't like it."

"That's how you described it, isn't it?"

"I never used that word . . . WITHER!" she glared at me, then closed her eyes.

"Are you dozing off? . . . It's almost time to get dressed for your birthday party."

"I'm already dressed," her eyes remained closed.

"I heard your daughter say she's laid out a special outfit for you on the foot of your bed."

"There's nothing wrong with this pants-suit I've got on! It just takes too much energy to change clothes—it exhausts me—and I don't like people dressing me," she let the remote control fall from her hand as she breathed more deeply, relaxing into the recliner.

386

CHAPTER **19**

FLEA WAS HIT by a car in late November of 1960, just four weeks before Alyce welcomed her second grandchild. In that same week Alyce saw Billy slipping into a steady decline.

"Jesus just grabbed that child outta my hand and threw her across the road like she be a *tree branch* tossed around in one of them hurricanes!" Josephine stood at the kitchen stove with a pot holder in hand and with an expression of bewilderment on her face.

After finishing her ironing for the day, she monitored the yellow 'pan-bread' she was fixing for Rappy who would arrive home momentarily. Alyce sat at the kitchen table clipping coupons in the newspaper's Thursday food section.

"The Lord didn't hit Flea, Josephine. That *car* hit her!"

"The policeman say he be driving drunk! Dat boy ain't nothin' but lowlife from down the dirt road where I lives. He ain't got no daddy, and his mama don't have *no* money!"

"Do they have car insurance, Josephine?"

"Miz Pee-rez, nobody in Trinity Gardens gots insurance!"

"How long's Flea gonna stay in the hospital?"

"Another week the doctor say. And I surely be ready to bring her home!

"Now, if you're cooking that cornbread to soften up Mr. Perez, you better hurry. Any minute he's gonna breeze in here and grab something to eat so he can get to Margie's store."

Legally, Flea was Josephine's great-niece. Because Josie's older sister, Rosie, was 'soft in the head' and not responsible to raise her three children—one of them being Flea's mother—Josie assumed the role of mother for her sister's clan. Rosie didn't resist. While Josie worked in town everyday as a domestic, Rosie kept the children at her ramshackle house located at the corner of the Trinity Gardens slum adjacent to Highway 45. Across the road stood the bus stop where Josie arrived every night after making two transfers from Laurel Street or wherever she had worked in town that day.

In the 1940s and early 50s the three children—Betty Jo, Bernice, and June-Boy—were met at Rosie's house and walked to Josephine's shotgun house a half-mile down the dirt road. Even if Rosie had fed the children only cereal and potato chips all day long, they would enjoy a nourishing meal with Aunt Jo before being bathed and tucked in bed between clean sheets and enough quilts to keep warm.

A generation later, after the two nieces and nephew had grown up and left for better jobs in Detroit, Josephine found herself at age sixty-six raising four small children left behind by Betty Jo and Bernice. The three girls were nicknamed Flea, Judy, and Chintzy-Lou. The boy was called Tick.

Fifteen years after raising Rosie's children, Josie was now stopping by the corner house at night to fetch Rosie's *grandchildren* to walk home, feed supper, bathe, and put to bed. In the winter it was dark when Aunt Jo arrived at Rosie's to guide the four little ones to her house. And on this particular November night, the sun had barely set when Josephine started down the dirt road carrying the baby in her arms and pulling the middle two children in a beat-up Radio Flyer wagon. The oldest, six year-old Flea, was walking beside her great-aunt, but instead of hanging next to the ditch, Flea skipped along the road dangerously close to the path of the vehicles.

The car came from behind—out of nowhere. Josie glanced up in time to see Flea sailing across the road where she bounced her head off a fence post and she landed in a clump of dewberry bushes.

Josephine heard only a barely audible 'thump' when the fender hit the child's body.

"The doctor say Flea's got *damage* to the head!" Josephine turned off the burner while flipping the cornbread onto a dinner plate.

"They call it 'brain damage', Josephine. But if she's managed to live two weeks on her own—and she's regained consciousness—then she's not gonna die. At least we don't have to worry about that!"

"No'm. . . . She ain't gonna die but she gonna be feeble-minded like her grand-mama, Rosie—and like little Billy in dat bed."

"Billy can't walk, Josephine. Flea'll be able to walk in a few months."

"The doctor say she gonna need some metal on her leg."

"A leg brace. The left side of her body is paralyzed—just like a stroke victim—but the physical therapists can teach her to walk again."

"I can't afford no metal for my child's leg, Miz Pee-rez! All I do is work for white folks! I ain't like Mr. Pee-rez working for the bank dat gots all the money locked up behind the steel doors!"

"I'm gonna make some phone calls to the Crippled Children's Association for you. The Rotary Club will help. Probably you won't have to pay anything. . . . Just stop worrying, Josie! All you gotta do is help Flea get better so you can take her home."

"I just don't want Flea to end up like little Billy in there."

♪♪♪

Eight weeks later, February of 1961, Alyce noticed a drastic decline in Billy's health. He fell asleep in his chair as early as 7:00 p.m., and he often asked to lie in bed for an hour after waking from his nap.

"Miz Pee-rez," Josephine greeted Alyce at the front door when she returned from picking up the children at St. Mary's school. "I done got Billy up after his nap—like you tole me—but maybe you needs to call the doctor!"

"Does he have a fever?" Alyce glanced at Billy in his chair, both hands propping up his wobbly head.

389

"No'm, he ain't hot, but them legs is in bad shape," Josie whispered to keep Billy from hearing her.

"I know," Alyce tried to sound nonchalant as she dropped her purse in the captain's chair in the dining room. "They're called 'bedsores' and there's nothing we can do about it."

"One of 'em's so bad you can see the red meat! . . . And I knows I saw the bone down there!"

"It's caused by poor circulation. The blood doesn't run through the veins fast enough. And it's caused by pressure! When he sleeps on his side—he can't sleep on his back because of that growth—his thighs rub together. He can't feel it but his legs put pressure on each other."

"I don't know nothin' about no 'bedsore', but it do look mighty bad!"

"Let's don't' talk about it, Josephine!" Alyce muttered, resisting an urge to shout.

"If it be my baby, I call the *doctor*!"

"Hush, Josephine! I've already called the doctor! He's coming tomorrow!"

It was a lie. The doctor wasn't coming tomorrow. Alyce had called Vaughan Adams that morning to say that Billy was becoming weaker by the day, but he said there was no urgency for him to come immediately. From what Alyce described on the phone, there was nothing a doctor could do. Adams promised to drop by Friday afternoon before he left for the weekend to his Point Clear home.

Later, after the younger children were in bed, Alyce sat on the living room sofa watching *Medic* with Tommy, now a high school senior. Shirley was out on a date with her fiancée. Alyce had put Billy to bed at 8:30. As soon as the program was over at 10:00, she scooted Tommy off to bed so she could have the living room to herself before Rappy got home from Serda's store.

After flipping the channel selector to find some show to distract her from Billy's plight, she hurried to the kitchen for her greatest self-indulgence. She positioned the step-ladder under a wall cabinet and climbed to reach the mix-master bowls on the top shelf. The three bowls—nestled inside of each other—were made of milk-glass. If a child stood on the floor and glanced up, he couldn't see what Alyce concealed inside the bowls. She realized that if the younger children discovered what treasure was hidden in the mix-master bowls, they would surely decry their mother packing mere vanilla wafers in their brown-bag lunches every day.

On her tip-toes, Alyce pulled from the bowl a bag of Nabisco Devil's Food Squares.

"There's just no way they could understand," she reasoned. "A box of chocolate snaps in their lunch-bags, carefully doled out, can last a week. This package has only twenty-four Devil's Food cookies! At two cookies per lunch-bag, it'd last only two days!"

She poured a tall glass of cold milk and returned with the bag of cookies to the living room sofa where she rationed herself two Devil's Food Squares—for the moment. She nibbled the chocolate delicacies, oblivious to what program she was watching on T-V. She was trying to figure out how she would give Billy all the attention he needed in his last days while still getting the younger children to the Mardi Gras parades next week. Probably she could depend upon Shirley and Tommy to take the children to the parades, but she and Rappy would have to limit the number of balls they attended, even if the bank expected them to show up at four in a row because it looked good for business.

At 10:15 Rappy had not yet returned from the store. First of the month, it took a long time to go over the orders to make sure the three managers didn't overstock inventory. She awarded herself two more Devil's Food Squares.

♪♪♪

On Friday Dr. Adams appeared unannounced at Laurel Street as the family was finishing supper. Rappy and Alyce left Shirley in charge of the dinner table and led the doctor to their bedroom where Billy still lay in bed after his afternoon nap. Adams examined the child, spending a lot of time listening to his lungs and pressing gently on his chest. Billy made not a sound but his eyes, opened wide, locked onto his mother's in fear.

"It won't be long now," the doctor predicted as they walked through the central hall to the front door.

"How will we know, doctor?" Alyce asked, trying to hide any emotion in her voice.

"His breathing will become labored—shallow. The tips of his fingers will turn blue."

"Can we do anything?" Alyce glanced at her husband.

"Exactly what *I* want to know, Dr. Adams," Rappy's voice was not deferential as usual. "It seems like you doctors could've cured this boy over the past ten years!"

"There's no cure for *spina bifida*, Rappy!"

"There's a boy at McGill—two years behind Tommy—with the same problem Billy's got. He's making good grades, serves on the Student Council, walks around with leg braces and crutches!"

"His *bifida* was probably removed. Your child's neurological anatomy at birth was so complex that Dr. Patton couldn't remove it. Now, Billy's . . . failing."

"I prayed that he wouldn't *wither*," Alyce murmured to herself.

"What's that Alyce?" Rappy focused on his wife.

"Rappy's still praying for a miracle, Doctor," she gave a weak smile.

"Rappy, it's much too late for a miracle," the doctor pushed open the screen door.

"We don't know that, Dr. Adams, we just don't know," Rappy grabbed his windbreaker and brown fedora to escort the doctor to his car as he left for Serda's store.

Alyce stood in the dark on the front steps as the two men got into separate cars. Neither turned to wave goodbye—not at each other, not at Alyce standing in the February chill with her lamb's wool cardigan draped around her shoulders. As soon as the two cars were out of sight, she found herself again sitting on the top step in the dark—her arms clasped around her shins.

392

"Mama, are you all right?" the voice inside the screen door was Shirley's.

"Tell 'em to finish their supper—I'll be in soon," Alyce realized how shaky her voice was.

"Tommy's in there—he's dividing up the last snapper. I'll wait here by the door so nobody tries to get outside."

"Yeah, please keep the little ones inside," Alyce acquiesced.

She realized there'd be no turning back. Once she started sobbing, she wouldn't be able to stop. Leaning over—her head buried in her wool skirt—she tried to muffle her moans, but her chest heaved profoundly. Her shoulders trembled. She squeezed her calves with all her strength as she sobbed.

Knowing Shirley stood guard at the door while Tommy held the younger children at the table for five minutes more, Alyce gave in and let loose. Her sobs could've been heard by neighbors on both sides, maybe even by Mrs. Bramlett across the street. But it didn't matter. She had told Mrs. Bramlett that Billy was dying. Rebecca Bramlett had watched her husband wither away after an automobile crash that left him a bedridden invalid for thirty years as he slowly declined. If anyone could sympathize with Alyce moaning on the front steps in the dark, it would be Mrs. Bramlett. But it didn't matter if anyone sympathized or not.

Alyce needed that five minutes to indulge her grief. She always knew she could accept God's Will if Billy died young and found relief from his misery. What she found hard to accept was that, despite all her prayers, she was forced to watch her child fade away before her eyes.

♩♩♩♩

One week later Billy died at age ten on Valentine's Day, 1961.

Also it was Cathy's twelfth birthday.

And it was Fat Tuesday.

Alyce and Rappy considered staying home on Mardi Gras Day in case Billy took a turn for the worse, but Miss Alice convinced them to take the little ones downtown to enjoy the final and most festive day of the Mardi Gras season.

After Bill Serda's death two years ago, Margie started a tradition of renting a room at the Cawthon Hotel every Fat Tuesday so that her teenagers would have a base on the parade route as they roamed downtown partying with their friends. Alyce and Rappy's teenagers, as well as Joe and Mary's, used the hotel room for lunch and a bathroom pit stop. Margie stocked the room with Coca-Cola and mountains of food—hams, roast beef, potato salad, and French bread—in hopes of discouraging the teens from buying corndogs from street vendors. She also provided an ice chest full of Budweiser for her two brothers, Rappy and Joe—food and beverages courtesy of Serda's Store.

The younger children stayed in the hotel room with their parents and watched the parades from the second story window overlooking Bienville Square. The Cawthon Hotel was a perfect solution for the three families: the teens were allowed to run the streets as long as they reported back to the hotel every three hours; the parents could watch the parades from the hotel window without having to take the little ones down among the throngs in the street; and everybody ate well.

To avoid being blocked from the parade route by the traffic police at nine in the morning, the three families arrived at the hotel by 8:30 a.m. and parked in the Cawthon's private lot. Later that night, after the *Order of Myths* paraded by the hotel at 7:00, everybody helped Margie clean up the hotel room, headed back home, and went to bed early to start Lent the next day with ashes on the forehead.

"Mama, if Billy gets tired, just put him back to bed," Alyce sat down at the dining room table with her breakfast of tea-and-toast.

"You and Rappy get those children downtown before they block off the streets! I can get Billy up after I change his dressing" Miss Alice dropped her purse on the table, sat down, and reached for the teapot to pour herself a cup.

"Now if he takes a turn for the worse, you call the Cawthon. The room's registered under 'Mrs. Bill Serda'."

"I just took a peek at Billy in bed. He's awake, and he smiled and said 'Hi, Grandma!' He doesn't look like he's failed anymore since I saw him Sunday—or was it Saturday?"

"He's holding his own, but I don't want to get caught downtown and not be able to get home through the traffic barriers if Billy takes a turn for the worse."

"You'll be home by eight after the *OOMs* pass by, and I'll be here if he does take a turn, but Alyce, his breathing sounds stronger than just two days ago on Sunday. And, it's not as if you're going off and leaving him with a stranger!"

"We ought to stay home, but Rappy and I cut back on taking the children to parades this year—they've been neglected while Rappy and I've been so concerned over Billy."

"Alyce, we can't ask the little children to stop living while we care for Billy. He could linger for another month," Miss Alice finished her tea and headed for the bedroom to bathe Billy, change his dressing, and lift him into his chair.

♪♪♪♪

After the afternoon parades passed the Cawthon, Rappy and Alyce usually stayed downtown to wait for the *OOM* parade at 7:00 p.m. But this year they took advantage of the break in traffic to get home to see about Billy and to get dressed for the *OOM* ball at nine. With the six youngest children in the station wagon, they headed west on Congress Street four blocks north of the parade route to avoid the traffic barriers. In another hour the police would block the streets again for the *OOM's* night parade, the last event of the Mardi Gras season.

"I got him up at ten," Miss Alice said, but he wanted to go back to bed by eleven—he didn't touch his breakfast—so I put him back to bed."

"You did right, Mama," Alyce was helping three year-old Richard unzip his parka.

"It seems to me, Alyce, his breathing's gotten a little shallow," Miss Alice looked up from the straight-backed dining room chair she had positioned next to Billy's bed where she held his hand through the vertical rungs in the baby-bed.

"Maybe I should put more bricks under the bed," Rappy bent over and looked under the crib.

"Land sakes, Rappy! That isn't gonna help!" Miss Alice rose from the chair so Alyce could sit next to Billy and hold his hand. "When the Lord's ready, He's ready!"

> *More bricks?!*
>
> *Rappy's still hoping for a miracle. Last week he put bricks under one end of the bed so it'd tilt, hoping Billy would be able to breathe more easily. If he were a normal child, it'd be like he's propped up on pillows, half-sitting up. But due to that growth on his back—now as big as a grapefruit—Billy's has to sleep on his side. Two layers of bricks at one end of the crib aren't stopping his lungs from filling up.*
>
> *And if we did get a miracle, would it reverse those horrible bedsores inside his thighs? The flesh has deteriorated so much that I can see the bone.*
>
> *I don't want a miracle. I just want an end to this slow death. We've had enough withering away.*
>
> *This child has never hurt a soul, Lord! He doesn't deserve this agony!*

At 5:30 Mickey and her husband arrived to take the six youngest children to the *OOM* parade. As soon as they drove off, Alyce stood in the doorway and realized the house was strangely silent and empty, except for Billy in his bed. She and Rappy returned to the bedroom to dress for the *OOM* ball beginning at nine after the parade.

"I don't want you to go," Billy spoke hoarsely from the bed as he saw his daddy struggling with the white bowtie around his neck.

Alyce paused where she was taking her red tulle ball-gown off the padded blue satin hanger.

Both of them stared at the child lying on his side.

396

"I want you to stay home," the child's breathing had become even shallower since his grandmother had left two hours earlier.

"We're not going anywhere, Billy," Rappy reached up and with a single tug untied the bowtie.

"You can go, Rappy, if you think the bank expects you to show up," Alyce threw the gown on the foot of the double bed.

"*I'm* not going anywhere."

"I'm calling Dr. Adams," Alyce headed for the phone in the central hall.

♪♪♪♪

"Thank you for calling back so fast, Dr. Adams. The woman at your answering service said that—," Alyce stood in the hallway in her slip.

"What kind of changes have you seen?" Vaughan Adams interrupted calmly.

"His breathing's gotten shallow. His eyes are open wide—he's staring into space—and he looks scared."

"What about his fingertips? Are they turning blue?"

"I didn't check but if you hold on, I can—"

"No, Alyce, it doesn't matter. I can't come right now, even if I thought I could do any good. I'm getting ready to get on the float."

"Oh, I didn't know you were a *OOM*," she felt foolish to have momentarily forgotten that Mardi Gras in Mobile takes over everyone's life.

"Yeah, I'm using the phone at our den. We're in costume waiting to get on the bus to Canal Street so we can start the parade, but I'll try to call you right after the Grand March."

"Well, I hope you have a good ride," she felt frivolous.

"If you don't hear from me by ten, call the answering service. I plan to check with her before eleven because I have two children at Mobile Infirmary."

By 8:30 Mickey and Pal dropped off the children after the parade and went home to their own two babies. Rappy found his file of burial policies and seated himself in the living room under a reading lamp to see what Billy's policy covered. The four youngest boys—Romie, Jimbo, David, and Richard—were scattered on the floor watching a western. Rappy and Alyce didn't think it prudent to tell the younger children what was going on in their parents' bedroom.

Little Rappy, now twenty-three and engaged to be married in December, was standing next to the vanity talking to his mother about his wedding plans. Alyce sat next to the baby-bed in the dining room chair while Billy, now with labored breathing, clutched her forefinger with one tiny fist.

Little Rappy talked quietly as he gazed down at Billy staring straight ahead and breathing audibly. It appeared that the child was counting his breaths as he stared into his oldest brother's eyes. Alyce was looking at Little Rappy as he listed his buddies he was considering as groomsmen.

He stopped in mid-sentence. His eyes remain transfixed on the child in the baby-bed. The labored breathing could no longer be heard. Neither Rappy nor his mother moved.

Abruptly Alyce turned on the chair and stared at the child still gripping her finger. His eyes remained fixed in a wild stare. His small lips—having become bluish an hour earlier—were parted slightly, his upper teeth gleaming with saliva. His frail chest no longer heaved.

Little Rappy hurried to the living room to summon his father. Alyce remained seated, calmly deciding how to remove her finger from the child's fist.

Rappy burst into the room and dashed to the baby-bed. Before Alyce could say anything, her husband lifted the child into his arms and started mouth-to-mouth resuscitation. She didn't dare dissuade Rappy from his hope of a miracle, but she couldn't bear to watch. She left the room.

In the hallway the younger children were emerging from all corners of the house to see what the problem was. Neither Shirley nor Tommy had arrived home after the *OOM* parade, so Alyce put fourteen year-old Snookums in charge of her five younger siblings before she returned to her bedroom where Rappy was still hovering over Billy as their oldest son struggled to close shut the dead child's eyelids.

In the hallway Snookums had the five children on their knees where she led them in the Hail Mary. Three of them were crying for their brother, but the two youngest—ages five and three—were bewildered by the confusion.

Alyce closed the bedroom door to keep the children in the hallway while she dealt with Rappy still clutching Billy in his arms. He desperately blew into the dead child's mouth. Alyce sat on the edge of the bed and allowed her husband to continue praying for his miracle.

Realizing that she wouldn't let the mortuary pick up the body until Shirley and Tommy returned home to view the child they had helped care for the past ten years—and that Dr. Adams would need to know the time of death to sign the certificate—she made a note of the alarm clock on her vanity.

Time of Death: 9:05 p.m.

The first person she called was her mother. Then she called Margie, knowing Rappy's sister would call the entire Perez family as well as the Gonzales's. She called Mickey, Father Oliver Adams, and Dr. Vaughn Adams' answering service. Within minutes the pediatrician returned the call. The phone conversation was brief, almost cordial:

"You have to sign a death certificate, don't you?" Alyce was matter-of-fact.

"I can do that in the morning."

"That's great! I don't want you to leave the ball."

"Have you called the mortuary yet?"

"No, Rappy's still sorting through the burial policy."

"If you want some time with Billy, don't call the mortuary yet cuz they'll come right away."

"Shirley's out on a date—I want to wait till she gets here."

"Then take your time. . . . Who're you using?"

"Roche."

"Just down the street from my office. I'll walk over first thing in the morning to sign the death certificate. I'll take care of everything."

"We appreciate it, Dr. Adams."

"And, Alyce, this is for the best, you know."

"I know. . . . Rappy and I thank you for everything you did for Billy. Now, go back to your dance."

Within fifteen minutes both the living room and the dining room were filled with the Hicks, Fanane, Serda, and Perez families. Everyone who came through the door hugged Alyce and spoke to Rappy who remained seated in his chair poring over policies. He looked up and greeted each person warmly but quickly returned to his insurance folder.

Alyce was holding up well until Aunt Olivia walked through the front door with Uncle Joe Midgette. This was the man who had let her sit on his shoulders at Mardi Gras parades when she was five years old, the father she never had, the rock in her life. As he clutched her to his chest, they swayed back and forth as if locked in a tribal dance. She gave herself license to sob.

By ten o'clock Shirley still had not arrived. People had scattered all over the house in small clusters. Father Adams went from room to room to see who needed comforting. Finally he sat at the head of the dining table, Alyce on his right, to enjoy a cup of coffee. He encouraged the children to talk freely about Billy. Between sniffles and sobs, the little ones shared.

"Billy's not crippled anymore!" the seven year-old Jimbo declared with his eyes opened wide as he discovered this revelation. "He's gone to heaven! In heaven everybody's perfect. You have to be perfect to go to heaven. Father Adams says Billy's better off cuz he's in heaven with no more headaches! If he's in heaven, then he's perfect and . . . he's not crippled anymore!"

After Shirley returned home at eleven and spent time alone with Billy, all the women and girls were ushered into Shirley's room where they admired her wedding trousseau as she displayed each piece behind the closed bedroom door. Across the hall the men gathered in Alyce and Rappy's bedroom as the crew from Roche Mortuary arrived to remove Billy's body. Finally at midnight Rappy and Alyce lay down

400

for a few hours sleep before they would awake on Ash Wednesday to two days of Catholic rituals to bury their child.

Five minutes after turning off the light, Alyce felt Rappy spring from the bed and rush to the new bathroom behind the back room.

He never got his miracle. He's in the bathroom crying. I could go to him, but he wants to be alone. Alone, like me crying in the dark on the front steps, the only place where I could escape in this busy house.

Everybody here tonight said I'm so brave. So many people said the same thing: "It must be terrible losing a child! I just can't imagine it! And you're holding up so well!"

What they don't know is that I did all my grieving on the front steps over the past several months as I saw my child wither away before my eyes. . . . What's brave about that?

A couple of people whispered that I must be relieved Billy's finally out of his misery. I AM relieved . . . for him. And also for the other children. We can take a longer vacation in August in Uncle Joe's cottage at Hollinger's Island. I'm relieved for Mama who won't have to stay two weeks with Billy every summer and make uniforms on my sewing machine which hasn't been maintained nearly as well as hers. I've gotta get that bobbin-winding-thing fixed.

I won't have to depend on Shirley or Tommy to baby-sit Billy when the little boys are playing Little League. I can go to the ball field to cheer them on when Rappy's at the store or doing something else and can't make the game. I'll have more time for the Ladies of Charity. I'll feel free to jump in the station wagon and go.

But mainly, Billy's out of his misery. No more spinal taps. No more rides in the car to the doctor's office.

Best of all, no more of those brutal headaches.

The child-sized coffin on display was covered in pleated white crepe. Billy was lying on his side in a white First Communion suit. His legs were covered with a child's blanket of snow-white lamb's wool. His tiny fist, no longer clutching his mother's finger, was wrapped around a single spray of white Lily of the Valley. The other hand held white rosary beads. At the funeral Mass the priest wore white vestments—not the usual requiem-black—because the Catholic Church believed there was nothing to mourn. In the eulogy Father Adams declared that God had brought his angel back to heaven. The congregation, many of whom were parish members who had never met Billy, celebrated the reunion with a White Mass.

Alyce insisted no one wear black. At the wake on Ash Wednesday night she wore a print dress of Alice-blue, Billy's favorite color. While Rappy and his brothers gathered in the foyer where the smokers felt free to indulge, the rest of the family were scattered around Parlor A. Only fifteen minutes into the visitation, so many friends and family had descended upon the mortuary that the management was forced to slide open the folding doors leading to Parlor B to accommodate the overflow.

The older children, without consultation, had instinctively stationed themselves in the corners of the two rooms. Mickey, with her husband at her side, stood near the coffin greeting her former classmates from COM, many who arrived with their own new husbands. Shirley and Rappy, both scheduled to marry later that year, stood in opposite corners with their fiancées hosting their own friends and colleagues from the offices where they worked. Tommy, a high school senior, carried messages back and forth between Alyce and Rappy.

Next to the coffin where the upper lid was open, Alyce stood as a receiving line of one person. As each guest approached—usually with trepidation of seeing a child with severe deformities laid out in mortal repose—Alyce opened her arms in compassion and understanding. She never insisted the guests view Billy in the coffin, but she urged them to do so.

"We hadn't planned to have the casket open because he had been so sick, but when I saw him today—looking so peaceful at last—I thought he really does look like he's sleeping. Why don't you take a peek?"

She glanced toward the hall door and saw Tommy making his way through the crowd with a Dixie paper cup of water for her when she noticed the trio of nuns approaching the coffin—Sister Mary of Mercy, Sister Mary Dorothy, and the fat nun whose name she could never recall.

"Ahh, Alyce!" Sister Dorothy exclaimed in her Irish brogue. "He looks like an angel! I've never seen a corpse this beautiful in all my days—not even in Ireland!"

"What a blessing!" Sister Mercy folded her hands as if praying. "God has relieved you of your burden!"

"Burden?" Alyce took the paper cup of water from Tommy. "It was my duty, Sister. It was God's Will. . . . I never saw Billy as a *burden!*"

_____

Two months later Alyce threw herself into planning Shirley's wedding scheduled for late August. With her spiral notebook organized with lists and prices from Mickey's wedding, Alyce acted as her second daughter's bridal consultant. She promised Shirley she wouldn't be half as pushy as Flossie Barrington who had served as Mickey's professional bridal consultant.

Because Shirley's fiancée was non-Catholic, the couple could not be married with a holy Mass. A further slight against the non-Catholic was that he and his Catholic bride could not enter the sanctuary to exchange vows at the foot of the altar. They were required to remain outside the communion rail to receive the Sacrament of Matrimony among the congregation.

After the bridesmaids proceeded up the aisle to the communion rail—followed by the bride on her father's arm—the ceremony itself lasted only ten minutes, not much longer than it took the wedding party to walk the length of St. Mary's Church. The upside was that the many non-Catholic guests were spared the Catholic rituals of genuflecting, sitting, rising, and kneeling at odd times during the typical Catholic Mass.

Three months before the wedding Shirley asked her mother and grandmother to help her browse through a few downtown stores for some ideas on designing her wedding dress. Shirley had already asked Grandma Hicks to fashion the wedding gown and Miss Alice, still spry at seventy-five, agreed to come up with ideas for an original gown that would suit her grand-daughter with the jet-black shoulder-length hair, so petite at age twenty that she still resembled Elizabeth Taylor in *National Velvet*.

But when the trio arrived on the second floor of Gayfer's Department Store, Shirley fell in love with a lace and tulle creation on one of the mannequins in the Bridal Corner. Shirley modeled the dress while her grandmother scurried around her with a tape-measure calculating how many yards of lace and tulle it would take to make the same dress.

"Now, you're gonna have to wear a hoop-skirt under that dress, Shirley," Alyce spoke from the armchair where she was resting her feet. "The skirt on that dress is much fuller than Mickey's wedding dress."

"Not just full," Miss Alice said as she held up Shirley's arm to measure the long-sleeve of lace, "but this skirt's made of *several* layers of tulle."

"There's a lot of lace too, Grandma," Shirley flounced the skirt with both hands to imagine a hoop-skirt underneath.

"How much do they want for this dress?" Miss Alice stepped back to get an overall view of her grand-daughter in the gown.

"It's $39.98," Shirley said as she read the price tag.

"My stars, Alyce, I could never make this dress for that! Why, the lace alone would cost that much! Look at all those panels!" Miss Alice rolled up her tape measure and returned it to her purse.

"Shirley," Alyce said, "if you're saying you want Grandma to make a dress exactly like this one, we'll just buy it! . . . Then she can concentrate on the bridesmaid dresses."

"How many bridesmaids do you have, Shirley? . . . Five?" Miss Alice ventured.

"Four bridesmaids and Snookums and Cathy."

"They're too old to be flower girls, aren't they?" Miss Alice sat in the armchair next to her daughter.

"They're called 'junior' bridesmaids, Mama."

"I declare! . . . So, Shirley, I've got six bridesmaids and your mama's outfit to make. I'll be glad to make your wedding dress, but I agree with your mama. Let's *buy* this dress!"

"Good! . . . I love this dress!" Shirley headed for the dressing room to change.

"It looks good on her, Alyce," Miss Alice sat back and relaxed.

"She's got a real tiny waist, Mama, so that full skirt is perfect. It wouldn't look good on a heavy girl."

"Well," Miss Alice let out a loud laugh of relief, "*that* was easy!"

"Yeah!" Alyce chuckled quietly.

"What's the matter? Are you still wishing she'd marry a Catholic boy?"

"No, Mama, I've gotten over that. And I understand why they can't have a Mass at the wedding, but I do wish the Church would let them inside the sanctuary and not make 'em stand on the other side of the communion rail like lepers!"

"Well, that's better than Betty Midgette's wedding! She and Jimmy had to get married in the rectory! They weren't allowed inside St. Mary's *Church*!"

"Mama, that was over ten years ago!"

"It was *only* ten years ago! . . . That means some progress has been made. Before you know it, they're gonna let non-Catholics marry Catholic girls with a *Mass*!"

"Did you write back to Aunt Eloise? . . . What'd she say?"

"She wants me to visit right after the wedding, but I need to save some more money. A train ticket to Los Angeles costs more than I've got in savings right now."

"I'm sure Bubber and Rappy'll help with the ticket when you're ready to go."

"I'm gonna wait till fall of next year so I can have another year to make some uniform money. Say a prayer I'll pick up a society wedding with twelve bridesmaids next spring."

"You need a break, Mama. A few months in California will do you good."

"Eloise wants me to stay *six* months, or longer."

"So, why don't you?"

"I probably will! . . . It might do my legs some good. Sitting behind a sewing machine all day's given my legs some cramps. I need to walk more. Out there in Los Angeles—actually, Eloise and Geraldine live near Beverly Hills—the weather's so mild you can walk outside all year long."

"Mama, you need to have a doctor look at your legs!"

"No, Alyce, I just need to walk more."

Fawn River
South Mobile County, Alabama
January 21, 2012

"IS THE SUN starting to go down? It goes down early in January, you know," she had been dozing only ten minutes when she opened her eyes and picked up the remote control

"You know, I *knew* Joe Midgette."

"That's not surprising—he had lots of friends."

"He called on Olivia at Bayou and Savannah after your mother and I were married."

"He was a good man, like a father to me."

"What were you thinking as he held you in his arms when your son died?"

"I wasn't thinking anything—I was just happy he got there so fast. He and Lee-Lee lived around the corner on Monterey—they could've walked if it hadn't been winter."

"Were you wishing that it had been your own father—instead of Joe Midgette—to hold you?"

"I never had a father," she stared me down.

"But if you had, would it have been more comforting?"

"I don't deal with WHAT IF! . . . Uncle Joe was always there for me—and that was good enough for me!"

"There's an automobile coming up the carriage path."

"Shirley and Rusty—we're all going together to St. Mary's!"

"To church?"

"To the parish hall! . . . That's where my birthday parties are held. Nobody has a house big enough to host everybody. If it were summer, we could have the party outside, right here on the river, but it's too cold for that."

"So, how many descendants do you have?"

"About seventy-five. Hard to keep track because of my grandchildren—and I have about twenty-eight of *them*! From that bunch of grandchildren I get at least one new baby every year!"

"You mean seventy-five counting their spouses?"

"Seventy-five *blood* descendants! . . . Don't ask me about spouses. Folks get divorced at the drop of a hat these days!"

"Someone might ask what kept you going to age ninety-nine. What gets you out of bed in the morning?"

"I'm not a *quitter*," she said softly, as if she were speaking to herself—as if I weren't standing at the window only a few feet away.

"Somebody's coming down in the elevator. . . . Time for you to get out of that chair."

"Look out the window!" she struggled to pull the recliner to a sitting position. "Look in the marsh! . . . The blue heron's back!"

CHAPTER **20**

TWO YEARS AFTER Billy died, Alyce was still driving to the Catholic Cemetery about once a month to be alone with him. On this particular April morning, she turned off the engine and remained at the steering wheel of the station wagon parked on the asphalt lane which rambled through the grassy plots. She searched the open space under the live-oak until she could focus on the large tombstone engraved 'PEREZ' which marked the family plot.

To the right of the granite tombstone lay Rappy's mother, father and his brother, Romie. To the left was Billy's grave. One day she and Rappy would lie on either side of him.

Well, Billy, today's Holy Thursday, so I'm gonna count this as my Easter visit. Everybody's excited about the bunny rabbit and I haven't even finished sewing the Easter dresses for Snookums and Cathy. You know that Grandma is in California visiting Aunt Eloise so I'll have to put in the zippers without her help.

It's over two years since you left us. A lot's happened in our family since you went away. I've already told you Shirley got married that summer, and then Rappy in December. Up till now, you have three nieces and a nephew, and more on the way.

Tommy's away at Auburn, and Snookums is a sophomore at the Convent of Mercy dying to date but I'm gonna make her wait till next fall when the football games start up—and then probably only double dates.

Your daddy's still going out to Uncle Bill's store almost every night, but I think that's gonna stop soon. One of the checkers—she'd been with Bill for over fifteen years—was discovered pocketing twenty-dollar bills from her till. She'd been at it for six months before they caught her. That took the wind out of everybody's sails. Then Daddy had a run-in with the butcher. Margie feels she should be home in the afternoons now that Bobby and Eddie are sophomores at McGill and getting their driver's licenses this year. With teenage twin boys, you've got double-trouble! And no daddy at home to help with discipline.

Greer's made another offer on the store. I think Daddy'll take it this time. He realizes that he and Margie together still can't replace Bill. That store needs somebody there all day who KNOWS the business or else the help'll steal you blind. It's just too much for Margie. And your Daddy's starting to realize he doesn't know enough to keep a business afloat. He's a great banker, but he's just not an entrepreneur.

We miss you, Billy. But I'm glad you're not hurting anymore.

She was about to start the car when she saw a nun crossing through the PEREZ plot, weaving among the headstones, intent on not stepping on anyone's grave. Holding up her long navy skirt to keep the hem dry, the sister scurried through the wet, tall grass as she waved her arm to flag down Alyce.

A Daughter-of-Charity! With that cornette-thing on her head—those two wings flapping like some huge, awkward white bird—you can spot 'em a mile away!

I hate to admit it, Billy, but ever since we had Sr. Catherine

Peter and the other two sisters at the house teaching you cat-
echism, I've become partial to the Trinitarians over any other
order of nuns. In the twelve months they came to our house
to help you, those three sisters never asked for a thing except
a drink of water.

Now, Billy, what do you suppose this sister wants?

"I think my battery's dead!" the young nun said breathlessly as
she approached the driver's window.

"Where's your car?" Alyce had already rolled down the window.

"Around the bend behind that oak tree!" she pointed.

"Get in, Sister," Alyce turned her back on the nun and reached
over to unlock the other front door.

"Oh, I'll just wait in our car until the mechanic comes. When you
get home, please call Providence Hospital and have Mother Superior
send help," the nun smiled as she stuffed her hands inside the flowing
sleeves of her habit.

"It's gonna rain any minute, Sister! It's *April*!"

"I'm new to Mobile!" the slight nun beamed. "Does it rain a lot
in April?"

"Please, get in the car!"

A few minutes later Alyce had maneuvered her Ford station wagon through narrow trails of the cemetery and was exiting onto Stone
Street.

"Now, look at this neighborhood, Sister. If you're new to Mobile,
you must realize this cemetery is in a bad neighborhood. I never visit
after two in the afternoon because I want to be out of here before the
schools let out. A woman alone in this cemetery in the late afternoon
can get into serious trouble."

"Oh, I never thought of that!" the young nun put her hand to her
mouth in surprise.

"Someone should tell your Mother Superior that Mobile isn't as
safe as it used to be. We all have to be on our guard."

"Well, since I'm tending the graves of our holy sisters who've gone to their heavenly reward, don't you think they'll protect me from any danger?" the naive nun asked with the innocence of a child.

"I'd surely hope so!" Alyce laughed. "But the Lord expects us to use common sense and take care of *ourselves*. He needs His guardian angels to look after all the drunks, fools, and politicians who seriously need divine protection!"

♪♪♪♪

After Alyce stopped by Providence to drop off the stranded nun, Sister Jane Logan, she arrived home to find Josephine on the front porch clutching the hem of her white apron and scanning Laurel Street as the station wagon approached.

"It's Miss Alice! . . . They's called from California! Miss Alice be sick in the hospital!" Josephine waved a used envelope where she had scribbled down a barely legible phone number.

"It's okay, Josephine, I'll call right now," Alyce tried to calm the near-hysterical woman. She grabbed the envelope as she breezed through the front door and headed for the phone in the central hall.

"You ain't gonna be able to read my writin', Miz Pee-rez!" Josephine remained on the threshold propping open the screen door with her fanny as she kneaded and folded the skirt of her apron.

"It's okay! . . . I've got the number written down in the back of the phone book!"

After Alyce talked with Aunt Eloise—her father's sister whom she had seen only twice since Eloise married and moved to California in the late 1930s—she called Rappy. He needed to book her flight reservation and withdraw some cash because she planned to be on a jet plane to Los Angeles the next day.

Arteriosclerosis! . . . What in the world is that?

Call Vaughan Adams to find out? . . . No, he's too busy. Look it up in the dictionary? . . . Emma! She's a nurse—she'd know!

Bubber! I need to call Bubber! Maybe he wants to go with

412

me. *Did Aunt Eloise call him first? Does she expect me to call him? I forgot to ask!*

It's Mama's legs. Those cramps. Aunt Eloise said it was a blood clot in her calf. Sitting at the sewing machine all these years. Edmund DeCelle, and the Crewe of Columbus costumes at our house on Bayou and Savannah, the school uniforms, the wedding gowns, bridesmaids!

But Mama doesn't sew when she visits California. Not the last time she visited—that was over ten years ago. Aunt Eloise said this time Mama's out there walking all over the place. Too much walking? . . . Or, too much sitting?

Amputation. . . . To save her life. Can't let the clot get to the heart! The leg'll be gone by the time I get there. Mama needs me.

I'm bringing her home on the airplane—no train this time. Mama's never flown on an airplane. Neither have I.

Where's Rappy? Did his silly secretary give him my message? I told her it was an EMERGENCY! . . . I've never had to take care of Mama before. It's always been the other way around.

What will Snookums and Cathy wear for Easter?! Tonight I've gotta pack and show Rappy what I've got frozen in the freezer for him to cook while I'm gone. I won't find time to finish those two dresses!

Lord, give me strength to get through this—to be a help to Mama.

♪♪♪

In Los Angeles Alyce spent Easter Sunday sitting at her mother's bedside while Miss Alice, still heavily sedated for pain, slept all day. Alyce had a thirty minute bus ride from Aunt Eloise's house to the hospital where her mother was recuperating. For the next three weeks she had breakfast with Eloise and Geraldine before they left for their business where they owned kennels for dogs and cats of the Beverly

413

Hills' rich. Alyce arrived at the hospital by nine-thirty every day.

On the initial visit she was surprised to find her mother still groggy three days after the amputation.

"It's morphine," the head nurse assured Alyce. "When someone as old as your mother has this surgery, we don't want her to feel intense pain. It might create undue stress on the heart, even a heart attack. In your mother's case, the blood clot was caused by poor circulation in the first place."

"Is *arteriosclerosis* the same as 'hardening of the arteries'"?

"It's more than that, but blood clots are one *result* of arteriosclerosis," the charge-nurse remained in the doorway to Miss Alice's room, anxious to return to her station but agreeable to answer each of Alyce's questions on her first visit.

"Is this the only blood clot she has?" Alyce asked.

"So far, this is the only one they've *found*," the nurse struggled to remain patient.

"You mean there could be others? . . . When is a blood clot fatal?"

"When it reaches a major organ, such as the heart . . . or the lungs."

"So how do we prevent another clot?"

"We have medication to thin the blood, but right now let's concentrate on your mother's recovery."

"I can't imagine Mama with a wooden leg."

"At her age she'd probably be confined to a wheelchair," the nurse edged towards her station.

"If she can't sew, she'll shrivel up and die," Alyce glanced at her mother asleep in the hospital bed.

♪♪♪♪

Three weeks later Alyce brought her mother home to Mobile.

The flight from Los Angeles required certain logistics to assure Miss Alice was comfortable. The airline rearranged four seats in the rear of the Economy Class section so that Miss Alice could lie on a stretcher for the five-hour flight to New Orleans.

Since Miss Alice was still taking medication for pain, she slept most of the flight. Alyce never even dozed. As soon as she felt the plane descending and saw the verdant Louisiana marshes brilliant green with new growth of spring, she relaxed a bit.

Almost home . . . and Mama never had to use the bathroom. Thank God! Even though that nice stewardess said she'd help me get Mama to the bathroom, it would've been a terrible chore to have her hop down the aisle holding onto the two of us.

Bubber's supposed to meet us with his station wagon so Mama can lie down in the back on the way to Mobile. It's only a 2 ½ hour drive, but it's gonna seem much longer on that bumpy Highway 90.

I'm not gonna rest easy till we get to Bubber's house and Mama's back in her own bed. Then we talk about rehabilitation and the possibility of an artificial leg, but right now she's too weak to even consider it.

As a trained nurse, Bubber's wife, Emma, became the primary caretaker for Miss Alice. Emma took responsibility for bathing her mother–in–law, serving her meals in bed, as well as the usual hygiene routine for a bedridden patient. But Emma's skills were crucial for changing the dressing on the wound where the leg had been removed above the knee.

Alyce drove to Bubber's house daily to help out. With only five year-old Richard still at home during school hours, she took him with her to visit Grandma in bed. Alyce tried to time her visit at noon to serve her mother's lunch so Emma could have a break and take a nap. Alyce made sure to hang around to help Emma change the bed-sheets—a chore requiring two people since Miss Alice wasn't able to move to a chair on her own. And Alyce handled the bedpan duties as often as she could.

Only a month home, Miss Alice was gradually being weaned off the morphine and even talking about visiting the Rotary Rehabilitation Center to see about an artificial leg. It seemed that God was answering everyone's prayers.

Thank God Emma's here! I could never change that dressing everyday on Mama's leg. Now I know why they call it a 'stump'. Those black stitches across the bottom are something from a Frankenstein movie! I can't imagine where they find thread that thick!

It feels so strange for me to be taking care of Mama . . . as if SHE were the child and I'm the parent. All my life she's been at my side whenever I've had a problem, and I don't mean just showing me how to put in a zipper every time I make a dress.

Lord, let her get strong enough to sit at her machine and sew again—even if she's in a wheelchair.

ﺩﺩﺩﺩ

Six weeks after arriving home Miss Alice developed a blood clot in her other leg. By the time she was admitted to Providence Hospital at noon, her foot had become icy cold and her toes had turned blue. All afternoon Alyce and Bubber watched doctors come and go from their mother's room as the physicians monitored the leg in hopes the clot would dissipate without need for surgery.

Miss Alice received injections of Demerol every four hours, but in between doses she moaned in pain and prayed aloud to the Sacred Heart of Jesus for relief. Her two children could do little but stand by her bed, hold her hand, and wipe her sweaty brow.

Because Miss Alice quickly became delirious with pain, at seven that evening Alyce and Bubber had to sign the authorization for a second amputation scheduled the next morning. At that point the mission was to help their mother get through the night with as little pain as possible.

Alyce's three oldest children arrived separately with their spouses—Mickey, Shirley, and Little Rappy—but they left after short visits when they realized their grandmother was in such pain she had no idea who was in the room. All three promised to return in the morning for the surgery. At eight Bubber left to grab a bite in the cafeteria before it closed. Alyce remained at her mother's bedside with her son, Tommy.

"Mama!" Tommy stood at the foot of the bed with his hand on his grandmother's foot. "This foot is frigid!"

"The clot in her leg has stopped any blood from circulating to her foot."

"Is that why she's in so much pain?"

"The doctor says she probably has clots somewhere else," Alyce moved her mother's hand from her left to her right.

"Why don't they give her some morphine?!" the nineteen year-old had become frantic at the site of his grandmother writhing in pain under the bedsheet.

"She's not due for an injection for another hour," Alyce glanced at her wristwatch.

"This is ridiculous!" Tommy's eyes were filling with tears. "I'm going to the nurses' station!"

Five minutes later he returned with a nurse holding a syringe at waist level. She injected the morphine into Miss Alice's thin arm and waited for two minutes to see if there'd be any reaction. When the nurse left the room, Alyce and Tommy stood opposite each other gazing at Miss Alice until she drifted to sleep within five minutes.

After the second leg was removed the next morning, Miss Alice remained in the recovery room as the anesthesiologist came and went in an effort to bring her back from sedation. After three hours the attending physician appeared in the waiting room to tell Bubber and Alyce that Miss Alice was dead.

"We want to do a post-mortem if you give us permission," the doctor said.

"What's that?" Alyce asked.

"It's like an autopsy, isn't it?" Bubber glanced at the doctor.

"Bubber, she's gone through so much! Why let them cut on her body again?"

"Mrs. Perez," the doctor smiled, "unlike an autopsy, a post-mortem is not that invasive. We're not looking for a *cause* of death—we already know that. We want to see if she had other blood clots, how many, and in which organs. You see, we know so little about arteriosclerosis. What we discover in the post-mortem might help us treat other patients, or even help to prevent the disease before it's too late."

"Alyce," Bubber put his arm around his younger sister, "Mama would want this post-mortem."

"Yeah, she was always helping people."

♪♪♪♪

Twenty-eight blood clots, Billy! That's how many they found in Grandma when they did that post-mortem. And half of 'em were in her lungs. No wonder she never came out of the anesthesia!

But she's out of her pain, Billy. You know she'd never have adapted to life without legs. She'd have ended up like you, Billy, just sitting in a chair all day long. Even if the chair was scooted up under her sewing machine, she wouldn't have been able to get down on the floor to pin the hem on an evening dress or pin up the cuffs when altering somebody's pants.

She's right above you, Billy. Soon your daddy and I are gonna be next to you. But right now Grandma's above you. Reach up and touch her, Billy! Say hello to your Grandma! Make her feel welcome!

♪♪♪♪

A month later Alyce was in her bedroom hurrying to finish a dress for herself when she ran into the usual problem putting in the zipper. On the third try she snatched the powder-pink silk dress from the sewing machine and threw the unfinished garment across the room where it landed on one of the four posters.

She was exasperated that she wouldn't have the dress completed before the family left for the annual three week summer vacation Down-the-Bay. The new dress was meant for an upcoming bank party on Labor Day weekend, just days after the family would return from Uncle Joe's rental cottage on Hollinger's Island.

Like her mother's White sewing machine, Alyce's machine also sat in a cherry cabinet the size of a small bookcase. It was ridiculous to consider packing the bulky cabinet in the boat, whose trailer was pulled behind the station wagon, and carting the sewing machine to Uncle Joe's cottage. Besides, she'd be spending most of her time on the end of the wharf making sure her preteens didn't ski into a piling as they tried out new maneuvers behind the faster Homelite 35 outboard motor.

At ages eleven and ten, Romie and Jimbo would surely want to advance to one ski this summer. And Cathy at age fourteen was often over-confident as she tried to ski on a Beaver paddle to keep up with Snookums, two years older. Snookums herself would be entertaining McGill high school boys from down the beach with two much time on their hands. Even if Alyce did have a sewing machine in the cottage to finish the dress, she wouldn't feel responsible working on it while the six children played in the water and Rappy, driving the boat, concentrated on the water-skier, oblivious to the other children and their friends at the foot of the wharf.

And then there were those McGill boys sniffing around Snookums on the beach where she lay soaking up a suntan as well as all that male attention.

A week later as the sun set on the first Sunday of vacation at Hollingers Island Alyce sat at the end of the wharf and kept one eye on Snookums sunbathing on the beach. The teenager lay giggling on a towel while four McGill seniors circled her like cocky blue jays performing a mating ritual. Alternately, Alyce monitored the crowd of preteens frolicking in the waist-deep water at the foot of the wharf's ladder.

Because the tide was going out, Rappy had steered the boat into deeper water where at top speed Cathy was skimming across the glassy surface on the slalom-ski. Her tanned arms stretched taut as she pulled on the tow-rope. She leaned to the side to create an impressive rooster tail of spray whose droplets glistened like diamonds reflected in rays from the setting sun behind Alyce. The skier had become a silhouette as she ventured further across the horizon.

When I drive to town tomorrow to shop for groceries, I'm gonna drop by the house and finish that dress. Mama's not here to rip out the zipper and put it in right. I can't give up. If I put my mind to it, I can figure out how to make it look as professional as if Alice Fanane Hicks had put it in!

Look at Cathy on that single ski. I would love to do that. Just like that day at Point Clear when I rode the surfboard behind John Quigley's boat waving at all those society people at the end of the Grand Hotel wharf. And they waved back!

Rappy's pulling her further across the bay. A mere speck on the horizon.

Too late for me to learn to water-ski. I'm fifty this year. But I'm content.

I wonder what's over that horizon for me?

Ackowledgments

For those cherished souls who provided
food, shelter, transportation,
and moral support,
Mary Frances H.
Mary Helen A.
Snookums
David H.
Fran L.

Especially for editing,
Mary Ann T.
And, of course,
for Hickory's gift of life.

August, 2010
Mobile, Alabama

421

CPSIA information can be obtained
at www.ICGtesting.com
Printed in the USA
FFOW02n0704200116
20595FF